CINEMA
ITALIANO

CINEMA ITALIANO

THE COMPLETE GUIDE FROM CLASSICS TO CULT

HOWARD HUGHES

I.B. TAURIS
LONDON · NEW YORK

Published in 2011 by I.B.Tauris & Co Ltd
6 Salem Road, London W2 4BU
175 Fifth Avenue, New York NY 10010
www.ibtauris.com

Distributed in the United States and Canada
Exclusively by Palgrave Macmillan
175 Fifth Avenue, New York NY 10010

Copyright © Howard Hughes, 2011

The right of Howard Hughes to be identified as the author of this work has been asserted by him in accordance with the Copyright, Designs and Patents Act 1988.

All rights reserved. Except for brief quotations in a review, this book, or any part thereof, may not be reproduced, stored in or introduced into a retrieval system, or transmitted, in any form or by any means, electronic, mechanical, photocopying, recording or otherwise, without the prior written permission of the publisher.

ISBN: 978 1 84885 607 3 (hb)
        978 1 84885 608 0 (pb)

A full CIP record for this book is available from the British Library
A full CIP record is available from the Library of Congress

Library of Congress Catalog Card Number: available

To Clara

CONTENTS

Art and Artifice: An Introduction to Italian Cinema ... ix

Acknowledgements ... xv

Chapter One	Hercules Conquers the Box Office: Mythological Epics	1
Chapter Two	Historical Escapades, High Seas and Low B's: Costume Adventures	29
Chapter Three	Fall of the Empire: Sword and Sandal Spectacles	49
Chapter Four	Tales from the Tomb: Gothic Horrors	77
Chapter Five	Battle of the Worlds: Science Fact and Fiction	101
Chapter Six	Vita All'Italiana: Love and Death	119
Chapter Seven	Shoot, Gringo...Shoot!: Italian Westerns	143
Chapter Eight	Passports to Hell: Euro Crime and Crimebusters	167
Chapter Nine	Anarchy and Allegory: Political Cinema	191
Chapter Ten	Mission Improbable: World War II Movies	209

Chapter Eleven	Knives in the Dark: Gialli Thrillers	223
Chapter Twelve	A Funny Thing Happened: Italian Comedy	245
Chapter Thirteen	Splats Entertainment: Italian Cinema Eats Itself	267

Bibliography and Sources	297
Index of Key Directors	301
Index of Film Titles	303

ART AND ARTIFICE
AN INTRODUCTION TO ITALIAN CINEMA

'For what we see', Bazin said, 'the cinema substitutes a world that conforms to our desires'. *Cinema Italiano* is the story of that world.

In its heyday – beginning in the late 1950s and lasting for over 20 years – Italy was second only to Hollywood as a popular film factory, exporting cinematic dreams worldwide. Italian filmmakers, backed by international finance and fielding multinational casts, crafted dramas, horror films, westerns, spy movies, sword and sandal epics, costume adventures, war movies, crime films, science fiction, political thrillers and comedies with equal gusto and in inimitable style. Many of these films became great international successes, but the cliché of Italian cinema is that it predominantly fed off other movies, adopting found ideas, plots and actors, and making whole genres its own. A common criticism of Italian genre filmmakers is that their films are not as good as the Hollywood films they imitate, when in many cases they are actually superior to the 'genuine article'.

Cinema Italiano discuses both Italian 'popular' and 'arthouse' cinema. Mythological sword and sandal epics, gothic horrors, sci-fi, crime films and spaghetti westerns are analysed alongside the best of Luchino Visconti, Federico Fellini and Michelangelo Antonioni. Some of the films discussed in this book are internationally famous, even infamous, while others are forgotten gems. I've sought to demonstrate that the work of world cinema heavyweights – Fellini et al. – has much in common with popularist filmmakers such as Sergio Leone and Dario Argento. In this respect, I've tried to treat everyone equally, from Pier Paolo Pasolini to Gianfranco Parolini, and from *The Leopard* to *Puma Man*.

The story of Italian cinema is essentially a series of creative explosions, interspersed with fallow periods of audience exhaustion. If a film was popular, literally dozens of imitations would be made to cash-in at the domestic and international box office. This intense technique often resulted in each fad enjoying

Starlet Sylvia Rank (Anita Ekberg) and companion in Federico Fellini's once-scandalous *La dolce vita* (1960). US poster courtesy Ian Caunce Collection.

rather limited longevity, as the glut quickly satisfied audience interest. Only the most talented directors, the biggest stars or the most imaginative gimmicks prevailed. Mythological muscleman films starring Steve Reeves as Hercules became the first Italian popular genre to enjoy widespread international success. This craze lasted from 1958 to 1964. It was superseded by Italian 'spaghetti' westerns, which took off in 1965 – with the massive success of Sergio Leone's 'Dollars' films starring Clint Eastwood as The Man With No Name – and lasted until 1970 when comedy, horror-thrillers [gialli] and crime films [poliziotteschi] coaxed audiences to pastures new. Gothic horror, Hammer-style, was popular in Italy from 1960 to 1965 and the James Bond movies inspired a spy cycle from 1963 to 1967. Within each of these frantic cycles there were many imaginative hybrid crossovers, which brought out the best in the fevered imaginations of Italian filmmakers. One trend is obvious: Italian genre cinema is obsessed with caped crusading superheroes. Even the most mercenary of Italian supermen are on the side of 'good', helping the exploited, downtrodden and victimised. It's no coincidence that everyone – from Hercules to The Man With No Name – wears a cape.

During most of these genre explosions, primary influence came from elsewhere. Time and again big international hits, regardless of their country of origin, were copied by Italian filmmakers – gothic horrors and Bondian espionage are good examples, both being inspired by already established formulas. Mythological epics, spaghetti westerns and gialli were reboots of classic Hollywood film genres. The trigger films in each case – *Hercules* (1958), *A Fistful of Dollars* (1964) and *The Bird with the Crystal Plumage* (1969) – are quite unlike their Hollywood counterparts. As soon as films and genres became hits, they also became targets for ridicule. Italian clown Totò parodied *La dolce vita* (1960) in Sergio Corbucci's *Totò, Peppino and la dolce vita* (1960), and Franchi and Ingrassia's goofy stock-in-trade were movie spoofs. Each of the chapters of *Cinema Italiano* maps out how various Italian genres rose, prospered and played out and analyses each cycle's most interesting, influential and financially successful examples, with plot resumes and cast, location, production and release details.

During the boom years of the 1960s and early 1970s, Italian film studios exceeded even Hollywood's film output. For example, there were 242 Italian films made in 1962, compared to 174 in the US; 245 Italian films to 168 American in 1966; and 237 productions to 156 in 1974. The Italian's cinematic assembly line – based in studios such as Rome's Cinecittà, Titanus, Dinocittà, Incir-De Paolis and Elios – churned out everything from sumptuous international epics to low-budget potboilers and action movies. In addition to Italy's own output, from 1957 to 1967 US companies spent approximately $35 million per year to finance or buy the distribution rights to Italian films, or to make their own films, with Italian studios as their production base. This enabled US filmmakers to take advantage of the Mediterranean weather and picturesque filming locations in Italy, Spain, North Africa and the former Yugoslavia. Often European casts and crews adopted anglicised pseudonyms to deceive audiences both at home and abroad. Films were

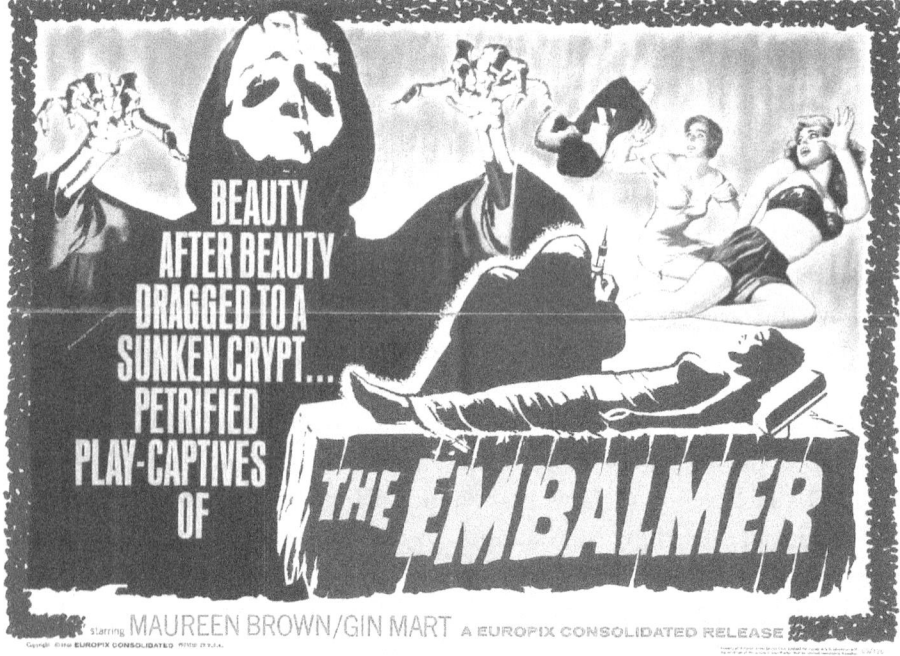

US double-bill poster for Michael Reeves' *The She Beast* (1965 – starring Barbara Steele) and Dino Tavella's *The Embalmer* (1965). Poster courtesy Ian Caunce Collection.

sometimes co-directed, with an Italian director working alongside a Hollywood counterpart. In the Italian versions of the film, the Italian director would be credited, while the international version would trumpet the Hollywood 'name'.

US companies' investments often took the form of co-productions with Italian partners, though French, West German, Spanish or Yugoslavian financiers also participated in such ventures. Stars from these countries were cast, in an effort to appeal to as broad a market as possible, with poster billing altered accordingly for different markets. Throughout the 1950s and 1960s, Italy had a rich crop of home-grown stars, with Sophia Loren and Marcello Mastroianni pre-eminent among them. Popular Italian stars who broke through internationally – and sometimes appeared in Hollywood films – included Gina Lollobrigida, Claudia Cardinale, Mario Girotti/'Terence Hill', Silvana Mangano, Alida Valli, Monica Vitti and Franco Nero.

But with American money came American stars. These included some genuine Hollywood legends – Burt Lancaster (*The Leopard*, *Moses* and *1900*), Orson Welles (*David and Goliath*, *The Tartars* and *Tepepa*) and Henry Fonda (*Once Upon a Time in the West*, *My Name Is Nobody* and *Tentacles*) – but usually meant supporting players, lesser stars and minor celebrities such as Henry Silva, Charles Bronson, Steve Reeves, Guy Madison and Jack Palance. Italian cinema afforded them star billing, fan adoration and lucrative careers as box office draws in Europe. Cameron Mitchell is a good example: a stage actor and minor Hollywood star, he travelled to Italy in 1961 to headline in a brace of Viking movies and never looked back. Several stars forgotten by Hollywood – such as Broderick Crawford, Joseph Cotton, Stewart Granger and Alan Ladd – enjoyed rejuvenated careers in Italy. Their Italian films were then truncated and dubbed for US and UK audiences and often released as ersatz Hollywood productions. There were several British performers – bodybuilding champion Reg Park, Wirral-born actress Barbara Steele and thespian Edmund Purdom – who became famous in Italy, and Italian cinema created a global superstar in Clint Eastwood (an American TV actor who became an overnight sensation in Italian westerns).

In his *Psychotronic Video Guide*, a comprehensive roundup of the best in world, cult and exploitation cinema, Michael J. Weldon compiled a list of the ten most prolific 'psychotronic movie directors'. It is headed by Spaniard Jesus 'Jess' Franco and includes such luminaries as Al Adamson, Fred Olen Ray, William 'One Shot' Beaudine and Jim Wynorski. Weldon notes that the list 'does not include Italians or serial directors'. Italy has produced more cult genres and movies than any other country in the world. During the writing of *Cinema Italiano* I collated a 'Top 20' of essential Italian films which in my view no collection should be without:

> *La dolce vita* (Fellini, 1960), *The Mask of Satan* (Bava, 1960), *Hercules Conquers Atlantis* (Cottafavi, 1961), *The Horrible Secret of Dr Hichcock* (Freda, 1962), *The Leopard* (Visconti, 1963), *Contempt* (Godard, 1963), *The Gospel according to St Matthew* (Pasolini, 1964), *Castle of Blood*

(Margheriti, 1964), *Fists in the Pocket* (Bellocchio, 1965), *Battle of Algiers* (Pontecorvo, 1966), *Blowup* (Antonioni, 1966), *The Good, the Bad and the Ugly* (Leone, 1966), *The Big Silence* (Corbucci, 1967), *Diabolik* (Bava, 1968), *The Bird with the Crystal Plumage* (Argento, 1970), *The Conformist* (Bertolucci, 1970), *Violent City* (Sollima, 1970), *The Marseilles Connection* (Castellari, 1973), *Illustrious Corpses* (Rosi, 1975), *Suspiria* (Argento, 1977)

I also compiled a further list of offbeat items. Some of these are perhaps less known than the previous titles and feature the work of journeymen directors who ploughed many furrows. The films' subject matter includes four-armed space mutants, coffin-dragging gunfighters, hardened criminals, Greek myths, reanimated flesh-eating zombies, secret agents, giant octopi, orgiastic Roman decadence, World War II action, gothic horror, slapstick comedy, incompetent superheroes, horror-muscleman epics and the world's first (and last) spaghetti western hero to be pitted against the Moors and the Vikings:

The Trojan War (Ferroni, 1961), *Maciste in Hell* (Freda, 1962), *Sons of Thunder* (Tessari, 1962), *Blood and Black Lace* (Bava, 1964), *The Castle of the Living Dead* (Kiefer, 1964), *The Last Man on Earth* (Salkow/Ragona, 1964), *The Wild, Wild Planet* (Margheriti, 1966), *Django* (Corbucci, 1966), *Special Mission Lady Chaplin* (De Martino, 1966), *Django, Kill! (If You Live Shoot!)* (Questi, 1967), *Fellini Satyricon* (Fellini, 1969), *They Call Me Trinity* (Barboni, 1970), *Milan Calibre 9* (Di Leo, 1972), *Deep Red* (Argento, 1975), *Get Mean* (Baldi, 1976), *Tentacles* (Assonitis, 1976), *The Inglorious Bastards* (Castellari, 1977), *Zombie Flesh Eaters* (Fulci, 1979), *Puma Man* (De Martino, 1980), *1990: The Bronx Warriors* (Castellari, 1982).

In my opinion, the archetypal Italian cult film would be directed by Enzo G. Castellari, Antonio Margheriti or Sergio Corbucci and would star Franco Nero, Tomas Milian, Klaus Kinski or Jack Palance. It would feature at least one bottle of J&B (Justerini & Brooks) whisky – the tipple of choice in Italian cinema – would have a score by Ennio Morricone or the De Angelis brothers and have been shot in a quarry in Lazio. Today such movies have been reclaimed by the cultists. It was once possible to encounter these films by accident on TV, often in the late-night schedule, but if you want to see most of the movies discussed in this book, you will have to buy or rent them. With the boom in DVD collecting worldwide, the best of this cinema has never been more accessible and popular. Many of these films are now available in pristine DVD editions – where were all these flawless, uncut, widescreen prints in the 1980s and 1990s, when collectors often had to make do with grainy, truncated, jumpy, faded, cropped and 'panned-and-scanned' releases? There will be films in this book you would have seen. There will be films you would want to see and even films you may never want to see. My only hope is that *Cinema Italiano* ignites or re-ignites your passion for this fantastic cinema.

HOWARD HUGHES

ACKNOWLEDGEMENTS

I'd like to thank Philippa Brewster, my editor at I.B.Tauris, for her efforts and ideas in bringing this project to fruition. I'd also like to thank Paul Davighi, Stuart Weir, Cecile Rault and Alan Bridger at I.B.Tauris, and Rohini Krishnan at Newgen for their hard work.

For providing most of the fantastic archive of advertising material reproduced in *Cinema Italiano* I'd like to thank archivist Ian Caunce, who has an amazing collection of film posters and a true passion for and knowledge of Italian cinema. Andy Hanratty has again done a great job on the restoration of many of these posters and stills. Further images were provided by Gary Smith and William Connolly. The remainder of the images are from my own collection.

For the research and sourcing of many of the rare films discussed in this book, special mention goes to Andy Hanratty, Mike Coppack, William Connolly, Alex Cox and Rene Hogguer, among many others. Italian soundtrack specialist Lionel Woodman of Hillside CD has also proved most helpful with his expertise over the years. Thanks to Tom Betts for research help and for his inspiring articles in *Westerns All'Italiana!* Thanks also to William Connolly and Mike Eustace (*Spaghetti Cinema*), Lee Pfeiffer and Dave Worrall (*Cinema Retro*) and Tim Lucas (*Video Watchdog*).

For their help – realised or otherwise – in the writing and researching of this book, I'd like to thank Belinda and Chris Skinner, Sir Christopher Frayling, Ann Jackson, Paul Duncan, Alex Cox, Kim Newman, Gareth Jones, Phil Cox, Kevin Wilkinson, Frankie Holmes, Rhian Coppack, Dave Lewis, Alex and Isabel Coe, Mark Chester and Vicky Millington, Nicki and John Cosgrove, David Weaver, Mike Oak, Peter Jones, Paul Moss and Daphne Newton.

Many thanks to mum (for proofing manuscripts) and dad. And as always to Clara, for her continued help with research, proofing, opinions and ideas.

Chapter One

Hercules Conquers the Box Office
Mythological Epics

Though they had been making impressive ancient spectacles since the silent era, the Italians' craze for mythological epics began in earnest in 1958. Making these epics was partly a way of utilising sets and costumes from Hollywood productions – including *Quo Vadis* (1951) and *Helen of Troy* (1955) – which had been filmed at Cinecittà Studios in Rome. Christened 'Hollywood on the Tiber', Cinecittà was a vast studio complex opened by Mussolini in 1937. Italian productions capitalised on the vogue for ancient spectacles ('Big Screens Mean Big Themes' went the publicity for *Helen*) by taking an already popular genre – the sword and sandal epic – and making it their own. Such films were christened 'peplum' (plural 'pepla') by French critics after the Greek word 'peplos', the name of the short skirts worn by the heroes.

The most popular stars were Steve Reeves, Reg Park and Gordon Scott: muscly outdoor types whose sheer bulk and screen presence compensated for their thespian shortcomings. Several of these musclemen – including Mickey Hargitay, Reg Lewis, Gordon Mitchell and Dan Vadis – had been bodybuilders in Mae West's risqué touring stage review in the US. There was also a phalanx of pseudonymous Italian musclemen – for example, stuntman Sergio Ciani became 'Alan Steel' and ex-gondolier Adriano Bellini was billed as 'Kirk Morris'. They played heroes named Hercules, Goliath, Ursus, Samson and Maciste. Ursus and Maciste were unfamiliar to English-speaking audiences, so many of their adventures were dubbed into Hercules or Goliath vehicles. Embassy Pictures released several as the 'Sons of Hercules' series, with a rip-roaring 'Sons of Hercules' title song: 'On land or on the sea, as long as there is need, they'll be Sons of Hercules!' If the truly 'epic' biblical epics of Hollywood director Cecil B. De Mille were famous for giving cinemagoers more than their money's worth, then peplum audiences sometimes felt a little short-changed.

The central theme of pepla is man's freedom. Often an oppressive overlord is misruling with vigour, enslaving the populace. With help from the hero the slaves cast off the shackles of oppression, an act representing a symbolic image of freedom that was a genre signature. There is often a wily, morally bankrupt queen (who desires the hero) and a virtuous heroine (for him to save from danger). Recurrent elements include torture, tests of strength, a cataclysm (usually an earthquake) and at least one cabaret spot by a group of dancing girls as court entertainment, to eat up the running time. Sometimes the hero is lifted completely out of his mythological context – *Hercules against the Sons of the Sun* shipwrecks its hero in South America, *Maciste in Hell* is set in Scotland – but to paraphrase Oscar Wilde, it's possible to believe anything provided it is incredible.

Hercules the Mighty

The trigger film for these 'bicepics' was Pietro Francisci's **Hercules** (1958), 'freely adapted' by Francisci from *The Argonauts* written by Appollonius of Rhodes in the third century BC. Francisci cast American Mr Universe winner Steve Reeves as Hercules opposite Yugoslavian starlet Sylva Koscina as Iole, King Pelias' daughter. Francisci had already had success with *Attila the Hun* (1954), which paired Anthony Quinn and Sophia Loren. Immortal Hercules is summoned to the city of Iolcus in Thessaly by Pelias (Ivo Garrani) to teach his braggart heir Iphitus (Mimmo Palmera) the art of war. Iphitus is savaged to death by a lion while in Hercules' care and the hero renounces his immortality. Jason (Fabrizio Mioni), the rightful heir to Pelias's throne, is sent to retrieve the Golden Fleece from Colchis. On board the *Argo*, built by Argos (Aldo Fiorelli), Jason gathers the Argonauts – the musician Orpheus (Gino Mattera), the Dioscuri (twin heroes) Castor and Pollux (Fulvio Carrara and Willi Columbini), Ulysses (Gabriele Antonini) the son of Laertes (Andrea Fantasia), Tifi the pilot (Aldo Pini) and Hercules. Pelias's henchman Eurystheus (Arturo Dominici) tags along to sabotage the trip. The questers are distracted on Lemnos, Island of the Women, where Jason falls for Antea, alluring Queen of the Amazons (Gianna Maria Canale). Later the Argonauts are ambushed by ape men in Colchis and Jason fights a dragon guarding the fleece, before returning to Iolcus to claim his throne.

Hercules was shot in Eastmancolor and French widescreen process Dyaliscope and is accompanied by a score by Enzo Masetti. Musical highlights include the lush title theme; the jaunty 'Athletes' theme; a lusty sailors' choir led by Orpheus; the theramin-led Sirens' theme; and love themes for Hercules and Iole, and Jason and Antea. Lidia Alfonsi played oracle 'the Sybil' and future Bond girl Luciana Paluzzi was Iole's handmaiden. Exterior footage was lensed at the Nature Reserve and beach at Tor Caldara, Anzio Cape, with palace interiors at Titanus Studios, Rome. Hercules' farewell to Iole was filmed at the arching fountains in Rome's EUR district; the athletes' games, where Hercules humiliates Iphitus, were also staged in EUR. Mario Bava's lighting and special effects are impressive and there are some memorable settings: the volcanic Island of Lemnos (a tropical paradise of palm trees, parrots and cascading flowers) and the tiered waterfall at Monte Gelato in the Treja Valley, Lazio. Antea's glittering grotto is festooned with stalactites, flowers (courtesy of Sgaravatti of Rome) and what appear to be strips of shimmering clingfilm. The Italian title (*Le fatiche di Ercole*) translates as 'The Labours of Hercules', though only two of the Twelve Labours feature: the strangling of the Nemean lion and the capture of the Cretan Bull (represented by a North American bison).

Hercules was a colossal success, especially in the US in 1959 where it grossed $20 million when independent Boston producer Joseph E. Levine bought the US rights for $120,000 and spent $1.2 million on advertising, including the precedent-setting use of TV ads in what William Goldman called 'the most aggressive campaign any film ever had'. Two different English language dubs of the film exist: the UK print opens with the titles over a Greek frieze, while the US version substitutes an animated starfield and a superior dubbing track. Distributed by Warner Bros, *Hercules* was one of their biggest hits of the year. Levine formed Embassy Pictures (later Avco-Embassy) as a result of this success and was later the producer of the Oscar-winning *The Graduate* (1967) and *The Lion in Winter* (1968).

Francisci's sequel, **Hercules Unchained** (1959), was based on *Oedipus at Colonus* by Sophocles (a dramatisation of the last hours of King Oedipus), *The Seven against Thebes* by Aeschylus (recounting the Theban Wars) and *The Legends of Hercules and Omphale*, again 'freely adapted' by Francisci. Hercules and his wife Iole (Reeves and Koscina), with Ulysses (Gabriele Antonini), land in Attica, Hercules' home, to find King Oedipus (Cesare Fantoni) at odds with his sons, Eteocles (Sergio Fantoni) and Polyneices (Mimmo Palmera). Oedipus has decreed that each will rule Thebes for a year, but Eteocles refuses to cede

Steve Reeves flexes muscle in Pietro Francisci's *Hercules Unchained* (1959), the first sequel to the phenomenally successful *Hercules* (1958).

power. Polyneices has laid siege to the city with his mercenary Argives. Francisci crowbarred Hercules into the story, casting him as a peace envoy. Hercules and Ulysses take a truce from Eteocles to Polyneices, but they are kidnapped en route by Lydian soldiers, who brainwash Hercules with 'the waters of forgetfulness'. He becomes the love slave of Omphale (Sylvia Lopez), the Queen of Lydia. As Omphale tires of her lovers they are transformed into human statues by her Egyptian henchmen, in a steamy vitrification process. One critic noted, 'Such a fate would have made little difference to Reeves' performance'. Eventually a rescue party led by King Laertes frees Hercules, who rushes to Thebes where Iole is about to become tiger food in Eteocles' arena.

Hercules Unchained is superior to its predecessor, with tighter plotting, punchier action and superior acting. Carlo D'Angelo appeared as Theban high priest Creon, Daniele Vargas played an Argive general, Gianni Loti was Sandone (Captain of Omphale's guard) and future peplum stars Alan Steel and Giuliano Gemma appeared as officers. Ballerina Colleen Bennet was the Lydian court dance soloist and Patrizia Della Rovere played Penelope, Ulysses' girl. Iole, plucking Orpheus's lyre (called a 'lute' in the slapdash dubbing) serenades Hercules by miming to June Valli's 'Evening Star' (lyrics by Mitchell Parish), the melody of which was used as the root of the film's title music. En route to Thebes Hercules fights Antaeus, the son of the earth goddess (played by world champion boxer and wrestler Primo Carnera, 'The Ambling Alp'). The film's impressive finale features a pitched battle as the Argives wheel their siege towers to the gates of Thebes. Hercules leads the Theban counter-attack across the plain in a four-horse quadriga chariot, lassoing and toppling the Argive towers.

Mario Bava was again in charge of lighting and effects and the Dyaliscope cinematography in crisp Eastmancolor is a major asset. The sunny Italian exteriors – beaches, cliffs, valleys, cities and woodland – are amongst the finest in pepla. Exteriors were filmed in Lazio (including the coast at Tor Caldara and the Treja Valley), with interiors at Titanus Appia Studios. It is in the exotic landscape of Lydia where the production really scores. When Hercules drinks from a bewitched woodland spring, there's a gnarly tree root shaped like a grotesque troll, with water pouring from its eye and the moss glistening magically. The Monte Gelato waterfall on the River Treja is bedecked with flowers for Hercules and Omphale's tranquil idyll. During a scene between Hercules and Omphale in her grotto beneath a waterfall, the flowery backdrop changes colour as the seductive mood changes. Omphale, as played by French actress Sylvia Lopez, is a red-haired seductress. She sashays across the screen in a variety of diaphanous dresses and Ester Williams sequinned bathing suits, gossamer trailing in her wake, while Bava lushly bathes the sets in her radiated sensuality. Men, even the sons of gods such as Hercules, are hypnotised by her. Lopez's portrayal of the doomed queen is movingly effective, particularly in light of her death from leukaemia at the age of 28 in November 1959. Levine again bought the rights, distributing the film through Warner Bros in the US and the UK in 1960. It made a fortune, through an intense TV advertising campaign which magnetised huge audiences into theatres.

Francisci returned to the Hercules saga with **Hercules, Samson and Ulysses** (1963). In Ithaca, Hercules (Kirk Morris), Ulysses and crew embark on an expedition to kill the Great Sea Monster. They are shipwrecked in Judea where they become embroiled in the rebellion against the evil ruler, the Seran (Aldo Giuffre), who is battling his enemy Samson (Iloosh Khoshabe, billed as the more easily pronounceable 'Richard Lloyd'). In one of the most violent scenes in pepla, the Seran orders the razing of a village which has been sheltering Samson, crucifying many of the locals to the walls of their houses. Such horror is dissipated by the Seran's soldiers' World War II-era German helmets. The finale, shot at the beach and headland at Tor Caldara (decked with fake palm trees), had Hercules and Samson joining forces to jack up the Temple of Dagon, which collapses and buries the Seran's army. When Delilah (a deliciously duplicitous Liana Orfei) attempts to entice Hercules to bathe with her in the Monte Gelato waterfall, he politely refuses ('Not today Delilah') and Hercules and Samson evidently prefer each others oiled company. Samson is so lubricated he appears to have been lacquered. For their big fight, the pair hurl outsized cardboard boulders, columns and masonry at each other.

Mighty Feats: In the Footsteps of Hercules

Between the release of Francisci's first and last 'Hercules' movies, Italian pepla veered off in many directions. Carlo Ludovico Bragaglia's ***The Loves of Hercules*** (1960 – *Hercules Versus the Hydra*) is told without pretension, attention to myth or logic. Hungarian bodybuilder and ex-Mr Universe Mickey Hargitay and his wife, busty Hollywood bombshell Jayne Mansfield, were cast as Hercules and Queen Deianara of Acalia. Hercules' wife Megara and Deianara's father Eurystheus are murdered by Lico (Massimo Serato) and his henchman Philoctetes (Andrea Aureli) who plan to usurp the throne of Acalia, while Hercules is falsely accused of killing Deianara's lover, Achillos (Gil Vidal). Hercules slays the three-headed Hydra and falls under the spell of Amazon queen Hippolyta (Mansfield again), who transforms herself into the living image of Deianara. Escaping her domain, Hercules races back to the fortress of Acalia to lead the people in revolt against Lico.

Mansfield made the film in Italy when Hollywood studios refused to cast her opposite Hargitay. She had to diet during its making to conceal the fact that she was pregnant with her second child, but still looked fabulous in voluminous, colourful costumes, her blonde hair hidden beneath a black or purple hairpiece (for Deianara) and a burnished red wig (for Hippolyta). Giulio Donnini and Andrea Scotti were Lico's devious high priest and Hercules' faithful shield-bearer Temanthus respectively. Accompanied by a majestic score by Carlo Innocenzi and shot in the Italian countryside (the impressive gates of Acalia were built beside the Monte Gelato falls) and amid vast Acalian city sets at

Cinecittà, *Loves* has several memorable action scenes. Hercules saves Deianara from a wild bull (which had to be tranquillised for the scene when Hargitay wrestles it) and also from Halcyone, a snaggletoothed ape. Hercules beheads the fire-breathing Lernean hydra (a puppet dragon) in a hokey scene which can be glimpsed in the 1968 mondo documentary *The Wild, Wild World of Jayne Mansfield* (released after the actress's death by decapitation in a car accident in 1967). *Loves*'s surreal surprise is Hippolyta's 'Forest of Death', where men she has loved live on as wailing tree creatures. Eventually one of the damned exacts revenge and strangles the evil queen with its branches. This murky Valley of Tree Men, which contributes some of the movie's least wooden acting, was constructed at Tor Caldara.

Like Francisci's *Hercules*, Riccardo Freda's **The Giants of Thessaly** (1961) was inspired by the Golden Fleece saga. Set in 1250 BC, King Jason of Thessaly (Roland Carey) embarks on a quest to find the fleece – if he fails, the gods will destroy Iolcus with a volcanic eruption. Ziva Rodann played Jason's wife Queen Creusa, Massimo Girotti was Orpheus and Luciano Marin was Eurystheus. Alberto Farnese was pointy-bearded despot Adrastes, who fancies Creusa ('Her loveliness is ablaze in me like an open furnace') and Raf Baldassarre plays Adrastes' henchman Antius. The Argonauts land on an island of witches, ruled by Queen Gaia (Nadine Saunders), an enchantress who turns Jason's crew into talking sheep. Gaia and Jason traverse a bubbling pool in a grotto on a floating throne, which resembles a peplum pedalo. The Argonauts save a city from a giant one-eyed gorilla (special effects were by Carlo Rambaldi) and Jason scales a colossal statue to retrieve the fleece. Shot on interiors at Cinecittà and the Instituto Nazionale Luce, with exteriors on the steps of Palazzo Della Civilta, EUR, Rome (the storming of Iolcus's palace), *Giants* builds to a splendid conclusion. As Adrastes is about to marry Creusa, the Argonauts burst forth from statues in great plumes of fire.

Columbia Pictures' version of the Golden Fleece saga, *Jason and the Argonauts* (1963), was lensed in picturesque locations in Campania, Italy, and at SAFA Studios in Rome. It featured Ray Harryhausen's stop-motion special effects in Dynamation 90 and Eastmancolor, with Nigel Green's Hercules opposite Todd Armstrong's Jason.

Goliath was second only to Hercules in popularity in the US and Vittorio Cottafavi's **Goliath and the Dragon** (1960) was one of the most successful examples. The Italian version ('The Vengeance of Hercules') was a sequel to Francisci's Hercules films. Emilius the Mighty, the 'Goliath of Thebes' (Mark Forrest), descends into the Cave of Horrors to retrieve the Blood Diamond for the Goddess of Vengeance, battles Cerberus the three-headed fire-breathing hell-hound (a puppet) and then wrestles a giant bat (a man in a giant bat suit). Eurystheus the Tyrant (Broderick Crawford), the scar-faced King of Ocalia, wants to take over Thebes. He murders Goliath's parents and imprisons Goliath's brother, Ilus (Sandro Moretti). Eventually, the Sybil (Carla Calo) foretells that

Ilus will be King of Ocalia, but it will cost Goliath the life of his wife, Dejanira (Leonora Ruffo). Crawford is a fine villain, who dies in his own snake pit wrestling a large rubber python. Gaby Andre appeared as evil Ismene, in league with Eurystheus's advisor Tindar (Giancarlo Sbraglai). Wandisa Guida played slave Ancinoe, dispatched by Eurystheus to poison Goliath, and Federica Ranchi was Thea, Eurystheus's daughter. Salvatore Furnari, as Goliath's midget companion, was a peplum regular, working often with Cottafavi. Goliath wrestles a bear, prevents Ilus from being crushed by an elephant's foot and tears down his own house when he realises he can't enjoy a mortal's life: 'Collapse like my shattered dreams!' he rages. Goliath enters the city's underground caverns, smashing the stalactite support pillars, causing Ocalia to crumble. Dejanira is kidnapped by Polymorphus the Centaur (Claudio Undari), a less-than-convincing half man–half deer, though the spectacular setting for his arrival is the cascading Cascate Delle Marmore (Marmore Falls) in Umbria. Polymorphus escapes with Dejanira through billowing clouds of purple smoke. Goliath takes on the dragon, with stop-motion footage of the beast (animated by Jim Danforth) intercut with close-ups of Forest battling a puppet in the rock-hewn underground caverns at Grotte Di Salone, Lazio. The US release replaces Alexandre Derevitsky's original score with new Les Baxter compositions.

In Cottafavi's **Hercules Conquers Atlantis** (1961) the portents foretell that Greece is to be destroyed by an unknown menace from across the sea. King Androcles of Thebes (Ettore Manni) leads an expedition, taking Hercules (British bodybuilding champion Reg Park) with him. They are shipwrecked on Atlantis, which is ruled by Queen Antinea (Fay Spain), who has created a race of invincible warriors. Antinea gains her power from the blood of the god Uranus, now cast as a rock hidden deep in the Mountain of the Dead – Hercules destroys the rock with a sunbeam, causing the destruction of Atlantis, and saves the known world.

With lushly saturated cinematography by Carlo Carlini, in Technicolor and 70mm widescreen 'Super Technirama', *Hercules Conquers Atlantis* is one of the most visually sumptuous epics of the 1960s that holds its own with its Hollywood contemporaries. It was filmed in Italy at Tor Caldara (here a swirl of sulphurous yellow mist), in the cavernous Grotte Di Salone (used as Prophet Tresias's underground temple and the bowels of Atlantis) and various limestone quarries and coastal beaches, with interior sets at Cinecittà. Androcles's galley was constructed at Nettuno Naval Shipyard. The film's settings and décor by Franco Lolli are at their best in the Atlantean production design. For the temple interior, a statue of Atlas strains under the weight of the vaulted ceiling, and the temple's towering entrance doors dwarf even Hercules. Park, in his best role, plays Hercules as a lazybones, but when he's roused his strength is unsurpassed, as he battles monsters and men in Thebes' name. Park's Hercules is wily: he spits out the queen's drugged wine, while Reeves would have downed it. Luciano Marin played Hercules' son Hylus and Salvatore Furnari was their midget companion

Timotheus. The Theban Council featured Mino Doro as the head of the council, and guest stars Gian Maria Volonté, Ivo Garrani and Enrico Maria Salerno as Greek kings. Laura Altian played Antinea's daughter Ismene – if she outlives her mother, Atlantis will be destroyed. Hercules saves Ismene from sacrifice to the god Proteus (Maurizio Caffarelli), who transforms himself into a snake, a lion, a vulture and a horned lizard to battle Hercules. Mario Petri played Zenet, the priest of Uranus, and Mimmo Palmera was the zombified head of Antinea's black-cloaked guard. Scabby captives, imprisoned in a valley and fed animal carcasses, are massacred by the Atlantean Invincibles. Hercules dispatches the Invincibles with a fiery oil slick and destroys the Blood Stone, triggering mayhem. As the volcano erupts, water swamps the city and crumbling masonry and ash cascade – the special effects were by Galliano and Ricci, with actual volcano stock from Haroun Terzieff, whose footage cropped up in many pepla.

For its US release by Woolner Brothers *Atlantis* was cut and retitled *Hercules and the Captive Women*. This version begins with a wobbly Filmation title sequence (which bills the director as 'Cottafani') and a tacked-on prologue, with voiceover narration by Leon Selznick. The score was re-edited by Gordon Zahler, and it partially replaced the original score with stock 'epic' music: Armando Trovajoli's pastoral themes for the sea voyage are now accompanied by triumphant trumpet fanfares.

Dark Worlds: Peplum Horror

Melding disparate genres was Mario Bava's forte, so when he was approached to direct a Hercules film, it was no surprise that the results were genre-twisting. The working title was 'Hercules in the Realm of the Dead', but the release title in the UK was **Hercules in the Centre of the Earth** (1961). Hercules (Reg Park) returns to Icalia to find Deianara (Eleonora Ruffo) bewitched by King Lico (Christopher Lee). Warned by chancellor Keros (Mino Dora) that the city is under the curse of 'Forces of Evil', Hercules learns from seer Medea that he must travel to the Island of the Hesperides to find a golden apple, so he can pass into Hades, the Kingdom of the Dead. Hercules and his companions Theseus (Giorgio Ardisson) and Telemachus (Franco Giacobini) retrieve the apple and travel to the Underworld, where Theseus falls for Pluto's favourite daughter Persephone (Ida Galli) and Hercules steals Pluto's magic stone. Lico plans to drink Deianara's blood during an eclipse to become 'King for all Eternity'.

Bava reused the palace interior and exterior sets at Cinecittà from *Hercules Conquers Atlantis*. The film opens with a band of brigands (led by Raf Baldassarre) ambushing Hercules at the Monte Gelato waterfalls, while beach exteriors (when Telemachus is almost torn apart by wild horses) were lensed at Tor Caldara. Hades was filmed in the Grotte Di Castellana (the Grottoes of Castellana) and the toxic menace of Hell seeps across the screen. The caverns are festooned with jagged stalactites and swathed in throbbing, vibrant colours (red, green, purple and blue) and swirling dry ice, filmed in Technicolor and Super/100 Totalscope.

The heroes travel across the sea in Sunis' magic ship, which sails against the wind under a blood-red sky. In the Garden of the Hesperides, the Land of Endless Midnight, granite golem Procrustes tortures Theseus and Telemachus on bone-crunching racks. When the heroes arrive in Hades, a beautiful woman, naked and chained, attempts to waylay them, but she is an apparition, who laughs mockingly as she bursts into flames.

Hercules has been told by Arethusa, Queen of the Hesperides (Marisa Belli), 'Do not believe in what you think you see'. Hercules and Theseus hack through a dense tangle of vines, which scream as they are cut, the branches dripping blood. The melancholic, haunting music by Armando Trovajoli deploys grating gypsy violins as spellbound Deianara rises from her tomb and an eerie clarinet bodes ill. For the macabre finale, as the stone tombs of Lico's corpse army creak open, Hercules rushes through Lico's dank cave lair to save Deianara. He is attacked by translucent-shrouded ghouls, which emerge from cobweb draped coffins and fly, swooping and clawing through the mist. At Lico's mountain-top sacrificial altar, amid a ring of monoliths, Hercules kills Lico and fights the spectres. As the sun emerges, Lico's corpse burns. The US release by Woolner Brothers, as *Hercules in the Haunted World*, features livelier title music and an animated title sequence designed by Filmation, its hypnotic swirls and flying ghouls resembling a schlocky drive-in poster.

Maciste against the Vampire (1961) was co-directed by Giacomo Gentilomo and Sergio Corbucci, and co-scripted by Corbucci and Duccio Tessari. Maciste (Gordon Scott) returns to his village to find it has been razed by pirates led by slave trader Amahl (Van Aikens). Maciste's mother (Emma Baron) has been slain and his lover Giulia (Leonora Ruffo) sold into slavery in the faraway Arabian city of Salmanak. Maciste and Giulia's young brother Ciro (Rocco Vitolazzi) travel to Salmanak, where Sultan Abdul (Mario Feliciani) and his slave Astra (Gianna Maria Canale) are oppressed by Kobrak the Vampire, a master of black magic who lives on human blood. Maciste teams up with Kurtik (Jacques Sernas) and his clan of subterranean Blue Men. Astra (who is in league with Kobrak) takes Giulia hostage: Kobrak wants to use Maciste as the model for his race of zombies. Maciste leads the Blue Men in an attack on Kobrak's lair, but the Blue Men are no match for the massed ranks of Kobrak's zombie army.

Salmanak (with its minarets, palace and bazaar) was filmed at De Laurentiis Studios and the Kingdom of the Blue Men's azure grotto is typically Bavaesque. Kobrak's club-wielding zombies are 'slaves without a human soul', their skeletal faces a blank mask. Maciste survives sonic torture from a huge clanging bell by stuffing wax in his ears. The sacking of Maciste's coastal village, as the pirates slaughter and pillage, was filmed at Tor Caldara. Maciste's numerous acrobatic brawls with the Salmanak guard feature an imaginative set piece in Salmanak's bustling town square. Scott's athleticism and acting are way above average for the genre (he'd played Tarzan in four screen adventures). Angelo Lavagnino's score was replaced in the retitled US version (*Goliath and the Vampires*) with

Gordon Scott faces Kobrak the Vampire in Giacomo Gentilomo and Sergio Corbucci's imaginative peplum-horror. Italian poster for *Maciste against the Vampire* (1961), which was also released as *Goliath and the Vampires.* Poster courtesy Ian Caunce Collection.

one by Les Baxter, and an alternative English language dub. Lavagnino's weird atonal violins scrape eerily on the soundtrack whenever Kobrak materialises in a cloud of red smoke. Annabella Incontrera plays Giulia's friend Magda and Kobrak transforms himself into Maciste's twin. The Macistes fight, with stuntman Giovanni Cianfriglia doubling for Scott. Maciste reveals Kobrak's true identity (a skull-like face) and the vampire is dispatched with an exploding vial of deadly vapour.

Riccardo Freda's ***Maciste in Hell*** (1962 – *The Witch's Curse*) remains the wackiest peplum horror. On 1 November 1550 in the Scottish village of Loch Laird, witch Martha Gaunt is put to the stake by Justice Edgard Parrish (Andrea Bosić) for having 'Communion with the Devil'. A hundred years hence the locals are again witch-hunting – women are possessed by madness, while others try to hang themselves from a cursed tree, which flowers each time Martha Gaunt's hex claims another victim. Newlyweds Martha and Charles Law (Vira Silenti and Angelo Zanolli) arrive to take up residence in Martha's ancestral home, until the locals find out that her maiden name was Gaunt and sentence her to burn. So unravels the first 18 minutes of *Maciste in Hell*, made on atmospheric sets at Incir-De Paolis Studios and at Caldara Di Manziana. Then Maciste (Kirk Morris) rides in wearing a loincloth and the film swerves abruptly off-track, as he travels to Hell to convince witch Martha to remove her curse.

The Hell scenes were staged in the caves of Castellana, an underground network of dramatic caverns and corridors with concretions of stalactites and stalagmites. It is still open as a tourist attraction today. Freda bathes these caverns in red tints, sets fires billowing smoke through them and pits Maciste against a roster of obstacles: a lion; a troglodyte Goliath (Pietro Ceccarelli); a giant stone being rolled uphill for eternity by Sisyphus (Bosić again); laughing, mocking voices; and a giant eagle which is pecking the entrails of tortured Prometheus (Remo De Angelis). Further extraordinary sights served up in Freda's Tartarus are a great fiery iron door (The Gate of Death) and a cattle stampede, in which Maciste drives a herd off a cliff in a scene animal lovers will shudder at.

Maciste falls in love with beautiful Fania, but she's actually sorceress Martha, who bewitches him. He forgets his quest and is reminded by replays of his previous exploits which appear in a pool of water (via clips from *Atlas in the Land of the Cyclops* and *Samson and the 7 Miracles of the World*). Helene Chanel appeared as both youthful Fania and old hag Martha, and John Karlson played Loch Laird's mayor. English film critic John Francis Lane, disguised in a hat and long scarf, appears briefly as the coachman driving the honeymooners. The hero's name is pronounced Mash-ee-stay, though in view of the Scottish setting perhaps it should have been Mac-Sheest. Carlo Franci's score is a booming brass arrangement, augmented by an operatic choir who unleash a shrill salvo. Maciste picks his way through the writhing condemned, tormented by devils, who seem to have been influenced by Rodin's 'Gates to Hell'. Indestructible Maciste forges a path of fire through the caves and the whole violent exercise becomes an endurance test for both protagonist and audience – a hellish experience all-round.

Dan Vadis (real name Constantine Daniel Vafiadis) played Argolese in Alvaro Mancori's **Son of Hercules in the Land of Darkness** (1963). Argolese liberates a kingdom from the Dragon of the Mountains (which he achieves via stock footage from *Hercules*) and then travels to the city of Demios, deep inside a mountain, to save his lover Telca (Spela Rozin) and her people, enslaved by Queen Ella (Carla Calo) and henchman Kabal (Ken Clark). Virtually non-stop, noisy action ensues in this preposterous yarn which deploys stock footage from *Mole Men against the Son of Hercules* and sets from *Ursus in the Land of Fire*. Usurper Melissa (Maria Fiore) murders Ella and plans to drink Telca's blood, until Argolese lets fly, destroying the underground city as the creeping lava bubbles in. The warriors of Demios are flesh-eating cannibals, and tortured Argolese is chained between four elephants. The city is accessed by a stone drawbridge, which spans a chasm of lava. Argolese uses an uprooted tree as an improvised bridge, then for extra thrills he wrestles a bear whilst gingerly crossing the log.

Giuseppe Vari's **Rome against Rome** (1964 – *Night Star: Goddess of Electra* and *War of the Zombies*) was a unique take on Rome's civil wars. Centurion Gaius Quintilius (Ettore Manni) is sent to Salmatia, a haunted land cloaked in tales of human sacrifice, torture and voodoo witchcraft, to track down a missing treasure. Suspicion falls on Praetor Lutetius (Mino Dora) but the culprit is Aderbal (John Drew Barrymore), the sorcerer high priest to the Goddess of Gold, a cult who worship the Daughter of Osiris, a golden cyclops statue which fires a blinding laser beam from its eye. Aderbal plans to mobilise a reanimated army of zombie Roman soldiers. Lutetius's wife, Tullia (Susy Andersen), is in league with Aderbal, but Gaius has an ally in Tullia's handmaiden Rhama (Ida Galli). Roman Consul Lucilius leads his legions against Aderbal's forces, but the zombie hordes are indestructible. Gaius confronts Aderbal and Tullia in the sorcerer's lair, stabbing the statue's eye with his sword, which blinds Aderbal, causing the zombies to disperse.

Aberbal's torch-lit cavern lair, a mist-swathed underground set (filmed at CSC Studios), is dominated by the Goddess of the Night Star's statue. Roberto Nicolosi's score adds to the unsettling atmosphere. Barrymore (father of actress Drew Barrymore) was a hellraiser off-screen and his performance as Aderbal, the zealot with a hypnotic stare, is histrionic. Aderbal's minions are knobbly faced mutants, who roam the misty battlefields by night, looting the dead, stealing treasure and carting off corpses. When Aderbal drinks human blood, translucent corpses rise from their tombs, accompanied by dissonant choral chanting on the soundtrack. The film is undermined by sluggish scenes of court intrigue (as Roman senator Andrea Checchi discusses foreign policy) and by the liberal use of stock footage from *Hannibal* and *Constantine and the Cross*. When Aderbal conjures up wind and snow to slow down the invading legions, we're actually watching Hannibal's army crossing the Alps. The confrontation between Rome (living) and Rome (dead) is *Hannibal*'s Battle of Cannae, with the ghostly zombie cavalry galloping in slow motion.

Antonio Margheriti's cleverly plotted **Hercules Prisoner of Evil** (1964) cast Reg Park (minus his trademark beard) as Hercules (Ursus in the Italian print). In a vaguely medieval setting, evil Prince Zara (Furio Meniconi) and his Kirghiz tribe covet the land of Hercules' neighbouring Chircassian tribe. Hercules is in love with the Kirghiz princess, Amiko (Mireille Granelli), and they enjoy trysts in the Grotto of the Falcon. The countryside is being terrorised by a caped fiend. Zara accuses Hercules of the attacks and then sacks Maliba, Hercules' village, blaming the monster. But Amiko isn't the real princess of the Kirghiz – Hercules' slave Katia (Maria Teresa Orsini) is the true heir. Amiko is a witch who turns men into the monster with her potion. At various points Hercules, his brother Ilo (Ettore Manni) and tribesman Fredo (Claudio Ruffini) are transformed into the beast without knowing it. The monster, with its scarred face, hairy torso, muscly arms and a black cape, runs madly through the woods, squawking like a parrot. The film has a good, nocturnal atmosphere (filmed in Italian woodland undergrowth and torch-lit grottos) backed by Franco Trinacria's dramatic score. In the finale, Hercules (transformed into the monster) carries Katia to the top of a cliff, intending to throw her to her death. Ilo kills Amiko, breaking the spell, and Hercules (now himself) extinguishes a forest fire by bursting a dam.

Born from the Rock: Maciste

For **Son of Samson** (1960 – *Maciste the Mighty* or *Maciste in the Valley of the Kings*) Mark Forest resurrected Maciste, an Italian muscleman hero who had been popular since silent cinema, when Genovese docker Bartolomeo Pagano played him in 25 features, beginning with *Cabiria* (1914). Forest explains that 'Maciste' means 'I was born from the rock'. *Son of Samson* was directed by Carlo Campogalliani in Egypt, at the Sphinx and pyramids at Giza. Just as Samson smote the Philistines, his son Maciste pummels the Persians, the oppressive regime who are enslaving the Egyptians in the eleventh century BC. The Persian queen, Smedes (Chelo Alonso), and her conniving grand vizier (Peter Dorric) assassinate Pharaoh Armitee (Carlo Tamberlani) and take over his court at Tanis. The pharaoh's son Kenamun (Angelo Zanolli), bewitched by the Necklace of Forgetfulness, marries Smedes – until Maciste arrives and provokes a slave revolt.

The exquisite costumes and lavish sets appear to have been left over from a more expensive production. Alonso makes her evil role count and Smedes commits suicide by throwing herself into a crocodile pit. Formerly a dancer in the Folies Bergère in Paris, Alonso was known as the 'Cuban H-bomb'. Whatever her shortcomings as an actress, she was a terrific dancer, which she demonstrated with a hip-notic, sensual showstopper in each of her pepla. Good support is offered by Federica Randi as Kenamun's lover Nofret and Vira Silenti as her sister,

Maciste's lover Tekaet. Egyptian musical accompaniment was provided by Carlo Innocenzi and Maciste's feats include boulder hurling, lion and croc wrestling, ladder carrying and a bit of bar-bending and chain breaking. He escapes from the Cell of Death (as the walls close in), destroys a bridge as the Persian cavalry cross it and helps slaves erect a giant stone obelisk. The film also features some surprisingly gory action: in an arena a group of blindfolded slaves (including women and old men) are scythed down by a chariot with rotating knives on the wheels. Only in the final battle, shot in Yugoslavia, with extras poking each other with axes, pitchforks and spears, does the film falter.

In Tanio Boccia's **The Triumph of Maciste** (1961 – *Triumph of the Son of Hercules*), the hero again defied the gods – and a hernia – with feats of strength. In Memphis, Queen Teniphus (Ljubja Bodin) holds power with a magic sceptre and daily sacrifices to the God of Fire in the Temple of the Mountain of Thunder, the stronghold of the troglodyte Yuri Men. Maciste (Kirk Morris) is recruited to stop this barbarity – save the sacrificial victims, save the world. Joseph Nathanson created the matte shots of Memphis, Innocenzi provided a Chinese-sounding score, and Bodin played Teniphus as a sexy, low-rent Cleopatra. Maciste enters the Mountain of Fire and battles a lion, the burning gates of the inferno, a rockslide and a giant caveman – all stock footage from Morris' *Maciste in Hell*. Giorgio Ferroni was similarly thrifty in *Hercules against Moloch* (1963 – *The Conquest of Mycenae*), which pitted Gordon Scott as Prince Glaucus ('a Hercules') against the Cult of Moloch. Ferroni cobbled together extensive battle and burning city footage from his own *The Trojan War* and *The Last Glory of Troy*, while the women drummers in Moloch's Bavaesque lair were from *The Bacchantes* (1960). In fact, there's more stock than new footage.

Antonio Leonviola's **Mole Men against the Son of Hercules** (1961) cast Mark Forest as Maciste (here pronounced 'Machestus'), first seen on a beach reeling in a harpooned whale. He's attacked by the Mole Men – an anaemic subterranean-dwelling race dressed in white robes, masks, horned headdresses and grass skirts – who die when caught in sunlight. Maciste and black slave Bangor (Paul Wynter) are put to work as labour in the Mole Men's gold and diamond mine, driving The Great Wheel. Princess Saliura (Raffaella Carra) is to be sacrificed by Queen Halis Moyab (Moira Orfei) to appease the Moon Goddess.

Despite a second-rate plot and Armando Trovajoli's recycled score from *The Giant of Metropolis* (1961), *Mole Men* features some impressive sets. Location footage was shot at Tor Caldara and the spectacular Umbrian Marmore Falls (here wreathed in a rainbow), with interiors at Cinecittà. The Mole Men's caverns are filled with mining paraphernalia: water jets, conveyors, chutes, pulleys and a heavy stone crusher, as the slave drivers whip hundreds of labourers toiling at the Great Wheel. Torture and suffering are commonplace: as punishment, one lax Mole Man guard is chained in the sunshine and reduced to a skeleton, and Maciste is placed in a cage with an ape man. As the slave uprising is stalled by the Mole Men's accurate archery, Maciste uses the Great Wheel to demolish the cavern pillars. The film has added cult value for the early performance by future Euro-star Gianni Garko as villainous Katan the Mole Man.

Gordon Mitchell (billed as 'Mitchell Gordon') starred in Antonio Leonviola's ***Atlas in the Land of the Cyclops*** (1961 – *Monster from the Unknown World*). It opens on the Island of the Cyclops, the lair of the last descendant of Polyphemus. Queen Capys (Chelo Alonso) of Sadok is doomed with a curse which can be lifted only when the last heirs of Ulysses are dead. Capys' soldiers attack the village of King Agrisandro (Germano Longo), killing him and capturing his wife Penope (Vira Silenti), but their baby son (Ulysses' heir) survives. Efros (Massimo Righi) takes the boy to Maciste (Mitchell) – despite the title, Atlas is nowhere to be found, even in the English language dub. Maciste hides the boy on Mount Ramak and rides to Sadok. The villains include Dante De Paolo as henchman Ephetus and Paul Winter as brutal slave Mumba (who is eaten by a shark). Location scenes were shot on Tor Caldara beach. For a chase between two galleys towards the Cyclops' island, Maciste rows a galley by himself. The film remains a cult favourite for its towering title villain (played by Aldo Padinotti), whom Maciste blinds with a sword and buries in rubble.

Fury of the Gods: Ursus

Second only in popularity to Reeves' Hercules in Italy was Ed Fury's Ursus. Carlo Campogalliani's ***Ursus*** (1961 – *The Mighty Ursus* or *Ursus Son of Hercules*) saw 'The Hero of the Euphrates' return from war to Sakara, to find that his fiancée Attea (Moira Orfei) has been spirited away to the Island of Zais. With blind shepherdess Doreide (Maria Luisa Merlo), Ursus heads across the desert (Tor Caldara, Lazio) and then travels to the tropical island, where he battles its evil queen. A good 'mystery peplum', *Ursus* was shot on location in Italy and Spain (including on leftover sets from *King of Kings* [1961]) and has a score by Roman Vlad. Roberto Camardiel played innkeeper Cleonte, Luis Prendes was villainous Setas, and Christina Gajoni and Soledad Miranda appeared in supporting roles. The incredible arena finale had Doreide regain her sight and Ursus (or rather Fury's stuntman) convincingly tossed and trampled by an unleashed wild bull.

In Carlo Ludovico Bragaglia's ***Ursus in the Valley of the Lions*** (1961), Ursus (Fury), the infant son of a dethroned king, is abandoned in the desert and raised by a family of lions. Alberto Lupo played Ayak the usurping barbarian, Moira Orfei was Queen Theor, Gerard Herter played barbarian General Lothar and Mariangela Giordano was Ursus' love interest, slave girl Anya. Scenes were filmed on location at Tor Caldara, Grotte Di Salone and the Monte Gelato Falls, and at Incir-De Paolis and Olimpia Studios. Anya is lowered into a pool of quicksand by evil Lothar, who gets his comeuppance when he falls into an animal pit and dies abruptly of hyenas. Fury makes a great doomed hero, an unfaltering force to be reckoned with. The scene when Ursus returns to his desert grotto, only to find his beloved lion family slaughtered, deliberately killed by Lothar with poisoned meat, is one of the most poignant in pepla – in the climax Ursus' lion companion Simba takes revenge and mauls Ayak to death.

Fury followed this with his best outing, Giorgio Simonelli's **Ursus in the Land of Fire** (1963). Shepherd Ursus (Fury) and his people are oppressed by a warlike tribe from the Mountain of Fire, who covet the shepherds' land. Evil General Hamilar (Adriano Micantoni) murders good king Lothar (Giuseppe Addobatti). Hamilar, with his lover Mila (Claudia Mori) and henchman Lero (Pietro Ceccarelli), massacres the shepherds' village and leaves Ursus buried in a rockslide. Vengeful Ursus travels to the land of fire, fights tyranny and saves Princess Diana (Luciana Gilli).

Ursus in the Land of Fire is successful through its arresting combination of sets and violence. The region's volcanic atmosphere is evoked through Italian landscapes swathed in smoke, intercut with eruption stock footage. Location scenes were lensed at the Grotte Di Salone, Monte Gelato falls, the valley at Tolfa and at Tor Caldara, with studio work at Elios. The cavernous sets were decorated with giant gargoyle effigies of the Fire God Ayat and other grotesqueries, and Carlo Savina provided the lush score. Ursus takes part in Hamilar's grand tournament in a conspicuous disguise: a finned helmet and an outfit with leopard-skin trim. He takes on all comers in the quarry arena during a muscle-twisting Trial of the Chariots and battles Lero and five highly trained wrestlers (including stuntmen Nello Pazzafini and Giuseppe Mattei) near a spiked pit, before being put to work driving the city's millstones. When Hamilar murders the Fire God's High Priest (Nando Tamberlani), the volcano erupts, the cascading flames staged by Eros Bacciucchi. Fury is a fine hero, especially during the fight scenes and when he wanders, dazed, into the razed shepherds' village. Epitomising his indestructibility, colossal, lumbering Ursus, with his quiff, sheepskin jerkin and boots, emerges dusty but unscathed from beneath the rubble of a volcanic eruption.

Vengeance of Ursus (1961) headlined another muscleman contender as the hero – Canadian wrestler Samson Burke. With help from his little brother Darius (Robert Chevalier), Ursus escorts Sira (Wandisa Guida), princess of Lycia, to marry tyrant King Zagro (Livio Lorenzon) of Karia, though it's a ruse by Zagro to take over both kingdoms. Directed by Luigi Capuano, *Vengeance* featured Gianni Rizzo as advisor Lycurgus and fencing master Franco Fantasia as the captain of Zagro's guard. The film benefits from plenty of action: a bandit attack on a barge, Darius menaced by a hungry ocelot, a tavern brawl and the final storming of the city by Zagro's army (filmed at De Paolis Studios). Pugnacious, broken-nosed Burke for once looked like a man who wrestled lions, fought elephants and brawled with soldiers. He also played Hercules in *The Three Stooges Meet Hercules* (1962).

Alan Steel played Ursus in Gianfranco Parolini's knockabout **The Three Avengers** (1964), filmed at Elios Studios with costumes left over from *Maciste against the Vampire*. In Arabia Ursus is pitted against an Ursus impostor (Mimmo

Palmera), resulting in some Ursus-versus-Ursus action. The real Ursus is blinded by acid for many of the combat sequences and his companions have to direct his movements. Ursus also duels with Semur (Nello Pazzafini), the axe-wielding leader of the desert-dwelling Tanusi. Glamorous set dressing was provided by Lisa Gastoni (Alina) and Rosalba Neri (Demora), and Gianni Rizzo played villainous Tiamoco.

Samson Mounts a Mighty Challenge

The last Italian muscleman hero to appear was **Samson** (1961), the figure from the Bible. Samson (Brad Harris) arrives in the city of Sulam to visit Queen Mila (Irena Prosen), but she has been usurped by Queen Romilda (Mara Berni), in league with Warkalla and his mercenaries, who seek the Treasure of Sulem hidden beneath the Temple of Baal. With rebel strongman Hermes, nicknamed Millstone (Alan Steel), Millstone's sister Jamine (Brigitte Corey) and King Botan (Carlo Tamberlani), Samson takes on Warkalla, who has secretly imported his army, the Tribe of Var. With location footage lensed in Yugoslavia and the Sulam dancing girls played by the Ballet of the Zagreb Opera, *Samson* thrusts its muscleman hero into a familiar tale of court intrigue and civil war. What hoists *Samson* above standard fare is director Gianfranco Parolini's brisk staging of the two-fisted action. Samson wrestles Igor, a well-oiled Ural mountainman, and fights Millstone blindfolded. Warkalla flees on a raft but, weighed down by treasure, drowns and is eaten by sharks. The best reason for seeing *Samson* is nefarious Warkalla, played by Serge Gainsbourg (the French crooner of 'Je T'aime...Mais non Plus'), with his rodent-like features and creepy sadism – a peplum nosferatu.

Parolini and Harris also made ***The Fury of Hercules*** (1961) in Yugoslavia (at Dubrava Film, Zagreb) with Gainsbourg as the villain, Menistus. Hercules (Harris) returns to Arkad to find Queen Canidia on the throne and the city rife with rebellion. The film is a remake of *Samson* and Steel appears as villain Janek, who with his four Neanderthal brothers challenges Hercules.

Hit and Myth: Peplum Send-ups

As pepla gained popularity in Italy and abroad, overt self-parody crept into the formula. Vittorio Sala directed a spoof of *The Loves of Hercules* – **Colossus and the Amazon Queen** (1960 – *Love Slaves of the Amazons* and *Queen of the Amazons*) – starring Gianna Maria Canale as the eponymous ruler. All males who land on the Amazons' island are used for one night of passion and then put to work in a stone quarry guarded by bears. Amongst the male suitors are Rod Taylor as twitchy loveboat Pirrus and Ed Fury as Greek muscleman Glaucus. Shot in Italy and accompanied by a comic musical score that includes ragtime jazz and mambo, this intended romantic farce is an incoherent mess. Ignazio Leone appears as comic relief Egyptian Sofo who invents the boomerang. The plot hinges on the theft of the Amazons' Sacred Girdle and the arrival of some greedy pirates (led by Alberto Farnese), but the slapstick situations and broad comedy don't work in a peplum setting.

In Mario Caiano's ***Ulysses against the Son of Hercules*** (1962 – *Ulysses against Hercules*), following the Trojan War, Ulysses (Georges Marchal) blinds cyclops Polyphemus on Sicily. Heracles, the Son of Hercules (Michael Lane), is dispatched to bring Ulysses before the Gods. The two heroes find themselves shipwrecked and captured by the Bird Queen (Dominique Boschero in a feathered outfit, which resembles an ostrich). Ulysses hides in the caverns of King Lago (Gianni Santuccio), the head of a troglodyte army, and Heracles agrees to join King Icano, Lago's enemy, if he can marry the king's daughter Helen (Alessandra Panaro), an agreement that doesn't please her lover Adrastes (Raf Baldassarre). The film is self-parodic in its approach to the genre and its most memorable feature is the queen and her bird army (a flock of extras in feathery loincloths and beaks) who live in a tropical paradise. They prepare to sacrifice the heroes to their god, the Mighty Vulture. During the ritual the feathery fiends perform a frenzied sacrificial dance, which resembles synchronised aerobics. The film ends with an impressive dust-swathed desert battle scene between King Icano's forces and Lago's trog minions.

The finest parody peplum was Duccio Tessari's directorial debut ***Sons of Thunder*** (1962), which starred former stuntman Giuliano Gemma as Crios, the youngest and smartest of the Titans. King Cadmus of Crete (Pedro Armendariz) kills his wife and declares himself a god. With Queen Hermione (Antonella Lualdi) he makes himself immortal and will remain so until the day Cadmus' daughter Antiope (Jacqueline Sassard) falls in love. The gods release Crios from Hades with instructions to kidnap Cadmus and drag him to the Avernus, the entrance to Hades. *Sons of Thunder* was bankrolled by Franco Cristaldi for his Vides production company. It was shot in Italy and Spain on sets decked with palm trees from *King of Kings*. Carlo Rustichelli provided the score, which is as playful with peplum convention as Tessari is with the form. Gemma (his hair dyed blond) is brimming with confidence as the acrobatic lead, a trickster immortal posing as a country boy. Gemma's poetic love scenes with Sassard are the finest romantic interludes in pepla – 'All you need is love', he tells her in the fadeout, having sent Cadmus back to Hell with a thunderbolt. Fernando Rey was Cadmus' conniving high priest, Fernando Sancho was the captain of the Cretan guard and Antonio Molino Rojo was Cadmus' advisor Idomeneus. Gerard Sety was mute Achilles (Crios' ally in Cadmus' palace) and muscleman Serge Nubret played condemned prisoner Rator.

Tessari's bravura set pieces include Cadmus' soldiers chasing Crios through the marketplace (acrobatic Gemma trampolines on stall awnings), a corrida in a bullring and a manhunt with Rator the prey. There were 12 Titans in Greek myth and the youngest was called Kronos – here they are 10, who apart from Crios are bearded strongmen. The fantasy elements feature special effects by

Joseph Nathanson and photographic effects by Galliano and Ricci, deploying miniature sets, outré designs and matte shots. In Hades, Sisyphus rolls a stone uphill, Prometheus has his liver pecked out by a vulture and starving Tantalus is tantalised by fruit he'll never reach. Crios bribes a giant Hades' guard with a ring in order to enter the Underworld and steal Hades' helm, which endows invisibility. He rescues Antiope from her island prison by outwitting a snake-haired Gorgon sorceress, and to attack Cadmus he buys a quiver of lightning bolts from a Cyclops. In the white caverns below the city, the Titans face Cadmus' indestructible soldiers, but Crios breaks the spell by breaching a dam with a thunderbolt. *Sons of Thunder* is a masterpiece of Italian cult cinema, its vitality and imagination making it one of the top pepla. It was titled *Arrivano i titani* in Italy and was released as *My Son, the Hero* in the US, promoted with the tagline 'My Son...The Hero! Smarter than a Fox! Braver than a Lion! Cuter than a Pussy Cat!'

If *Sons of Thunder* strove to subvert pepla, there were those where the humour was wholly unintentional. In **Vulcan Son of Jupiter** (1962), Vulcan, the God of Fire (Rod Flash Ilush), and Mars, the God of War (Roger Browne), quarrel on Mount Olympus over Venus (Annie Gorassini). Jupiter (Furio Meniconi) decides to punish them, but Mars and Venus flee to earth where they enlist the help of Thracian general Milos to build a tower up to Olympus to obtain power. Vulcan foils their plan, falling for earthly Etna (Bella Cortez) in the process. Directed by Emimmo Salvi, *Vulcan* has some of the wildest footage in the genre. Vulcan is discovered by a group of sea nymphs on Tor Caldara beach. They are imprisoned by Lizard Men, with scaly backs and tails and vampire teeth, and saved by Neptune's Tritons, undersea fish-men. Gordon Mitchell had a supporting role as Pluto, the God of Darkness, and Salvatore Furnari appeared as Vulcan's midget sidekick, Jaho, who infiltrates the Thracian camp disguised as a bush. Vulcan, the Blacksmith of the Gods, tends his workshop (shot in Grotte Di Salone) where he forges on a giant anvil. Unfortunately, Browne and bombshell Gorassini's bland love scenes (backed by Marcello Giombini's smoochy sax) lack chemistry: Vulcan's anvil generates more sparks.

Browne reprised the role in **Mars, God of War** (1962 – *The Son of Hercules Versus Venus*) where his 'personification of Jupiter's thunderbolt' saves the city of Telvia from King Affro (John Kitzmiller) and his African warrior army. When Mars falls for mortal Daphne (Jocelyn Lane), his request to renounce his immortality is granted by Jupiter – 'Let it be done...you will remain a mortal man, forever' – and he later saves Daphne from being sacrificed to Perganto, a tentacled giant cactus.

Fire Monsters against the Son of Hercules (1963 – *Colossus of the Stone Age*) starred Reg Lewis (ex-Mr America and Mr Universe) as Maciste, the ancient world's first and last ginger muscleman. In probably the worst dubbing job of all time, Lewis delivers his dialogue with a condescending half-smile. For the English language version, Maciste's name is changed to Maxus.

To avoid redubbing the entire film, each time Maxus' name is mentioned, a completely different higher-registered voice dubs in the amended name. Set in prehistoric times, *Fire Monsters* tells of the peaceful valley-dwelling Tribe of Dorak (who worship the sun) and their war with the cave-dwelling Droods (who worship the moon), led by the evil Fuan (Andrea Aureli). The Droods kidnap Dorak's women, so Maxus, a freelance do-gooder with a ginger quiff, rescues them. Maxus falls for Moa (Margaret Lee) but when they are buried up to their necks by Fuan to be eaten by worms, a handy volcanic eruption splits the earth, freeing them. The Droods team up with the cannibalistic Ulma (led by Nello Pazzafini, wielding a rubber club) who wear headbands with two cow's horns attached.

Fire Monsters, directed by Guido Malatesta, is a prehysteric adventure set 1 million years BC ('Before Cinecittà'). It was shot in Incir-De Paolis Studios in Rome and on location in the lakes, forests and caves of Yugoslavia. After they've been out clubbing, the Dorak enjoy watching dancing girls twisting in hairy outfits which resemble a carwash, and romance isn't depicted very well in the film. Maxus and Moa enjoy romantic walks beside a swamp (accompanied by Mantovani strings) and during a wedding ceremony the groom is told that if his wife doesn't obey him, 'Then you have the right to put her to death'. The Fire Monsters of the title – a dragon in a lake, an underwater hydra and a monitor lizard that surprises Maxus and Moa in a cave – are puppet beasts, which Maxus easily dispatches.

Colossus and the Headhunters (1963) deployed the volcanic eruption from *Fire Monsters* as its opening apocalypse, when Maciste (Kirk Morris) helps a tribe flee their island home. Escaping on a raft, the refugees drift to the land of Urya – a lush, forested country (looking very much like Yugoslavia) which has been taken over by Kermes (Frank Leroy) in league with a cruel tribe of headhunters led by Goona (Nello Pazzafini). Kermes plans to marry the deposed queen, Amoa (Laura Brown), but Maciste leads the Urians to liberty. *Headhunters* is a by-the-numbers peplum, again directed by Malatesta, and Queen Amoa wears the shortest peplum censors would allow.

Delightfully Imaginative: Myths Remixed

Alberto De Martino's **Perseus the Invincible** (1963 – *Perseus against the Monsters* and *The Medusa against the Son of Hercules*) is an imaginative remix of Greek myths. According to mythology, Perseus defeated Medusa the Gorgon, a winged woman-beast with writhing serpents for hair, whose gaze turned her victims to stone. De Martino and his scriptwriters largely rewrite the story, with Perseus (Richard Harrison) caught between warring kingdoms, the cities of Seriphos and Argos. Acrisius, the evil king of Argos (Arturo Dominici), and his son, whip-lashing Prince Galinor (Leo Anchoriz), stop the merchants of Seriphus from using a trade route to the sea, which is guarded by a dragon and Medusa. Perseus, not knowing that he is the rightful ruler of Argos, sides with good king Cepheus of Seriphus (Roberto Camardiel) and woos his daughter, Princess Andromeda (Anna Ranalli).

Perseus was shot at Cinecittà (with set design by Franco Lolli), on location near Madrid and in Italy, notably at an almost unrecognisable Tor Caldara, here transformed with a matte shot and some mist into a magnificent jagged mountainscape: Medusa's Valley of Petrified Men. Carlo Franci provides a horror movie score, deploying swirling violins, drums and ominous, resounding chords. Elisa Cegani played Queen Danaë, Perseus' mother, who recognises her son by a birthmark, the Sign of Jupiter. The supporting cast includes Antonio Molino Rojo as Tarpetes (a traitor to Seriphus who is eaten by a dragon) and Lorenzo Robledo and Frank Braña as two princes. Legend has it that if the Medusa is killed, her petrified victims return to life, which will provide Seriphus with an army. Perseus kills the dragon and confronts Medusa, presented here not as a snake-haired woman but as a shuffling shrub-like creature with a mass of cascading tentacles and one glowing golden eye. Perseus hacks at its tendrils and uses his highly polished shield as a mirror. Eventually Perseus punctures Medusa's bulbous eye, slitting it like an egg yolk, and the beast dies twitching. The hideous Medusa was created by Carlo Rambaldi, who went on to work on some of the most disgustingly convincing Italian horror effects and created the lost alien in *ET The Extra-Terrestrial* for Steven Spielberg and the creature in *Alien* (1979).

In Osvaldo Civriani's **Hercules against the Sons of the Sun** (1964), Hercules (Mark Forest) is swept off course while crossing the Great Ocean from Hellas and is shipwrecked in Inca-period South America. He teams with rebel prince Maytha (Giuliano Gemma) to rid the kingdom of usurper king Atahualpa (Franco Fantasia), who has imprisoned the prince's father, King Huascar (Jose Riesgo), and sister, Princess Yamara. Using Hercules' modern know-how (including the invention of the wheel), Maytha's army attack the fortified city of Tiwanaka with war machines to restore democracy. The film is lifted by its unusual setting and Lallo Gori's Mexican-flavoured score. The cast look resplendent in their elaborate, colourful Inca costumes, with intricate ornamentation, gold decoration, beads, cloaks, skull masks and feathered headdresses, but the overlong dance sequences, choreographed by Gino Landi and Archie Savage, and showcasing the black dancer Audrey Anderson, slow the film's pace. Giulio Donnini played Atahualpa's high priest and Angel Rhu his queen. Anna-Maria Pace was cast as Maytha's sister Yamara, under threat of sacrifice to the great god Viracocha. By hiring a few llamas for the camp scenes, the Italian countryside was transformed into the Andes, though Hercules is shipwrecked, as always, at Tor Caldara, Anzio Cape.

Like Kirk Morris, Forest found that his peplum heroes were well-travelled, as in Michele Lupo's **Goliath and the Sins of Babylon** (1963). In 200 BC, Goliath (Forest) returns to Nefer on the Persian Gulf to find it under Babylonian rule. Pergaso (Piero Lulli), the king of Nefer, must pay a yearly gift of 30 virgins to Babylon, with Babylonian Morakeb (Erno Crisa) ensuring the tribute is paid.

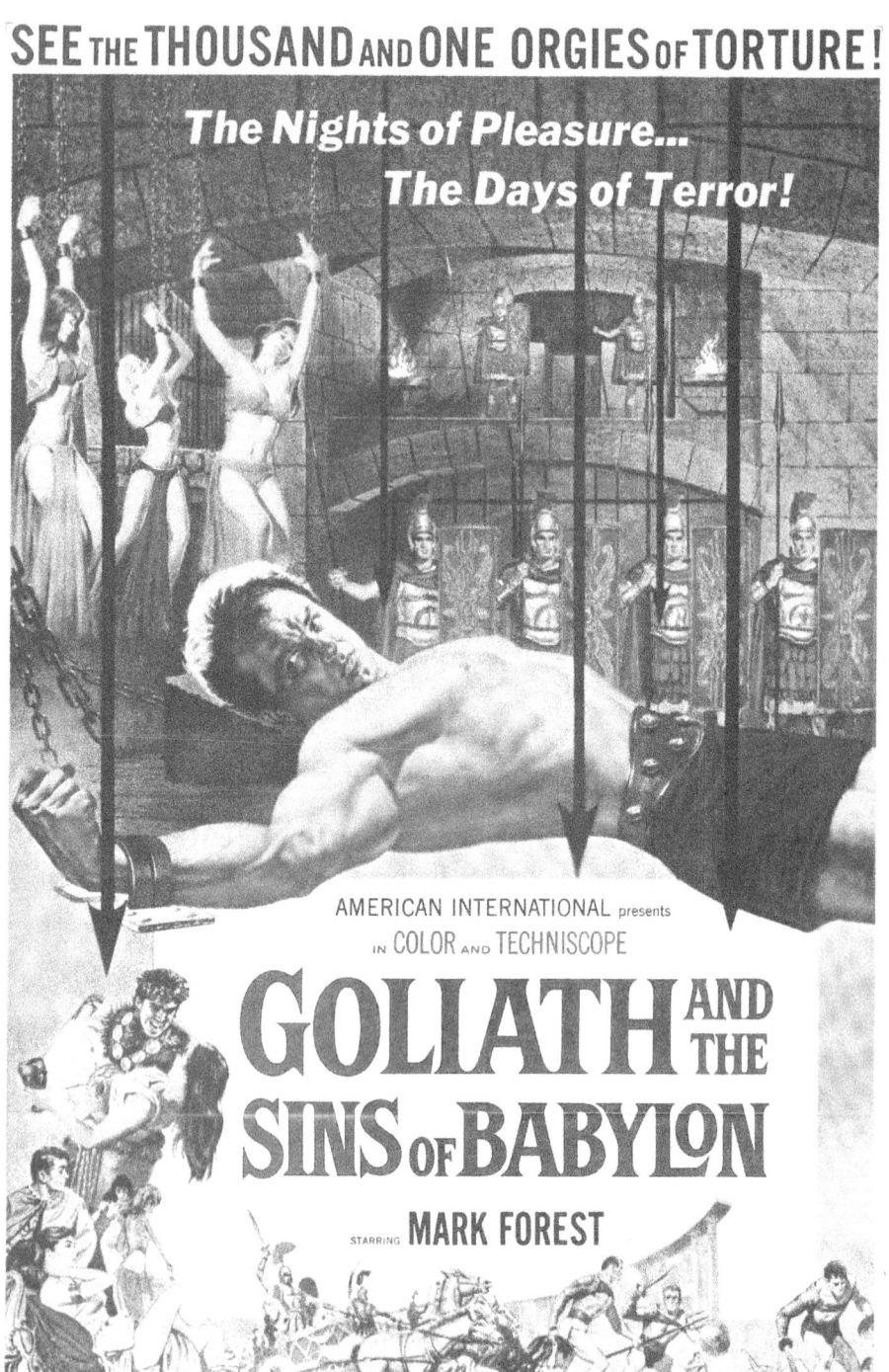

US artwork for Michele Lupo's *Goliath and the Sins of Babylon* (1963), starring Mark Forest as the imperilled hero. Poster courtesy Ian Caunce Collection.

Goliath teams up with rebel gladiators led by Evandro (Livio Lorenzon) and wins the hand of Princess Resya (Jose Greci) in a chariot race. Lupo cast Giuliano Gemma as acrobatic rebel Sandros and his gladiator compatriots included Mimmo Palmera as Arcao, Jeff Cameron and Nello Pazzafini, with Paul Muller as the Babylonian king Kafus. A sea battle and Babylon burning are stock footage from *Carthage in Flames* (1960). For the US release by American International Pictures (AIP), it had new theme music composed by Les Baxter (replacing Francesco De Masi's), tying it in with other 'Goliath' movies. Siro Marcellini's *The Hero of Babylon* (1963), another Babylonian-set movie, starred Gordon Scott as Nipur, up against King Balthazar (Piero Lulli) and Queen Ura (Moira Orfei). A great-looking but pedestrian peplum, shot in Italy at De Paolis, it was misleadingly called *The Beast of Babylon against the Son of Hercules* in the US.

The all-female Amazon tribe of Greek myth were understandably popular with peplum audiences. Antonio Leonviola's **Thor and the Amazon Women** (1963) starred Newcastle upon Tyne champion wrestler Joe Robinson as Thor. In Carol Reed's *A Kid for Two Farthings* (1955) Robinson had wrestled Primo Carnera, the 'Ambling Alp' from *Hercules Unchained.* Thor travels to the city of Babylos in the all-female country of Nalia, to free dethroned queen Tamar (Susy Andersen). Janine Hendy was the queen of Babylos, which forces its women captives to fight for their freedom in the Triangle of Death arena: the film was originally called *Le Gladiatrici* [The Gladiatrixes]. It was shot in Ceria Studios (Trieste), on location in Yugoslavia and in the Grottoes of Postumia. Black muscleman Harry Baird appeared as Thor's sidekick Ubaratutu. Clips from *Ursus in the Valley of the Lions* and *Mole Men against the Son of Hercules* crop up in stock footage, and Tamar's flashback to the death of her father is the attack on the Viking village from *Erik the Conqueror* (1961). Thor engages the entire female population of Nalia in an immense tug of war contest for his life, so that 'The authority of men will be restored'.

Dan Vadis played Hercules in Alberto De Martino's lively **The Triumph of Hercules** (1964), filmed at Incir-De Paolis' arena and city street sets, and on location at Tor Caldara. In the city of Mycenae, Prince Milo (Pierre Cressoy) has taken power by assassinating the king, the father of Princess Ate (Marilu Tolo). With a band of rebels led by Euristeo (Piero Lulli), Hercules plans to win Ate's hand, but Prince Milo is aided by his sorceress mother, Pasiphae (Moira Orfei). The witch has given Milo a magic dagger, the golden Dagger of Gaea, which when unsheathed conjures up seven indestructible muscleman mercenaries made of gold. The Seven Sons of Gaea – bald, beefy and sprayed gold – resemble towering Oscars. Milo's evil conspirators include Reto (Enzo Fiermonte) and Gordio (Renato Rossini), Jacques Stany played Erione (Hercules' ally) and Aldo Cecconi and Nazzareno Zamperla played two cut-purses, the film's comic relief. The witch lives in a mossy, misty cave and watches the action in a magic pool. For the finale, Pasiphae transforms herself into Ate – the only indication that she is an impostor is her orange eyes. For this scene Tolo wore tinted contact lenses.

The End of the Myth

As steamrollering pepla began to run out of puff, they ricocheted in ever more outlandish directions. Reg Park filmed his outdoor scenes for Piero Regnoli's **Maciste in King Solomon's Mines** (1964) in the Republic of South Africa. In the city of Zimba, evil Riad (Elio Jotta) overthrows the king with the help from Bedouin warrior queen Fazira (Wandisa Guida). The rightful heir, Vazma (Loris Loddi), is spirited away by Samara (Eleonora Bianchi) and sheltered in Bambara, with the Myedonga tribe. Maciste (Park), bewitched by a drugged garland of flowers and entranced by Fazira's magic ankle band, is put to work in the Zimban gold mines, a plodding zombie slave. When Samara is about to be gilded in molten gold, Maciste breaks loose and Riad and Fazira are smothered instead. With the Myedonga sporting Zulu-like oval shields, assegai spears and knobkerry clubs, and with liberal stock wildlife footage and a voiceover that resembles the TV series *The World About Us*, this Maciste entry is one of the most distinctive – the African footage is intercut with Italian location shots (Tor Caldara and De Paolis Studios), thus providing an unusual backdrop. Park is his usual muscular self – he won Mr Universe the following year for the third time.

Hercules the Avenger (1965) liberally reuses stock footage from previous Park adventures, cut-and-pasting to ingenious effect. In Syracuse, recently widowed Queen Lida (Gia Sandri) receives proposals from several suitors, but Anticleia the oracle dissuades her from a swift union. Hercules (Park) travels to the Sunerian Marsh, to cure his son Zanthus, who has gone mad following a mauling by a lion. Hercules' quest is footage from *Hercules Conquers Atlantis* and *Hercules in the Centre of the Earth*. The film also stars Giovanni Cianfriglia as the New Hercules, an impostor whose exploitation of the city leads to a revolt (footage from *Atlantis*). Hercules seeks out this impostor, who is revealed to be Antaeus, the son of the Earth goddess Gaia. Hercules plugs up a volcano, which erupts and destroys Syracuse (more footage from *Atlantis*), and then fights Antaeus in the Grotte Di Salone. Following *Hercules the Avenger* Park retired to South Africa to concentrate on his chain of bodybuilding gyms.

Gordon Scott's final contribution to pepla was the title role in the 47-minute pilot for a TV series called *Hercules*, produced by Joseph E. Levine in 1965. **Hercules and the Princess of Troy** featured an Anglo-Italian cast: Paul Stevens (Diogenes), Roger Browne (Ortag), Gordon Mitchell (a pirate captain), Diana Hyland (Princess Diana) and Giorgio Ardisson (Leanda, Diana's lover). Photographed by Enzo Barboni on authentic peplum locations (the beach at Tor Caldara and the Grotte Di Salone), the show's saving grace was its sea monster, a bug-eyed, stickle-backed, insect-like beast with pincers, which resembled a giant prawn. The show's weekly format would have served up a different adventure, as Hercules voyages to Thebes on his ship, the *Olympia*, but the peplum fad had passed and the series was never commissioned.

Giorgio Capitani's comedic *Hercules, Samson, Maciste and Ursus the Invincibles* (1964) was released internationally as **Samson and the Mighty**

Challenge. Alan Steel starred as Hercules, Howard Ross was Maciste, Nadir Moretti was Samson and Yann L'Arvor played Ursus. Elisa Montes (Omphale) and Luciano Marin (Inor) were the young lovers, Helene Chanel was the oracle and Livio Lorenzon a whip-cracking brigand. This shot-in-Spain production welded Greek mythology to the Old Testament.

It was this film that was chosen for spoof dubbing in the Australian send-up ***Hercules Returns*** (1992). In Melbourne, disillusioned Brad McBain (Dave Argue) resigns from his job at the Kent Cinema Corporation and refurbishes a rundown cinema, with help from projectionist Sprocket (Bruce Spence) and maverick publicist Lisa (Mary Coustas). For the gala opening they show the last film that was screened at the cinema, billed as *Hercules* but actually Capitani's movie. Too late they discover that their Italian language print is not subtitled, so the trio dub the film themselves. *Hercules Returns* was based on the live show 'Double Take meets Hercules', which was performed by Des Mangan and Sally Patience, who provide most of the principle voices here. In their story Hercules ('The dumbest man in the world') saves heroine Labia (Elisa Montes) from drowning, on his way to the city of Climidia. Muriel, Labia's mother, owns the Pink Parthenon nightclub and won't allow her to marry Testiculi (Luciano Marin), the son of a rival beer garden proprietor (Livio Lorenzon). Samson, with a weedy voice and pigtails, is now henpecked by Delilah, Ursus is a tavern brawler with a Glaswegian accent, and Maciste (now Machismo) has an effeminate voice and a horse named Cyril. The Oracle (Helene Chanel), with her smoking skillet, is cleverly redubbed as a crepe chef.

It was the unlikely figure of Pier Paolo Pasolini who had the last word on Greek myths in 1960s Italian cinema. ***Oedipus Rex*** (1967) was inspired by Sophocles' plays *Oedipus Rex* and *Oedipus at Colonus* (also a source for *Hercules Unchained*). Abandoned as a child on Mount Cithaeron by a herdsman (Francesco Leonetti), Oedipus is found by a shepherd (Giandomenico Davoli) and is adopted by King Polybus (Ahmed Bellachmi) and Queen Merope (Alida Valli) of Corinth. Adult Oedipus (Franco Citti) travels to the Oracle at Delphi and learns that he is fated to murder his father and make love to his mother. En route to Thebes, where three roads meet, Oedipus murders a rich traveller. In Thebes, Oedipus kills the city's tormentor, a monster called the Sphinx, and marries Queen Jocasta (Silvana Mangano), the widow of Laius (Luciano Bartoli), the recently murdered king. But Thebes is scourged with a plague which won't lift until Laius' murderer is found. Oedipus is implicated in the killing and suspects that Jocasta's brother Creon (Carmelo Bene) is trying to take power. Tiresias the blind prophet (Julian Beck) identifies Oedipus as the culprit – King Laius and Queen Jocasta had tried to dispose of their newborn baby when they heard the evil prophecy, but fate brought cursed Oedipus back to Thebes. Jocasta hangs herself and Oedipus pokes out his own eyes with a pin from her dress, wandering into exile as a blind beggar.

As one would expect from idiosyncratic Pasolini, this isn't regular peplum fare. The story is bookended by scenes set in modern Italy (shot in Bologna), but the majority takes place in the desert lands between Corinth and Thebes, which Pasolini shot on spectacular locations in Morocco. *Oedipus* was lensed by Giuseppe Ruzzolini, the grand cities and crumbling villages of Morocco more believable than Cinecittà's cardboard palaces. Most of the extras are North Africans, with desert life etched into their faces. The costumes by Danilo Donati are stylised, almost to the point of distraction, the chunky woven fabrics, armour, helmets and crowns looking at once authentic and risibly bogus. Pasolini is a filmmaker with a fine eye for visuals. The Oracle at Delphi resembles an African tribal witch doctor, with a gourd-like headdress decorated with sticks and straw, while the Sphinx is similarly indigenous, not a monster but a man bedecked in straw, animal hair and necklaces. When we first meet Queen Jocasta, she is being pushed ahead of her entourage in a wheelbarrow, and victims of the contagion are tossed onto funeral pyres. Laius' servant carries baby Oedipus tied to a spear over his shoulder – the child's feet are tightly bound, which inspires his name: 'Little Swollen Feet' (Oedipus). Pasolini favourite Ninetto Davoli appears as Angelo, a Theban messenger boy who becomes blind Oedipus' companion, while Pasolini has a cameo as a Theban spokesman. Mangano, one of the great faces of Italian cinema who shot to stardom in Giuseppe De Santis' *Bitter Rice* (1949), makes a flawless Jocasta. The musical score is a string 'Quartet in C Major' by Mozart (used when Oedipus first meets Tiresias), a selection of Romanian folk songs (for village celebrations and ceremonies) and ancient Japanese music – a hollow beating drum and whistling flutes – which accompanies Oedipus on his desert odyssey.

Pasolini followed *Oedipus Rex* with **Medea** (1969), loosely based on the play by Euripides. Jason (Giuseppe Gentile) is raised by a centaur (Laurent Terzieff) and returns to Iolcus to claim his throne from King Pelias (Paul Jabara). The king sends Jason on a quest to retrieve the Golden Fleece. In Colchis, sorceress Medea (opera diva Maria Callas), the daughter of King Aeëtes, helps Jason to steal the fleece and runs away with him to Iolcus. In Corinth Jason falls in love with Glauce (Margareth Clementi), the daughter of King Creon (Massimo Girotti), and Medea uses her magic to take revenge. Partly based on the same source material as *Hercules* and *The Giants of Thessaly*, it is almost unrecognisable as the same story. The costumes are a mixture of Middle Eastern, African, Japanese and Medieval, giving the film a distinctive visual style. A chariot used by Medea looks nothing like its peplum equivalent, but rather a rickety construction of animal skins and timber, with solid wooden wheels, while the *Argo* is simply a raft with a livestock pen and oars. Pasolini filmed in Turkey (cave dwellings represent Colchis and weird tepee-like rock formations at Goreme) and Syria (the citadel fortress of Aleppo as Corinth's walls). Pasolini also shot in Italy: the Camposanto (cemetery) with its distinctive arched wall in the Piazza Dei Miracoli (Square of Miracles) in Pisa became Corinth and the coast at Grado (in the Friuli-Venezia Giulia region) was the setting for Jason's upbringing. Pasolini even uses the beach at Tor Caldara, when Jason and his Argonauts leave Colchis.

Pasolini stages some incredible brutality in *Medea*. In Colchis, a sacrificial victim is dismembered with an axe – his blood is dabbed on the crops, his vital organs are rubbed against fruit trees and his body parts are burned on a fire, to guarantee a good harvest. When King Aeëtes leads a posse after the fleece thieves, Medea hacks up her brother Absyrtus (Sergio Tramonti) and leaves a trail of body parts through the desert, slowing the pursuers down, as the king collects the bits of his son for burial. Fearful of the sorceress, King Creon exiles Medea, who takes revenge on Jason by killing Glauce. Pasolini includes two versions of this: one as described by Euripides, one his own interpretation. Medea gives a dress to Glauce, but as the princess puts it on, it catches fire, immolating her. In Pasolini's variation, Medea gives Glauce a bewitched dress which compels Glauce to jump to her death from Corinth's walls. For her final vengeance, Medea murders her three sons by Jason and burns their house: 'You will suffer with me', she tells Jason. Callas, in her only film, is a powerful screen presence. That face, with its strong forehead, noble nose and deep eyes, is the living image of classical Greek vase artwork. *Medea* is powerful, intellectual filmmaking – *Hercules* with subtitles it ain't.

Chapter Two

Historical Escapades, High Seas and Low B's
Costume Adventures

During the boom in Italian popular cinema, Italy, Spain and the former Yugoslavia were passed off as many locations, from the plains of Troy to the Russian steppes. Yugoslavia was an attractive location for international co-productions in the 1960s, due to its wide range of majestic, picturesque landscapes (from rolling, lush valleys and woodland to mountains and waterfalls) and its hoards of cheap extras. Italian cinema produced many disparate costume adventures, usually inspired by big budget Hollywood productions of the day, including pirate movies set in the Caribbean, swashbuckling cavalier and musketeer films, Napoleonic and Risorgimento epics, desert-set Arabian adventures and tales of rampaging Tartar and Mongol hordes.

Comes a Norseman: Viking Adventures

An unexpectedly popular sub-genre of Italian adventure cinema was the Viking saga. Richard Fleischer's *The Vikings* (1958) was the trigger film, with Kirk Douglas' scar-faced Einar (one eye plucked out by a falcon) and Tony Curtis' slave Eric (who has his left hand chopped off) fighting over Welsh princess Morgana (Curtis' then-wife Janet Leigh). Mario Nascimbene's fine score and the siege finale proved particularly influential and the film spawned half a dozen Italian derivatives starring Cameron Mitchell, Gordon Mitchell, Giorgio Ardisson or Giuliano Gemma, and also Richard Widmark's Hollywood vehicle *The Long Ships* (1964), which was shot in Yugoslavia.

Giacomo Gentilomo's **Last of the Vikings** (1961) cast Hollywood star Cameron Mitchell as Viking leader Harald. Viken, his village, is destroyed and his father murdered by Sveno (Edmund Purdom), the king of Norway. Harald poses as Danish emissary 'Prince Ragmar' to kidnap Sveno's daughter, Princess

Hilda (Isabelle Corey). Aakon (Andrea Aureli, with one eye and a scarred face) seizes control of Viken, but Harald kills his usurper. The Vikings construct war machines (a battering ram tower and catapults that fire flaming logs) to attack Sveno's castle.

Last of the Vikings is the best of the Italian cycle. Instead of the model trireme often deployed in pepla, it has full-sized Viking ships with dragon prows 'Furnished by Nettuno Navy Yard'. It also has a percussion-driven Roberto Nicolosi score and vivid costumes and set design. This is especially apparent in the Vikings' return to Viken (a crow-pecked, arrow-riddled misty ruin) and in Sveno's labyrinthine stone castle and torture chamber (interiors were filmed at Cinecittà and Titanus), where Harold's brother Guntag (Giorgio Ardisson) is crucified by Sveno on an X-shaped cross. The bloodletting is frequent, with death by arrow in the eye, hatchet to the head, torch to the face and sword through the chest, complete with blood spurts. Viking formula ingredients include boisterous feasts and funeral pyre send-offs to Valhalla. London-born Edmund Purdom, cast as Sveno, had worked with Laurence Olivier on the Broadway stage in *Caesar and Cleopatra* and *Anthony and Cleopatra*. His histrionic shambling transforms Sveno into Richard III; Purdom portrayed several historical figures in Italian spectacles, including Herod and Rasputin. The supporting cast features Mario Feliciani and Piero Lulli as Sveno's henchmen Simon and Hardak, and Aldo Buffo Landi as Harald's lieutenant Longborg, while fencing master Benito Stefanelli appears as Viking Lorik. Mitchell turns in an effective performance as the dynamic Harald, who in one scene dispatches a bear about to ravage Hilda.

The success of *Last of the Vikings* in Italy resulted in Mitchell being called back to make **Erik the Conqueror** (1961), directed by Mario Bava. It was released as *Fury of the Vikings* in the UK, and has been known variously as *The Invaders*, *Viking Invaders* and *Conquest of the Normans*. This is not to be confused with Giuseppe Vari's *Attack of the Normans* (1962), with Mitchell as the villain, which was set in the time of the Norman Conquest. *Erik the Conqueror* begins in 786 AD with a spectacular action sequence staged on the beach at Tor Caldara, Anzio Cape (depicting the coast of Northern Britain), as Sir Ruthford's British army pillage a Viking village. Viking Erik (Giorgio Ardisson) is captured and raised by British queen Alice (Françoise Christophe). In adulthood he becomes Duke of Helford, commander of the British navy, while his brother Eron (Cameron Mitchell) becomes a Viking chief and leads an expedition against Britain. Eventually Erik and Eron face each other in a duel.

Filmed from August to October 1961, the film's interiors were at Cinecittà and Titanus Studios, including a vast Viking great hall (dominated by a gnarly root from *Hercules in the Centre of the Earth*). The colour-drenched Bava compositions in widescreen Dyaliscope visually enhance the film. Bava staged his sea battles indoors on studio soundstages – to suggest the forward movement of

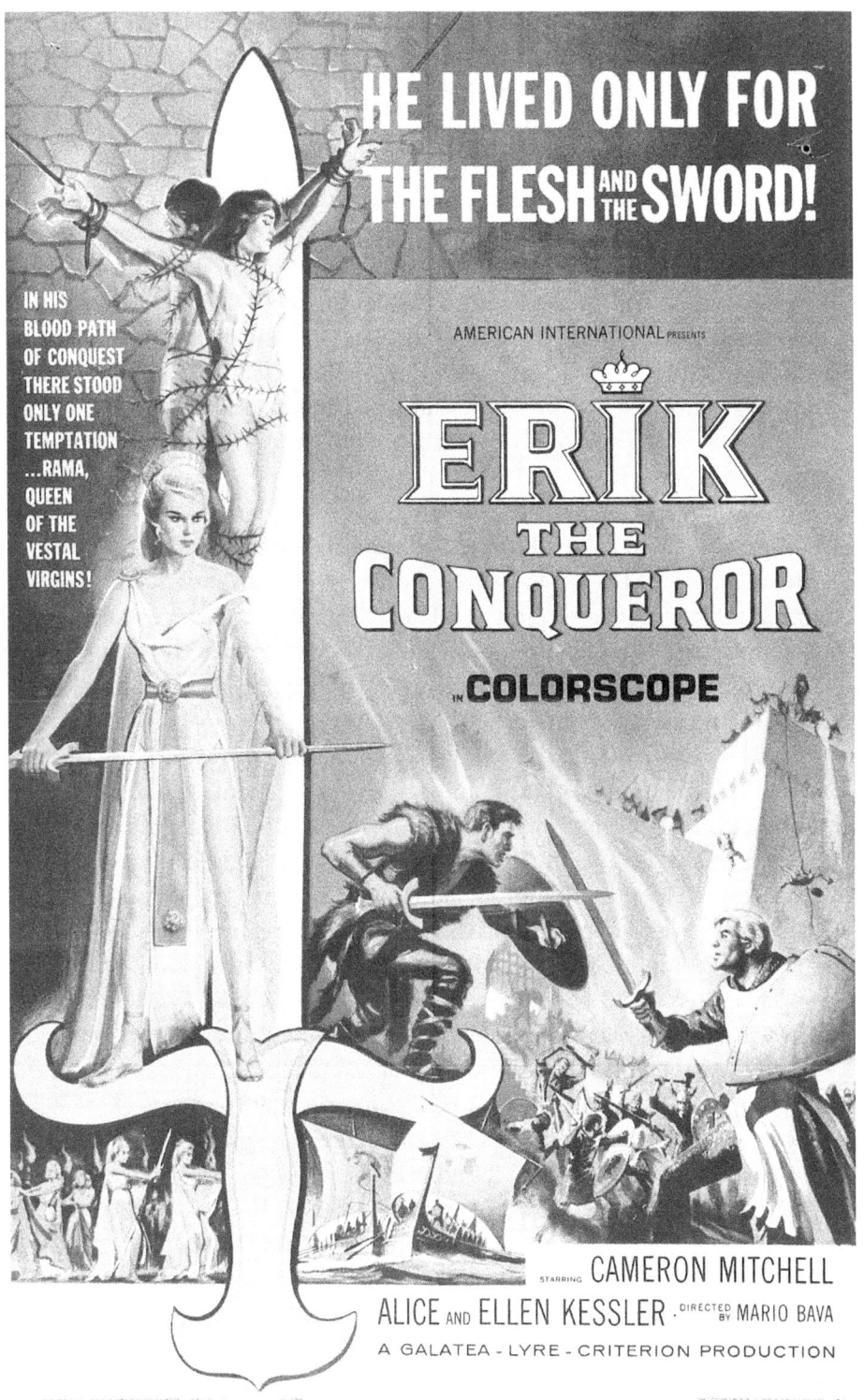

US poster for AIP's release of the Viking epic *Erik the Conqueror* (1961), directed by Mario Bava and starring Cameron Mitchell and the Kessler twins. Poster courtesy Ian Caunce Collection.

the ship, he dollied his camera alongside a stationary vessel. Bava created a castle atop the bluffs of Tor Caldara by simply cutting an image from the *National Geographic* and aligning it in the frame. The final battle, as the Vikings storm Queen Alice's fortress, is a convincing swirl of fire and sword (plus stock footage from *Last of the Vikings*). The cast included Andrea Checchi as Sir Ruthford, Raf Baldassarre as his trusty bowman assassin, Folco Lulli as Erik and Eron's father, Joe Robinson as Viking warrior Garion and Franco Ressel as King Lothar (Queen Alice's murdered husband). Lothar is king of the Britons in the English language print, but of Scotland in the Italian version. A casting coup was the beautiful East German Kessler twins, Alice and Ellen, as white-robed Vestal Virgins. Erik falls for Rama (Alice) and Eron loves Daya (Ellen). The Kesslers were cabaret stars (they perform a synchronised dance routine in *Erik*) and later appeared briefly in *The Last Days of Sodom and Gomorrah*. AIP trailers for *Erik* billed them as '*Life*'s Cover Girls'.

In Mario Caiano's **Erik the Viking** (1965 – *Vengeance of the Vikings*), Erik (Giuliano Gemma) leads an expedition across the Sea of Darkness and discovers America. Lucio De Santis, Gordon Mitchell and Eduardo Fajardo covet the Indians' gold and Elisa Montes is Erik's Indian princess love interest. Photographed by Enzo Barboni and scored by Carlo Franci, the film is notable for its tropical greenery, shot in the botanical gardens of Finca (country house) La Concepcion, north of Malaga.

Bava's **Knives of the Avenger** (1966) is a western in Viking garb. Although his penchant for gore, mist and shadow is more than evident in the film, it was yet another Bava hybrid, coining 'Viking horror'. Karin (Elissa Pichelli, billed as 'Lisa Wagner' or 'Lissa') and her little son Moki (Luciano Polletin) are warned by seer Shula to go into hiding. Aghen (Fausto Tozzi) is trying to kill them, so Karin and Moki relocate to a hut in the mountains. They are visited by a wandering stranger (Cameron Mitchell), an expert crossbowman and knifethrower. He is vengeance-seeking Rurig (some sources call him Rurik) – Aghen beheaded Rurig's wife and son years before. Filmed in a week in February 1966 for $75,000, *Knives of the Avenger* is another visually sumptuous Technicolor adventure from Bava, shot in 2.35:1 Techniscope on period interiors at Titanus Studios, Rome, and at the Tor Caldara Nature Reserve and the lush grassland of Manziana, Lazio. The Viking village set is a disguised US cavalry fort and a village tavern is a wild west Mexican cantina set. Giacomo Rossi-Stuart played Karin's husband, King Arald; stuntmen Bruno Arié, Goffredo Unger and Osiride Pevarello played Aghen's henchmen. Viking favourite Mitchell – his hair was red or blond in these adventures, depending on the quality of the print viewed – is dubbed in the English language version by Paul Frees. Rurig is essentially a revenge-seeking stranger in town who's quick on the draw: he can throw three daggers simultaneously. As the trailers stated, 'The *Knives of the Avenger* – They Hit Dead Centre'. Marcello Giombini's score even resembles a western, with strident horn 'riding themes' and a harmonica melody.

Wind from the East: The Hordes Is Coming

Muscleman Steve Reeves starred as Hadji Murad in ***The White Warrior*** (1959), which was based on a Leo Tolstoy novel. Murad was a rebel who in 1850 led the mountain peoples of the Caucuses in the steppes against the tyrannical rule of Tsar Nicholas I (Milivoje Zivanovic). Though it deploys great costumes and settings (in Yugoslavia), a score by Roberto Nicolosi and photography by Mario Bava, this is a formula Reeves vehicle. The familiar story trapped Reeves between a good woman – lowly peasant Sultanet (Giorgia Moll) – and a bad one, Russian Princess Maria (Scilla Gabel). Villainy was supplied by Gerard Herter as Prince Sergei (Maria's husband), who captures Murad, submitting Reeves to his obligatory onscreen flogging. Director Riccardo Freda occasionally manages some rousing scenes: the Russian attack on a peasant village; Murad's massed cavalry attack on Fort Tabarasan (a stronghold that controls the Black Mountains); Murad's escape from the Russian HQ (when he rides his horse through a packed ballroom); and the final duel between Murad and traitorous rebel Akmet Khan (Renato Baldini). For this scene, Reeves was doubled by Alan Steel. Reeves' acting isn't up to much – any emotional turmoil is conveyed by clenched fists, gritted teeth and frowning – but the film was successful in the US in 1961 when released by Warner Bros. As publicity stated, 'Make Way For Steve "Hercules" Reeves!'

For Carlo Campogalliani's ***Goliath and the Barbarians*** (1959 – *Colossus and the Golden Horde*), Reeves was in muscles mode in 568 AD, as Lombard hordes led by Alboin (guest star Bruce Cabot) invaded Italy. Emilius (Reeves), 'a Goliath', sees his father murdered by the Lombards and swears revenge on culprit Igor (Livio Lorenzon). Emilius disguises himself as a growling monster – in a lion mask with pointed teeth, a cloak and clawed 'paws' – and attacks the Lombards. A love story subplot sees Emilius involved with barbarian Landa, played by Chelo Alonso, who performs a snaky dance routine. Giulia Rubini and Luciano Marin were the peasant lovers Sabina (Emilius' sister) and Marco. The Lombards, sporting animal skin outfits, featured Furio Meniconi as Dencerico, Arturo Dominici as Svevo and Andrea Checchi as Delfo (Landa's father). Stuntmen Pietro Ceccarelli and Nello Pazzafini appeared as barbarians and busy stunt-coordinator Remo De Angelis can be spotted in three supporting roles (as Igor's sidekick, a blond barbarian and a peasant archer). *Goliath* was filmed in Yugoslavia and at Incir-De Paolis Studios. Much of the woodland footage was filmed indoors. In costume Reeves resembles a hulking Robin Hood and his stunt double was Giovanni Cianfriglia/'Ken Wood'. The opening caption called 568 AD 'A time when if you didn't love or fight...life was a very short and dull affair'. In the US Carlo Innocenzi's score was replaced by Les Baxter themes and it was a great success when it was released by AIP in 1960, cut from 100 minutes to a barely coherent 85.

The Tartars (1961 – co-directed by Richard Thorpe and Ferdinando Baldi) offers a once-in-a-lifetime pairing of Orson Welles and Victor Mature. Set on the banks of the Volga in Russia, the film tells of battles between Vikings, led by Oleg the Brave (Mature) and the Tartar hordes, commanded by their khan, Burundai (Welles). Oleg kills Burundai's brother Tobro (Folco Lulli) and takes Tobro's daughter Samya (Bella Cortez) hostage. Burundai kidnaps Oleg's wife Helga (Liana Orfei), while Oleg's brother Erik (Luciano Marin) falls in love with Samya. Eventually the Tartars attack the Viking stockade: both Oleg and Burundai are killed and Samya and Erik float away together in a longboat. Shot in collaboration with Dabrava Film, in Zagreb, amid sweeping Yugoslavian landscapes (with interiors at Titanus Studios), *The Tartars* is backed by a flavourful Russian-sounding score by Renzo Rossellini. What sinks the film as credible entertainment are the leads. With his oil slick hair and Mediterranean complexion, Mature makes an unconvincing Viking. It is a prime example of Mature's talent for reducing historical figures to grinning idiots, and when he's not smiling, he wears a slightly troubled expression, as though something unpleasant is wafting across the Volga. It's wonderful to hear the rich tones of Welles enunciate: 'So the Viking wolf has ventured into the den of the Tartar bear'.

The Tartars shouldn't be confused with *The Tartars* (1963 – *Plains of Battle* and *Taras Bulba, the Cossack*) starring Vladimir Medar as Taras Bulba, which in turn shouldn't be confused with *Taras Bulba* (1962), Hollywood's Argentinian-shot version of the same story, featuring Yul Brynner as Taras. Ursus muscled in on the act with Remigio Del Grosso's **Ursus and the Tartar Princess** (1963), a displaced western set on the Crimean frontier in the seventeenth century. A patrol of red-jacketed Polish knights led by Prince Stefan (Ettore Manni) take on roving bands of Tartars. Stefan, captured by the Tartars, falls for Princess Ila (Yoko Tani), the daughter of the Great Khan (Akim Tamiroff). Tom Felleghi and Andrea Aureli appeared as the Tartar villains. Axe-wielding woodcutter Ursus (Joe Robinson) is almost an afterthought in his own movie, as the accent is placed on a religious conflict between Christian Poles and Pagan Tartars. *Atlas Versus the Czar* (1964) cast Kirk Morris as Atlas and Massimo Serato as the czar, while Sergio Grieco's *Queen of the Tartars* (1961 – *The Huns*) saw Chelo Alonso in the title role as Tanya. Both these films used the hokey Welles-Mature model as their Tartar source.

Samson and the 7 Miracles of the World (1961 – originally 'Maciste in the Court of the Great Khan') was set in thirteenth-century China, when the Mongols invaded and the Mighty Garak (Leonardo Severini) ruled with tyranny. When Garak attempts to murder the rightful heirs to the throne – Prince Tsai-sung and his sister, Princess Lai-ling (Yoko Tani) – Samson (Gordon Scott) intervenes, despite looking completely out of place in his Tarzan loincloth amongst the opulent Far Eastern décor. *7 Miracles* is one of Riccardo Freda's better pepla. It was greatly aided by the leftover sets, costumes and a multitude of Asian extras from *Marco Polo* (1961), which starred Tani opposite Rory Calhoun as the Venetian explorer. During a punch-up Samson destroys a tavern like a human-wrecking ball and wrestles with a bladed chariot about to behead five unlucky rebels (in footage so impressive that it reappeared in *Maciste in Hell*). For the film's US release several musical cues were replaced by Les Baxter 'Goliath' themes; fortunately Carlo Innocenzi's tinkling Chinese-flavoured main theme was retained. The cast included Helene Chanel as Garak's villainous lover Kiutai, Valery Inkijinoff as the high priest and Gabriele Antonini as rebel leader Cho. Samson performs only two miracles: first, he finds and tolls the Great Bell of Freedom, calling the oppressed to arms against Garak. Unfortunately the Great Bell's Great Clapper knocks Samson out. Garak buries Samson alive deep in the foundation bowls of the city in a tiny stone chamber. But ancient mystic the Wise One calls on Samson to perform the 'Seventh Miracle'. Mighty Samson musters all his strength and ruptures the earth, causing a mighty earthquake which destroys the city, enabling Lai-ling and Cho to found a new dynasty.

Domenico Paolella's **Hercules against the Mongols** (1963) cast Mark Forest as Hercules, a dislocated BC Greek muscleman hero transported to 1227 AD. Genghis Khan is dead and his three sons stir up trouble, fomenting war between the Mongols and the Christian west. The trio are Sayan, a peerless archer (Ken Clark), Susdal, an expert with a whip (Renato Rossini) and Kihan, meaning 'The Hurricane', a strongman (Nadir Moretti), all of whom wear drooping Fu Manchu moustaches. They launch a stock footage attack on the Christian city of Tudela, killing the king and capturing his daughter Bianca (Jose Greci), but her little brother Alexander (Loris Loddi), the heir to the throne, is taken to safety by his nurse (Bianca Doria). Enter Hercules, who resolves to restore Alexander to his throne and kick the Mongols out of Tudela, as foretold by a Chinese seer in the film's pretitle sequence. A subplot details the villains' search for the treasure of Tudela, which is hidden in a grist mill. Maria Grazia Spina appeared as the evil Mongol warrior Li-Wan and Tullio Altamura was Adolphus, a spy. Hercules' feats of strength are average stuff, except for a lively scene when he defends himself with an iron bar against a lion. Christian Bratislavan knights led by their king (Giuseppe Addobbati) storm Tudela and Hercules bursts a dam, routing the Mongols. It was filmed on sunny Yugoslavian exteriors and at Incir-De Paolis Studios interiors: the Mongol torture chamber is the familiar peplum arched stone wall set.

One of many great things about Italian cinema is that even the most innocuous looking film can deliver the unexpected. Paolella's **Hercules against the Barbarians** (1964) would be expected to be a 'muscleman-Mongol' hybrid, with the Greek hero adrift in Poland. It opens in the twelfth century with the Mongols under Genghis Khan (Roldano Lupi) storming Krakow and being repulsed by 'Hercules the Hurricane' (Mark Forest). Soon Paolella's film drifts further from logic and history, with a subplot detailing a witch hunt in a peasant village, complete with torch-bearing locals. Hercules' lover Armina (Jose Greci) is kidnapped by the Mongols (she is the heir to the Polish throne), so Hercules is dispatched with Arias (the accused witch, played by Gloria Milland, a regular in Paolella productions) to save Armina from the Mongol fortress at Tarnopol.

As in *Hercules against the Mongols*, Paolella makes much use of stock footage and recasts many of the earlier film's actors. Ken Clark played Kublai the Mongol villain (eventually crushed beneath a descending portcullis) and Renato Rossini was Mongol Gasan, while Mirko Ellis appeared as the Polish king Vladimir, Tullio Altamura was a priest and Ugo Sasso was the leader of a band of roving acrobats, who entertain the Mongol court with gymnastics, lance duels and plate spinning. Obviously a budget production filmed at Incir-De Paolis Studios, the film had music that was lifted from *Maciste in Hell*. Hercules wrestles a rubber crocodile and crosses a fiery chasm on a log (filmed at Tor Caldara) in this cross-genera movie that doesn't quite gel. Hollywood also shot its own Mongol epic in Yugoslavia. *Genghis Khan* (1964) boasted spectacular settings and costumes, and some spectacular miscasting, with Egyptian Omar Sharif in the title role and James Mason and Robert Morley as caricatured Chinese.

A Thousand and One Fights: Arabian Adventures

A minor cycle of Arabian adventures fused themes found in muscleman epics with '1001 Nights' settings and stories. **The Conqueror of the Orient** (1960), a mercifully brief, overly chatty adventure from Tanio Boccia, is set in an unspecified eastern Orient created at De Laurentiis Studios. In the City of the Golden Dome, evil Dakar (Paul Muller) and his lover Dynazeze (Gianna Maria Canale) rule. Nadir (Rik Battaglia), a lowly fisherman, saves the life of a fugitive princess, Fatima (Irene Tunc), and discovers that he is the throne's rightful heir. The film is noteworthy for its insufficient sound effects: as dozens of rebel horsemen hurtle through lush green countryside, two coconuts clatter on the soundtrack.

Mario Bava provided the imaginative special effects for Henry Levin's colourful children's film **The Wonders of Aladdin** (1961), photographed by Tonino Delli Colli at Kairouan, Tunisia and Titanus Studios, Rome. Donald O'Connor starred as Aladdin, heading a cast which included Michele Mercier as Princess Zaina, Vittorio De Sica as the genie and young Mario Girotti (later 'Terence Hill') as Prince Moluk.

Steve Reeves' contribution to the cycle was **The Thief of Baghdad** (1961), directed by Arthur Lubin. Cutpurse Karim (Reeves) embarks on a quest to pass through the Seven Doors to find where a magical Blue Rose grows – it is the only cure for the bedevilled princess, Amina (Giorgia Moll). The film is essentially *Hercules in the Centre of the Earth* in turbans. Arturo Dominici guested as the evil prince, Osman, Edy Vessel was a sexy distraction for Karim and George Chamarat was a friendly magician who helps Karim. Colourfully shot in the Tunisian desert by Tonino Delli Colli and scored by Angelo Lavagnino, *Thief* is one of Reeves' finest vehicles, featuring an array of mythological creations, including tentacled trees which come to life, a cloak of invisibility, a Pegasus, blank-faced egg-headed swordsmen, fiery caverns, earthquakes, petrified stone men, a duel between Karim and a bald, gummy wrestler on a clifftop bridge, and Karim's magical army, which takes on Osman's forces in the final attack on Baghdad.

Perhaps the sub-genre's greatest moment was Antonio Margheriti's ***The Golden Arrow*** (1962), with teen idol Tab Hunter as robber Hassan. In Damascus, Princess Jamilia (Rosanna Podesta) must choose her suitor from among three princes. Hassan poses as Prince Hassan of the Islands of Flame and kidnaps Jamilia, but instead of ransoming her, he falls in love. He is the son of Karim the Just and with help from three genies he embarks on a quest to retrieve the Golden Arrow, which once fired magically returns to its owner's hand. The Prince of Bassora takes over Damascus with his army, forcing Jamilia to marry him. The colourful cinematography, detailed interiors and exotic costumes make this a visual delight. Desert and mountain location footage was shot in Egypt, with interiors filmed at Titanus Studios. Jose Jaspe and Claudio Scarchilli played Hassan's robber cohorts, Sabrath and Abdul; Franco Pesce was an elderly flying carpet merchant, Dominique Boschero played the queen of a realm frozen in stone and Mario Feliciani was Baktiar, the wily grand vizier. Renato Baldini was excellent as the power-hungry prince of Bassora, with Calisto Calisti as his sidekick. When a hermit refuses to hand over his elixir of life, the villains stab him, though not mortally, waiting to see where the vial is hidden and then testing it on the dying man. The trio of comical genies in outsized turbans (Giustino Durano, Umberto Filiciani and Franco Scandurra) provide the daftest moments, as they conjure Hassan out of various scrapes – like *The Wonders of Aladdin*, *Arrow* was aimed squarely at the children's market. Hassan navigates the cave realm of the Fire Queen (Gloria Milland) who is protected by the Flaming Monsters – flailing stuntmen in blazing fireproof suits. In the pitched battle finale Hassan and the genies (on flying carpets) launch an aerial assault, flattening Bassoran soldiers by dropping enormous clay jars on them.

Anthar the Invincible (1964 – *The Devil of the Desert against the Son of Hercules*) was also directed by Margheriti. Anthar (Kirk Morris) of the Bathaya tribe saves Princess Soraya (Michele Girardon) from Akrim (Jose Jaspe). Soraya's father, the king of Baral, has been killed and her brother, Prince Daikor (Manuel Gallardo), imprisoned by wicked Ganor and his henchman Rabek (Goffredo Unger). Renato Baldini appeared as Kamal, who buys Soraya from Akrim in a slave market, Mario Feliciani played slaver Ganor and young Roberto Dell'Acqua played Anthar's mute sidekick Aimu 'The Mosquito'. The straightforward story is enhanced by the Arabian setting – the city of Baral (with interiors and exteriors filmed at Incir-De Paolis Studios) and desert location footage shot in Algeria – but Morris is given little opportunity to flex muscle until the climax. Anthar wrestles a wild Indian rhino and incites the populace to revolt and then duels with Ganor in the villain's Chamber of Death hall of mirrors.

In ***Kindar the Invulnerable*** (1964), Kindar is born in the city of Uthor. His mother dies in childbirth when she is struck by lighting, but Kindar survives, imbued with super strength and invulnerability. Little Kindar is stolen by rebel nomads and raised by Chief Seymuth (Mimmo Palmera), never knowing that he is really the king of Uthor's son. After 20 years pass, Kindar (Mark Forrest) is to lead the attack on besieged Uthor, but on discovering his real parentage he switches sides. Seymuth discovers that the hero's weakness is fire (he's 'Kindar the Inflammable') and tries to kill him in the Temple of Horus. Osvaldo Civriani's *Kindar* was shot at De Paolis Studios and amidst real pyramids in Egypt. The film features a Russian-sounding chanted score by Lallo Gori; Rosalba Neri appears as Seymuth's lover Kira, Renato Rossini played Kindar's brother Siro and Mimmo Palmera's overplayed wicked laugh grates on the nerves: 'Kindar Ha Ha Ha Ha! Your opponent challenges you! Ha Ha! To the death!'

Emimmo Salvi's **Ali Baba and the Seven Saracens** (1964) starred Gordon Mitchell as Omar, who rules the city of Kufar. For Omar to accede to the Gold Throne he must defeat seven tribal challengers. Omar's enemy is Ali Baba (Bruno Piergentili/'Dan Harrison') from the Mahariti tribe. Ali falls for Princess Fatima (Bella Cortez) and faces Omar in the grand tournament: thus Ali Baba faces the Seven Saracens. Franco Doria played Omar's chief adviser Sherif, Carla Calo appeared as Omar's lover Farinda, while Ali's jailbreaks are masterminded by a eunuch with a nervous twitch (Attilio Severini) and dwarf Jookie (Tony Di Mitri, who resembles a miniature Frank Sinatra). *Ali Baba* doesn't hang around: look out for the torture scene where Mahariti tribesmen are throttled with chains, repeated shots of the same quarry (used for all the film's exteriors) and the climactic tournament (an eight-man 'It's a Knockout') with contestants deploying anything that comes to hand – including swords, forks, lances, chains, knives, maces and bows – until only Omar and Ali are left standing. Mitchell is in fine evil form as Omar, his rock-faced grimace fixed, until he's run over by a chariot. Salvi later directed Mitchell and Mickey Hargitay in the lively western-gothic horror peplum hybrid *3 Bullets for Ringo* (1966).

All For One: Pirates and Swashbucklers

The successful Hollywood production *The Crimson Pirate* (1952), starring Burt Lancaster as Captain Vallo, the acrobatic gunrunner, was filmed around the island of Ischia in the Bay of Naples (subbing for the Caribbean). Italian adventure filmmakers capitalised on its lively formula with a short-lived cycle of derivatives, with titles such as *Guns of the Black Witch* (1961) and *Cold Steel for Tortuga* (1965). In Mario Costa's **Gordon the Black Pirate** (1961) Ricardo Montalban played the title role, a buccaneer who battles slave traders led by governor's aide Romero (Vincent Price) from the Caribbean island of Novesperanza. Thinking he has put the trafficker, Captain Tortuga (Jose Jaspe), out of business, Gordon discovers otherwise when a slave's corpse is washed ashore. The trader's base, 'a vulture's nest', is the island of San Salvador and the Black Pirate sets sail on his galleon *The Indomitable*. Gordon impersonates 'Don Carlos Bastia', a rich Cuban plantation owner with 'labour problems', and attempts to woo the governor's daughter, Manuela Cortez de Castilla (Giuliana Rubini).

Gordon the Black Pirate is flamboyant costume adventure at its best. Montalban cuts a dash, while Price does his usual crafty scene-stealing. Liana

Orfei played Novesperanza villager Luana, who loves scallywag Gordon. Jaspe, a regular in buccaneering fare, played Tortuga with an eye patch and a prodigious beard and girth. The pirates include stuntmen Bruno Arié, Riccardo Pizzuti (as *The Indomitable*'s helmsman) and Gino Marturano (as Gordon's second-in-command). In one unpleasant scene, an English slaver throws its live cargo overboard, still bound, rather than let them go free. Filmed on Mediterranean locations, *Gordon the Black Pirate* includes all the expected buccaneering ingredients, accompanied by a jaunty pirate score by Angelo Lavagnino. There are elegant balls; a Caribbean 'Fiesta of the Dragon'; chained, downtrodden plantation slaves; pirate raids on peasant villages; and an array of authentic weapons including flintlock pistols, halberds (a spear-battleaxe combo), rapiers, daggers and cannon. The sea battles never involve more than two ships, which look as though they were the only ones available to the production. The storming of Don Pedro's castle is a picturesque sequence – as Gordon's vessels bombard the fortress, his men scale the castle walls with grappling hooks and the Spanish defenders shell the galleons.

Many peplum stars tried their hand at swashbucklers. Steve Reeves starred as Captain Morgan in Andre De Toth and Primo Zeglio's *Morgan the Pirate* (1960), with Valerie Lagrange, Ivo Garrani, Giorgio Ardisson, Lydia Alfonsi and Chelo Alonso. He also portrayed turbaned rebel pirate Sandokan fighting British imperialism in the South China Sea and the jungles of Borneo in Umberto Lenzi's *Sandokan the Great* (1963) and *The Pirates of Malaysia* (1964). **Sandokan the Great**, based on Emilio Salgari's novel *The Tigers of Mompracem*, saw the hero kidnap Mary Anne (Genevieve Grad), the niece of Sandokan's arch enemy, Lord Guillonk (Leo Anchoriz). Sandokan's band trek across the island, braving rivers, poisoned arrows, wild animals, swamps and a tribe of headhunters, but are captured on a beach as they attempt to escape by fishing boat. Antonio Molino Rojo, Enzo Fiermonte and Mario Valdemarin played Queen Victoria's finest, and Sandokan's pirates featured action stars and stuntmen: Rik Battaglia, Nazzareno Zamperla, Dakar, Maurice Poli, Gino Marturano and Giovanni Cianfriglia (Reeves' acrobatic stunt double). Yugoslavian actor Andrea Bosić played Sandokan's sidekick, Portuguese adventurer Yanez De Gomera.

Released internationally by MGM, this excellent adventure had a good score by Giovanni Fusco, a sense of exoticism and scale in its Malaysian locations, colourful costumes and Techniscope location photography which featured much jungle wildlife footage. The colonial milieu of pith helmets and turbans makes a pleasant change for Reeves, who wrestles a tiger, avoids an elephant stampede and wields a mean machine-gun in the all-action finale, as Sandokan's pirates and the headhunters storm to the rescue at Fort Victoria to defeat Guillonk's sepoys. Ray Danton took over as Sandokan in *Sandokan Fights Back* and *Sandokan against the Leopard of Sarawak* (both 1964), with Guy Madison as Yanez. Kabir Bedi played the lead in Sergio Sollima's six-part TV miniseries *Sandokan* (1976), with Philippe Leroy as Yanez, Carole Andre as Marianne and a catchy theme tune by the De Angelis brothers.

Gordon Scott and Gianna Maria Canale appeared in Luigi Capuano's impressive, Venetian-set *The Lion of Saint Mark* (1963 – *The Marauder*). Canale starred as Sandra in *Queen of the Pirates* (1960 – with Massimo Serato, Scilla Gabel and Livio Lorenzon) and its sequel *Tiger of the Seven Seas* (1963). Richard Harrison was the *Avenger of the Seven Seas* (1961) and Alan Steel starred in *Hercules and the Black Pirate* (1964). Lisa Gastoni was female buccaneer Mary Read in *Hell Below Deck* (1961 – *Queen of the Seas*), Mijanou Bardot (Brigitte's sister) starred in *Pirate of the Black Hawk* (1958) and Robert Alda tortured Pier Angeli in *Musketeers of the Seas* (1960). Singer Johnny Desmond was the *Hawk of the Caribbean* (1963) and George Hilton starred in *The Masked Man against the Pirates* (1962 – *The Black Pirate*). Lex Barker carved an elegant niche for himself in Italy in such fare, starring in *Captain Falcon* (1958), *Son of the Red Corsair* (1959), *The Pirate and the Slave Girl* (1960) and *Secret of the Black Falcon* and *Pirates of the Coast* (both 1961).

One of the most widely seen Italian swashbucklers is **Seven Seas to Calais** (1962), co-directed by Rudolph Maté and Primo Zeglio. An entertaining skip through Tudor history, the film is a biopic of Francis Drake: mariner, explorer and queen's privateer. In 1577 Drake embarks on a three-year expedition in the *Golden Hind* to loot Spanish gold from their Pacific ports, with the blessing of Protestant queen Elizabeth I (Irene Worth). Drake returns with a mountain of Spanish gold, which earns him a knighthood. In 1587, Spanish plotters led by Lord Babbington (Terence Hill) attempt to assassinate the queen and free Mary Queen of Scots (Esmeralda Ruspoli), a Catholic, from jail in Tutbury Castle. But Mary, Babbington and the conspirators are beheaded. In 1588 King Philip II of Spain (Umberto Raho) attacks England with an armada, but en route to Calais to pick up the Duke of Parma's army, Drake defeats them.

Seven Seas was shot in Rome at Titanus Appia Studios, with a few well-placed establishing shots of key English locations (including the exterior of Saint James's Palace). The nautical scenes were shot in the Bay of Naples. The film benefits from fine Eastmancolor and CinemaScope photography, some good sets and ships, and authentic Tudor costumes (designed by Filippo Sanjust) with doublets, hose and ruffs de rigueur. Two athletic Australian-born actors played the main roles: Rod Taylor made an excellent Drake and Keith Michell (later of 'Captain Beaky and his Band' fame) was his roisterous sidekick, Malcolm Marsh. Edy Vessel was French exile Arabella who is involved in a love triangle between Marsh and snivelling Babbington. Anthony Dawson and Basil Dignam were cast as the queen's trusted advisors Lord High Treasurer William Burghley and spymaster Sir Francis Walsingham. Drake's crew featured Gianni Cajafa as bosun Tom Moon and Marco Guglielmi as Parson Fletcher. During Drake's three-year voyage they land in America (New Albion) and bring back potatoes and tobacco. This sequence includes Marsh's humorous relationship with an Indian chief's daughter, 'Potato' (Rosella D'Aquino). Only in the armada finale does the film fall flat, with an unconvincing sea battle staged by burning model ships in a choppy water tank.

In 1935 Errol Flynn sprang acrobatically onto the scene as the lead in *Captain Blood*, based on the novel by Rafael Sabatini; 27 years later Tullio Demichelli's **The Son of Captain Blood** cast Errol's 21-year-old son Sean as Robert Blood, the dead buccaneer's son. In Port Royal, Jamaica, Lady Arabella (Ann Todd) wants her son Robert to study medicine in Edinburgh, but he goes to sea. During his eventful voyage, Robert falls for Abigail McBride (Alessandra Panaro) and encounters his father's old pirate crew, including Oglethorpe (Roberto Camardiel), Kirby (Barta Barry), Lynch (Angel Ortiz) and Timothy Thomas (Fernando Sancho, dubbed with an Irish accent). They battle Robert's father's arch enemies Capitan De Malagon (Jose Niento) and henchman Bruno (Raf Baldassarre). In Port Royal, Governor Townsend has enslaved Arabella's black plantation labourers and the pirates attack as an earthquake strikes. Robert saves his mother and her servants, including Moses (John Kitzmiller), and heads for high ground, as Port Royal is engulfed in a tidal wave. Handsome blond Flynn makes a fine swashbuckling lead (he also appeared in *The Sign of Zorro* [1964]). Antonio Casas appeared as the captain of a British slave ship and Riccardo Pizzuti and Alvaro De Luna loitered as pirates. Port Royal was filmed on the seafront of Denia harbour (País Valenciano, Spain), on the Gulf of Valencia. This location was also used for *Cervantes* (1967), a dull biopic of poet Miguel De Cervantes (Horst Buchholz), which features a re-enactment of the sea battle at Lepanto (1571) in the Gulf of Corinth, between Turks and the Holy League. *Cervantes* thanked the general staff of the Spanish naval base at Cartagena for their assistance in staging the engagement.

Sergio Corbucci's **The Man Who Laughs** (1966) was an adaptation of Victor Hugo's novel. In Renaissance Italy, Cesare Borgia (Edmund Purdom) and his sister Lucrezia (Lisa Gastoni) spread terror across the land. Astore Manfredi, the Duke of Faenza and an enemy of the Borgias', hides out with a group of travelling players, including blind Dea (Ilaria Occhini) and tightrope walker Angelo, who wears a leather mask to conceal his disfigured, grotesquely grinning face. Most of the players are killed during an attack on the Borgias' stronghold and Angelo swears revenge on Astore: the duke steals Dea from him when she regains her sight. Corbucci cast French actor Jean Sorel as both handsome aristocrat Astore and red-haired acrobat 'freak' Angelo. This dual casting is explained. Cesare's physician experiments on human physiognomies, using lepers as guinea pigs, and alters Angelo's features with cosmetic surgery, transforming him into Astore. At Astore and Dea's wedding ceremony in Faenza, the Borgias swap Angelo for Astore, who will reign as their puppet. It was filmed at Tor Caldara beach and at Cinecittà and Titanus Appia Studios. Corbucci regular Gino Pernice appeared as Borgia henchman Galliaco. There is plenty of action from Corbucci and some macabre touches: a sadistic Borgia torture chamber and lepers dragging their death cart through the countryside. Purdom is excellent as cultured sadist Cesare, who notes, 'As painting is an art, so is killing'. Cameron Mitchell also played Cesare in Pino Mercati's *The Black Duke* (1963), with Gloria Milland as his adversary, Caterina Sforza.

Terence Hill starred in Vincent Thomas' **The Black Pirate** (1971 – *Blackie the Pirate*), an oddly listless swashbuckler, with fleeting swash and scant buckle. Hill played Captain Blackie, an English corsair fighting on the Spanish Main, who tries to steal a shipment of gold from the viceroy (Edmond Purdom). Bud Spencer played rival pirate Captain Skull, who sides with Blackie. Hill's sidekicks are his burly bearded bosun (Fernando Bilbao) and scallywag Don Pedro (George Martin). Silvia Monti was Hill's love interest, viceroy's wife Isabel De Mendoza y Laguna and Diana Lorys was posada owner Manuela. The hornpipe score (including a terrible title song, 'Ship Ahoy!') was provided by Gino Peguri and any excitement generated during the sea battles is dissipated by the obvious use of grainy stock footage from previous pirate adventures.

Musketeers and cavaliers were also popular subject matter in Italy, in such films as *The Devil's Cavaliers* (1959), starring Anthony Steffen, Gianna Maria Canale and Frank Latimore (later the star of Spanish 'Zorro' westerns), *The Cavaliers of Devil's Castle* (1959), *Revenge of the Musketeers* (1963 – with Fernando Lamas as D'Artagnan), *The Secret Mark of D'Artagnan* (1962) and *The Four Musketeers* (1963). Pierre Brice starred as Zorro in *Terror of the Black Mask* (1963) and Lex Barker appeared in *Terror of the Red Mask* (1960) and *The Executioner of Venice* (1963 – *Blood of the Executioner*). Brice and Barker later teamed up in the German 'Winnetou' westerns. Gordon Scott appeared in *Mask of the Musketeers* (1960 – *Zorro and the Three Musketeers*) with Giacomo Rossi-Stuart, Livio Lorenzon and Nazzareno Zamperla as Athos, Porthos and D'Artagnan. *The Devils of Spartivento* (1963) was sumptuously photographed and costumed entertainment, starring Scilla Gabel and John Drew Barrymore, who sports distracting black and white striped 'humbug' tights.

Hollywood legend Stewart Granger starred in Etienne Perier's **Swordsman of Sienna** (1962). Granger was English mercenary freebooter Thomas Stanwood in sixteenth-century Tuscany, though the film was shot at Titanus Studios and in the Lazio countryside. It has a sweeping score by Mario Nascimbene and was photographed in CinemaScope and Metrocolor by Tonino Delli Colli. Stanwood arrives in Siena, then under Spanish occupation, to act as bodyguard to Lady Orietta Arconti (Sylva Koscina), who is to marry the tyrannical Spanish governor, Don Carlos (Riccardo Garrone). Realising that the populace oppose the marriage, Stanwood joins a group of Italian rebel patriots, The Ten, led by Councillor Andrea Paresi (Alberto Lupo). Riddled with court intrigue and subterfuge, *Swordsman* is one of the best of its type, with Granger excellent as the wisecracking mercenary. His duel with Lupo in a stable demonstrates his expertise with a rapier. Claudio Gora appeared as Councillor Leoni, who is murdered by the Ten, his corpse hung from the town's bell tower. Fausto Tozzi played Carlos' villainous henchman Captain Hugo and Christine Kaufman played Orietta'a sister, Serenella (Stanwood's love interest). The film's best sequence is Siena's Palio horserace, a pageant of colour and movement. This dangerous steeplechase through the city streets and across the countryside is excitingly staged, as the stunt riders (including arch enemies Hugo and Stanwood) negotiate the obstacle-strewn course – speared fences, spiked logs, crossbow marksmen and a booby-trapped bridge at Monte Gelato Falls.

From pirate and musketeer films to pepla and horror films, Italian audiences loved masked heroes and villains. Sometimes these genres collided, in such unlikely pairings as Umberto Lenzi's *Zorro against Maciste* (1963 – *Samson and the Slave Queen*), which cast Pierre Brice as Zorro and Alan Steel as Maciste, and *Samson and the Treasure of the Incas* (1965), a peplum-western, also starring Steel. In Piero Pierotti's **Hercules and the Masked Rider** (1964), Hercules (Alan Steel) is a member of a rebel gypsy band. Set in Spain during the war in Flanders, the film details conflicts between greedy Don Romero (Arturo Dominici), the Duke of Medina, and Don Francisco, the Prince of Valverde. Romero murders Francisco; thus Francisco's nephew Don Juan (Mimmo Palmera) seeks revenge. Juan strikes as the Masked Rider, in scarlet Zorro mask, cape and gauntlets, to win back the hand of his lover, Doña Blanca (Jose Greci). Ettore Manni appeared as Captain Blasco, Romero's henchman, who has a change of heart when he falls in love with gypsy witch Estella (Pilar Cansino), and Nello Pazzafini and Sal Borgese appeared as rebels in this action-filled, cheap, shot-in-Italy production, which was backed by a flamenco score by Lavagnino. As to be expected, Hercules looks lost when hauled out of historical context.

Rebellion and Risorgimento: Leopards and Lions

There were several mammoth international productions – involving Italian finance, studios or stars – set during the Napoleonic Wars. They were defined by impressive star casts, resplendent costumes and sets, and plodding historical plots leavened periodically by epic battle scenes. King Vidor's mammoth *War and Peace* (1956) was filmed at De Laurentiis Studios and headlined Audrey Hepburn, Henry Fonda, Mel Ferrer, Vittorio Gassman, John Mills and Anita Ekberg. The romance was set against Napoleon's (Herbert Lom) 1812 invasion of Russia. Abel Gance's French-Italian-Yugoslavian-Liechtenstein *The Battle of Austerlitz* (1960) was a stagy, studio-bound affair which reduced Napoleon's 1805 victory over Austro-Russian forces to the level of pantomime. Claudia Cardinale, Ettore Manni, Jean-Louis Trintignant, Leslie Caron and Jack Palance were wasted in fleeting, badly dubbed cameos. Pierre Mondy played Napoleon, Orson Welles appeared as an American inventor and Vittorio De Sica was the pope.

Stanley Kramer's 1810 Peninsular War epic **The Pride and the Passion** (1957) cast Italian star Sophia Loren, who provided the 'passion'. It was a $5 million US production shot on spectacular locations near Madrid – including Toledo, the cathedral in Santiago De Campostela, the mountains at Manzanares El Real and the mushroom rocks at Cuidad Encantada – with a cast of thousands. Spanish guerrilleros haul a massive seven-ton, 42-foot-long cannon 1,000 km across a landscape of dust, rivers, rocks and windmills, to breach the walls of fortified Avila, the French headquarters in Spain. A British admiralty agent,

Captain Anthony Trumbull, 'a cold piece of English mutton' (Cary Grant) and 'son of a shoemaker' guerilla Miguel (Frank Sinatra) fight the French and quarrel over spicy gypsy girl Juana (Loren). The film influenced later Italian political adventure films, such as *A Professional Gun* and *Burn!*, which teamed a foreign mercenary or weapons expert with a peasant rebel. Trumbull is indispensable to the guerrilleros as the only man who knows how to fire the cannon.

Sergei Bondarchuk's Italian-Russian co-production **Waterloo** (1970) was produced by Dino De Laurentiis and Mosfilm. It was made on a $25 million budget at De Laurentiis Studios and on location in Ukraine. Nino Rota provided the dramatic score. The Soviet army in period costume re-enacted the famous battle, where Napoleon (Rod Steiger) faced the Duke of Wellington (Christopher Plummer) on 18 June 1815. The eclectic cast featured Virginia McKenna, Michael Wilding, Jack Hawkins, Gianni Garko, Ivo Garrani, Andrea Checchi and Ian Ogilvy, with Orson Welles as a corpulent King Louis XVIII.

After a slow first section, the second half of the film is virtually non-stop action, as the encounter unfolds in colourful, knockout battle scenes. Cannons thunder, rank upon rank of infantry advance and galloping cavalry sweep across the smoky landscape; 20,000 men and 3,000 horses were deployed in these crunching re-enactments. The film's stunt coordinator was Franco Fantasia. The two cavalry charges – a frontal assault by the Scots Greys and the French cavalry assault under Marshal Ney (Dan O'Herlihy) which engulfs the British redcoat infantry squares (filmed in an impressive helicopter shot) – have been shorn of their dangerous horse stunts on UK DVD releases, diminishing their power. As Napoleon prepares to deliver the coup de grâce, the Prussians under Marshal Blucher (Serghej Zakhariadze) arrive to save the day. Having refused to surrender, the French Old Guard are mown down at point-blank range by British cannons. In the aftermath of the battle, Napoleon escapes, while looters and crows scavenge the dead. Photographed in Panavision and Technicolor by Armando Nannuzzi, *Waterloo* resembles period paintings brought to life by the rich cinematography and is a perfect marriage of Italian style and Russian scale.

Luchino Visconti's operatic **Senso** (1954 – *Wanton Contessa* and *The Wanton Countess*) was set in 1866, during the Austrian occupation of Venice. Countess Livia Serpieri (Alida Valli) becomes the lover of an Austrian artillery officer, Leutnant Franz Mahler (Farley Granger), initially to save her cousin, Marquis Ussoni (Massimo Girotti), who is a rebel fighting against Austrian rule. Livia loans Franz thousands of florins which were supposed to help the rebels' cause, so he can bribe a doctor to exempt him from service. When she visits him in Verona, she discovers he's nothing more than a drunken, unfaithful wastrel, who has frittered the money away on women, booze and gambling. As revenge she reports his desertion to his superiors and he is summarily shot. The film is notable for great central performances by Valli and Granger, for its Technicolor photography of the Italian locations and for the convincing albeit brief battle scenes, which Visconti seamlessly interweaves into his melodrama.

Don Fabrizio (Burt Lancaster) waltzes with Angelica Sedara (Claudia Cardinale) in this Italian poster for Luchino Visconti's sumptuous Sicilian epic *The Leopard* (1963).

An earlier episode in the Risorgimento (Resurgence), the political upheaval which resulted in the unification of Italy, was the backdrop to Visconti's meticulous ***The Leopard*** (1963), which was touted in pre-production as Europe's *Gone with the Wind*. Adapted from Giuseppe Tomasi Di Lampedusa's 1958 novel *Il Gattopardo*, it tells the story of the Prince of Salina, Sicilian Don Fabrizio (Burt Lancaster), 'The Leopard'. It begins in May 1860 as Giuseppe Garibaldi invades Sicily with his red-shirted Garibaldini. Don Fabrizio is a member of the old ruling class caught between two worlds and finds that his credo – 'Things will have to change in order that they remain the same' – now has added resonance. Don Fabrizio's nephew Count Tancredi (Alain Delon) joins the Garibaldini and rejects his lover Concetta (Lucilla Morlacchi), Don Fabrizio's daughter, to become engaged to 'new-rich' Angelica Sedara (Claudia Cardinale), the heiress daughter of wealthy Don Calogero Sedara (Paolo Stoppa). Emissary Cavalier Chevally (Leslie French) asks Fabrizio to join the Italian senate, but he refuses, suggesting Don Calogero for the post. 'We were the leopards, the lions', says the prince, 'Those who take our place will be jackals and sheep'.

Goffredo Lombardo of Titanus Films acquired the book rights and Twentieth Century-Fox co-produced. Milanese aristocrat Count Don Luchino Visconti di Modrone ('The Red Duke') told Lampedusa's story with vivid imagery and peerless attention to period detail. It was shot over five months from May 1962 on location in Sicily, at Donnafugata and the village of Ciminna. The exterior of Villa Salina with its tree-lined avenues was Villa Boscogrande, near Palermo. The Battle of Palermo was staged with hundreds of extras, while the Ponteleone ball sequence was shot amidst the golden chandeliered opulence of Palazzo Gangi in Palermo. For this scene Visconti's attention to lavish mise-en-scène went into overload, with the exquisite ball gowns by Oscar-nominated Pietro Tosi. Nino Rota's music swirls as Visconti orchestrates a sea of bobbing, waltzing couples. Rota's majestic, swelling score showcases the composer at his most epic. The cinematography in Technicolor and Super Technirama-70 by Giuseppe Rotunno – of sun-scorched ochre countryside, swathes of blue sky and dusty, grand architecture – captured 'the violence of the landscape' and the luxury of aristocracy.

The Leopard has one of the finest casts assembled for an Italian production. Delon's dashing Tancredi is ambitious, loveable, but 'a sieve with money', while Cardinale's soft-eyed Angelica, with her raucous laugh, is displaced among the effete diners at Don Fabrizio's table. Rina Morelli played Princess Maria Stella (Fabrizio's wife), Serge Reggiani was Fabrizio's shooting partner Don Ciccio Tumeo, Ida Galli and Pierre Clémenti were two of the prince's seven children, Marino Masé played their tutor and Romolo Valli was the House of Salina's priest, Father Pirrone. Ivo Garrani played Colonel Pallavicino, the hero of Aspromonte, who hates Red Shirts. When Tancredi returns from the Battle of Palermo, he is accompanied by General Bardi (Giuliano Gemma) and Count Cavriaghi (Terence Hill), who unsuccessfully courts Concetta. *The Leopard* is notable for the noble performance by Lancaster as a man of contradictions, based partly on Visconti himself. As melancholy Don Fabrizio contemplates Greuze's *Death of a Just Man*, a deathbed painting, and waltzes with Angelica, the old and new worlds meet. In the novel the prince dies, but Visconti's film ends with the tired prince wandering Palermo and fading into a darkened street.

The film was cut by 40 minutes to 165 minutes and dubbed for its English language release, with the inferior print processed in CinemaScope and DeLuxe colour. In 1987 *The Film Club* on BBC2 screened a unique 165-minute print, in Technirama and Technicolor, dubbed into English – this is the definitive English language cut, with Lancaster and Cardinale dubbing themselves. The Italian print, running 205 minutes, won the 1963 Palme d'Or at Cannes for Best Film but the English dub was an international flop, almost bankrupting Titanus, and was critically panned. It wasn't until its reissue at 185 minutes in 1983 that it enjoyed the praise it deserved as one of the towering achievements of Italian, indeed world, cinema.

Chapter Three

Fall of the Empire
Sword and Sandal Spectacles

In addition to mythological pepla, Italian filmmakers also made admirable 'sword and sandal' epics which depicted ancient history. These films, inspired by the Hollywood model of *Quo Vadis* and *Helen of Troy* (both shot in Rome), were often dramas based on historical fact. *Helen of Troy* was particularly influential. It featured great sets (at Cinecittà), costumes and battle scenes staged in Lazio – the soldiers' flapping rubber shields excepted – though the plodding romance concentrates on Prince Paris (Jacques Sernas) and his lover Helen, queen of Sparta (Rosanna Podesta). Italian sword and sandal spectacles sometimes recreated actual military campaigns (the Invasion of Gaul, the Punic Wars) or staged half-myths (the Trojan War). There was also a trend for biblical epics and after *Cleopatra*, for Egyptian-set court intrigues. As important as the subject matter and cast were the visuals – there was always prominent billing for the productions' suppliers of weapons, costumes, wigs and footwear, even chariots and flowers – the visual pomp that defined the Italian filmmakers' over-attention to detail.

Greek Myths and History

Following Steve Reeves' Herculean success as the archetypal peplum hero, he appeared in ***The Giant of Marathon*** (1959), which was started by Jacques Tourneur but was completed by Mario Bava. It was filmed in Dyaliscope and Eastmancolor at Titanus Studios, with a score by Roberto Nicolosi. *Giant* was set in 490 BC and Reeves starred as Philippides the Athenian 'Hero of Olympia', whose feats inspired the Marathon race. Philippides courts two women – Andromeda (Mylene Demongeot) and Karis (Daniela Rocca), who is working for turncoat Greek Theocrates (Sergio Fantoni). The Persians invade Greece, led by King Darius (Daniele Vargas) and Greek traitor Hypias (Gerard Herter). Ten days before the film's Rome premiere, their climactic showdown at Marathon was still being ineptly shot in Yugoslavia. Bava maintains the footage was awful, with charioteers smoking cigarettes. Bava reshot the sequence in a quarry at Gottarossa in Italy, using only 100 extras. He filmed the sequence at five frames per second instead of 24, speeding up the action into a frenzy of hacking swords and raining arrows. The combat begins with the Persians firing a human skull from a catapult and beating their mighty war drum. When the Persians charge, their chariot horses fall into defensive pits. This action sequence and the final sea battle are the equal of many a Hollywood epic, at a fraction of the cost – Sparta's city is a simple matte shot of the Tor Caldara headland. Alberto Lupo played Athenian general Miltiades, Ivo Garrani appeared as Andromeda's father Cruces, muscleman Alan Steel played Spartan hero Iolas and Reeves was doubled in his fight scenes by Giovanni Cianfriglia (alias 'Ken Wood'). Philippides' heroic act sees him run from Marathon to warn Athens of an impending Persian surprise attack and then Philippides and the hundred-strong Sacred Guard attack the Persian fleet. As Philippides duels with Theocrates, imperilled Andromeda is bound to a ship's prow and Theocrates dies spectacularly when he falls onto the spiked jaws of his galley's crocodile-toothed ram.

The Colossus of Rhodes (1961), Sergio Leone's directorial debut, was filmed on location in Spain, with interiors at Cinecittà in Rome. The title refers to the massive bronze statue of the sun god Apollo erected overlooking Rhodes, bestriding the harbour. It was one of the Seven Wonders of the World and was destroyed by an earthquake, circa 224 BC. Rory Calhoun played Dario, a Greek visiting his uncle Lissipus (Jorge Rigaud) in Rhodes in 280 BC. Thar (Conrado Sanmartin) plans to overthrow King Xerses of Rhodes (Roberto Camardiel) with help from the Phoenician army, who have been smuggled into the Temple of Baal disguised as slaves. Dario becomes involved with rebels led by Peliocles (Georges Marchal). Eventually Thar assassinates Xerses and Dario helps the rebels to free the slave population, as an earthquake destroys the city and topples the Colossus.

The film's greatest asset is its visuals. As Leone commented, 'The accumulation of such bad taste enhanced its fascination: a film made of stucco and fake jewellery'. Leone filmed in Supertotalscope and Eastmancolor at the picturesque Laredo harbour, Cantabria, the Bay of Biscay. Further location scenes were shot at the rock formations at Manzanares El Real, north of Madrid (with the Santillana Reservoir standing in for the Med), while the rebels' hideout in the Caves of the Stone Desert was the mushroom rocks at Ciudad Encantada at Cuenca, west of Madrid. Leone includes some arena action featuring a chariot with blades on the wheels. There are numerous swordfights, punch-ups and torture scenes (involving a giant bell and molten lead) and the rebels storm the Colossus with a battering ram. Angelo Francesco Lavagnino composed the magisterial title music, orchestrating thudding drums and brass. During a swordfight, Dario climbs out of the Colossus's ear and runs down his right arm, pursued by Thar's soldiers, and makes his escape by diving into the harbour. Antonio Casas played the Phoenician ambassador and Angel Aranda, Mimmo Palmera and Alfio

Caltabiano (Charlton Heston's stunt double in *Ben-Hur*'s chariot race) played rebels. Mabel Karr was rebel Mirte, Dario's love interest. Felix Fernandez played Carete, the designer of the Colossus, who thought he was creating art, when it is actually a prison and harbour defence. Carete's daughter Diala (Lea Massari) appears sympathetic, but she betrays Dario to Thar. The Italian version runs for 142 minutes – the English language print is 14 minutes shorter but is still long-winded and only vaguely hints at Leone's directorial prowess.

Giorgio Ferroni's **The Trojan War** (1961 – *The Trojan Horse* and *The Wooden Horse of Troy*) was based on Homer's *The Iliad* and *The Odyssey*. It told of how Helen, King Menelaus's wife, was kidnapped from Sparta by Prince Paris (Warner Bentivegna). Menelaus (Carlo Tamberlani) sailed for Troy and besieged the city for 10 years. The story begins in the tenth year of the siege, as Greek hero Achilles (Arturo Dominici) has slain Hector (Paris' brother) for killing his friend Patroclus. Ferroni narrates from the perspective of Trojan hero Aeneas (Steve Reeves), who is sent to recruit help from Phrygia. When Aeneas returns with the Dardanian cavalry, the Trojans rout the Greeks, but crafty Ulysses (John Drew Barrymore) concocts a plan: they construct a huge wooden horse. The Trojans believe it is sacred to the sea god Poseidon, so they take it inside Troy as booty. That night soldiers hidden inside the horse open the gates, allowing the Greek army to ransack the city, kill Paris and reclaim Helen.

The Wooden Horse is hauled inside the walls of Troy on set at Cinecittà Studios. US lobby card for Giorgio Ferroni's *The Trojan War* (1961) under the alternative international title *The Trojan Horse*. Image courtesy Gary Smith Archive.

Reeves is reduced to a guest-starring role amongst an eye-catching cast. Nerio Bernardi played Agamemnon, king of Mycenae, and 'weapons consultant' Benito Stefanelli played Greek officer Diomedes. Hedy Vessel was the screen's most beautiful Helen; Lidia Alfonsi appeared as the Trojan prophetess Cassandra and Juliette Mayniel was Aeneas's pregnant wife Creusa. Both the Greeks *and* the Trojans are the villains: Aeneas is the film's sole sympathetic protagonist and there are several trademark Reeves moments, as when Aeneas takes on Greek hero Ajax (Mimmo Palmera) in a wrestling match. Right from its bleak opening, with Achilles dragging Hector's corpse in the dust around Troy, *Trojan War* benefits from a poetic script. Helen of Sparta is described by Aeneas as 'our gravedigger', while the Trojan king, Priam (Nando Tamberlani), visits the Greeks to claim his son's body, 'Armed only with my tears'. The Trojan walls (with its impressive Scaean Gate), the Greeks' stockaded camps and the battle scenes were shot on Yugoslavian plains. Interiors and the Troy exteriors were shot at Cinecittà. The six-wheeled Trojan Horse is dragged into Troy and Giovanni Fusco's triumphal marches, punctuated by choral blasts and bursts of brass and timpani, invoke epic traditions. The middle section of the film is a series of immense confrontations, as Aeneas leads his Dardanians into battle against the Greeks. The massed extras (the Greeks in red cloaks, the Trojans in white) are impressive, the Dardanians' Smurf-like helmets notwithstanding. By 'The End', Troy is sacked and Aeneas, his infant son in his arms, leads the survivors away. This climactic imagery of the city in flames recalls convoys of refugees during World War II. Is Paris burning? – Yes he probably is.

Marino Girolami's **Fury of Achilles** (1962) was told from the Greek hero's perspective. Achilles, the king of Phthea in Thessaly, fought in the Trojan War knowing that he wouldn't survive. When the Greeks attack the town of Lirnesso, Achilles (Gordon Mitchell) takes Trojan Briseis (Gloria Milland) as his slave and King Agamemnon (Mario Petri) takes Chryseis, the daughter of the Trojan priest Chryses. Apollo inflicts a plague on the Greeks, so Agamemnon returns Chryseis to her father, taking Briseis from Achilles instead. Achilles refuses to fight, so Patroclus (Enio Girolami, the director's son) impersonates Achilles, leading the Myrmidon warriors into battle. Hector (Jacques Bergerac) kills Patroclus and Achilles vows revenge, killing Hector in a duel and allowing King Priam (Fosco Giachetti) to retrieve his son's body.

In Ultrascoped Eastmancolor, *Fury of Achilles*' production design, costumes and weapons look authentic, even if the Trojan army's shields are inaccurately adorned with horses' heads. The mythological element is kept to a minimum, making the crunching battle scenes more effective: the sacking of Lirnesso; the Trojan attack on the Greek's beached fleet (filmed at Tor Caldara); the Trojans assaulting the Greek stockades; and the twin duels between Hector and Patroclus (filmed at Caldara Di Manziana) and Achilles and Hector. Achilles looks particularly awesome in this scene – 'a servant of the avenging furies' – arriving by chariot hollering 'Phthea! Phthea!' Joseph Nathanson created matte shots of Troy, with studio work filmed at Incir-De Paolis. Piero Lulli played Ulysses, Remo De Angelis was Trojan hero Sarpedon, Edith Peters played a Nubian slave, and Cristina Gajoni was Xenia, who commits suicide on Patroclus' funeral pyre. Director Girolami chose to miss out Achilles' brutal treatment of Hector's corpse (which he dragged around Troy) and ends the film before Achilles' death. The US release of *Fury of Achilles* is superior to the UK print retitled *Achilles*, which is 20 minutes shorter. The UK version omits the Greeks' attack on the town of Lirnesso (battle footage from *Trojan War*), the sacking of the town (outtakes from *Trojan War*), the introduction of the Trojan protagonists and the Trojans' assault on Ulysses' camp (more *Trojan War* stock).

Set in 400 BC, Curtis Bernhardt's ***Damon and Pythias*** (1962) told the story of Athenian Pythias (Don Burnett) who journeys to Syracuse. Pythias must find Arcanos (Andrea Bosić), a teacher of the outlawed Philosophy of Pythagoras so that Arcanos can return to Athens to become ruler. Pythias is befriended by thief Damon (Guy Williams) and when Pythias is captured as a result of Damon's betrayal, guilty Damon offers himself as hostage, enabling Pythias to return home to see his ailing wife Nerissa (Ilaria Occhini) and newborn son. Pythias promises to return two months later to face his execution. Liana Orfei was Damon's lover Adriana. The film's best asset was its photography (with city matte shots by Nathanson). The city sets were at Cinecittà, with location footage filmed in the Grotte Di Salone, on a bridge spanning the Monte Gelato waterfall, the valley at Tolfa, the towering cliffs at Gaeta and the seaside at Terracina. *Damon and Pythias* was presented internationally by MGM, though the lion at the film's opening should have winced rather than roared.

Duelling Titans: The Founding of Rome

By far the most popular subject matter for Italian-made sword and sandal epics was the Roman Empire. Albert Band's ***The Last Glory of Troy*** (1962 – *War of the Trojans*), the sequel to *The Trojan War*, depicted Aeneas' founding of Rome and was based on Virgil's poem *The Aeneid*. A cheap effort shot in Yugoslavia and at Incir-De Paolis in Rome, *Last Glory* had Steve Reeves reprise his role as Aeneas, now leading the Trojan survivors through the marshes of Latium in Italy. The wanderers camp on arable land at the fork of the River Tiber. King Latino (Mario Ferrari) is happy to allow the foreigners to settle. His wife, Queen Amata (Lulla Selli), doesn't want their daughter Lavinia (Carla Marlier) marrying Aeneas, preferring King Turno of the Rutili (Gianni Garko). Aeneas defeats Turno in single combat, allowing him to marry Lavinia and found Rome. A slapdash Reeves vehicle crowbarred into a classical narrative, *Last Glory* focuses on its colourless hero. Aeneas again embarks on a mission to get help – here from the neighbouring Etruscans. Benito Stefanelli appeared as Trojan Nisio, Enzo Fiermonte and Giacomo Rossi-Stuart played Trojans Agathon and Eurialo, and Maurice Poli played Turno's henchman Mezensio. In a chariot battle between Aeneas and Turno, the real competition is to decide who has the most ridiculous helmet: Aeneas' giant metal quiff or Turno's spiky stickleback. The film's highpoint occurs during this duel, when Aeneas knocks the wheels off Turno's chariot and the villain attempts to make his escape through a wood on what now resembles a sledge. It was also known as *The Avenger*, which is a cut version in black and white. A fresco triggers Aeneas' flashbacks to Troy, cuing stock footage from Ferroni's *Trojan War*: the Wooden Horse and Aeneas' duel with Achilles.

Sergio Leone and Duccio Tessari contributed to the script for Sergio Corbucci's **Duel of the Titans** (1961 – *Romulus and Remus*). It was photographed in CinemaScope by Enzo Barboni, with the moving score composed by Piero Piccioni. Filmed in Lazio and at Titanus Studios, *Duel* told an alternative legend of the founding of Rome, 'The greatest city in the world'. Romulus (Steve Reeves) and Remus (Gordon Scott) are abandoned by their mother Rhea Silvia (Laura Solari) and are raised by a she-wolf. Later they are fostered by shepherd Faustalus (Andrea Bosić). In 753 BC they rebel against tyrannical Amulius (Franco Volpi), the king of Albalonga, and incur the wrath of Sabine king Tacius (Massimo Serato); his daughter Julia (Virna Lisi) sides with the brothers, angering her betrothed, Curtius (Jacques Sernas). Romulus and Remus lead their caravan through the Great Marsh (a swampy Tor Caldara), across the Mountain of Fire and towards the fertile Valley of the Seven Hills. The brothers quarrel and part, but Remus' caravan is destroyed when the volcano erupts – bodies fall down chasms and cartwheeling boulders flatten extras, intercut with stock footage of spitting lava and black smoke. In the Valley of the Seven Hills, Romulus makes peace with the Sabines, ploughs the first furrow and kills his brother in single combat.

Corbucci's movie was a great success in Italy. Reeves and Scott, in their only film together, acquit themselves well as the mythical heroes. Authentic sets designed by Carlo Simi include a log stockade arena, where Romulus wrestles a bear. There's much talk of 'destiny' and 'fate': 'It's fate, not the horses, that move the wheels of the cart', says Julia, while cautious Curtius observes, 'But to the cruelty of fate the wise surrender'. The supporting cast includes Piero Lulli, Franco Balducci, Germano Longo and Enzo Cerusico as rebels Sulpicius, Acilius, Servius and Numa. Jose Greci appeared as Hestia (Julia's handmaiden) and Ornella Vanini was memorable as Tarpeia (Remus's warrior lover). Giovanni Cianfriglia doubled Reeves in the stunt scenes. Diverting action includes the Burning Hurdles steeplechase, a frenzied pagan rite of Lupercalia (filmed in the caverns at Salone), a rebel attack on Albalonga, a bridge demolition and the battle in the Valley of the Seven Hills, where the Sabine cavalry attack Romulus's entrenched camp and fall victim to spiked defences, nets and water-filled pits.

Richard Pottier's **Romulus and the Sabines** (1961), starring Roger Moore as Romulus, was a misguided light romantic comedy version of the Rape of the Sabine Women. The all-male Roman community face extinction if they don't acquire some females, so during the Sabine harvest festival to the god Consus, the Romans steal their women. The Sabines attack Rome, but the Sabine women mediate and a truce is reached. The good cast – Mylene Demongeot as Sabine princess Rhea, the daughter of King Titus Tacius (Folco Lulli), Scilla Gabel as Romulus' Phoenician lover Dujya and Giorgia Moll as Sabine Lavinia – can't save the film. Moore, who sports a quiff and dubbed himself in the English print, is completely miscast, though there is early evidence of the acting technique known as 'Moore's Eyebrow'.

The story of the early conflict between Rome and Alba was filmed as ***Duel of Champions*** (1961). Following an ambush by Albans on the Fourth Legion, Roman hero Horatio (Alan Ladd) is missing, presumed dead. The oracle proclaims that the Horatii and the Curiatii (two trios of brothers) will settle the conflict between Rome and Alba in a duel. Horatio, the eldest of the Horatii, returns from the mountains where he has been convalescing and, with his brothers Marcus (Jacques Sernas) and Elio (Luciano Marin), takes on the Curiatii. Franca Bettoja appeared as Roman princess Marcia, Franco Fabrizi played Curazio, with Osvaldo Ruggieri and Piero Palmeri as his fellow Alban champions. Jacqueline Derval played the Horatiis' sister, Horatia, who is in love with Curazio. King Tullius Hostilius of Rome was played by Robert Keith and Andrea Aureli appeared as Nezio, king of Alba. It was co-directed by Terence Young (immediately before he helmed *Dr No*) and Ferdinando Baldi. The Albans are presented as barbarians who throw their prisoners into a wolf pit. Ladd was hired by Tiberia Films, but they couldn't pay him his full salary. Financier Lux Films stepped in, so filming could be completed in Italy, Yugoslavia and at Cinecittà Studios.

Arm of Fire (1964 – *The Colossus of Rome*) was set in 500 BC, when banished Tarquin the Proud (Massimo Serato) besieged Rome with aid from Etruscan King Porsena. Gordon Scott starred as Roman hero Caius Mucius – their 'last minute savior', according to the opening blurb. When his attempted assassination of Porsena fails, Mucius plunges his right hand into a brazier. Thereafter he wears an iron gauntlet on his disfigured hand and is known as Scaevola ('left-handed'). Directed by Giorgio Ferroni, this by-the-numbers peplum is particularly difficult to follow in some video prints, as the reels are in the wrong order.

Hannibal and Carthage

The Rome-versus-Carthage Punic Wars provided spectacular fodder for Italian epics. ***Hannibal*** (1959) was co-directed by Edgar G. Ulmer and Carlo Ludovico Bragaglia. In 218 BC, Carthaginian general Hannibal Barca (Victor Mature) leads his forces out of Spain into the Rhone valley and across the Alps to invade Italy, his motto – 'Conquer or Die!' As they campaign through Italy, enjoying victory at the Battle of Lake Trasimene (217 BC), Hannibal falls in love with Sylvia (Rita Gam), the niece of Fabius Maximus (Gabriele Ferzetti), a powerful Roman senator. Hannibal's forces face the Romans, under the joint command of consuls Varro (Andrea Aureli) and Aemilius (Andrea Fantasia), on the plains of Cannae (216 BC).

Hannibal is the story of the Second Punic War, peplum-style, with little attention to historical accuracy. Victor Mature made a formidable eye-patched hero, his brylcreamed quiff and kiss curl notwithstanding. Filmed in SuperCinescope and Eastmancolor, *Hannibal*'s set pieces were staged on location in Italy and Yugoslavia. The mountain crossing begins Hannibal's campaign in style, as the Carthaginian army coax their elephants over the Alps and long lines of frostbitten troops snake their way through a snowbound landscape. Those who fall by the wayside become wolf food. The elephants' scenes were filmed in an impressive studio interior Alp set (at Incir-De Paolis Studios), with fake snow. Shots of Hannibal's army on campaign are accompanied by Carlo Rustichelli's jaunty march, with elephant-like trumpets and brass. The battle scenes are a mixture of large-scale location scenes, intercut with studio-bound re-enactments. Cannae is particularly impressive, with the Roman legions advancing across a yellowing grass valley when the Carthaginians spring their ambush, leading to a melee involving hundreds of extras.

The plot strikes a balance between politicised debate in the Roman senate, the romantic Hannibal-Sylvia subplot (their trysts were filmed at Tor Caldara, Anzio) and Hannibal's invasion. Milly Vitale appeared as Danila (the mother of Hannibal's son) whose arrival causes Sylvia to flee to Rome, where she is imprisoned for treason and buried alive. Rik Battaglia played Hannibal's brother Hasdrubal, Mirko Ellis was General Mago and Franco Silva was Numidian general Maharbal. Several stuntmen appear in acting roles, including Gino Marturano (a Roman general), Remo De Angelis (a Carthaginian general), Pietro Ceccarelli (a Carthaginian officer) and Benito Stefanelli and Nello Pazzafini (as wrestlers at Capua). The film also featured Terence Hill as Fabius' son, Quintilius Maximus, and Bud Spencer as barbarian chief Lutarius (in a red beard and horned helmet), years before their success together.

Also set during the Punic Wars, Pietro Francisci's **The Siege of Syracuse** (1960) takes us to Sicily, a vital objective for the Romans and Carthaginians. It was filmed on location on the Anzio coast and at Cinecittà and NIS Studios, with the accent on romance, as inventor Archimedes (heartthrob Rossano Brazzi) forsakes his betrothed Clio (Sylva Koscina), the daughter of King Hieron, for spicy dancer Diana (Tina Louise). Enrico Maria Salerno was Diana's treacherous brother Gorgia, a spy in Syracuse. Angelo Francesco Lavagnino provided the lush score. Only in the climax, when Archimedes' inventions (mirrored contraptions that look like satellite dishes, which harness the suns rays into blinding laser beams) burn the Roman fleet, does the film come alive, though the tragedy of the story marks this out as a more mature work from Francisci. Clio's first child is stillborn and she is killed in a chariot accident when her cloak tangles around the wheel and the vehicle plunges off a cliff.

Directed by Carmine Gallone, who had made *Scipio Africanus* (1937 – historical propaganda which boasted Mussolini among its fans), **Carthage in Flames** (1960) was one of the most expensive Italian epics of the 1960s. Despite the film's pomp and grandeur, Gallone was from an earlier generation of filmmakers and his static camera style labours through the 107-minute story. An international cast headed by Anne Heywood enact the talky melodrama, which is set in 146 BC at the end of the Third Punic War. Besieged by the Romans under Scipio Emilianus for three years, Carthage is doomed. The central love story is between Carthaginian Hiram (Jose Suarez) and Roman Fulvia (Heywood), but Hiram also loves Carthaginian Ophir (Ilaria Occhini), who is betrothed to Carthaginian Tsour (Terence Hill, sporting one dangly earring and a costume that resembles a genie's). Paolo Stoppa was Hiram's cohort Astarito and Pierre Brasseur was good as pessimistic Sidone. The production design – especially the Temple of Baal Moloch – and costumes are resplendent and the sea battle between Hiram's ship, the *Hemiolia*, and a Carthaginian war vessel (with a battering ram and fortified turret) is one of the most impressive scenes in sword and sandal cinema. The sacking of Carthage was staged at Cinecittà, with the set torched and extras scrambling for safety through the blazing streets.

The Empire Strikes Back: Roman Conquests

Cameron Mitchell played Julius Caesar in Amerigo Anton's ***Caesar the Conqueror*** (1962), based on *De Bella Gallico*, Caesar's recollections of the Gaulish Invasion. The film benefits from plush visuals and large-scale battle scenes, shot on location in Yugoslavia. *Conqueror* begins in 54 BC with Caesar vanquishing the Gauls. Caesar pardons Chief Vercingetorix, who then leads his people in revolt. With interiors filmed at De Laurentiis Studios, *Conqueror* includes recreations of two key engagements: the Battles of Gergovia and Alesia, in 52 BC. Alesia is one of the most studied sieges in tactical military history and the sequence includes impressive matte shots by Joseph Nathanson of fortress Alesia on the horizon. Caesar besieges the city with an earthwork stockade and the Gauls emerge from their defences to face the Romans in open country. Rik Battaglia (Vercingetorix) and Dominique Wilms (warrior queen Astrid) were charismatic villains. The film is most notable for some fair moments of brutality: a blinded Roman soldier is discovered wandering a corpse-strewn battlefield and Vercingetorix puts captured Roman soldiers to the sword and tortures others with hot irons and floggings.

In Antonio Margheriti's ***The Giants of Rome*** (1964), Chief Vercingetorix has holed up in the hill fortress of Alesia. Julius Caesar (Alessandro Sperli) plans to send his legions through the Mountains of Alesia, but the pass is guarded by Gaul's secret weapon. Caesar sends a crack squad of soldiers into the domain of the mystical Druids to destroy it. The film is a derivative of *The Magnificent Seven* and *The Guns of Navarone*. Caesar's 'special squad' consists of knife-thrower Verus ('Only Jove is faster') played by Goffredo Unger, acrobat Valerius (Alberto Dell'Aqua), Castor (Ettore Manni), muscled, pony-tailed Goth axe-man Germanicus (Rulph Hudson) and their leader, Claudius Marcellus (Harrison). Margheriti shot most of the action in the Nature Reserve at Tor Caldara and the caves of Grotte Di Salone, with interiors at Olimpia Studios and NC Studios, Rome. The secret weapon is an immense catapult hidden in a cliffside cave, which is capable of firing bags of rocks and two pitch balls which explode on impact. There's almost non-stop action (as the squad negotiate Gaul-infested territory) and moments of pathos (young Valerius is discovered crucified to a tree). Germanicus takes on a bunch of Gallic cavalry with his axe in a scene notable for its violent horsefalls. Wandisa Guida played Livia and Philippe Hersent was Drusus (two Roman hostages freed from the Gauls during the squad's mission), Piero Lulli appeared briefly as Caesar's opponent Pompey, and Renato Baldini played the grand druid. As Caesar's legions arrive, Marcellus manages to destroy the catapult by rolling it off a cliff.

Giacomo Gentilomo's **Brennus Enemy of Rome** (1963 – *Battle of the Spartans*) was shot in Ultrascope at Olimpia Studios. It's a dose of 'history as adventure', Italian-style, with muscleman Gordon Mitchell cast as Gaulish chieftain Brennus. The film begins in 391 BC, with Brennus taking the Roman town of Clusium. The Roman populace huddles on the Capitoline Hill (one of the Seven Hills of Rome), prepared for the worst. The film also details the mission of Quintus Fabius (Tony Kendall) to rescue Nissia (Ursula Davis), a Roman kidnapped to be Brennus' wife. The battles are bolstered with stock footage and the destruction left in the Gauls' wake – fields of massacred dead, smouldering towns and scavenging survivors – is convincing. Carlo Franci's score is based partly on themes from his earlier work, particularly *Maciste in Hell*. Mitchell (real name Charles Allen Pendleton) in his imposing barbarian regalia dominates whenever he appears, his hewn-from-rock screen persona tailor-made for snarling Brennus – the Ruler of the Dark Lands. Carla Calo appears as Gaulish priestess Ahmed, Erno Crisa played disingenuous senator Lutinius, Andrea Aureli was traitorous Turam the Etruscan and Lucio De Santis and Goffredo Unger were Gallic raiders. Massimo Serato played General Marcus Furius Camillus, who becomes a farmer, only to return to lead the army when all seems lost. As the besieged Romans pay off Brennus with a thousand pounds of gold, weighed on a giant set of scales, they complain the Gauls are cheating them. Brennus tosses his sword onto the pile, shouting his famous line: 'Woe to the vanquished!'

Richard Harrison starred in Mario Caiano's **The Two Gladiators** (1964 – *Fight or Die*) as Centurion Lucius Crassus, the twin brother of Commodus (Mimmo Palmera), the violent emperor. Rome is in the grip of a famine. Crassus, with his officers Horatius Devaticus (Giuliano Gemma) and Marcus Panuncius (Alvaro De Luna), returns from battling the Gauls and foments rebellion. The film was cheaply shot on location in the greenery of Lazio (including Tor Caldara, where Crassus leads the Praetorian cavalry into quicksand) and on familiar streets and palaces at De Paolis Studios. Piero Lulli played Cleander (the Praetorian commander) and the love interest (Moira Orfei as evil Marcia; Ivy Holzer as virginal Emilia) hardly feature. Palmera hams it up as Commodus and spouts some awful lines ('By the precious girdle of Venus!'). Harrison and Palmera don't look like twins, but their arena combat is effective, as both wear identical face-concealing Thracian helmets and are left-handed, generating a fair amount of tension. The film's political message is simple: Crassus refuses to become emperor and appoints experienced senator Pertinax (Mirko Ellis), reasoning, 'Power is a dangerous potion and I might get drunk on it'.

Roman history was garbled by virtually the same cast in Alfonso Brescia's ***The Revolt of the Pretorians*** (1964). Valerius Rufus (Harrison), centurion of the Praetorian Guard, leads a revolt against Domitian (Lulli), the despotic emperor. Orfei played Domitian's consort Artomne. Gemma played Senator Nerva, Ivy Holzer was handmaiden Zuza and Paola Pitti was Lucilla (Valerius' lover), who Domitian plans to execute in a cauldron of boiling lead. The main plot details a furry-masked Valerius terrorising the palace as his alter ego the Red Wolf. Domitian is overthrown by the Praetorian Guard and a troupe of circus entertainers (jugglers, strongmen and acrobats) who attack the Imperial Palace (an Incir-De Paolis set). Midget Salvatore Furnari played Caesar's court jester Elpidion, while Orfei's costume designs surreally colour-coordinated with her vivid hairstyles.

Fellini Satyricon (1969) is a more stylised depiction of life in the Roman Empire than its low-budget Cinecittà cousins. Fellini's narrative is episodic, shambolic, almost nonexistent, which is fitting as only fragments of Petronius' source text remain. Encolpio (Martin Potter) and Ascilto (Hiram Keller), and their lover Gitone (Max Born), drift through a strange Roman landscape. Encolpio meets poet Eumolpo (Salvo Randone) and attends a gluttonous feast hosted by Gaius Pompeius Trimalcione (Mario Romagnoli). Encolpio, Gitone and Ascilto are captured by slave trader Lichas of Taranto (Alain Cuny) aboard his merchant ship. Usurped Caesar (Tanya Lopert) commits suicide on the island of Taunia, his corpse held aloft on spear points by treacherous soldiers. Encolpio and Ascilto arrive at a villa where a husband and wife (Joseph Wheeler and Lucia Bose) have committed suicide. Gordon Mitchell appears as a brigand who helps Encolpio and Ascilto steal an anaemic hermaphrodite oracle, who dies of sunstroke in the desert. Luigi Montefiori played the Minotaur – Encolpio is forced to fight the beast in the labyrinth for the honour of Ariadne. To cure his impotence, Encolpio visits Enotea, a powerful good witch (*Vogue* model Donyale Luna) who transforms herself into an earth goddess, played by Maria Antonietta Beluzzi (later the tobacconist in *Amarcord*). The cast is filled with Fellini grotesques – dwarves, musclemen, hunchbacks, harlots, varlets and monsters. The aquiline beauty of Capucine, as priestess Trifena, is a rare example of Fellini using an established international name, as he often cast actors for their faces, not their acting ability. Famed variety performer 'Fanfulla' (Luigi Visconti) played raucous, farting actor Vernacchio. Mario Romagnoli (Trimalcione) was a Roman restaurateur known as 'The Moor' and rather than recite his lines, he read out a menu (his correct lines were dubbed in post-production). The script was a mixture of profanity ('Wretched fate has me by the balls again, swinging on them' complains Encolpio) and poetry ('Life passes like a shadow', observes a bard), with Vulgar Latin and theatrical gesture conveying the dialogue's meaning.

Fellini filmed from November 1968 to late May 1969. Bankrolled by Italian producer Alberto Grimaldi, it was the biggest production at Cinecittà since *Ben-Hur* (1959), with 89 interior and exterior sets. The fantastical costumes and settings, designed by Danilo Donati, were photographed by Giuseppe Rotunno, with optical effects by Joseph Nathanson. The sets included the wide streets of Rome and the tiered tenements of the 'Suburra' (red-light district) which is levelled by that peplum staple, an earthquake. Fellini created windblown deserts, burnished horizons and opulent villas – his aim was to make 'a sci-fi movie about the past'. A giant statue's head is towed through the streets of Rome by horses; a whale is landed on the deck of Lichas' galley; the new Caesar's army arrive in Rome in a triumphant, cacophonous parade; and Encolpio fights the Minotaur in a vast, dusty desert arena cheered on by a clattering, chanting crowd. Fellini shot the slave ship sequences and Caesar's murder on and around the island of Ponza (including the beach and cliffs at Chiaia Di Luna). For the scene when poet Eumolpo dies (to be cannibalistically devoured by his own benefactors), Fellini filmed on the flat beach and dunes of Focene in Fiumicino. The film closes with the protagonists depicted as frescos on ruined walls, as 'Roman Life' becomes 'Roman History'.

Satyricon's atonal musical score was by Nino Rota, in collaboration with Ihlan Mimaroglu, Tod Dockstader and Andrew Rudin. 'The Drums of the Niegpadouda Dance', which accompanied a frenzied dance by Fortunata (Magali Noël) at Trimalcione's orgy, was from 'Anthology of Music of Black Africa'. Natural sounds – the wind, bird trills and squawks – proliferate on the soundtrack. The film's title doesn't arise from its director's vanity, but because the rights to the title *Satyricon* were owned by producer Alfredo Bini, who mounted his own version directed by Gian Luigi Polidoro. *Fellini Satyricon* was released internationally in 1970, promoted by the tagline 'Rome. Before Christ. After Fellini'. It remains one of the most financially successful Italian films and is the epitome of Fellini's carnivalesque, unique cinema.

Circus Maximus: Gladiators

Perhaps the liveliest Italian historical epics were gladiator movies. Hollywood's *Demetrius and the Gladiators* (1954) starring Victor Mature was a key influence on the Italian sub-genre, as was Riccardo Freda's *Sins of Rome* (1953), starring Massimo Girotti. But it was the international success of Stanley Kubrick's *Spartacus* (1960), depicting the slave revolt in 73 BC (the Third Servile War) led by Thracian Spartacus (Kirk Douglas), that prompted many derivatives. A familiar tale of armour and *amore*, Alberto De Martino's **Gladiators Seven** (1962 – or *Gladiators 7*) starred Richard Harrison as gladiator hero Darius, who is granted his freedom and returns to Sparta. Darius learns that his father has been murdered and Hiarba (Gerard Tichy) has taken power as first emperor. Hiarba plans to marry Aglaia (Loredana Nusciak), Darius' girl, with help from her father Milon (Edoardo Toniolo), henchman Macrobius (Antonio Molino Rojo) and an army of mercenaries. Darius and Livius (Enrique Avila) recruit gladiators: drunkard knifethrower Flaccus (Barta Barri), strongman Mados (Antonio Rubio), archer Xeno (Jose Marco), slingshot-wielding blacksmith Panurgus of Thrace (Livio Lorenzon) and acrobatic Vargas (Nazzareno Zamperla). They are aided by Panurgus' daughter Licia (Franca Badeschi) and hide out in the mountains at Fezda.

Though set in the first century AD, *Gladiators Seven* closely resembles *The Magnificent Seven*, while the dusty Madrid exteriors at Manzanares El Real and La Pedriza would be reused for spaghetti westerns. Marcello Giombini's score resembles a western, with its horn-led 'love theme' for Aglaia and a galloping 'riding theme'. Interiors were filmed at Rome's De Paolis Studios and Madrid's Sevilla Films Studios. The arena combat scenes, with Darius and his men taking on Hiraba's mercenaries, are inventively staged: bowman Xeno fires four arrows simultaneously and Vargas gymnastically avoids the attention of a wild bull. *Gladiators Seven* benefits from clever perspectival special effects by 'Emilio Ruiz' (full name Emilio Ruiz Del Rio) – he later worked on the 'Conan the Barbarian' movies, *Dune*, *The Devil's Backbone* and *Pan's Labyrinth*. His work is especially noteworthy in the panorama dominated by Hiarba's jagged eagle's nest fortress perched on a mountain. Darius fights bullwhipping Hiarba atop the fortress's tower and Hiarba plunges to his death. Rather than it being a film about gladiators fighting for freedom and democracy, this is a tale of revenge – any righting-of-wrongs is a by-product of the hero's vendetta.

Anthony Momplet and Alberto De Martino's **The Invincible Gladiator** (1962) was also filmed in Spain. Set in the Roman city of Acastus in the third century AD, the film starred Harrison as gladiator Restius, who saves the life of ruler Rabirius (Leo Anchoriz). Prime minister Rabirius is ruling until the dead king's children, Princess Sira (Isabelle Corey) and 12-year-old Darius, come of age. Rabirius plans to marry Sira and become regent. Restius is appointed head of a campaign to flush out mountain brigand opponents of Rabirius but discovers that Sira is their leader. Restius joins Sira in her fight to dethrone Rabirius, releasing from servitude his gladiator friends. The supporting cast includes Jose Marco as Restius' companion Vibius, Livio Lorenzon as gladiator trainer Itus, George Martin as a gladiator and Antonio Molino Rojo as Rabirius' advisor, Euphante. It was shot at Sevilla Film Studios for Acastus's exterior sets, with De Paolis for interiors. Restius' convoy surprises the ambushing rebels with archer-filled carts (filmed at La Pedriza, Manzanares El Real) and there's a cross-country chariot race which ends with Restius' vehicle plummeting off a cliff. The gladiator sequences, set in an impressive arena and deploying some eye-catching helmets, were choreographed by Giorgio Ubaldi and pitted swordsmen against 'Retiarri' (armed with nets and tridents). Vibius is attacked by a squad of gladiator midgets, which is an accurate depiction of ancient Rome's perverse entertainment.

Harrison's action-packed *Messalina against the Son of Hercules* (1963) cast Lisa Gastoni as the wanton empress and Harrison as gladiator Glaucus, while Dan Vadis and Alan Steel starred in Domenico Paolella's *The Rebel Gladiators* (1962). Mario Caiano's lively *Maciste, Gladiator of Sparta* (1964 – *The Terror of Rome against the Son of Hercules*) featured Mark Forest and Marilu Tolo, who also co-starred in Alfonso Brescia's *The Magnificent Gladiator* (1964). The cheap **Gladiator of Rome** (1962 – *Battles of the Gladiators*) cast Gordon Scott as slave Marcus, who attempts to protect Princess Nisa (Wandisa Guida) from a Phoenician assassin, General Astade (Piero Lulli), at the time of Christian-pagan conflicts during Emperor Caracalla's reign. Marcus is sent to gladiator school (a sort of 'Maim Academy') and sides with the mocked, persecuted Christian 'fanatics'. A low-rent gladiator revolt saves Marcus and Nisa from crucifixion.

A key addition to the cycle was the 'Ten Gladiators' trilogy, which began with Gianfranco Parolini's **The Ten Gladiators** (1963). Roccia (Dan Vadis) and his Thracian gladiators – en route from Herculaneum to perform in Rome – become embroiled in a plot to assassinate Emperor Claudius Nero (Gianni Rizzo). Glaucus Valerius (Roger Browne) is the head of the conspiracy to install Servius Galba (Mirko Ellis) on the throne. With help from the gladiators, Glaucus' plan succeeds, but at the cost of Roccia's life. The familiar cast included Jose Greci as Livia (Glaucus' love interest), Ugo Sasso as Restius (the gladiators' trainer) and Sal Borgese as mute gladiator Minos, with stuntmen Aldo Canti, Pietro Torrisi, Emilio Messina and Giuseppe Mattei as gladiators. Vassili Karis appeared as Epaphoritos, Nero's food taster who eventually stabs his master. Nero's death was filmed on the steps of the Palazzo Della Civilta, EUR in Rome, part of Mussolini's monument to fascism. Tigelinus (Mimmo Palmera), centurion of the Praetorian Guard, is stabbed by the gladiators, his chest porcupined with swords. Parolini appears as Senator Lucius Verus, a Christian who is thrown to the lions. The murder of Nero's wife, Poppea (Margaret Taylor), is noteworthy. Tigelinus, who loves Poppea and is being tested by Nero, arrives at her picturesque island palace by boat (filmed on the lake at Villa Borghese, Rome). Poppea, in a white dress, greets him, they embrace, he stabs her and she falls bleeding into a beautiful arching fountain (at EUR). Parolini uses stock footage from *The Colossus of Rhodes* and *The Last Days of Pompeii* and his eye for picturesque settings and action – Nero's mountaintop palace garden at Capua bursting with floral colour; Restius' rain-drenched funeral; and the final battle amid burning crucified Christians – raises the scenes visually, but the film is too dependent on stock footage to be successful in its own right.

Ten Gladiators was followed by two sequels. Both starred Vadis as Roccia, were directed by Nick Nostro and had stirring scores by Carlo Savina. In **Spartacus and the Ten Gladiators** (1964 – *Day of Vengeance*), Roccia and his gladiators save Lydia (Ursula Davis), the daughter of villainous senator Julius Varro (Gianni Rizzo), who is using slave labour to build the Great Aqueduct (stock footage from *Pontius Pilate*). The gladiators are dispatched by Varro to capture bandit Spartacus (John Heston), but they side with him. Varro mobilises the Roman army (footage from *Hannibal*) and in a pitched battle (footage from *Sign of the Gladiator*), the rebel slaves defeat the legions and Varro is killed. Filmed in the familiar Lazio landscape – Tor Caldara for Spartacus' camp and Caldara Di Manziana for Varro's aqueduct work camp – the film is littered with punch ups, staged *con brio*. Enzo Fiermonte played gladiator Restius (resurrected from the first film) with Sal Borgese, Emilio Messina, Aldo Canti and Pietro Torrisi as Roccia's bunch. Pietro Ceccarelli played gladiatorial impresario Terapsis, Helga Line was slave Daria (Roccia's lover) and British wrestler Milton Reid was memorable as Varro's bulldog henchman Cimbro, who kidnaps Daria in a quadriga and is chased along a picturesque lakeside by the heroes.

Triumph of the Ten Gladiators (1964) thriftily reuses stock footage – a cave battle (from *The Colossus of Rhodes*); Steve Reeves riding into Pompeii and the arena crowd (both from *The Last Days of Pompeii*) – in the best of the trilogy. Roccia and his gladiators are sent on tour by Publius Quintilius Rufus (Carlo Tamberlani), pro consul of Syria, to Arbela – ostensibly to entertain the court, but really to kidnap the queen, Moluya (Helga Line). They are accompanied by centurion Glaucus (Stelio Candelli) and must combat the evil prime minister, Prince Aramandro (John Heston), and his Parthian mercenaries. Moluya is the masked rebel leader who is attempting to overthrow Aramandro. Action sequences were again staged in EUR (including the arched fountain), with interiors at ATC Studios. *Triumph* features a well-mounted scene when the rebel army appear from behind the rubbled architecture in a ruined city, surprising the gladiators. Gianni Rizzo played the queen's advisor Sextus Vittorius, Enzo Fiermonte was Restius, Halina Zalewska played Myrta (Restius' niece, who falls for Glaucus), Pietro Ceccarelli played Antioch impresario Navatao, Leontine May was evil Parthian princess Salima, with Canti, Borgese, Messina and Torrisi as the gladiators. The 'Ten Gladiators' films feature exciting scenes of gladiatorial combat and are powered along by their own dumb, illogical momentum.

In **The Spartan Gladiators** (1964 – *The Secret Seven*) Spartan Keros (Tony Russel) searches for a statuette containing a treaty which incriminates Sar (Nando Gazzolo). Keros is joined by several freedom fighters – rebels Baxo (Massimo Serato), Silone (Piero Lulli) and Renato Rossini (Croto), ex-gladiator Mardok (Pietro Capanna), and travelling actor Nemete (Livio Lorenzon) and fire-eater Jagul (Dakar). Filmed at Incir-De Paolis Studios and in the Lazio countryside, the meandering narrative consisted of Kero's band hiding out with Nemete's travelling players. There are comedy moments (Keros and company appear in drag), a herd of longhorn cattle is stampeded at Sar's cavalry (though a row of telegraph poles can be seen in the background) and the rebels deploy a flamethrower. The finale has Keros and Sar duelling in a swampy Caldara Di Manziana. Paola Pitti was Elea (Keros' lover) and Helga Line was bigamous Aspasia, Sar's lover who is also married to Baxo.

Steve Reeves as Centurion Randus duels with an Iscian warrior in Sergio Corbucci's *The Son of Spartacus* (1963). UK poster courtesy William Connolly Archive.

Sergio Corbucci's ***The Son of Spartacus*** (1963) was retitled *The Slave* in the US. It is 20 years since Spartacus's uprising and his vanquisher – slave trader Marcus Licinius Crassus (Claudio Gora) – is now consul of the African province of Iscia. Crassus is preparing to strike against Rome, so Caesar sends Centurion Randus (Steve Reeves) and his Germanic scout Barros (Franco Balducci) to Zudma to investigate. When he meets ex-gladiator Gular (Enzo Fiermonte), Randus is identified as Spartacus's son by the Thracian amulet around his neck.

Corbucci's best peplum, *Son of Spartacus* is also one of Reeves' finest vehicles. It's a big-budget production photographed on location in Egypt in Eastmancolor and CinemaScope by Enzo Barboni. Interiors were filmed at Titanus Studios in Rome and at Studi MISR Guizeh Le Caire, in Cairo. Piero Piccioni composed the edifying score, which is recycled from *Romulus and Remus*. Memorable settings include Caesar's camp beside the pyramids and Sphinx; bustling Alexandria; sail boats on the Nile; and the sun-crumbled, dune-buried ruins of the City of the Sun – a refuge for escaped slaves, wherein lies Spartacus's tomb. Jacques Sernas played Crassus' greedy henchman Vertius and Gianna Maria Canale was Vertius' easily flattered sister Claudia (Crassus' consort). Ombretta Colli played slave Saida with whom Randus falls in love and Benito Stefanelli played Zorak, the leader of Crassus' leopardskin-clad, black-cloaked Iscian warriors. Randus dons his father's famous armour – including a huge, visored helmet – to raid Crassus' property. Spartacus leaves a large red 'S' as his calling card (like Zorro), while his quick-change act owes much to Superman. Crassus drowns slaves in the rising tide and asphyxiates them in a giant bubble with a red-hued deadly vapour as court entertainment. In revenge, the revolting slaves melt down Crassus' gold and force him to swallow his molten wealth. Randus is sentenced by Caesar to be crucified as 'an example' to other insurgents, but in an ending that echoes Kubrick's *Spartacus*, the populace curtail the execution, stating that they must all be crucified – 'We are Spartacus!'

One God: Romans versus Christians

One of the great early Italian epics was *Fabiola* (1948), Alessandro Blasetti's tale of persecuted Christians in fourth-century Rome. In the wake of Hollywood epics such as *Ben-Hur*, Italian filmmakers made several variations on the pagan Romans versus devout Christians discord – ***The Last Days of Pompeii*** (1959) being the most famous example. When director Mario Bonnard fell ill, it was completed by Sergio Leone, who also collaborated on the screenplay (based on the 1834 Bulwer-Lytton novel of the same name) with Duccio Tessari and Sergio Corbucci. In 79 AD Centurion Glaucus Lito (Steve Reeves), the conqueror of Palestine and Syria, returns to Pompeii, under the shadow of rumbling Vesuvius. Murderous hooded fanatics are attacking Roman villas and Glaucus' father has fallen victim to them. Consul Ascanius (Guillermo Marin) suspects the Christians and persecutes the sect, but Glaucus, with the help of street thief Antoninus Marcus (Angel Aranda), discovers that the culprits operate from the sacred Temple of Isis, presided over by Arbaces (Fernando Rey), the Egyptian high priest. Ascanius' Egyptian concubine Julia Lavinia (Annemarie Baumann) is the ringleader – with Arbaces she plans to return to Egypt and oust the Roman invaders. Glaucus falls for Ascanius' daughter, Ione (Christine Kauffman), a Christian, but as Glaucus, Ione and the Christians are about to be fed to the lions in the arena, Vesuvius goes bang.

Filmed at CEA Studios (Madrid) and Cinecittà (Rome), *Pompeii* is a slow 97 minutes. Reeves was again pitted against Mimmo Palmera (as Gallinus, a Praetorian Guard) and Carlo Tamberlani was dignified as the leader of the Christians. In a typically Reeves-ian resolution, Glaucus saves the Christians in the arena by wrestling a lion. Barbara Carroll garnered sympathy as Ione's blind servant, Nydia, who inadvertently discloses the Christians' catacomb hideout. The Supertotalscope Eastmancolor cinematography showcased the great sets, notably the authentic-looking streets of Pompeii, with cobbles and flagged paviors, market stalls and hefty curb stones. Pompeii had already been destroyed by an earthquake in 62 AD and was a half-built city in rejuvenation when it was levelled in 79 AD. Its destruction redeems the film, the street sets demolished en masse. The Temple of Isis collapses and the town is showered with cascading hot coals and cinders and is torn asunder by yawning fissures, intercut with spewing lava stock footage (courtesy of Haroun Terzieff), resulting in an impressive Acropolis Now.

A great success in Italy, *Pompeii* was much imitated, with Gianfranco Parolini's **79 AD** (1962 – *The Destruction of Herculaneum*) the most obvious example. Starring Brad Harris and featuring raft-bourn gladiatorial combat on a fiery, crocodile-infested lake, it was retitled *The Last Days of Herculaneum* in France. Herculaneum was a small township also engulfed by the famous eruption. *Last Days of Pompeii* remains the best-known version of the story, despite the appearance in 1984 of a seven-hour UK-Italian TV series of the same story starring Anthony Quayle, Ned Beatty, Lesley-Anne Down, Laurence Olivier, Marilu Tolo, Brian Blessed, Ernest Borgnine and Franco Nero.

The title of **Sign of the Gladiator** (1959) is somewhat misleading, as there is no sign of a gladiator in Guido Brignone's tale of Rome's battles with Zenobia (Anita Ekberg), queen of Palmyra: 'The City of Palms'. Marcus Valerius (Georges Marchal), the vanquished commander of Rome's forces, is put to work in the Syrian mines. As part of a plan to dethrone Zenobia he embarks on 'a love campaign', seducing her. Zenobia is betrayed by her counsellor Semantius (Folco Lulli), who plans to seize power with the aid of King Shapur of neighbouring Persia. The Romans defeat the Palmyrans in a pitched battle at Jaffa Gorge, leaving Zenobia the Romans' prisoner. A subplot had Roman Decurion Julian (Jacques Sernas) fall in love with Vestal Virgin Bathsheba (Lorella De Luca), a believer in Christianity. Lator, the leader of the Christians, was a rare sympathetic role for Mimmo Palmera. Chelo Alonso was Erika, Semantius' lover, who twirls her waist-length hair through an explosive belly dance. Gino Cervi played Emperor Aurelian and Arturo Dominici appeared as the mine's overseer. When Brignone fell ill,

Sign was completed by Michelangelo Antonioni, a director who cut his teeth in popular cinema but went on to gain international 'arthouse' success. Riccardo Freda directed the big battle sequence, staged in a valley in Yugoslavia, which with the addition of a few palm trees passed for the Syrian desert. The Palmyran mine exterior was the entrance to Grotte Di Salone in Italy and the palace scenes were shot at Incir-De Paolis. The Battle of Jaffa Gorge was pilfered by cheaper pepla as stock footage. The outnumbered Romans ambush the Palmyrans in a valley and bombard them with catapults which shoot fireballs and flaming javelins, while a huge booby-trapped pit swallows the Palmyran cavalry charge.

Lionella De Felice's **Constantine and the Cross** (1962 – *Constantine the Great*) cast Hollywood star Cornel Wilde as the first Christian emperor of the Roman Empire. Filmed in Lazio and Yugoslavia, this is the film *Last Days of Pompeii* should have been. Set 'Three Centuries after the birth of Christ', the Roman Empire is on the verge of implosion, with Diocletian ruling the eastern domain and Maximanus ruling the west. Infighting in Rome has resulted in civil war, with prefect of the Praetorians Maxentius (Massimo Serato) seizing power. Constantine is in love with Fausta (Belinda Lee), Maxentius' sister. Christine Kaufman played persecuted Christian Livia. Kaufman's performance and the drama that unfolds as the Romans seek to exterminate the threat to their pagan gods make the film superior to all other peplum treatments of the subject. The Christians are thrown to the lions and tortured in scenes which are still powerful – there's no Steve Reeves to wrestle the lions here. Their unshakable faith ('I believe in one God') impresses Constantine, a wise man torn between pagan Rome and what he feels is morally right. It is revealed that he is the son of a Christian, Elena (Elisa Cegani), and his friend Centurion Hadrian (Fausto Tozzi) falls in love with Livia, drawing Constantine closer to the Christian faith.

Constantine's forces are trapped between Maxentius and his ally Licinius (Nando Gazzolo). On the eve of the battle at Milvian Bridge, Constantine witnesses a vision of a bright cross in the sky during a storm and hears the voice of God telling him, 'Heed this sign – ye shall conquer' (the actual quote, attributed to Constantine's biographer Eusebius, was 'Hoc signo vince' – 'By this sign, win your victory'). Constantine's forces fight under standards based on the Christian cross and are victorious. Made with considerable resources, the film opens in Treviri, Southern Germany, with Constantine's legions sacking a barbarian settlement – this isn't the usual three barbarian extras running past the camera 10 times but is staged on a rather grand scale. The final re-enactment of the Battle of the Milvian Bridge (312 AD) deploys multitudes of well-drilled extras. Much of this stirring footage, of marching legions in square formation and columns of cavalry, reappeared as stock in lesser pepla.

Tales of the Nile

The publicity surrounding the making of *Cleopatra* (1963) resulted in a minor Italian fad for Egyptian-set epics. The Liz Taylor-Richard Burton film, financed by Twentieth Century-Fox, had begun shooting in Pinewood Studios, London, in September 1960 and was completed, after relocating to Cinecittà, in March 1963, at a cost of $44 million. Taylor donned 65 costumes in the title role – enough outfits to clothe the casts of three low-budget pepla. *Cleopatra* boasted two tremendous set-pieces: Cleopatra's entrance into Rome on a sphinx drawn by hundreds of slaves (filmed at Cinecittà) and the sea battle of Actium, filmed near the island of Ischia.

Vittorio Cottafavi's *Legions of the Nile* (1960), starring Argentinian Linda Cristal as Cleopatra and Georges Marchal as Mark Anthony, was suppressed by Fox for $500,000, to avoid having two Cleos at the box office. Pascale Petit played Cleo in *A Queen for Caesar* (1962) with Gordon Scott as her beefy Caesar and Italian filmmakers ensured that all Cleopatra's relatives were catered for. Mark Damon starred as rebel El Kebir fighting the Romans in Ferdinando Baldi's *Son of Cleopatra* (1964), which also starred Scilla Gabel; Fernando Cerchio directed *Cleopatra's Daughter* (1960) and *Nefertite – Queen of the Nile* (1961).

Debra Paget was cast as Shila, the regent's daughter, in **Cleopatra's Daughter**. Shila is forced to marry hypochondriac pharaoh Nemorat (Corrado Pani) by his pushy mother Tegi (Yvette Lebon), but pharaoh's right-hand-man Kefron has other ideas, framing Shila for pharaoh's murder and seizing power. Pietro Ceccarelli had a cameo as Tutek, the royal mummifier, and Ettore Manni was the hero, physician Razi. Shila is given a potion by Razi which induces a temporary coma and is buried in a sarcophagus in the pharaoh's tomb. To save Shila, Razi kidnaps architect Inuni (Robert Alda) and negotiates the network of booby traps designed to kill tomb raiders.

Cerchio's **Nefertite – Queen of the Nile** cast former 'Miss Long Beach' Jeanne Crain as Tanit, who is anointed high priestess Nefertite in Thebes. She is torn between sculptor Tumos (Edmond Purdon, here resembling footballer George Best) and a forced marriage to Pharaoh Amenophis (Amedeo Nazzari). Shot at Incir-De Paolis Studios, it epitomises the Italian 'Cleopatra' movies, with great sets, lighting, costumes and eyeliner disguising a paper-thin plot. Lovestruck Tumos is commissioned to produce a bust of his beloved, while inter-religion rivalry foments rebellion. Liana Orfei performed an exotic dance at an oasis as Tumos' admirer Merith; Carlo D'Angelo played Saper (heretic to the sun god Aten) and Umberto Raho was a priest to Amon. *Nefertite*'s trump card is the presence of Vincent Price as the villain, Benakon, the high priest of Amon. Kitted out in a black braided wig, eyeliner, dramatic eyebrows, a leopardskin cloak and a spangly swimming cap, Price struggles to play it straight.

Fernando Cerchio's Ancient Egyptian set **Totò Versus Maciste** (1962) starred Samson Burke as Maciste, the lover of Nefertite (Gabriella Andreini). Pharaoh's wife Faraona (Nadine Saunders) aims to topple her husband Ramses (Nerio Bernardi). Weedy strongman Totòkamen (Totò) and his manager Tarantakamen (Nino Taranto) arrive in Thebes and Totò is appointed commander of the Theban army. *Totò Versus Maciste* is a passable genre pastiche, with great costumes and hieroglyphic-etched sets (filmed in Totalscope at De Paolis) augmented with stock footage. A highlight is Totò's act – in a stripy strongman leotard, he demonstrates his inflatable bicep, bends an iron bar, spits fire, spouts steam from his ears and escapes from binding chains. Totò and Cerchio also made *Totò and Cleopatra* (1963), with Magali Noël as Cleo.

In Giorgio Ferroni's **The Lion of Thebes** (1964), Mark Forest played Arion (who possesses the 'Strength of Hercules'), who is escorting Helen (Yvonne Furneaux) to safety following the sacking of Troy. Shipwrecked on the shores of Egypt (Tor Caldara beach), they are taken to Pharaoh Ramses (Pierre Cressoy). The pharaoh is knocked out by Helen's beauty, while his fiancée, Nais (Rosalba Neri), is less impressed by the interloper. Arion becomes the Lion of Thebes when the Mighty Gaor (Nello Pazzafini) is killed by a poisonous snake. A power struggle between the pharaoh and Tutmes (Massimo Serato) results in Ramses' murder. Thebes is attacked by rival Menophis (Carlo Tamberlani), who arrives with Helen's vengeful husband, Menelaus (Alberto Lupo). The film becomes bogged down in labyrinthine court intrigue, though the Egyptian army's outsized pickle fork spears leaven the monotony. Unconvincing 'exterior' desert scenes were filmed in De Paolis Studios and the civil war consists entirely of stock footage. The UK print begins with a printed scrawl explaining Helen and Arion's plight. When Helen experiences a traumatic flashback, she (and the audience) endures another reuse of footage from Ferroni's *The Trojan War*.

Thus It Was Written: The Old Testament

There were several Italian Old and New Testament biblical epics patterned on the American model, with impressive spectacle and much dialogue, but little action. **Esther and the King** (1960) cast Joan Collins as Esther and Richard Egan as Ahasuerus, the Persian king. Returning to Shushan from his war with the Egyptians, Ahasuerus discovers that his wife, Queen Vashti (Daniela Rocca), has been unfaithful with Prince Haman (Sergio Fantoni). Haman and General Klidrates (Renato Baldini) convince the good king to persecute the Judean settlements in Persia, until Esther exposes Haman's duplicity. *Esther* deployed Mario Bava as cinematographer; his signature lighting effects are apparent, particularly in a dancing girls' routine (accompanied by a Lavagnino-Nicolosi composition sung by Gianna Spagnolo). Rik Battaglia appeared as Esther's husband-to-be, Simon, and Rosalba Neri was memorable as sultry Karesh, Haman's seductive pawn.

Gianfranco De Bosio's violent, six-hour, Italian-UK TV series **Moses the Lawgiver** (1975) is best remembered for its excellent locations (photographed by Marcello Gatti in the Israeli desert, at Tor Caldara and at Cinecittà) and for Ennio Morricone's hymnal score featuring haunting vocal solos by Gianna Spagnolo. Burt Lancaster starred as Moses and also dubbed the Voice of God (via the burning bush). The series depicted Moses leading the Israelites' exodus out of Egypt to the Promised Land of Canaan and includes recreations of the parting of the

Red Sea and Moses receiving the Ten Commandments on Mount Sinai. Mario Bava directed the special effects. The literate script had Moses observing, 'A miracle, I suppose, is something you need, happening when you need it'. Lancaster's son William played young Moses and the cast included Anthony Quayle, Irene Papas, Ingrid Thulin, Jacques Herlin and Umberto Raho. It was also released as a choppy 136-minute feature, *Moses*.

Joseph and his Brethren (1960 – *Sold into Egypt*) told the story of Joseph and his 'coat of many colours', with Geoffrey Horne as Joseph, Robert Morley as Potifar, and Belinda Lee, Vira Silenti, Arturo Dominici and Terence Hill. **David and Goliath** (1961), co-directed by Richard Pottier and Ferdinando Baldi, and presented by Beaver-Champion Attractions Inc., was shot on location in Jerusalem and Yugoslavia, with interiors at Amato Studio and De Paolis. Yugoslav actor Ivo Payer starred as 'David, Son of Jesse', a shepherd who stands up for the Israelites against the Philistines, led by King Asrod (Furio Meniconi) and his champion Goliath (Kronos). Massimo Serato played duplicitous Abner and Edward Hilton was a worthy Prophet Samuel. With dialogue bristling with thee's and thou's, the film manages an authentic biblical flavour and is worth seeing for David's final slingshot-versus-spear shootout with Goliath. The film is best remembered today for Orson Welles, wearing a false nose and what appears to be a tent, as King Saul, in one of his first Italian acting jobs to raise funds for his pet directorial projects.

Robert Aldrich's **The Last Days of Sodom and Gomorrah** (1962 – *Sodom and Gomorrah* and *Sodom and Gomorrah: Twin Cities of Sin*) was the last word in Italian biblical spectacles and one that proved costly to the Italian film industry. Due to a difficult shoot in Morocco and financial wrangles between producer Goffredo Lombardo (for Titanus), Joseph E. Levine (the US distributor) and Aldrich, the cost escalated from $2 million to $5 million. Second-unit director Sergio Leone was fired for taking extended lunch breaks and Oscar Rudolph took over. Lot (Stewart Granger) leads the Hebrews into the Jordan Valley, in the shadow of iniquitous Sodom and Gomorrah, which is ruled by Queen Bera (Anouk Aimee) and her brother, Prince Astaroth (Stanley Baker). Following an attack by nomadic Helamite raiders led by Segur (Daniele Vargas), the Hebrews shelter in Sodom and Gomorrah. They become wealthy salt sellers when vast mineral deposits are discovered on their land and soon the corrupted Hebrews are indistinguishable from the Sodomites. Lot kills Astaroth when he discovers that his virtuous daughters Shuah (Rosanna Podesta) and Maleb (Claudia Mori) have been dishonoured by the prince. In prison Lot is visited by celestial envoys of Jehovah. Lot leads his people to safety, as vengeful Jehovah destroys Sodom and Gomorrah and its people in a cataclysm. Though the Hebrews have been warned not to look back at Sodom, Lot's wife, ex-slave Ildith (Pier Angeli), can't help herself and is transformed into a pillar of salt.

Sodom and Gomorrah was filmed at the impressive fortified desert town at Ait Ben Haddou, on the Ouarzazate River (with interiors at Titanus). The production design was by Ken Adam and the music was composed by Miklos Rozsa. Antonio De Teffé/'Anthony Steffen' played a Sodomite captain, Giacomo Rossi-Stuart was Ishmael and Rik Battaglia was Melchior. The film highlights some grim torture chamber scenes. Sodomite slave girl Tamar (Scilla Gabel) is hugged to death by Arno (Mimmo Palmera) – a blind man wearing a spiked leather jerkin – and slaves are burned to death on a huge revolving wheel. During Lot and Ildith's wedding, the Helamite cavalry attack the Hebrew settlement as Segur yells, 'The word of the day is kill!' This impressive sequence was filmed in Marrakech, Morocco, by Leone's second unit. The Helamites burn the Hebrews' camp and charge across a plain, and the Hebrews halt them with slingshots, arrows and a fiery oil-filled trench. Having built the Great Dam to irrigate the valley using water from the Jordan, Lot destroys it, sluicing away the Helamites. The uncut print of this opulent, overblown classic runs 143 minutes, while a more widely seen truncated print, some 30 minutes shorter, plays like a 'highlights-of-the-action' trailer. On its release in Italy in October 1962, the film was a costly flop, marking the 'Last Days of Hollywood on the Tiber', as US producers and directors pulled out of Rome en masse. Leone later reused the plot of worthless desert land which becomes valuable in *Once Upon a Time in the West* (1968).

Dino De Laurentiis, who styled himself the Italian Cecil B. De Mille, partially stemmed this exodus with **The Bible...in the Beginning** (1966). John Huston directed this mammoth $18 million production on location in Rome (at De Laurentiis Studios, 'Dinocittà'), Sicily (Mount Etna), Egypt and Tunisia. The film depicted the first 22 chapters of the Book of Genesis, including the Creation, the Garden of Eden, the Great Flood, the Tower of Babel and the destruction of Sodom and Gomorrah. The all-star cast included George C. Scott (Abraham), Ava Gardner (Sarah), Peter O'Toole (the Angel of the Lord), Stephen Boyd (Nimrod), Gabriele Ferzetti (Lot), Eleanora Rossi Drago (Lot's wife), Richard Harris (Cain) and Franco Nero (Abel). Huston played Noah, whose segment featured a replica ark costing $300,000 and animals imported from a zoo in Germany. It was released to critical ridicule but remains one of the most financially successful Italian films.

Tales of the Christ: The New Testament

The New Testament also provided plenty of material for Italian epics. Edmund Purdom starred as **Herod the Great** (1959), the King of Judea. The film begins with the defeat of Cleopatra and Mark Anthony at Actium – Herod was allied to them and must now suffer reprisals from Octavian (Massimo Girotti). Most of the story is talky court intrigue, staged on vast Jerusalem palace interior sets at Cinecittà (with some good exteriors of the city created in matte by Joseph Nathanson). Sylvia Lopez made a luscious Miriam (Herod's wife) and Fellini favourite Sandra Milo played Sarah, the lover of Herod's commander of the guard, Aaron (Alberto Lupo). Jealous Herod suspects Aaron and Miriam of having an affair, so he tortures Aaron and has his wife stoned to death, whilst also drowning Miriam's brother Daniel. The film ends with Herod, now insane, receiving news from a shepherd (Carlo D'Angelo) of the birth of the King of the Jews in Bethlehem. The despot orders all newborns to be killed, before collapsing and dying during a storm signifying the wrath of God. Irving Rapper's *Pontius Pilate* (1961) focussed on the Roman prefect of Judea (played by Jean Marais) who quells an uprising by Barabbas (Livio Lorenzon).

Telling the story of the robber who was freed so that Christ would die wasn't going to be easy, but director Richard Fleischer pulled it off, with an all-star cast and an excellent script by Christopher Fry. **Barabbas** (1961), produced by Dino De Laurentiis and filmed at Dinocittà, was based on the novel by Nobel Prize winner Pär Lagerkvist. The story follows Barabbas (Anthony Quinn) in the first century AD, commencing with his pardon by Pilate (Arthur Kennedy). He witnesses Christ's crucifixion (filmed during an actual eclipse on 15 February 1961) but returns to a life of outlawry, until he's sentenced to life imprisonment in the Sicilian sulphur mines (filmed on barren Mount Etna, Sicily). Having spent 20 years choking below ground, Barabbas and his companion Sahak (Vittorio Gassman) survive a mine disaster and are taken by Senator Rufio (Norman Woodland) and his wife, Julia (Valentina Cortese), to Rome, where they are trained by Torvald (a manic Jack Palance) to become gladiators. Granted his freedom, Barabbas is arrested during the Great Fire of Rome and executed as a persecuted Christian.

Fleischer's film concerns Barabbas' struggle with faith – through his association with Christian Sahak, he learns about Christianity. When Sahak is executed by Torvald for sedition and treason, Barabbas avengers his friend's death in the arena. The gladiatorial scenes – filmed in the Arena Di Verona, Piazza Bra – are spectacular, with gladiators, mocking clowns, wild animals, dwarves and elephants presented as carnivalesque entertainment. The requisite peplum finale (with Dinocittà's sets burning) was undercut by Barabbas' execution on a hillside, amid a sea of crucifixions. Katy Jurado appeared as tavern keeper Sara (Barabbas' lover), Ernest Borgnine played Christian servant Luke, Paolo Pitagora was Mary Magdalene and Harry Andrews was fisherman/apostle Peter. Silvana Mangano (De Laurentiis' wife) was Rachel, Barabbas' friend who converts to Christianity and is stoned for blasphemy. The film is accompanied by what the soundtrack LP sleeve-notes describe as 'The most innovative movie score ever recorded' by Mario Nascimbene. With the booming gong and eerie whine of 'Eclipse', the searing sonic lashes and wails of 'The Whipping of Christ', the booming, clanking 'The Mines' and the majestic main theme, it remains Nascimbene's masterpiece.

Marxist director Pier Paolo Pasolini made two films which depicted Christ's crucifixion. The first was 'La Ricotta' [Curd Cheese], his contribution to the four-story **RoGoPaG** (1962 – directed by Roberto Rossellini, Jean-Luc Godard, Pasolini, and Ugo Gregoretti). In 'La Ricotta', film director Orson Welles is shooting a version of the crucifixion on the outskirts of Rome, on a ridge near Acqua

Santa spring, between the Via Appia Nuova and the Via Appia Antica. Stracci, a local who is playing the Good Thief (crucified beside Christ), gorges himself on curd cheese during a break in filming; when the time comes to shoot the scene, he dies on the cross. The crucifixion scenes are in colour, the scenes of the crew at work are monochrome. The satire features speeded-up footage and a talking dog. The actors and extras have no reverence for their subject, giggling and breaking up, looking at the camera and picking their noses. The crucifixion is supposed to be scored by Scarlatti, but the sound man keeps playing the wrong record, a twist. Welles sits reading Pasolini's script for *Mamma Roma* between takes. As a result of the film's ridiculing tone, Pasolini was tried for blasphemy in March 1963 and was sentenced to four months in prison, though the verdict was overturned in May.

Atheist Pasolini then decided to make a biblical feature film. He adapted the first book of the New Testament, **The Gospel according to St Matthew** (1964) – the 'Saint' was added by the producers against Pasolini's wishes – and dedicated it 'To the dear, joyous, familiar memory of Pope John XXIII'. A faithful telling of the gospel, the film begins with the birth of Jesus in Bethlehem to the Virgin Mary (Margherita Caruso) and carpenter Joseph (Marcello Morante). Fearing reprisals from King Herod the Great (Herod I, played by Amerigo Belivacque) when Jesus is proclaimed King of the Jews, the family flee to Egypt, returning to Israel years later. Jesus is recognised by John the Baptist (Mario

Via Dolorosa: Jesus Christ (Enrique Irazoqui) in Pier Paolo Pasolini's *The Gospel According to St Matthew* (1964).

Socrate) as the Messiah, the Son of God. Following his ordeal in the wilderness, where he is tempted by Satan, Jesus begins spreading the Word of the Lord. He gathers 12 disciples, but his popularity and views bring him into conflict with Caiphas (Rodolfo Wilcock) and the Pharisees in Jerusalem. Betrayed by Judas Iscariot (Otello Sestili), one of his followers, for thirty pieces of silver, Jesus is tried for blasphemy and crucified by Pontius Pilate (Alessandro Clerici) at Golgotha.

Pasolini planned to film in Africa, then Palestine, but eventually settled on Italy. He commenced shooting in spring 1964 with Jesus' baptism – the River Jordan was a gorge and waterfall between Orte and Viterbo. The Mount of Olives was in Lazio, near Tivoli, and Christ's temptations were filmed on volcanic Mount Etna, Sicily. When Joseph and his family flee to Egypt, Pasolini used Tor Caldara, so familiar from 'Hercules' movies. Other locations include the ruins at Canale Monterano in Lazio and Catania in Sicily (for some Jerusalem scenes). He also filmed at Crotone in Calabria and at Barile, Potenza and Matera in Basilicata, with its distinctive rock-hewn hovels, the Sassi Di Matera (Pasolini's Bethlehem). Pasolini depicted some magnificent, empty landscapes – sandy wastes of sparse rolling desert country, swept by whistling winds. The film was photographed in monochrome by Tonino Delli Colli and edited by Nino Baragli, both of whom worked on another great 'desert' film – *The Good, the Bad and the Ugly*. Pasolini cast many rural Italians as the Judean people, their costumes designed by Danilo Donati. Convincing locales and locals gave the film a documentary-like, neo-realist quality absent from all other versions of Christ's life on film, as Pasolini trained his camera on these portraits of poverty.

Gospel portrays a Human Christ, a Jesus of the People, almost a revolutionary. The Sermon on the Mount is presented as a dramatic montage of Christ's message, the Beatitudes becoming slogans. During Jesus' ride into Jerusalem on an ass, the cheering, smiling throng waving palms see him as hero. His actions – casting out those who have made his house of prayer 'a den of thieves' – place him in opposition to the lawgivers and the government and constitutes a revolutionary act. Pasolini underplays Christ's miracles – Jesus cures the possessed, lepers and the lame with none of the showmanship of his Hollywood equivalents. Even Pasolini's earthquake is low-key, while the first communion during the Last Supper is similarly understated. The feeding of the 5,000 with five loaves and two fishes and Christ's walk on the Sea of Galilee are more moving for their simplicity. Pasolini's depiction of the attack by Herod's soldiers on Bethlehem, slaughtering the village's firstborn, is one of the most horrific scenes in cinema. Christ's harrowing walk to Calvary along the Via Dolorosa – wearing a crown of thorns and burdened by a cross mockingly inscribed 'INRI' (King) – and his crucifixion at Golgotha are leavened by his climatic Resurrection.

Pasolini used only quotations from Matthew's 28-chapter text. There are no time or place captions ('Jerusalem' or 'Three Day's Later') and few character names are mentioned. Pasolini cast Enrique Irazoqui, a Spanish economics student from Barcelona, as Christ. In addition to Irazoqui – his hallowed, cowled countenance a living El Greco and his voice dubbed by Enrico Maria Salerno – Natalia Ginzburg played Mary of Bethany (Mary Magdalene), Rosanna Di Rocco was the Angel of the Lord (with dark curly hair and no wings) and Eliseo Boschi played Joseph of Arimathea (who inters Jesus in the tomb). Francesco Leonetti was Herod Antipas (Herod II), Franca Cupane his wife, Herodiade, and Paola Tedesco played Salome, who danced for Herod and asked for John the Baptist's head on a dish. The Apostles were played by Settimo Di Porto (Peter), Ferrucio Nuzzo (Matthew), Giacomo Morante (John) and Alfonso Gatto (Andrew). Enzo Siciliano, later Pasolini's biographer, played Simon. Pasolini's mother Susanna played the aged Madonna, Mary, at the time of Jesus' death.

Some incidental themes were written by Luis Enriquez Bacalov, but the bulk of the score was stirring pieces from Bach ('Matthew's Passion'), Mozart, Prokofiev and Anton Webern. 'Gloria' (Missa Luba) was an African interpretation of the Latin Mass and the emotionally wracked spiritual 'Sometimes I Feel Like a Motherless Child' (used for Jesus' Nativity and baptism) was sung by Odetta. *Gospel* premiered in September 1964 at the Venice Film Festival, where it won a Special Jury Prize. The OCIC (the Catholic International Film Office) noted that Pasolini 'has made a fine film, a Christian film that produces a profound impression'. Originally 135 minutes long, it has since been released on DVD in a 90-minute colourised version dubbed in English. Pasolini made violent, questioning, unsettling cinema, but he was also a poet. Together with *The Leopard*, *The Gospel according to St Matthew* is the finest film discussed in this book and one of cinema's few works of art.

Chapter Four

Tales from the Tomb
Gothic Horrors

The golden age of Italian gothic horror was 1960–65. Though they were influenced by the Technicolor horror of Hammer Studios and Roger Corman's CinemaScoped Edgar Allan Poe adaptations, many 1960s Italian horror films opted for monochrome. As director Mario Bava noted, 'In a horror film, lighting is 70% of the effectiveness; it's essential in creating the atmosphere'. Bava conjured his exquisite effects with 'smoke and mirrors' camera trickery, but crucial to his success were atmospheric scores by Roberto Nicolosi and Carlo Rustichelli. Their contributions were at least as important as those of Ennio Morricone and Luis Bacalov to Italian westerns and Carlo Innocenzi and Enzo Masetti to pepla.

The Master of Horror: Mario Bava

The son of special effects master Eugenio Bava, Mario Bava had worked in Italian cinema as a photographer since 1939. Bava made his directorial debut with ***The Mask of Satan*** (1960), a grim fairytale of folklore and gore. In seventeenth-century Moldavia, vampires Asa the Witch (Barbara Steele) and her lover Igor Javutich (Arturo Dominici) are executed by the High Court of the Inquisition of Moldavia led by her brother, Grayarvé. Two centuries later, on 'The Day of the Damned', the pair wreak revenge on the House of Vadja's descendants, with Asa possessing Princess Katja (Steele again). On their way to Moscow, Professor Choma Kruvajan (Andrea Checchi) and his assistant Dr Andre Gorovek (John Richardson) stay in an inn at Mirgorod. The professor is called to Castle Vajda to treat Prince Vajda (Ivo Garrani) for shock but is vampirised. As Asa transforms into Katja, Andre arrives to save her – Katja is wearing a crucifix, the only way he can tell which witch is which.

Mask of Satan was based on *The Vij* by Nikolai Vasilevich Gogol. Bava wanted the villains to wear vampire fangs (they appeared in cast publicity photos), but the film's vampirism is implied: victims have colon puncture holes in their necks.

Scream Queen: Asa the Witch (Barbara Steele) is put to death by the Inquisition of Moldavia. French poster for Mario Bava's trendsetting Italian gothic horror *The Mask of Satan* (1960).

Bava created impressive special effects, as when Steele's cloak falls open to reveal a fleshless ribcage and guts, and when Asa is burned at the stake by torch-bearing villagers. In the film's now infamous opening, the hooded inquisitors brand Asa with a sizzling 'S' (the Mark of Satan) and hammer a spiked devil mask onto her face with a huge mallet. The 'Mask of Satan' was designed by Eugenio Bava in bronze. When Asa is resurrected, she explosively blasts out of the coffin. Steele is excellent as the witch, her face grotesquely punctured by the mask's spikes. As

Katja she's dubbed with a rather flat vocal, but Steele's beauty and spellbinding stare were primal forces to be reckoned with, her marble eyes and aquiline face equally suited to soulful beauty and soulless horror. Antonio Pierfederici played the Rasputin-like parish priest who helps Andre dispatch the vampires: he pokes out the professor's eye with a stick. Enrico Olivieri played Katja's brother, Constantine. Renato Terra played Vadja's coachmen Boris, who is drowned in a stream, and Tino Bianchi was manservant Ivan, who's found hanged.

Mask was shot on interiors at Titanus Studios. Atmospheric scenes depicted coachman Nikita (Mario Passante) driving nervously through the misty, tangled forest, amid howling wolves and moaning winds, and Javutich's ghostly coach gliding silently through the mist. The ruined chapel has crumbling arches, cobwebs, tombs and a crypt, and the castle interior, with its great hall dominated by an ornate fireplace and portraits of Asa and Javutich, conceals a network of secret passages and trapdoors. Mirgorod's graveyard is the setting for Javutich's resurrection: the earth cleaves and the coffin lid yawns open, as the cadaver's clammy hands reach from beyond the grave, in the first of many undead rebirths in Bava's cinema.

Released in Italy in August 1960, *Mask of Satan* announced Bava as a talented director. In the United States it was retitled *Black Sunday* by AIP, who replaced Roberto Nicolosi's score with an inferior one by Les Baxter and recorded a different dubbing track to the UK print. Steele is misspelt 'Steel' in the title sequence of some versions. It was rejected a UK certificate in February 1961 and was retitled *Revenge of the Vampire* for its belated X-rated UK release, cut, in June 1968.

Bava's next gothic was part of his three-part 'demonthology': **Black Sabbath** (1963), which exists in two very different versions – one tailored to the Italian market, one to the US audience. Both were shot at Titanus Studios and the US print replaces Nicolosi's score with lesser compositions by Baxter. All three tales deal with ghosts and the supernatural. In the order they appear in the US version, the episodes were 'The Drop of Water', 'The Telephone' and 'The Wurdulak'. In the Italian print the running order is 'The Telephone', 'The Wurdulak' and 'The Drop of Water'. In 'A Drop of Water', nurse Helen Corey (Jacqueline Pierreaux) is summoned to the mansion of Madame Zena, a medium who has died of a heart attack during a séance. While she dresses the corpse for burial, Helen steals Zena's ring. In her apartment, Helen hears dripping water and is eventually scared to death by an apparition of Madame Zena. When the police arrive, Helen has throttled herself and a shifty neighbour (Harriet White Medin) has stolen the ring. Zena's grotesque, rigid face was created in wax by Bava's father.

In the US version of 'The Telephone', prostitute Rosy (Michele Mercier) is menaced in her apartment by threatening phone calls from Frank, her ex-lover who has been dead for three months. Rosy phones Mary (Lydia Alfonsi) and asks her to come over. Ghostly Frank (Milo Quesada) breaks in and kills Mary by mistake, so Rosy stabs him to death. In the fadeout, the mysterious calls continue. The Italian print of this story is quite different. Now it is Rosy's ex-lover Mary

'The Most Gruesome Day in the Calendar of the Undead': A headless horseman and a misty castle adorn this US poster for AIP's release of Mario Bava's *Black Sabbath* (1963) starring horror icon Boris Karloff. Poster courtesy Ian Caunce Collection.

who makes the threatening phone calls, in an effort to renew their relationship. Frank Rainer (Quesada) is a criminal who seeks revenge on Rosy for his betrayal to the police. In the US print, Rosy receives a mysterious note under her door ('It won't be long now!'), while in the Italian print she receives a newspaper cutting detailing Frank's prison escape. The most telling difference is the omission of any lesbian subtext to Mary and Rosy's relationship, which in the US version plays as a ghost story.

In the Russian tale 'The Wurdulak', Count Vladimir D'Urfe (Mark Damon) discovers the headless corpse of Turkish bandit Alibek on the road to Yessey. Vladimir finds a peasant family living in fear of their father, Gorka (Boris Karloff), who is hunting the bandit. The family are Gorka's grown-up children Peter (Massimo Righi), Sdenka (Susy Andersen) and Gregor (Glauco Onorato), and Gregor's wife Maria (Rica Dialina) and their little son Ivan. Alibek is a vampire, a 'Wurdulak', and when Gorka returns, clomping across the bridge on the stroke of ten, he too has joined the walking dead. Gorka roams the house, vampirising the family, including Ivan who rises from the dead, calling out 'Mama, I'm cold, let me in'. Vladimir and Sdenka flee, but Gorka and the Wurdulaks follow, taking Sdenka back with them – in a final kiss, Sdenka sinks her teeth into Vladimir's neck. Bava sets the story in frozen wastes, replete with howling dogs, whistling wind and gliding fog. Damon is excellent as the young nobleman and Karloff is ideally cast as the caped cadaver.

With their threatening roving camerawork, urban settings, thunderstorms and throbbing neon lights, 'A Drop of Water' and 'The Telephone' anticipate giallo thrillers, while 'The Wurdulak' harks back to *Mask of Satan* (Bava reused the ruined chapel set). Karloff introduces each of the stories in jokily macabre fashion: 'Come closer, I have something to tell you – this is Black Sabbath'. For the Italian print, Karloff reappears at the end in a visual gag. He's seen being filmed on a dummy horse in Titanus Studios, in costume as Gorka, in front of a wind machine, while the crew run around him brandishing fir branches, making it appear as though Gorka is galloping through a wood. The US version was a great success when released by AIP with a poster campaign featuring Karloff's severed head. It was Bava's favourite film, no doubt due to the presence of horror icon Karloff. In 1969 Ozzy Osbourne's British heavy metal band Black Sabbath took their name from a poster for Bava's film.

The Whip and the Body (1963) was Bava's most controversial film of the 1960s. Kurt Menliff (Christopher Lee) returns to his family castle. He's not welcome, having caused the suicide of housekeeper Georgia's daughter, Tanya. In Kurt's absence, his brother Christian (Tony Kendall) has married Nevenka (Daliah Lavi), Kurt's one-time paramour, while cousin Katia (Ida Galli) still loves Christian. Count Menliff (Gustavo De Nardo) decides that Christian will inherit the estate. Vengeful Kurt assaults Nevenka on a beach and is murdered with Tanya's suicide dagger. But Kurt isn't dead, returning to torment Nevenka and knife the count. *Whip* is Bava's most poetic period film, which is enhanced by Carlo Rustichelli's score. Billed as 'Jim Murphy', Rustichelli composed 'The Windsor Concerto', a dramatic, richly romantic piano composition. Israeli actress Lavi vaguely resembles Barbara Steele and Bava plays up their similarities. With the castle's interiors saturated with colour, Bava expanded the style he'd deployed in *Black Sabbath*. Through intense compositions, vibrantly matching the tale's passion, this is Bava's best-photographed film. Its style influenced Dario Argento's shifting floods of colour (for example, in Jessica Harper's stormy taxi ride at the beginning of *Suspiria*).

Whip was shot on the beach and coast at Tor Caldara, Lazio, for approximately $66,000, with a matte shot creating cliff top Castle Menliff; its interiors were in Rome. Harriet White Medin appeared as housekeeper Georgia and Luciano Pigozzi was servant Losat. The English language version is cursed with a facile script and flat dubbing. Even Lee is voiced by someone else, as he drives a nail through the heart of his rigid Dracula impersonations. In the dead of night, Kurt visits Nevenka in her bedchamber. His hand reaches out of the darkness like a claw, tearing her nightgown. Those familiar with Lee only via the 'Star Wars' and 'Lord of the Rings' series will be surprised to see him whipping Nevenka with such demonic relish. Nevenka enjoys these sadomasochistic activities and is revealed to be the unbalanced murderer of both Kurt and the count.

The horror here is monstrous Kurt's fetish and Nevenka's fevered imagination, willing Kurt back to life. The film was released as *Night Is the Phantom* in the UK in 1964 (shorn of the whipping scenes and rated X) and as *What* in the US.

In Bava's **Kill, Baby...Kill!** (1966 – *Curse of the Dead*), Kernigan is a village cursed, living and dying in fear. Following the apparent suicide of Irena Hollander (Mirella Panfili), who is found impaled on spiked railings, coroner Dr Paul Eswai (Giacomo Rossi-Stuart) arrives to conduct an autopsy and discovers a coin embedded in her heart to ward off evil spirits. Eswai joins Inspector Kruger (Piero Lulli) and burgomaster Karl (Luciano Catenacci) in their investigation. The village is haunted by Melissa Graps, a seven-year-old girl who, during a village festival 20 years ago, was trampled by drunken locals as she tried to retrieve her bouncing ball and bled to death. Ghostly Melissa's revenge is orchestrated by her mother, Baroness Graps (Giana Vivaldi), a medium. Death is heralded by Melissa's stuttering laughter, a tolling bell and a ghostly white bouncing ball, and whoever sees Melissa dies of self-inflicted wounds – Kruger shoots himself and Karl slits his own throat with a sickle.

Several of Bava's early films were tailored to the American market, but *Kill* is an Italian horror movie that plays best in Italian with English subtitles. Rossi-Stuart, stiff and awkward when dubbed into English, gives a better performance in Italian. Hawk-faced Lulli and bald-headed Catenacci are more charismatic and survive the English dubbing. Erika Blanc played Monica Schuftan who is revealed to be Melissa's sister. The cast also includes Giuseppe Addobatti and Franca Dominici as Hans and Martha (the local innkeepers) and Micaela Esdra as their daughter Nadine, who kills herself on a spiked candle stand. Fabienne Dali was witch Ruth (Karl's lover) on whom Kernigan relies for magic spell cure-alls – their substitute for religion in the face of superstition, ignorance and poverty. Raven-haired sorceress Ruth is a good witch, while Melissa (who resembles an undead Alice in Wonderland) is the killer. In a bizarre piece of casting Melissa was played by a boy, Valerio Valeri in a flowing blonde wig.

Bava filmed Kernigan on location in Calcata, a medieval fortress town perched atop a rocky promontory (overlooking the Treja Valley in Viterbo, Lazio), a higgledy-piggledy warren of narrow streets, mossy steps and decaying walls. Nearby village Faleria is equally distinctive, with its old town, gate portals, arches, crumbling walls and steep winding streets. Bava bathed these locations in bold colours and wafting mist. He also created an atmospheric graveyard in Titanus Studios (where he lensed the interiors). The coffin-strewn undertaker's, the inn, Ruth's house (decorated with stuffed birds) and Villa Graps (its faded grandeur filmed at Villa Frascati, Rome, with its spiral staircase, corridors, webby crypt and Melissa's doll-filled room) are littered with ephemera and authentic-looking artefacts. Nobody does clutter like Bava. The score by Carlo Rustichelli includes an excerpt of 'The Windsor Concerto' and a tinkling music box melody, supported by odd, sliding bass, which accompanies Melissa's ghostly appearances. The US release was marred by a shoddy advertising campaign: 'KILL BABY

Gothic Horrors 83

'Operation Fear': Italian poster for Mario Bava's *Kill, Baby...Kill!* (1966). Monica Schuftan (Erika Blanc) is stalked by her sister, Melissa (Valerio Valeri). Poster courtesy Ian Caunce Collection.

KILL – Makes You Shiver & Quiver!' The English language print is a picturesque ghost story, but in Italian it is Bava's supernatural masterpiece.

Strange Love: The Horror of Riccardo Freda

Director Riccardo Freda cast Barbara Steele in two Technicolor gothics: *The Horrible Secret of Dr Hichcock* (1962) and its sequel, *The Ghost* (1963 – *The Spectre*). Freda and Bava had worked together as director and photographer on the early Italian horror movie *I vampiri* (1956 – *The Devil's Commandment* or *Lust of the Vampire*), which was set in contemporary Paris. In **The Horrible Secret of Dr Hichcock**, set in London in 1885, surgeon Dr Bernard Hichcock (Robert Flemyng) indulges his necrophiliac urges. He administers his patented serum, which slows the heart rate, to his willing wife, Margaretha (Maria Teresa Vianello), so that she replicates death during their lovemaking. But he ups the dose and she dies, so he entombs her in the family crypt. Arriving back at his London mansion after 12 years with his new wife, Cynthia (Steele), Hichcock finds the spirit of Margaretha abroad once more. With Jezebel, her black cat, the wraith cometh, seeking revenge.

Also called *The Horrible Dr Hichcock*, *The Terror of Dr Hichcock* and *Raptus – The Secret of Dr Hichcock*, Freda's Victorian 'necromance' is a unique Italian gothic. The Italian cast and crew hid behind English pseudonyms to make *Dr Hichcock* appear a Hammer horror movie: Freda became 'Robert Hampton', screenwriter Ernesto Gastaldi was 'Julyan Perry', and the crew included assistant director 'John M. Farquhar' and decorator 'Frank Smokecocks'. British actor Flemyng gives an artfully menacing performance, while young Dr Kurt Langer (Silvano Tranquilli) is Cynthia's cardboard love interest. Hichcock's sinister housekeeper Martha (Harriet White Medin) cares for her insane sister in the mansion's cottage, but her patient is actually Margaretha. Elegantly dressed and sumptuously photographed – in her only Italian gothic in which she didn't play a tormentor, murderess or ghost, but simply the victim – Steele has never looked better. Cynthia's wide-eyed horror is accentuated by Steele's catlike eyes, as when she's trapped in a coffin, her silent terror visible through a glass window in the lid.

Freda's meticulous Victoriana evokes the period convincingly. The bright white interiors at Hichcock's University College Hospital contrast with the funereal décor of his necrophiliac lair. With the memorable set pieces – Margaretha's rain drenched funeral, Hichcock's grave robbing, Cynthia's explorations of long corridors and crypts by flickering candlelight, and Margaretha's terrifying appearances wearing a white dress and veil – Freda out-Bava's Bava. Hichcock's ritualised sex games, with the chamber decorated with drapes and candles, are elevated to religious rites. Roman Vlad's romantic score, laced with dark undertones, lurks menacingly, ebbing like Hichcock's perverse urges. Freda floods the screen with bleeding, lustful reds, a visualisation of the doctor's fetish, as in the scene where Hichcock steals into the hospital morgue. This aspect of the film, in particular Hichcock's corpse-fondling activities, were toned down in US and UK prints, which ran 76 minutes – the full version is 8 minutes longer. In the fiery finale, Hichcock and Margaretha are revealed to be in league – he plans to restore her beauty with Cynthia's young blood. Kurt saves Cynthia from the burning mansion and pushes Hichcock off a balcony while Margaretha perishes in the flames: Poe-etic justice indeed.

The Ghost is set in Scotland in 1910 at the Hichcocks' coastal mansion near Dowbridge. Dr John Hichcock (Elio Jotta) is paralysed, a condition that is slowly killing him. Dr Charles Livingstone (Peter Baldwin), his live-in physician, treats him with a serum – a poison and then an antidote – which seems to be stimulating his limbs back to life. Hichcock's wife Margaret (Steele) and Charles are having an affair and dispose of John. They discover he has left most of his £150,000 fortune to the local orphanage, run by Canon Owens (Umberto Raho). Margaret becomes convinced that her husband is still alive, communicating through their housekeeper, Catherine Wood (Harriet White Medin), a medium. Driven to dementia by apparitions, greedy Margaret becomes suspicious of Charles and kills him, before John reappears and has the last laugh. The film provides a logical explanation for John's 'ghostly' appearances – John and Catherine engineer the scheme – and Steele's descent into wild-haired madness is convincing. Franco Mannino's score features an arching, romantic title theme. Freda's gothic touches include swivelling bookcases, exhumed corpses, crypts, a funeral and the expected nocturnal shenanigans: John's empty wheelchair careers downstairs, blood drips from the ceiling and oozes from a snuffbox. Eventually Margaret, paralysed with curare, watches John accidentally drink a dose of poison. *The Ghost* was a success for Steele in the US, swelling her cult of fans, but like most of her films, it wasn't released in the UK.

Castles of Terror: Antonio Margheriti

Antonio Margheriti directed three horrors in the mid-1960s as 'Anthony Dawson': *The Virgin of Nuremberg* (1963), *Castle of Blood* and *The Long Hair of Death* (both 1964). In **The Virgin of Nuremberg** (*The Castle of Terror* or *Horror Castle*) Max and Mary Hunter (Georges Riviere and Rossana Podesta) move into Max's ancestral castle on the Rhine. Mary witnesses shadows in the night and discovers a woman's corpse, her eyes poked out by the Virgin, a sarcophagus-like torture device. The castle houses a museum to a seventeenth-century torturer, The Punisher (dressed in a red cape, black hood and gauntlets), who seems to have been resurrected. Mary suspects Max is responsible, but the murderer is Max's father, the general (Mirko Valentin), a Nazi officer who took part in an assassination attempt on Hitler. His conspirators were shot, hanged or gassed, but the general was subjected to horrific experiments. He had facial tissue removed, leaving him resembling 'a living skull', with sunken eyes, no ears, nose or hair.

Filmed in three weeks on interiors at Incir-De Paolis Studios and at Villa Sciarra, Rome, *Virgin* is the most violent 1960s Italian horror. The Punisher ties a woman to a chair and notes that this method of torture has been forbidden since the fifteenth century, 'But the old ways are still the best'. He straps a caged rat to her face, which gnaws off half her nose. Amy Degli Uberti played housekeeper Frau Martha and Luciana Milone was housemaid Trudy. Christopher Lee played Erich, the general's once-time aide, now working as the custodian of the museum. Although Erich was also badly scarred in the war and is a likely candidate for the Punisher's alter ego, he is a sympathetic character, bringing the police to Max and Mary's rescue and dying whilst attempting to save his old comrade from the fire that engulfs the castle. The presence of FBI investigator John Selby (Jim Dolen) is a superfluous addition tacked on for international audiences, and Riz Ortolani's intrusive jazz score seems from another film entirely.

Castle of Blood (1964 – *La danza macabra* or *The Castle of Terror*) is set in nineteenth-century London. A tavern wager results in *Times* journalist Alan Foster (Georges Riviere) spending the Night of the Dead, the first midnight of November, in haunted Blackwood Castle. Foster's bet is made with Sir Thomas Blackwood (Umberto Raho) and author Edgar Allan Poe (Silvano Tranquilli). Foster encounters all manner of ghosts, who re-enact horrific murders from the castle's past. Dr Carmus (Arturo Dominici), the scientist author of *Elements of Metaphysics Medicine*, helps Foster make sense of the carnage, until he too is revealed to be a ghost. Foster falls in love with Elisabeth Blackwood (Barbara Steele) who seems to be in peril, but as the vengeful ghosts close in to kill Foster ('Your blood will be our life'), Elisabeth betrays him. With the ghosts' mad laughter ringing in his ears, Foster escapes through the graveyard and sees the trees festooned with lynched corpses – the first Lord Blackwood was a hangman. At dawn Sir Thomas and Poe find Foster impaled on the castle's iron gate and collect their winnings, 10 pounds Sterling, from his wallet.

Co-written by Margheriti, Gianni Grimaldi and Sergio Corbucci, *Castle of Blood* is scarily effective. Riz (billed as 'Ritz') Ortolani's score is suitably hair-raising and Riccardo Pallottini's monochrome cinematography lenses the castle in its gothic glory: the rising mist and ivy covered tombstones, the cobwebby parlour, hypnotic portraits, bedchambers and family crypt lit by candlelight. The ghostly supporting cast includes Benito Stefanelli as William (Elisabeth's husband), Giovanni Cianfriglia as the hulking gardener Herman (Elisabeth's lover) and Margarete Robsahn as Julia (also Elisabeth's lover). These spooks enact jealousy, adultery and gruesome murder before Foster's disbelieving eyes, but it's Steele you'll remember, making a spectre of herself in her finest role: a lost soul with no heartbeat and to whom life is a distant memory, haunting a decaying, long-abandoned castle. Steele's English language dubbing is better than usual and her strange beauty is lit to accentuate her long black hair, strong eyebrows, prominent cheekbones and big eyes. 'Kiss me, warm me', she lures Foster, until she returns to her corpse-like state. In the US the film was tenuously touted as another Poe adaptation.

The Long Hair of Death (1964) begins with accused witch Adel Karnstein burned to death by Count Humbolt (Jean Rafferty) for murdering his brother, Franz. Her daughters, Helen (Steele) and Lizabeth (Halina Zalewska), resolve to take revenge on Humbolt's family, including the real murderer, Humbolt's son Kurt (Giorgio Ardisson). Helen is killed by Humbolt when she's pushed over a waterfall, but later Mary (Steele again) arrives at the castle, the apparent survivor of a coach crash. Kurt has since married Lizabeth but begins an affair with Mary, until it's revealed that Mary is Helen's ghost, plotting revenge. *Long Hair of Death* is a superior monochrome gothic. Steele, with very long black hair, is excellent in two of her best roles. Umberto Raho was the district's ruler, Von Klarga, and Nello Pazzafini appeared as a servant. The fever-pitch score by 'Evirust' (Carlo Rustichelli) reuses cues from *Blood and Black Lace* for a scene depicting an outbreak of plague (which resembles *The Seventh Seal*). The opening execution sees Adel trapped in a labyrinth of burning sticks, until she dies atop the pyre, clinging to a wooden cross and spitting curses at the House of Humbolt. For Helen's resurrection, lightning strikes her grave, splitting the earth, then Steele appears dramatically in the chapel doorway, literally scaring Humbolt to death.

Long Hair is a familiar litany of cobwebby corridors, crypts, wormy cadavers and bumps in the night, but its finale was influential. To mark the end of the plague, Von Klarga holds a Day of Thanksgiving. The populace construct a large wooden Effigy of Death – carrying a scythe, topped with a skull head and decorated with long hair shorn from the women of the city – which is to be burned. Driven mad by Lizabeth and Helen, Kurt is captured by Helen who locks him inside 'Death'. Gagged and restrained, Kurt can only watch as Lizabeth is given the honour of lighting the effigy: 'Burn as my mother did', she sneers. It's largely forgotten in Italian horror that most witches were hanged, not burned.

Barbara Is Abroad: Scream Queen Steele

Barbara Steele's next Italian gothic was Massimo Pupillo's ***Five Graves for a Medium*** (1965), which cast her as Cleo Hauff, the widow of Dr Jeronimus Hauff. A year since his death, Hauff, a spiritualist, resurrects plague victims to avenge his murder. His killers include solicitor Joseph Morgan (Riccardo Garrone) who is having an affair with Cleo. Morgan's assistant, Albert Kovac (Walter Brandi), is summoned to Villa Hauff. Each murderer's death is heralded by the squeaky wheels of the corpse carriers' cart: Oscar Stinnel (Ennio Balbo) commits suicide by driving his wheelchair headlong into a sabre, impaling himself on the blade. Horror regular Luciano Pigozzi played Kurt the gardener who ensures that 'The Vengeance of Jeronimus' comes to pass. Alfredo Rizzo was Dr Nemek, Hauff's replacement as doctor of Gradenville, Tilde Till was Villa Hauff's nervous maid Louise, and Mirella Maravidi was Corrine Hauff, Kovac's love interest. Corrine sees apparitions of Jeronimus, and Kovac's car won't start because there's 'an owl caught in the engine'. A wax cylinder recording of an eerie lullaby tells Kovac that only 'pure water' will suppress the reanimated avengers. A heart in a jar and a display case of severed hands (the 'plague spreaders', who deliberately diffused the pestilence) twitch to life, until purifying rain saves Kovac and Corrine. Reputedly 'inspired by Edgar Allan Poe', it was retitled *Terror-Creatures from the Grave* and presented internationally by the aptly named 'Pacemaker Pictures'. With its 1911 setting, the film's monochrome film stock resembles grainy photographs come to life. Jeronimus' exhumation near a mausoleum in the drifting mist has Steele in black hat, veil and funeral attire, as skeletal, leafless trees clutch desperately towards the grey dawn sky.

Steele had a small but pivotal role in the low-budget **The She Beast** (1965 – *Revenge of the Blood Beast*), written and directed by Michael Reeves, one of the great horror talents of the 1960s. Steele was hired for one day's work for $1,000; the producer didn't mention how long the day would be and made her work for 18 hours. Newlyweds Philip (Ian Ogilvy) and Veronica (Steele) are on their honeymoon in Transylvania, but their black VW Beetle plummets into a lake and Veronica is drowned. Her spirit passes into the body of witch Vardalla, who was put to death in 1765 in 'the seat of chastisement', a ducking stool. Steele sends up her horror image – when she hears the name Van Helsing, she can't place the name. Though padded with humour – bumbling Count Van Helsing (John Karlsen) pursues Vardalla – the film is most memorable for its violence. The flashback to Vardalla's execution is the most excessive scene. A child with a blood smeared forehead interrupts a funeral and tells the congregation that he has found Vardalla hiding in a cave. The torch-bearing peasants trap the screeching witch, a 'Sister of Satan', tie her to the ducking stool, drive a spike through her and drown her. The witch herself (played by a man) is a hideous creature, boasting a long robe, chopped liver complexion, straggly hair and tombstone teeth. Between takes, the actor would terrify drivers by hitchhiking on the road in costume.

In 'Alan Grünewald'/Mario Caiano's **Night of the Doomed** (1965) Steele played Muriel Arrowsmith, the wife of Dr Stephen Arrowsmith (Paul Muller), who lives in Hampton Castle. The doctor, an archetypal 'mad scientist', is experimenting in blood rejuvenation and discovers that Muriel is having an affair with servant David (Rik Battaglia). The doctor tortures them with firebrands, electrocutes and cremates them. Dr Arrowsmith cuts Muriel's heart out, keeping it in a glass case, and uses her blood to rejuvenate his elderly lover, Solange (Helga Line). Muriel has willed her castle to her mentally fragile stepsister, Jenny Hampton (Steele in a blonde wig), so the doctor marries her and later administers hallucinogens which cause Jenny nightmarish apparitions. Her doctor, Joyse Derek ('Laurence Clift'/Marino Masé), realises that Jenny is possessed by Muriel. He removes a scalpel from Muriel's suspended heart, unleashing the vengeful spirits of Muriel and David. During a botched blood transfusion, Solange disintegrates to instant old age and beyond, while Dr Arrowsmith is strapped to a chair and immolated.

Steele really suffers as Muriel in this sadistic movie, while as Jenny she used her own voice in the English language dub. Dr Arrowsmith wires Derek's cast-iron bath to the mains, but butler Jonathan (Giuseppe Addobatti) drops the soap into the water and is electrocuted instead. It is as resurrected Muriel that Steele appears in one of her most famous guises, her long cascade of black hair brushed over the right hand side of her face, concealing gruesome facial disfigurement. *Night of the Doomed* benefits from fine monochrome photography by Enzo Barboni, effective makeup, special effects (which include a pot plant fertilized with Muriel's ashes that drips blood) and a torturous organ fugue from Ennio Morricone. *Night of the Doomed* (100 minutes long) was released as *The Faceless Monster* in the UK in 1969 (cut by 25 minutes). *Nightmare Castle* was the 81-minute US print.

Steele's final Italian gothic, Camillo Mastrocinque's **An Angel for Satan** (1966) again saw her in two roles, as heiress Harriet and her violent, seductive alter ego Belinda. Claudio Gora played Count Montebruno (Harriet's uncle, an evil hypnotist) and Anthony Steffen (who in his hat, scarf and long coat resembles Django) was artist Roberto Merigi, who arrives by boat to restore a naked statue of Steele which has been retrieved from a lake. The film's dreamlike mood is enhanced by Francesco De Masi's forlorn score and the monochrome cinematography. Steele is at her most sensuous as Belinda, who takes pleasure in splitting up her maid Rita (Ursula Davis) and Rita's beau, schoolteacher Dario (Vassili Karis), driving the latter to suicide. She also compels tavern ruffian Carlos (Mario Brega) to burn his own house down with his children inside and turns gardener Victor (Aldo Berti) into a mad axe man. Falling in love with Steele does that to you.

Visions and Nightmares, Italian style

With the template of Italian gothic horror established by Bava, Freda and Margheriti, many filmmakers ghosted in their wake. In Giorgio Ferroni's **Mill of the Stone Women** (1960) student Hans Von Arnim (Pierre Brice) arrives at a windmill in the Dutch canal system. His assignment is to write a monograph on the history of the mill's famous carousel, a macabre revolving display of life-sized waxworks. Professor Wahl (Herbert Boehme), a sculptor, lives with his beautiful daughter Elfie (Scilla Gabel) and a mysterious doctor, Bohlem (Wolfgang Preiss). The statuary that litter the mill are, in fact, preserved corpses. Elfie is terminally ill and needs regular blood transfusions, and their next victim is Hans' girl Liselotte (Dany Carrel).

The opening – depicting Hans' journey to the mill by barge, accompanied by Carlo Innocenzi's eerie score (subtle percussion, repetitive piano and ghostly vocals) – begins the film in style. It was based on a short story in *Flemish Tales* by Pieter Van Weigen. The film adaptation is a little slow and confusing in the first half (what's it all about, Elfie?) but gathers momentum in the second. Gabel makes one of the most beautiful heroines in Italian gothic horror, her black hair and pale skin contrasting vividly with her red dress. Marco Guglielmi played Hans' friend, art student Ralf, Liana Orfei was tavern singer and dancer Annelore (who winds up on display on the professor's carousel) and Olga Solbelli was

Angel of Death: Camillo Mastrocinque's *An Angel for Satan* (1966), the last of Barbara Steele's Italian gothics. Italian poster courtesy Ian Caunce Collection.

sinister housekeeper Thelma. The 1912 mise-en-scène of crosses, frozen clutching hands and severed anatomy in jars provides a suitably twisted backdrop to the action. The star of the show is the sinister carousel – Joan of Arc, Elizabeth I and Cleopatra mix with a beheading, a hanging, and other grotesqueries enacted by mummified cadavers wearing wax masks. The revolving carousel catches fire and springs to life, the figures waltzing in a slow, fiery dance of death as their faces bubble, melt and drip from their human skulls. *Mill of the Stone Women* was released internationally in 1963 with the tagline 'See a beautiful girl changed into a petrified monster before your very eyes!'

Camillo Mastrocinque's ***Crypt of Horror*** (1964) is an adaptation of Sheridan LeFanu's *Carmilla*. It depicts the Karnstein family: Count Ludwig (Christopher Lee), his lover Annette (Vera Valmont) and his daughter Countess Laura (Adriana Ambesi), at Castle Karnstein (filmed at Piccolomini Castle at Balsorano, L'Aquila, Abruzzo). Ludwig is convinced that Laura will be possessed by her ancestor, witch Seera Karnstein, and employs historian Friedrich Klaus (Jose Campos) to research the family archives. Following a coach crash, beautiful Lyuba (Ursula Davis) stays at the castle. She is revealed to be the reincarnation of Seera, who tries to kidnap Laura in a sinister black coach. The film mixes witchcraft, possession, vampirism and mystery. Lee uses his own voice in the English dub, which adds to his performance. Jose Villasante played a hunchback beggar who is discovered hanged from the ruined church's bell rope, his hands severed. The scenes of Laura and Lyuba running through ruins, their white dresses billowing in the wind, recall Bava and Margheriti's imagery, and a flashback to witch Seera's crucifixion replays *Mask of Satan*. Housekeeper Rowena (Nela Conjiu) dabbles in black magic: she wanders the corridors of Castle Karnstein brandishing the beggar's severed hand, lit with candles, a satanic 'Hand of Glory'; having been killed, she later jerks bolt upright at her own funeral, pointing out her murderer in the lightning-strobed chapel.

Lee also appeared in ***The Castle of the Living Dead*** (1964), set in post-Napoleonic War Europe. A band of travelling gypsy players are invited to perform their fake hanging act at the castle of Count Drago (Lee), until they discover they are to be immortalised in the count's 'Eternal Theatre'. The count experiments with a new embalming fluid, extracted from a tropical plant, which induces instant suspension of life at the moment of death. Credits indicate that the film was directed by 'Warren Kiefer'/Lorenzo Sabatini, though he had uncredited help from his assistant Michael Reeves. The gypsies were Bruno (Jacques Stany), his sister Laura (Gaia Germani), fire-breathing strongman Gianni (Ennio Antonelli), harlequin Dart (Luciano Pigozzi) and dwarf Neep (Antonio De Martino). When Dart is fired from the troupe, wandering hussar captain Eric (Philippe Leroy) takes his harlequin role. Their act consists of condemned harlequin duping a hooded executioner into hanging himself.

Angelo Francisco Lavagnino supplied the score, which deployed a melancholy gypsy violin to unsettling effect. Castle Drago's grounds are represented by the Parco Di Mostri ('Park of the Monsters') in Bomarzo, Viterbo, an unusual collection of giant statuary, including elephants, dragons, a tortoise and a monstrous face with a cave as its mouth. As the players' wagon passes through a wood, they discover a rigid, petrified raven on a branch and Castle Drago (Odelscalchi Castle, near Lake Bracciano, Lazio) is decorated with all manner of embalmed wildlife. Mirko Valentin played Sandro, the count's leering, cloaked coachman who wields a mean scythe. Sandro fires a dart dipped in the embalming serum from a miniature catapult into Gianni's eye and the coachman throws Neep off the castle's tower, only for the fortunate dwarf to land in a haystack. Drago's embalmed wife lies in bed, staring forever into a looking glass, while spiders crawl across her pillow and rats gnaw at her fingers. Lee is on good form as the gaunt, sunken-eyed count. The strange goings-on at the castle are investigated by three policemen, played by Renato Terra, Luigi Bonos and Donald Sutherland (in his film debut). A heavily disguised Sutherland also plays an old witch who talks in rhymes and warns the troupe to steer clear of Drago: 'Some will live and some will die before tomorrow's sun is high'. Later the hag tells Dart, 'The harlequin who eats my bread will soon be dead'. Sutherland was reputedly so pleased to be given his first film roles that when his son was born in December 1966, he named him Kiefer in honour of this film's director.

If Barbara Steele's vehicles were the classier face of Italian horror, then Massimo Pupillo's **Bloody Pit of Horror** (1965 – *A Tale of Torture* and *The Crimson Executioner*) was their trashy antithesis. Publisher Max Parks (Alfredo Rizzo) and his entourage arrive at a castle for a photo shoot promoting lurid horror novels. Author Rick (Walter Brandi) is accompanied by Edith (Luisa Baratto), photographers and several scantily clad models, the Lover Girls: Annie (Femi Benussi), Kanujo (Moa Tahi), Nancy (Rita Klein) and Suzy (Barbara Nelli). The castle is occupied by Travis Anderson (Mickey Hargitay), an ex-actor who had been famous as a muscleman in costume films. The Crimson Executioner, a torturer put to death in a sword-lined Iron Maiden in 1648, possesses Travis, who runs amok, sadistically torturing to death most of the cast. Travis is obsessed with his 'perfect body' and takes sadistic pleasure from defiling others. One model has boiling tar poured on her, another is stretched on a rack, while other members of the party are hacked, slashed and speared to death. Edith is tied to a metal furnace, Max is roasted in an iron cage and Kanujo, trapped in a giant web, is menaced by a mechanical spider. The Crimson Executioner is a memorably berserk creation: oiled and bare-chested, Hargitay dons red leggings, a hefty belt, a gold medallion, a tight-fitting red hood and a Zorro mask to terrorise his victims. Exterior location scenes were filmed in PSYCHOVISION at Piccolomini Castle at Balsorano in Abruzzo, with interiors at Palazzo Borghese, Artena (Rome). The film is so cheap that at one point the music soundtrack sticks, like a scratched record.

In Dino Tavella's **The Embalmer** (1965 – *The Monster of Venice*) a killer is stalking the canals of Venice, murdering women and embalming them in his subterranean laboratory, to be preserved as white-robed statues. Journalist Andrea (Luigi Martocci) discovers that the 'monster' is a deranged hotel manager, Mr Torre. The killer wears a frogman suit and flippers to snatch women and drag them underwater. In his catacomb lair he wears a hooded monk's habit and a skull mask, and a cabaret spot features an Elvis impersonator emerging from a coffin. A group of female students staying at Torre's hotel are taken sightseeing by Andrea, via travelogue shots of the city. The killer frogman shadows the students' gondola and upends their boat, slipping away with another victim. The film ends on a surreal note, as Andrea (dressed as a frogman) chases the monk through the streets of Venice. Financed by Gondola Film and shot at Ceria Studios, Trieste, *The Embalmer* played on double bills in the US with *The She Beast*.

Histoires Extraordinaires (1968 – *Force of Evil* and *Tales of Mystery and Imagination*) was a three-part horror anthology based on Edgar Allan Poe's work. 'Metzengerstein' was a medieval *Barbarella* from Roger Vadim and Jane Fonda. Frederica (Fonda), countess of Metzengerstein and a 'Lady Caligula', falls in love with her cousin, Count Wilhelm (played by Fonda's brother, Peter). She causes his death when she orders the torching of his stables. Out of the inferno emerges a wild-eyed ebony stallion, which becomes the melancholy countess' companion, eventually carrying her to her death in a heath fire. Despite an apt score by Jean Prodrimides (echoing flutes and harpsichord), autumnal French coastal locations (including Kerouzéré Castle, Brittany) and a memorable final shot (as fire bleeds into the setting sun), this is a half-hearted Roger Corman imitation. The second story – Louis Malle's 'William Wilson', filmed in Bergamo, Lombardia, Italy – starred Alain Delon as Lieutenant Wilson, a bully who has been haunted throughout his life by a mysterious doppelganger (also Delon). His double causes William to commit suicide, throwing himself from a bell tower after he has publicly humiliated Josephina (Brigitte Bardot) and been exposed by his double as a cheat.

'Liberally adapted' from Poe's 'Don't Wager Your Head to the Devil', the third episode, Federico Fellini's 'Toby Dammit' was shot over the winter of 1967–68, on location in Rome and at Elios Studios, with interiors at CSC. In a role written for Peter O'Toole and offered to Richard Burton and James Fox, Terence Stamp starred as burnt-out English actor Toby Dammit. He arrives in Rome to star in the first Catholic western: 'The return of Christ to earth in a desolate frontier land', shot in the style of Carl Dreyer and Pasolini, 'with a touch of John Ford'. It is Toby's drug-addled vision of Rome that we see at Fiumicino Airport. His car journey through orange-tinted Rome is a hallucination: a butcher's truck hung with carcases, traffic jams, builders, fashion shoots, accidents, a *Sergeant Pepper*-era John Lennon look-alike, and two blind nuns driving a car. A gypsy fortune teller refuses to read Toby's palm. Toby hates the lights of the TV studio where he's interviewed ('I only live during the night') and reveals that he believes in the Devil: 'I'm English, not Catholic. To me the Devil is cheerful, agile – he looks like a little girl'. The troubled actor is haunted by this devil, a blonde girl in a white dress playing with a ball, an apparition only he can see.

At the self-congratulatory Golden Wolf Awards, awash with beautiful women, dinner-jacketed producers, handshakers and yes men, fazed Toby is hailed as a great Shakespearian actor, but while reciting a speech from *Macbeth*, he forgets his lines. From his producer, Toby receives a red Ferrari convertible and he speeds off into the night through the foggy streets of Roma and into the countryside. Lost, Toby lets out a tormented scream, gunning the engine as though possessed by the devil, and tries to find his way back to the city. His journey to the end of the night terminates at a collapsed bridge. He sees the little girl on the other side of the chasm and attempts to leap the Ferrari across the gap. He makes the jump, but a wire suspended across the road decapitates him and the little devil retrieves a new ball from the tarmac. With Nino Rota's carnivalesque organ score, 'Toby Dammit' is Fellini *in excelsis* – the costumes and sets were by Piero Tosi (anaemic Toby resembles a Byronic vampire), the visual effects (including a ruined bridge) were staged by Joseph Nathanson and the cinematographer was Giuseppe Rotunno. A scene depicting Toby's western being shot at Elios Studios was cut from the finished version of the film (a snippet can be seen in the trailer). *Histoires Extraordinaires* was released by AIP as *Spirits of the Dead* in the US, narrated by Vincent Price.

The Dead Exhumed: The 1970s

As censorship relaxed in the late 1960s, allowing more grue and gore, Italian gothic horror lived again, revived by Jean Rollin's sexy French vampire movies (*Le Frisson Des Vampires* and *Requiem pour un Vampire*), feudal British horror (*Matthew Hopkins – Witchfinder General* and *Blood on Satan's Claw*) and the Spanish-Portuguese 'Knights Templar' series (notably *Tombs of the Blind Dead* and *Return of the Evil Dead*).

Directed by schlock-horror maestro Jesus Franco, **The Bloody Judge** (1969 – *Night of the Bloody Monster*) emulated the witch hunts of Michael Reeves' *Matthew Hopkins – Witchfinder General* (1968). Infamous judge George Jeffreys (Christopher Lee), Lord Chief Justice, presides over the 'Bloody Assizes', the trials of rebels during the Monmouth Rebellion in 1685. It was led by the Duke of Monmouth, who landed at Lyme Regis and was defeated by James II at the Battle of Sedgemoor, an engagement which Franco frugally recreates with a battery of cannon, some extras and swathes of smoke. This is one of Franco's better productions, thanks to its costumes, Techniscope photography and a romantic score by Bruno Nicolai. The love affair between Monmouth plotter Harry Sefton (Hans Hass) and Mary Gray (Maria Rohm) is torn asunder by despotic Jeffreys. Lee is excellent as the judge, who spends his time 'smelling out witches' and sentencing his victims: 'To dangle until you are dead'. Jeffreys' sadistic cronies are Satchel (Milo Quesada) and spidery chief torturer Jack Ketch (Howard Vernon), dressed menacingly in a tight black leotard, gauntlets and hood. Mary's sister,

Alicia (Margaret Lee), is stretched on a rack, flogged and branded with a 'W', before being burned atop a ladder, while other victims are whipped, branded, poked, prodded, slapped and shredded, irrespective of 'whether witch or wench'. Leo Genn played Lord Wessex and Diana Lorys was victim Sally Downs. The 89-minute English language release, shorn of 10 minutes, is still strong stuff.

Bram Stoker's Count Dracula (1970) feebly claims to be 'exactly as [Stoker] wrote it'. London lawyer Jonathan Harker (Frederick Williams) travels to the Carpathian Mountains to visit Count Dracula (Christopher Lee). Weeks later Harker is found, mad and with a bite on his neck. At an asylum, Harker and madman Renfield (Klaus Kinski), another victim of the count, recover, while Professor Van Helsing (Herbert Lom) resolves to discover the secret of Castle Dracula. Jesus Franco's film was produced by Harry Alan Towers ('A Towers of London Production') and is tortoise-paced, with the mid-section consisting mainly of people lying in bed recuperating and Renfield eating flies. Franco regulars include Maria Rohm (as Mina Harker), Soledad Miranda as Lucy Westenra (who is vampirised and becomes a soulless killer of children) and Jack Taylor as Quincey Morris (Lucy's fiancé). Franco strives for Bavaesque imagery during Jonathan's misty coach journey in the Borgo Pass. All the locations, including Carpathian Bistritz and London, have suspiciously Spanish-looking architecture. The scene where a roomful of stuffed mammals, fish and birds (including an emu) 'come to life' and attack the heroes has to be seen to be believed, and the enticing unholy trinity of Lee, Lom and Kinski fails to deliver. Lee's incarnation of the count adopts a Hungarian Magyar look, with a drooping moustache. Lom (concealed behind a Lenin beard) is nondescript as Van Helsing, but untamed Kinski's periodic appearances as Renfield are the film's saving grace. The count travels from London to Transylvania, via Varna on the Black Sea, in a cart guarded by gypsies. The heroes ambush the convoy at Castle Dracula, setting fire to the count and pushing his burning crate off a high wall.

Antonio Margheriti remade his own *Castle of Blood* as **Web of the Spider** (1971), this time in colour. Anthony Franciosa played American reporter Alan Foster who makes a wager with Lord Thomas Blackwood (Enrico Osterman) to spend the night in his castle. The murderous re-enactments unfold exactly as in *Castle*, with the ghosts seeking Foster's blood, which will resurrect them for one night a year hence. Michele Mercier played ghostly Elisabeth Dollister Blackwood (now a blonde) and Karin Field was Julia. Raf Baldassarre played Elisabeth's lover Herbert, Peter Carsten was Dr Carmus and Silvano Tranquilli (Poe in *Castle of Blood*) was Elisabeth's husband, William. The film has a good gothic atmosphere and a menacing score, again by Ortolani. Its real plus is Klaus Kinski as Edgar Allan Poe, who in the opening sequence is depicted as the unhinged protagonist in one of his own tales, frantically searching a graveyard by torchlight, then exhuming the coffin of Berenice Morris.

Margheriti also supervised *Flesh for Frankenstein* (1973) and *Blood for Dracula* (1974), both 'presented' by Andy Warhol and credited to director-writer

Paul Morrissey. ***Flesh for Frankenstein*** stars Udo Kier as the Baron, Arno Juerging as his snivelling assistant Otto, Monique Van Vooren as Frankenstein's sex-maniac sister, and Joe Dallesandro as her manservant stud. Shot in Serbia and at Cinecittà with set design by Enrico Job, this is a blood-drenched send-up with nudity, spurting blood and dangling entrails (by Carlo Rambaldi), photographed in a garish 3D process called Spacevision. Once a Video Nasty in the UK, this tongue-in-cheek bloodbath should be taken with a pinch of snuff. ***Blood for Dracula*** is equally disgusting, its humorous central premise notwithstanding: Count Dracula (Kier) leaves his native Romania in a car with his coffin strapped to the roof and heads off to Italy with his secretary (Juerging) in search of 'Wirgins' blood. He stays at the villa of Marquis Di Fiore (Vittorio De Sica), who has four beautiful daughters though none of them are virgins, thanks to hunky handyman Joe Dallesandro. Look out for Roman Polanski, in flat cap and moustache, in a cameo as a peasant playing a mimicry game in a tavern.

Mel Welles' ***Lady Frankenstein*** (1971) had Baron Frankenstein (Joseph Cotten) and Dr Charles Marshall (Paul Muller) transplanting brains and hearts into reanimated cadavers. They create a monster (Paul Whiteman) but use a damaged brain and the creature crushes the baron to death. Frankenstein's daughter, Tania (Rosalba Neri), continues her father's experiments, jolting the dead to life with primitive jump leads. She sets about creating her perfect man, putting Charles' brain and heart into the body of brawny stable boy Thomas Stack (Marino Masé). Her creation eventually strangles her during their lovemaking, as angry villagers (led by Romano Puppo) torch the castle. Although it manages an occasional visual flourish (an atmospheric graveyard and snowy Castle Frankenstein), *Lady Frankenstein* adopts a sexploitative approach. The hideous bald creature, with one eye popping out of its socket, is eventually killed by cutting off its arm, stabbing it with a sword and putting an axe through its skull. Muscleman Mickey Hargitay played Captain Harris, investigating the graverobbing activities of Tom Lynch (Herbert Fux), the baron's supplier of stiffs. Esteemed actor Cotten looks bemused to be among such cheap special effects as bats on strings, shoddily staged on castle interiors at Incir-De Paolis and accompanied by a dramatic score by Alessandro Alessandroni. Further Italian versions of the Frankenstein story include *Frankenstein '80* (1973 – with Gordon Mitchell as Dr Albrechtstein) and *Frankenstein's Castle of Freaks* (1973) which saw Rossano Brazzi's Count Frankenstein cast alongside dwarf Genz (Michael Nunn), cavemen Ook (Boris Lugosi) and hunchback Igor (Gordon Mitchell).

The Devil's Nightmare (1971 – *The Devil's Longest Night*) was a cheap but effective modern gothic, directed by Jean Brismée and scored by Alessandroni. Seven bus travellers, including a trainee priest, find themselves stranded in the bedevilled castle of Baron Von Rhoneberg (Jean Servais). Mysterious beauty Lisa Müller (Erika Blanc) transforms herself into a ghastly, green-faced succubus, with black lipstick and a variety of revealing black outfits, and each of the guests succumbs to her tantalising. Each victim represents one of the Seven Deadly

Sins – for example, a fat glutton gorges on a banquet and chokes to death. The murders are revealed to have been a horrible dream – the Devil's nightmare – endured by the priest, who decides to stay with Lisa. His fellow passengers board the bus and are killed. Their vehicle plummets off a mountain road when it swerves to avoid a hearse driven by the spindly, bald, rodent-toothed Devil (Daniel Emilfork).

Guido Zurli's ***The Strangler of Vienna*** (1971) was a stab at jet-black cannibal comedy. In 1930, corpulent butcher Otto Lehman (Victor Buono) is released from an asylum. Soon afterwards he strangles his wife Hannah (Karin Field). Inflation is high and supplies of meat low, so Otto hatches a plan involving his wife's corpse and a sausage-making machine. His tasty sausages are the talk of Vienna, but women begin vanishing. Bertha (Franca Polesello), Otto's latest prospective sausage-filling, manages to warn the police by sneaking buttons and a ring into the sausages served in the police mess hall. It was shot at ICET De Paolis Studios in Milan and on location in Vienna itself, including the Ferris wheel and roller coaster (in the Prater Amusement Park) and the gardens of Schönbrunn Palace. Brad Harris played investigating reporter Mike Loring. Most interesting is Alessandroni's score, which includes a pastiche of Anton Karas' *Third Man* zither theme and a barrel organ ragtime that resembles 'Mack the Knife'.

Bava Rises Again

Following a series of westerns, comedies and sci-fi movies, Bava returned to the genre with which he'd made his name for ***Baron Blood*** (1972). Arriving in Vienna, Peter Kleist (Antonio Cantafora) visits his ancestral home, the 'Castle of the Devil', where 300 years ago Baron Otto Von Kleist tortured victims. The castle is being converted into a hotel, but Peter, with help from history student Eva Arnold (Elke Sommer), resurrects the Baron by reciting an ancient incantation. The Baron begins to claim fresh victims, including the hotel developer, Herr Dortmund (Dieter Tressler), and the caretaker, Fritz (Luciano Pigozzi). The castle is bought at auction by wheelchair-bound Alfred Becker (Joseph Cotten), who plans to renovate it. With his uncle, Professor Karl Hummel (Massimo Girotti), and an occultist, Christina Hoffman (Rada Rassimov), Peter and Eva break the curse. During a bonfire ritual, Christine invokes the spirit of witch Elizabeth Holly (also played by Rassimov). Eva reanimates the Baron's victims with an amulet – only by their hands can he die.

The Bloody Baron's castle was filmed on location from September to November 1971 in Austria at Burg Kreuzenstein, a fairytale fortification in the Lower Danube Valley, with turrets, slate roofs, crenellations and arches. It was this film that established Sommer as a scream queen. No one can react like Sommer – a frightened look, a rigid twitch, followed by a glass-shattering shriek. The dubbing studio must have shuddered. Sommer has to endure a garish selection of miniskirts, tight sweaters, smocks, headscarves and some bizarrely patterned knitwear. The baron is also the stuff of nightmares, in his broad-brimmed hat and cape, with burned, weeping hands and a blood-oozing face. The makeup was designed by Carlo Rambaldi and was applied to special effects man Franco Tocci (in costume as the baron). Professor Karl's daughter, Gretchen (Nicoletta Elmi), appears clutching a ball, recalling *Kill, Baby… Kill!* and the Baron's pursuit of Eva through fog-wreathed streets is Bava at his best. The Italian print took place in 'Nuremberg Castle' in Germany. For the US release, *Baron Blood* lost 8 minutes of footage and was re-scored by Les Baxter in place of Stelvio Cipriani's jaunty Euro-pop title music (which resembles Tom Jones's 'It's Not Unusual'). Posters denied any responsibility for patrons who suffered 'Apoplectic Strokes, Cerebral Hemorrhages, Cardiac Seizures, or Fainting Spells'.

With the success of *Baron Blood*, producer Alfredo Leone financed **Lisa and the Devil** (1972), which many count as Bava's masterpiece. In Toledo, tourist Lisa Reiner (Sommer) is separated from her friend Kathy (played by Leone's daughter, Kathy). Lost in the backstreets, Lisa hitches a lift with a wealthy couple: Francis Lehar (Eduardo Fajardo) and his wife, Sophie (Sylva Koscina), and their chauffeur, George (Gabriele Tinti). Their Packard breaks down and they take refuge in the villa of a blind countess (Alida Valli), her son, Maximilian (Alessio Orano), and their butler, Leandro (Telly Savalas), who closely resembles the Devil in a fresco in Toledo's square. Max is convinced that Lisa is Elena, lover of his dead step-father, Carlos, who himself appears to be alive, despite preparations being made for his funeral.

Lisa was photographed by Cecilio Paniagua and filmed from September to November 1972 on location in Toledo, at a villa outside Madrid (for the mansion's exterior shots), at Barcelona Airport, Villa Frascati and Faleria. Carlo Savina composed the loping, dreamy theme music (with piano, strings and Edda Dell'Orso's wilting soprano) heard over the animated title sequence of a tarot dealer. *Lisa* is a strange viewing experience, at once nightmarish, disjointed and illogical, but equally engrossing, horrific and perverse. To prevent Lisa from leaving the villa there are several gory deaths. George is stabbed in the neck with scissors, Francis is run over by the Packard, Sophie has her skull caved in, and Max stabs his own mother. Lisa encounters Leandro, who is carrying a wax dummy of Carlos (which is replaced in some shots by actor Espartaco Santoni) and Bava arranges the corpses of the Lehars, George, Carlos and Elena like Da Vinci's 'The Last Supper'. Impotent Max attempts to make love to sedated Lisa on a four-poster bed, beside the skeletal corpse of Elena, a scene which is choreographed to the second movement of 'Concierto De Aranjuez' by Joaquín Rodrigo. When Lisa awakens, she is alone in the ruined mansion, overgrown with tangled vegetation and seemingly long-abandoned. As she boards a TWA 747 home, the passengers are corpses from the villa and the pilot is Leandro. The film's oddest aspect, even among matricide and necrophilia, is Telly Savalas' butler, Leandro. Savalas, at Bava's suggestion, sucked lollipops throughout the film, and shortly afterwards he starred in TV cop show *Kojak* (1973–78), where the lollipop became his trademark.

In 1973 most distributors wouldn't release *Lisa*, despite a premiere at Cannes, and the only theatrical run it received was in Spain. Leone looked to capitalise on the current success of *The Exorcist* (1973) and reused Bava's footage in **The House of Exorcism** (1975). Leone shot for three and a half weeks with Bava and Sommer in Rome at a disused hospital. In Leone's mutation, while visiting Toledo, Lisa is possessed by the Devil (a Savalas stand-in) and taken to hospital, where a priest, Father Michael (Robert Alda), attempts to exorcise her. *Lisa* footage is spliced throughout the story, as Lisa's experiences in a haunted mansion. Father Michael goes to the villa (shot by Bava at Villa Frascati) for an impressive, whirlwind exorcism, featuring burning Bibles and flying snakes.

The new scenes in the hospital are of the gross-out variety, with Sommer convulsing on a bed, attacking the staff, vomiting luminous green bile and toads, and spitting some very strong language. *Exorcism* also features copious nudity, most notably in a gratuitous scene when Lisa is transformed into naked Anna (Carmen Silva), Father Michael's dead lover. When Leone assembled *Exorcism*, he used the full-length cut of *Lisa*, which has since been lost and several scenes play longer in this rehash. *House of Exorcism* is a schlocky vomitorium of a movie, typical of 1970s and 1980s Italian exploitation horror. There's no accounting for taste, but Leone certainly knew his business: it took $5 million when released in the US by distributor Peppercorn-Wormser in 1976. *La casa dell'esorcismo*, directed by 'Mickey Lion' (Bava had his name removed), opened in Italy in April 1975. There was something grimly ironic in Bava's dreamlike masterpiece being filleted into a gory bile-fest which brutally exorcised the ghosts of Barbara Steele and Elke Sommer.

The Italians brought style and elegance to gothic cinema. Some of the films aren't particularly frightening, but they look tremendous – straight from the cobwebbed pages of Poe. Steele noted in interviews that she couldn't fathom why, in the optimistic climate of Rome in the early 1960s, they ended up producing horror movies. Italy is a sunny country, with a turbulent history – perhaps it was this underlying history, lurking in the shadows, which informed these macabre movies. As Bava himself said, 'We have the Mediterranean sun to chase away all the shadows'. But sometimes the sun casts long, menacing shadows too.

Chapter Five

Battle of the Worlds
Science Fact and Fiction

In contrast to post-nuclear US or Japanese science-fiction films, which often deployed unconvincing rubber monsters, or bleak, low-key UK sci-fi, such as the 'Quatermass' films and *The Damned* (1961), Italian science-fiction presented a colourful, fantastic kaleidoscope of flashing lights, star fields and bizarre spacecraft. Filmmakers used a variety of tricks to create these cosmic worlds, but the most important feature of Italian sci-fi was the omnipresent space fog which wreathed sets, creating demonic, threatening atmospheres whilst shrouding budgetary shortcomings.

Blast-off: Early Italian Sci-fi

Paolo Heusch's ***The Day the Sky Exploded*** (1958) was the first significant Italian sci-fi movie, filmed in black and white by Mario Bava. John McLaren (Paul Hubschmid) pilots the atomic powered XZ rocket on a six-day mission from Cape Shark in Australia. But McLaren loses control of the craft to mysterious forces and abandons ship (his escape pod lands on Tor Caldara beach, masquerading as Australia). The rocket is now a drifting, pilot-less atomic missile. Cape Shark picks up an explosion in the 'Delta Asteroid Zone' and animals migrate inland, suggesting imminent tidal waves and floods. Professor Weisse (Ivo Garrani) ascertains that meteorites are heading for Earth. Heusch's film resembles a 1950s American B-movie, with its penny arcade control room, overexcited reporters and no-name cast. Subplots detail McLaren's strained relationship with his wife, Mary (Fiorella Mari), and son, Dennis (Massimo Zeppieri), and a love story between two technicians: smarmy Peter (Dario Michaelis) and shy Katy (Madeleine Fischer). Almost the entire film was made on one set: the Cape Shark control room and labs. Various natural disasters (stampeding livestock, burning cities and forest fires) are stock footage, as are the missile launch scenes. For the state of emergency, newsreel footage depicts

A Prophetic Motion Picture 100 Years Ahead of Its Time: US advertising for Antonio Margheriti's Italian sci-fi *Battle of the Worlds* (1961), where Earth is menaced by 'The Outsider'.

panicking crowds and convoys of refugees, which appears to be of WWII vintage.

'Based on an ancient Mexican legend', *Caltiki – The Immortal Monster* (1959) was a rare Italian creature feature, with an oozing, blob-like central performance from Caltiki – a 'crawling crushing colossus' of 'man-eating protoplasm', as the trailer put it. In Mexico archaeologists desecrate a deserted, misty Mayan sacred pyramid. One of the archaeologists, Max Günther (Gerard Herter), is attacked by monstrous Caltiki. Contact with the blob eats away the skin on his arm. Back in Mexico City, as a radioactive comet approaches Earth, a globular sample of Caltiki regenerates itself and grows to massive proportions, while deranged Max escapes from hospital. Caltiki devours Max and is dispatched by Mexican army flamethrowers and tanks. Although Riccardo Freda was billed as the director, this was cinematographer Mario Bava's directorial debut. The cast included John Merivale, Daniela Rocca, Arturo Dominici and Giacomo Rossi-Stuart, and the score was co-written by Roberto Nicolosi and Roman Vlad. Caltiki itself was made from tripe.

Anton Giulio Majano's *Atom Age Vampire* (1960) was a mad scientist scenario that depicted reparatory facial surgery. When stripper Jeanette Moreneau (Susanne Loret) is facially disfigured in a car accident, she is treated by Professor Albert Levin (Alberto Lupo) and his assistant, Monique (Franca Parisi), with his untested rejuvenation serum. It works only over short periods and he needs fresh female genes to make more. Another serum has the side-effect of tuning him into Seddok, a ferocious, werewolf-like creature. In this guise Levin roams the foggy streets, killing women, prolonging Jeanette's beauty, until her lover, Pierre (Sergio Fantoni), and Commissioner Bruchard (Ivo Garrani) corner him. Cheaply made, but with an effectively eerie Armando Trovajoli score and a fine turn by Roberto Bertea as Levin's mute henchman, Sacha, *Atom* is a mixture of gothic horror and sci-fi. Having studied post-atomic skin treatment at Hiroshima, Levin cures Jeanette and transforms himself back from Seddok with radiation. The police suspect that Seddok is a Hiroshima victim, 'a vampire of the atom age'. Levin's stop-motion transformation, with layers of hair and makeup applied between shots, is an effective technique that was used in many classic horror films.

Wild Planets: Antonio Margheriti

Antonio Margheriti was the leading Italian sci-fi director, often working under the pseudonyms 'Anthony Dawson' or 'Anthony M. Dawson'. The formula for Italian sci-fi was established by Margheriti's Technicolor *Assignment: Outer Space* (1960 – *Space Men*), made in four weeks for 24 million lira. Dateline: 17 December 2116. Reporter Ray Peterson (Rick Van Nutter) of New York's *Interplanetary News* is on spaceship Bravo Zulu 88 to cover a 10-day mission, a routine check of infra-radiation flux in Galaxy M-12. On a manned satellite, Peterson meets Lucy, the navigator, and clashes with her commander, George (David Montresor). The crew embark on a top-secret expedition – drifting spaceship Alpha Two isn't responding to radio contact. The mission diverts to Venus and discovers Alpha Two, its pilot dead, floating toward Earth. Its photonic generators have created a high-temperature force field, which will turn the Earth into 'a mass of boiling mud'. Pilot Al (Archie Savage) flies an atomic rocket at Alpha Two but perishes, and Peterson manages to board the errant ship and destroy its electronic brain. The acting is awful and the choppy plot difficult to follow. The special effects include a refuelling scene, an asteroid shower, Peterson's space walk through a star field towards the satellite, and a stricken ship's demise on satellite Phobos. Bravo Zulu 88's landing on Phobos, a misty, bubbling volcanic planet, hints at what the genre held in store, while the impressive interplanetary base on Venus (created in miniature), with its elliptical glass dome, missile launch sites and rockets, was reused in later Margheriti movies. Spaceship Alpha Two resembles a giant hypodermic needle with balloons attached. Astronauts utter typically B-movie curses ('By all the rings around Saturn'), though at least their bulbous space helmets facilitated dubbing.

In Margheriti's **Battle of the Worlds** (1961) scientists detect a planet heading towards Earth. Professor Benson (Claude Rains) is convinced it will miss Earth and is proved right when it begins to orbit. Benson terms it the Outsider, a planet from another solar system, and tells the United Commission they must destroy the interloper. Earth sends out an exploratory party, but flying saucers emerge from the Outsider and destroy them. The Outsider causes worldwide panic, volcanic eruptions, fires, whirlwinds and storms (all stock footage) and Benson destroys the Outsider's saucers with oscillating sound waves. Boarding the Outsider, Benson finds a grotto of insect-like corpses, 'fugitives from a dying world' – their Noah's Ark has 'become their tomb'. When Benson locates the planet's electronic brain he realises that he can divert the planet, but it's too late – the planet collapses around his ears and earth's missiles obliterate the Outsider.

Battle of the Worlds is impressively plotted and staged, with Margheriti's camera trickery noticeably evolving. The revolving flying saucers are rather poor, as are the animated white laser beams during aerial combat, but the general mise-en-scène, from the professor's flower-filled laboratory, to the monitors in the conference room and the cavernous, red-bathed arterial bowels of the Outsider, enhances the drama. The film's opening scenes at Earth's island observatory are eerie, as scientist Eve Barnett (Maya Brent) runs down the limestone steps to the beach where fellow scientist Fred Steele (Umberto Orsini) is swimming (their on-off love story subplot is the film's main weakness). This scene is accompanied by extraordinary avant-garde oscillations composed by Mario Migliardi, over which a female vocalist wails distorted lyrics, including, 'The Outsider is coming!' The cast features Bill Carter as Mars commander Bob Cole, Carol Danell as his wife, Cathy, Jacqueline Derval as the mysterious 'Black Widow' Mrs Collins, Carlo D'Angelo as impatient general Varreck and Massimo Righi as pilot Lewis Boyd, while future star Giuliano Gemma tried to get noticed as bit-part technician Moran. Feisty 72-year-old Rains was appearing in one of his last films before his death in 1967. As the old professor, himself a perpetual 'outsider', wearing thick glasses and smoking a cigar, Rains spends the film railing against

Science Fact and Fiction

the 'bigwigs' of government and thriving on his lifelong thirst for knowledge: 'What importance does life have', he asks, 'if to live means not to know?'

Antonio Margheriti continued to produce imaginative, colourful sci-fi movies: *War of the Planets* (1966 – *The Deadly Diaphanoids*), its sequel *The Wild, Wild Planet* (1966), *War between the Planets* (1966 – *Planet on the Prowl*) and *The Snow Devils* (1967 – *Space Devils*). The first two films starred Tony Russel as Commander Mike Halstead, while Giacomo Rossi-Stuart took over as the hero of *War between the Planets* and *Snow Devils*. These four films were made for US television (the first two were produced by MGM) using the same casts and sets, in 12 weeks.

The Wild, Wild Planet is a combination of futuristic crime film, horror and fantasy. On space station Gamma One, Commander Halstead is suspicious of the macabre experiments in organ miniaturisation by Professor Nurmi (Massimo Serato), who works for Chem-Bio-Med (CBM). On Earth, people are disappearing with no explanation, including General Fowler (Enzo Fiermonte). Mike's girlfriend, Lieutenant Connie Gomez (Lisa Gastoni), accepts Nurmi's offer to take a vacation on Delphos at Nurmi's research facility. At United Democratic Space Command (UDSCO), Mike realises that the kidnap victims are shipped to Delphos for Nurmi's experiments.

Wild, Wild Planet is a wild, wild film. The space stations, spacecraft and the metropolis of Earth's capital are the expected none-too-convincing miniatures present in all Margheriti's work. But the futuristic costumes (by Bernice Sparrow), makeup (by Euclid Santolis) and Eastmancolor cinematography are a feast for the eyes, from the sleek, domed space cars that glide along Earth's highways, to the interior sets (designed at De Paolis Studios by Piero Poletti) and outlandish props (such as the flamethrower laser guns). Angelo Lavagnino provided atmosphere with a mixture of lush space symphonies and atonal clangs. Carlo Giustini and Franco Nero played Mike's sidekicks, lieutenants Ken and Jake. Franco Ressel was Gamma One's Lieutenant Jeffries, stuntman Goffredo Unger helped out with the investigations on Earth and Umberto Raho was Paul Maitland, the UDSCO general who refuses to believe Nurmi's culpability.

The film's most imaginative features are allied to Nurmi's nefarious activities to create a race of perfect beings: the climax is the fusing of his own body with that of Connie's. To carry out the kidnappings, Nurmi dispatches squads of karate-kicking, robotic inflatable women to Earth, accompanied by equally inflatable henchmen – mysterious, anaemic, bald zombies wearing caps, shades and long grey macs. The police discover that these henchmen have four arms concealed beneath their coats, the result of Nurmi's fusion grafts. Their modus operandi has the deadly duos miniaturising earthlings to Barbie-doll size and transporting them to Delphos. Mike and his crew relax in a groovy space canteen-cum-disco and attend productions at the Proteo Theatre, where the dancers flit around the stage in capes. Mike and his squad infiltrate Delphos and are captured. They see lab assistants wheeling around trolleys carrying leftover 'scraps' (spare hands, arms and other anatomy) and Nurmi has a cell ('My private Hell') filled with the mutant results of earlier experiments. Nurmi resolves to destroy the master computer – he opens sluice gates and releases a vast swimming pool of blood, which swamps the entire facility in a plasma tidal wave. As rescue crafts arrive from Earth, Mike utters the most incredible line in Italian sci-fi: 'Just leave it to Maitland – he's sure to bollocks it up'.

Chariots and the Gods: Sci-fi Pepla

Another trend in Italian sci-fi was a series of sword and sandal epics that transported their heroes into futuristic subterranea or else pitted them against visitors from other worlds – as though Erich Von Daniken's *Chariot of the Gods* had been rewritten with real chariots. Umberto Scarpelli's **The Giant of Metropolis** (1961) starred Gordon Mitchell as Obro, who travels to Atlantis in 20,000 BC. King Yotar (Roldano Lupi), the ruler of the futuristic city of Metropolis, is experimenting with human brain transplants on his son, Elmos (Marietto). Yotar resurrects his elderly father, Egon (Furio Meniconi), but Yotar's wife, Queen Texen (Liana Orfei), and daughter, Princess Mercede (Bella Cortez), oppose him. Yotar tests Obro's endurance – Obro battles a club-wielding Neanderthal giant (massive actor Kronos), five wild pygmy men (who attempt to rip off his skin with their teeth) and Yotar's Black Guard (led by Ugo Sasso) with their cutlasses and crab-claw spears. Egon releases Obro, who manages to escape with Mercede and Elmos, as Atlantis is apocalyptically destroyed by flood and earthquake (partly footage from *Hercules Conquers Atlantis*).

The volcanic desert landscape of the outside world (shot on Mount Etna, Sicily) is as unnatural as the devilish depths of Metropolis, achieved with Bavaesque imagery and Armando Trovajoli's staccato piano, brass and woodwind score: the interiors were recreated at De Paolis Studios, with the palace's exterior façade at Olimpia Studios. Fantastical interior sets and matte shots (by Joseph Nathanson) include Yotar's impressive observatory (with its colossal telescope), the Hall of Arts and Sciences laboratory, stalactite strewn caverns and the Quartz Grotto. The dry-ice machines worked overtime, the Metropolis sets wreathed knee-deep in fog. Obro is 'tested' by being held in a tractor beam of blinding, scalding light and Obro's brothers are zapped by Yotar's 'Whirlwind of Death' ray. Obro battles these futuristic wonders with pure muscle and an array of spiky weaponry.

Alfonso Brescia's **The Conqueror of Atlantis** (1965 – *Kingdom in the Sand*) told a similar story, with Kirk Morris (in his final peplum) as Greek hero Heracles, who is shipwrecked in Egypt and becomes involved in inter-tribal rivalry. The plot veers off when nomad princess Virna (Luciana Gilli) is abducted to the Mountain of the Dead Ones, beyond which is the City of the Phantoms. Hercules and Prince Karr (Andrea Scotti) find themselves in a futuristic city populated by the survivors of Atlantis, ruled by Ramir (Piero Lulli), who has brainwashed Virna and crowned her queen. With impressive footage shot in Egypt (the film was an Italian-Egyptian co-production) and belly dancers adding local colour, *Conqueror*'s strength lies in the imaginative *Flash Gordon*-style production design of Ramir's royal palace, perched atop a smoking volcano and suspended on a 'cushion of gas'. The interiors feature a high-vaulted throne room, a turbine wheel, gas chambers and TV monitors, while Ramir and his evil queen Aming (Helene Chanel) brandish ray guns. Ramir wears black robes, a Mohican helmet headdress, spiky collar, arched eyebrows, eyeliner and a foot-long green pointy beard. His guards are Amazonian archers and Ramir's experiments change mortal men into immortal Golden Phantoms. Dressed in blue leotards and loincloths, these henchmen, with gold faces, hands and boots, are the most ridiculous creations in pepla. A pitched battle in a desert ravine between the Golden Phantoms and the nomads (armed with heavy balls and chains which they use like bolas) ends the film on a hilarious note.

Hercules against the Moon Men (1964), directed Giacomo Gentilomo, detailed the possible encounter between ancient civilisations and visitors from outer space. Hercules (Maciste in the Italian print, played by Alan Steel) is summoned to the Kingdom of Samar, where tyrant queen Samara (Jany Clair) rules with her household guard, commanded by Mogol (Goffredo Unger). A mysterious meteor has crashed into the Mountain of Samar. Strange Luna creatures have ensconced themselves in the bowels of the mountain and Samara's people sacrifice their children to the Mountain of Death to appease the Moon Men. Samara is about to sacrifice her sister, Princess Bilis (Delia D'Alberti). The Moon Men need her blood to resurrect their queen, Selena, whereupon they will become masters of the Earth. With the help of Agar (Hercules' lover, played by Anna Maria Polani), Bilis' fiancé, Prince Darix (played by Jean-Pierre Honoré), and a band of rebels operating from a tavern, Hercules foils Samara's plan and takes on Moon Man giant Redolphis (Roberto Ceccacci) and his army of ten-foot-high stone men.

Steel is a fine hero, with Clair his nefarious match as the red-haired queen Samara (recalling Sylvia Lopez in *Hercules Unchained*). Hercules fights a giant tusked ape, Queen Samara tries to squash Hercules between the jaws of a spiked mantrap and attempts to drug him with a 'love filter'. Sets were created at Cinecittà, with location footage shot in the Lazio caves and at Tor Caldara (where Samara's men herd the chained condemned towards the Mountain of Death). Tor Caldara is shown to best advantage in *Moon Men*, which shot the muddy inlet, the beach and headland, the low bluffs and surrounding woodland from every imaginable angle. The epic theme by Carlo Franci (with brass and strings accompanying a full-throttle Valkyrie choir) is an edit of his music for *Maciste in Hell*. A cataclysm sees the oceans rise, volcanoes erupt and lava gush forth (stock footage) coupled with a multicoloured sandstorm (recreated on studio sets). As Bilis's dripping blood begins to revive Selena, the stone men crush Samara, the throbbing emerald brain (the fulcrum of the *Moon Men*'s power) is toppled, Redolphis is destroyed and the caverns collapse on the stone men.

Future Fiction

If pepla looked to science past, then ***The Last Man on Earth*** (1964) peered nihilistically towards the future. An Italian-US co-production co-directed by

'I Am Legend': Dr Robert Morgan (Vincent Price) battles the virus-infected undead in *The Last Man on Earth* (1964), a US-Italian co-production released in the US by AIP.

Ubaldo B. Ragona and Sidney Salkow, *Last Man* starred Vincent Price as Dr Robert Morgan, the lone survivor of a worldwide plague. Apparently immune, he lives in his barricaded house by night, as hordes of vampirised undead attack his stronghold. During the day Morgan travels the city in his hearse-like station wagon, staking the vampires and throwing their bodies in a perpetually burning mass grave, the Pit. Set in 1968, flashbacks reveal how the windblown plague arrived in 1965 and how Morgan's daughter, Kathy (Christi Courtland), wife, Virginia (Emma Danieli), and Ben Cortman (Giacomo Rossi-Stuart) – his work colleague at the Mercer Chemical Research Institute – became victims. Ben now leads the nightly attack against Morgan's house. Through Ruth Collins (Franca Bettoia), Morgan finds that others have survived and are intent on forming a New Society. They see Morgan as a monster: 'You are a legend in the city', Ruth tells him, 'Living by day instead of night'. The New Society has become infected but keeps the virus in check with injections of 'defibrillated blood' plus a vaccine. Morgan gives Ruth a blood transfusion to save her, but the New Society hunts him, cornering him in a church. 'Freaks', shouts Morgan, 'I'm a man, the last man', as they stake him with an iron spike. Now immune, Ruth tells a weeping babe-in-arms, 'There's nothing to cry about. We're all safe now'.

The Last Man on Earth was based on *I Am Legend*, Richard Matheson's 1954 novel. The film opens with shots of deserted streets, littered with wrecked, abandoned cars and strewn with dead bodies. It was shot on location in Rome, including the steps of the grand Palazzo Della Civilta and the distinctive mushroom tower of Il Fungo in the EUR district. Price is excellent as Robert Morgan (Robert Neville in the novel), an insane avenger travelling the ruined city with his mallet and stakes for his repetitive daily routine. Society no longer exists, though Morgan still observes certain rituals. He visits the local supermarket jammed with abandoned trolleys (to collect more garlic) and a car showroom (to pick out a new car). Garlic, a wooden cross and mirrors are attached to his front door to ward off vampires. The explanation for Morgan's immunity is that when he was working in Panama he was bitten by a vampire bat and that 'the vampire germ' is already in his blood. The shambling vampires resemble zombies and some scenes look like rushes for George Romero's *Night of the Living Dead* (1968).

Moodily photographed in 2.35:1 widescreen by Franco Delli Colli, *Last Man* takes 'bleak' to another level. When a scraggy black dog offers Morgan companionship, it is infected and he has to stake it. The first symptom of the plague is blindness and Morgan's own daughter becomes afflicted and is tossed into the Pit. Morgan drives his wife's shrouded corpse to the suburbs to bury her. But that night, a voice calls to him from outside: 'Let me in Robert'. He opens the door and his resurrected wife attacks him. *Last Man* has aged well and its nihilistic ending is still powerful.

Elio Petri's ***The 10th Victim*** (1965), a satire on commercialism, TV and soulless living based on Robert Sheckley's short story *The Seventh Victim*, remains a highpoint in Italian futurism. In the twenty-first century, murder is legal as contestants in 'The Big Hunt' shoot it out in the streets. Contestants must undertake 10 hunts – five as hunter, five as prey – with a prize of $1 million and the title 'Decathon' for the first to claim 10 victims. Their opponents are randomly generated by a computer in Geneva. American Caroline Meredith (Ursula Andress) has one round to go before she becomes champion and her tenth victim is Italian contestant Marcello Poletti (Marcello Mastroianni, with his hair bleached blond). She travels to Rome but in the course of the chase they fall in love. She eventually manages to lure him to the Temple of Venus, where their duel is televised as part of an advert for her sponsor 'Ming Tea'. They can't kill each other and flee on an airliner, where Caroline forces Marcello to marry her at gunpoint.

The 10th Victim was filmed at Titanus Appia Studios and on location in Rome, including St Peter's Square, the Piazza Navona, the Colosseum and Fiumicino Airport. Marcello joins a cult of 'Sunset Worshippers' on Ostia beach and outwits his sixth victim, Baron Von Aschenberg (Wolfgang Hillinger), whom he dispatches with exploding riding boots at an equestrian event staged at the Villa Borghese's Piazza Di Sienna. The TV extravaganza, which features showgirls and dancing teacups, ends with a shootout in the ruins of the Temple of Venus, where Caroline and Marcello face Marcello's ex-wife, Lydia (Luce Bonifassy), and his mistress Olga (Elsa Martinelli). Massimo Serato played Marcello's lawyer, Milo Quesada was Rudy (Caroline's beau) and Jacques Herlin was the Big Hunt's adjudicator. The film opens with Caroline being pursued through the streets of New York by her ninth victim (George Wang). He tracks her to the Masoch Club, where Andress performs a striptease in a silver metallic bikini, before killing him with guns which protrude from her brassiere. Produced by Carlo Ponti and Joseph E. Levine, *The 10th Victim* is imaginatively Pop Art, with sets by Piero Poletti (who usually worked with Michelangelo Antonioni) and stylish, bold futuristic costumes by Coltellacci. Piero Piccioni provided the jaunty score, including the stuttering 'Spiral Waltz' title song performed by pop singer Mina.

Dark Star: Bava in Space

Much in the spirit of Margheriti's futuristic style, Mario Bava blended sci-fi and horror in **Planet of the Vampires** (1965 – *The Demon Planet*). The Argos and the Galliot investigate a strange signal emanating from the fog-shrouded planet of Aura. Both craft are dragged down by the gravitational pull. The crew of the Argos attack each other and only the quick thinking of Captain Mark Markary (Barry Sullivan) saves them. The Galliot isn't so lucky – Markary and his crew find their cohorts dead. Stranded on the supernatural planet, the astronauts find a gigantic wrecked spaceship. Meanwhile, the crew of the Galliot rise from the dead as zombies, possessed by the parasitic spirits of Aura, and attack the Argos, stealing its valuable Meteor Rejecter. The Aurean's sun is dying and they have been trying to lure a ship to transport them away. Argos's crew assault the Galliot, destroying the ship and its undead crew with plutonium, before making their escape.

Demon Planet: Spacecraft the Argos approaches the skeletal space mists of Aura in this Italian poster for Mario Bava's *Planet of the Vampires* (1965).

Bava's zombie space flick was based on Renato Pestiniero's 'One Night of 21 Hours', published in *Interplanet #3 Science Fiction Magazine*. Bava filmed entirely on Cinecittà soundstages, creating Aura's eerie world through swirling coloured fogs, jagged rock formations, bubbling lava beds and unsettling sound effects, as hovering lights flash and voices moan from the creeping fog. The film's sound design is suffused with humming generators, sonar blips, whooshing meteors and Aura's moaning wind; the electronic effects were created by Paolo Ketoff. Some international prints of *Planet* replaced Gino Marinuzzi's original score with electronic compositions by Kendall Schmidt. His astral title music consists of darting synthesizer arpeggios (imitating stuttering computer data) overlaid with piercing electronic feedback. The vast rusty space cruiser, with its throbbing red-lit interior and the giant skeletal remains of its crew slumped at the craft's controls, is one of Bava's most memorable creations and influenced Ridley Scott's *Alien* (1979).

Norma Bengell played crew member Sanya, Angel Aranda appeared as engineer Wes, with Ivan Rassimov (Carter), Evi Mirandi (Tiona), Mario Morales (Eldon), Stelio Candelli (Brad), Franco Andrei (Bert) and Fernando Villena (Dr Karan) filling out the Argos's crew. The Galliot team included Federico Boido (Keir), Massimo Righi (Captain Sallas) and Alberto Cevenini (as Markary's brother, Toby). Their gory undead face makeup was by Amato Garbibi, while the futuristic space suits, tight-fitting black leather with orange trim, were designed by Gabriele Mayer. Although identified as 'space vampires', these cadavers are zombies. Markary, Sanya and Wes escape on the Argos, but Markary and Sanya have been possessed and detour to the nearest planet, 'a puny civilisation': Earth. Even in outer space, Bava managed to recreate one of his beloved slow motion resurrection scenes. Markary and his crew bury the Galliot astronauts, but their monolith grave markers topple and the space fog swirls, as metal coffin lids creak open and the astronauts emerge, tearing apart their plastic body bag shrouds, before stumbling off into Aura's perpetual night.

Comic Book Heroes

Bava's comic strip adaptation **Diabolik** marked the moment when Italian cinema went psychedelic, as though Fellini had made a James Bond movie. It was the first and best of three European comic strip adaptations released in 1968, the other two being *Satanik* and *Barbarella*. *Diabolik* and *Barbarella* were made concurrently by the same production companies: De Laurentiis (Rome) and Marianne (Paris). John Phillip Law (who also played the blind angel, Pygar, in *Barbarella*) starred as Diabolik, a master thief always one step ahead of Inspector Jinko (Michel Piccoli). The authorities try everything to apprehend him, including restoring the death penalty and putting up a $1 million bounty. Crime lord Ralph Valmont's mob kidnap Diabolik's girl, Eva Kant (Marisa Mell), but Diabolik foils their scheme and kills Valmont. Eventually Diabolik steals a 20-ton gold ingot being transported by train in Operation Goldvan. The bullion is radioactive and

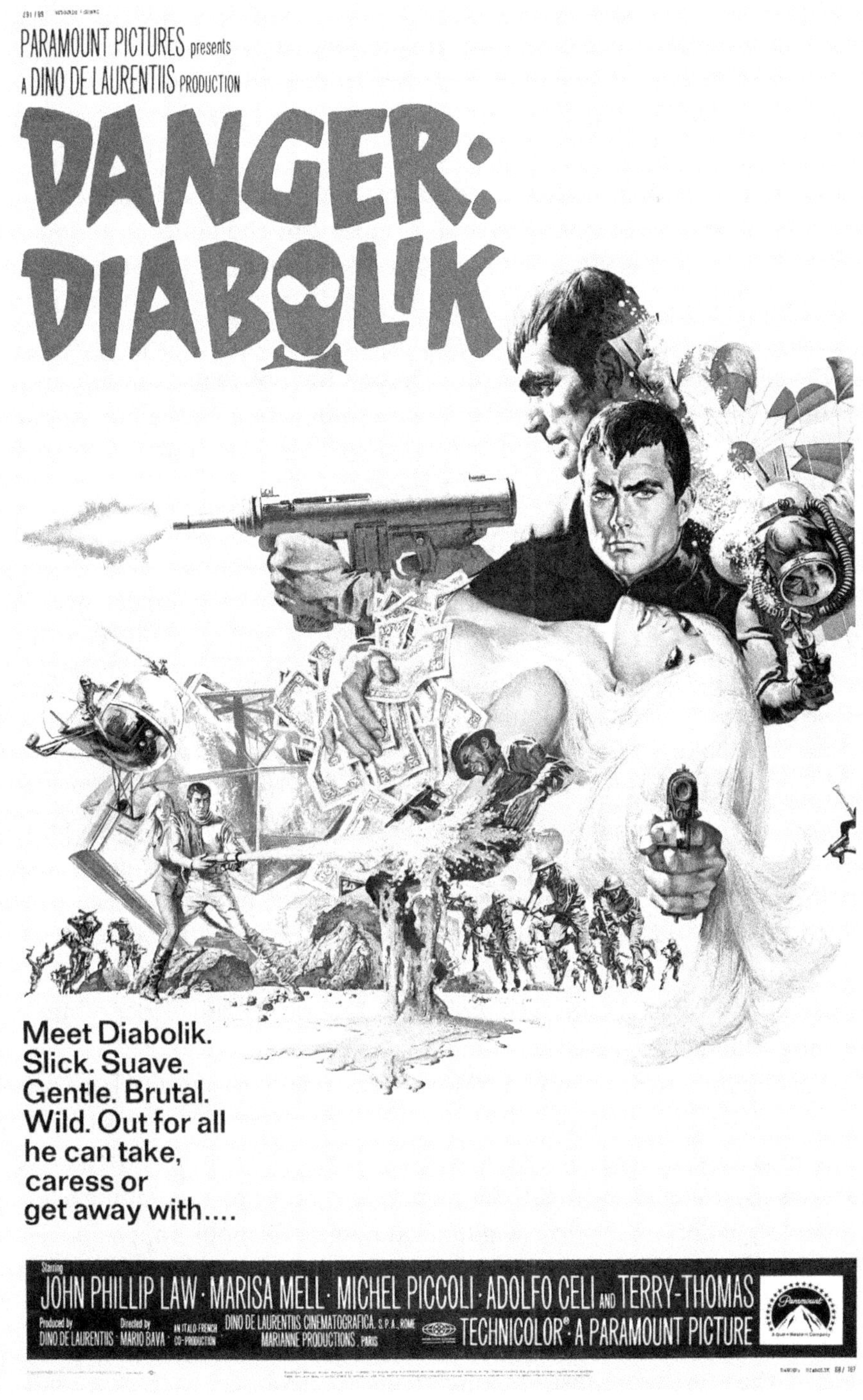

Science Fact and Fiction 113

US poster for Mario Bava's pop-art cult classic *Diabolik* (1968), starring John Phillip Law as the cunning masterthief and Marisa Mell as his bombshell lover Eva. Poster courtesy Ian Caunce Collection.

the police trace it to Diabolik's underground lair, where he is defeated when the molten ingot explodes, incarcerating him forever as a gold statue.

Offered a budget of $3 million by Dino De Laurentiis, Bava made *Diabolik* for $400,000. The film was shot from April to June 1967 at the Fiat plant in Turin, on location in Rome and in the Blue Grotto on Capri. Tor Caldara was used for clifftop St Just castle (a matte shot) and for the scene when Diabolik parachutes to save kidnapped Eva and is trapped by the police. Interiors were lensed at De Laurentiis Studios, Rome. *Thunderball* actor Adolfo Celi appeared as Valmont. The underwater heist (staged by Nicola Balini), when Diabolik tows away the gold ingot using inflatable balloons and a submersible jet sled, resembles *Thunderball*'s underwater scenes. Though the police use helicopters, cars and motorbikes and the costumery sets the film firmly in the pop-art 1960s, Diabolik's technology is futuristic. When Diabolik breaks into St Just castle to steal the famous Aksand emerald necklace, he scales the tower, Spiderman-style, using suction cups. To steal a $10 million cash shipment, he lifts the Rolls Royce carrying it with a dock crane and escapes by motor boat and E-Type Jag; he also demolishes the Lawrence Bridge to derail a train carrying the ingot. Bava and his scriptwriters concocted a witty, parodic script: 'With this suit I could swim through the centre of the sun', Diabolik tells Eva of his heatproof outfit.

Bava stages a succession of memorable set pieces, lensed in vivid Technicolor by Antonio Rinaldi, in a style defined by Bava's zooming, whip-panning, comic book verve and invention. Law is ideal as Diabolik, dressed in a variety of striking bodysuits and masks designed by Carlo Rambaldi. Mell (who replaced Catherine Deneuve, once the latter was fired from the role) is equally good as Eva. Terry-Thomas had a cameo as the incompetent minister of the interior. Claudio Gora played the chief of police, Andrea Bosić was the manager of the First International Bank Trust Company, Giulio Donnini was Dr Vernier, Annie Gorassini played Rose (Valmont's moll) and Federico Boido, Tiberio Mitri and Wolfgang Hillinger appeared as Valmont's gangsters.

Diabolik's unique score by Ennio Morricone is one of his finest. When Diabolik drives into his subterranean lair, Morricone's sinuous cue – mixing sitars, tabla, flutes and violins – sounds like Ravi Shankar-meets-The Velvet Underground. In Valmont's psychedelic nightclub, hippy patrons groove to a pounding acid-pop trumpet Deguello. Jarring electric guitars announce Diabolik's appearances and a frantic guitar riff scores speeding chases. The title song, the lilting 'Deep Down', was sung by Christy. The underwater heist features Edda Dell'Orso's soprano, which springs to life with vocal 'wah-wah-wahs', electric guitars and chunky drums, in the film's best musical moment: an 'ecstasy of gold' which sounds like the Good, the Bad and the Ugly doing the twist. For *Diabolik*'s English language release two different dubs were prepared. One version, entitled *Diabolik*, dubs the cast with American accents, while in the other, *Danger: Diabolik,* the accents sound British. In *Diabolik*, for instance, the thief's name is pronounced Dee-abolik, in *Danger: Diabolik* it's Die-abolik.

Glenn Saxson starred as a skull-faced super criminal in Umberto Lenzi's comic book adaptation *Kriminal* (1966) and Bava's film was parodied by ***Arriva Dorellik*** (1967), starring Johnny Dorelli as assassin Dorellik. Terry-Thomas was again the caped villain's nemesis. Also titled *How to Kill 400 Duponts*, this *Kind Hearts and Coronets*-inspired comedy featured the grooviest cabaret spot in Italian cult cinema, with shimmying Baby Eva (Margaret Lee) performing the onomatopoeic 'Crash-sci-sci-patapum!'

In Piero Vivarelli's ***Satanik*** (1968), an elderly, facially scarred doctor, Marnie Banister (Magda Konopka), concocts a regeneration serum ('the key to immortality') in Madrid. The potion transforms her into a beautiful young woman but unleashes her 'primordial instincts', turning her into a seductive, murderous killer. She leaves a trail of dead bodies, killing a rich diamond dealer (Umberto Raho) and stealing the identity of Stella Dexter, a gangster's moll. She flees to Lake Geneva, staying at the lakeside casino owned by crook Dodo La Roche (Luigi Montini), where she's eventually caught by Scotland Yard's Inspector Trent.

Backed by a groovy bossa nova score by Manuel Parada, *Satanik* melds sci-fi with jewel thievery, espionage, sexploitation and murder mystery. Armando Calvo was good as Madrid police chief Gonzales, Julio Peña equally so as the vacationing inspector, Trent, while sexy Konopka (known off-screen as The Magnetic Pole) was excellent as the lady killer, donning a variety of colourful, exotic fashion creations to stay one step ahead of the law. The ending is well handled, when Marnie reveals her true identity (and more besides) to Trent when she performs a striptease in the Casino 'Chez Moi' in a sultry Diabolik-styled outfit and mask, to the smoochy piano and sax of 'Strip-Blues' by Gepy and Gepy. She escapes on a paddle steamer but runs out of serum. Marnie changes into her older alter ego, which enables her to evade the police. Stealing a car with no brakes from a garage, she crashes while on a winding mountain road. In the wreckage, Marnie transforms into her younger self.

Star and No-Star Vehicles: The 1970s

For almost a decade no Italian sci-fi movies surfaced, but the global success of *Star Wars* (1977) relaunched the genre. Luigi Cozzi's ***Starcrash*** (1978) had smugglers Stella Star (Caroline Munro) and Akton (Marjoe Gortner) and their police android companion Elle (Judd Hamilton in a robot suit) dispatched by the Star Emperor (Christopher Plummer) to the heart of the Haunted Stars to investigate Count Zartharn (Joe Spinell), who has developed a Doom Machine. Stella locates Simon (David Hasselhoff), the Star Emperor's son, and together they take on Zartharn's axis of evil, destroying his planet, Demondia, and employing a tactic known as 'Starcrash: Fourth Dimensional Attack' to assault his space station headquarters. Filmed at Cinecittà Studios, *Starcrash*'s special effects are way above average for Italian sci-fi. Spaceships gracefully glide, rather than stutter, across vibrant star fields swathed in colour. Some effects still look as though the spacecraft are stuck inside a lava lamp, but the explosive ray gun finale exceeds expectations. John

Barry's score lifts the film and provides a suitably Bondian sweep to the intergalactic adventure, with voluminous orchestrations of strings and horns.

Starcrash opens with a spaceship passing overhead (identical to *Star Wars*) and an introductory scroll: 'In a time before time, life existed in the outer galaxies'. Akton uses a light sabre and Zartharn's minions are all-in-black stormtroopers. The heroes encounter beautiful Amazons led by Queen Corelia (Nadia Cassini), a giant robotic Amazon, two sword-wielding robotic 'golems', and grunting troglodytes. When Stella is caught smuggling by the Imperial Police, she is sentenced to hard labour in a radium mine. *Starcrash*'s cult popularity is due to ex-Bond girl and Hammer glamour queen Munro, here modelling a bikini and thigh-high boots. Robert Tessier played turncoat Imperial policeman Thor in green face makeup. Curly-haired Gortner and pre-*Baywatch* Hasselhoff are Stella's supposed love interest, though she prefers the company of Elle. Voiced by Hamilton Camp, Elle is the simple plot's narrator, explaining the blatantly obvious in a Midwestern drawl. Plummer's dignified imperial performance as the emperor of the First Circle of the Universe added moral gravity to an otherwise weightless scenario.

Special effects had improved immensely in the decade since Alfonso Brescia's *Conqueror of Atlantis*, but you'd never know from his 1970s work. His most notorious space opera is **Cosmos: War of the Planets** (1977), a remake of *Planet of the Vampires*. A spaceship commanded by Captain Fred Hamilton (John Richardson) on a mission in the Vega Sector picks up a strange signal from a strange planet. The planet's population is oppressed by a robot (The Immortal Monster) of the Texas Instruments variety. The green, bald, pointy-eared inhabitants are led by Amok (a disembodied voice) and their chief, Etor ('Nick Jordan'/ Aldo Canti), a six-foot goblin in a loincloth. The astronauts destroy the robot, the planet explodes and only Etor and the crew escape. Two astronauts have been possessed by the planet's ruler. Hamilton and his crew exterminate the zombies, but the robot takes control of their on-board computer as they return to Earth. *Cosmos* headlines a less-than-stellar cast, with everyone bar the leads wisely adopting pseudonyms. Mila, one of Hamilton's crew, was played by Yanti Somer, sporting an awful crew-cut. Although the film deploys some good starfield backdrops, it's what happens in the foreground that is the problem. The blipping score by Marcello Giombini consists of snatches of Bach toccatas played interminably on a synthesizer. The astronauts are kitted out in skin-tight white jumpsuits, coupled with red helmets (making them resemble human cannonballs); they enjoy non-interactive Cosmic Love on those lonely space nights; and their all-knowing computer at Base Orion is called WIZ. *Cosmos* is the most consistent Italian sci-fi movie: script, special effects, costumes, music and acting are all terrible. As Amok says of his planet's demise, 'I am talking about an atomic catastrophe'. Brescia certainly captured that on film.

Brescia followed this with another anti-classic, **The War of the Robots** (1978), starring Somer as space cadet Julie serving under Captain John Boyd (Antonio Sabato) on the spaceship Trissi. She has a crush on the captain, who loves Lois (Melissa Longo). Professor Carr (Jacques Herlin) and Lois are kidnapped from Earth by Gold Men from the planet Anthor. Carr has developed a secret formula for immortality. The Trissi sets off in pursuit, as a terrestrial reactor which only Carr can diffuse threatens to explode. Traitorous Lois, now the power-hungry empress of Anthor, attacks the Trissi, and Boyd, Julie and Lois resolve their love triangle with aerial combat.

Robots boasts some half-decent sets (at De Paolis Studios), *Space Invader* special effects and passable costumes. The PVC 'anti-radiation spacesuits' courtesy of Trissi Sport prominently bear the Trissi name on the front, which is probably why Brescia chose the name for his spacecraft. The Gold Men are androids in gold suits and blond wigs, a shiny, glam rock Abba tribute. The film's pumping synth score, again Giombini's responsibility, abandons Bach for more conventional orchestrations. Italian cult film regulars Giacomo Rossi-Stuart, Massimo Righi, Venantino Venantini and Roger Browne have been here before. Rossi-Stuart, by now 47, doesn't seem to care for the material at all, his mind visibly wandering. Aldo Canti tops his previous portrayal as Etor with a barnstorming, athletic turn as Kuba the Alien. An old enemy of the Gold Men, he's liberated from the planet Azar and is even entrusted with a few lines, in contrast to Etor who communicated telepathically. In one scene the Gold Men use light sabres (called Inderian swords) clearly modelled on *Star Wars*. And what were the English language dubbers thinking when they had the air assault by the Gold Men led by General Gonad? Perhaps Julie's comment best sums up the experience of sitting through Brescia's sci-fi movies: 'It's wonderful to be alive after being so near to death'.

The Humanoid (1979) was directed by Aldo Lado as George B. 'Lewis' (rather than Lucas). The second unit was helmed by Enzo G. Castellari, with special effects by Antonio Margheriti and models by Emilio Ruiz Del Rio. Both the model work and special effects – of spaceships and the Metropolis colony on planet Earth – are above average for Italian features. Interiors were shot at Cinecittà and DEAR Studios, with desert exteriors deploying matte shots as Metropolis. Inspired equally by *Star Wars* and *Frankenstein*, *Humanoid* had Dr Kraspin (Arthur Kennedy) working with a Darth Vader look-alike, Lord Graal (Ivan Rassimov), who aims to take over Earth. Having stolen the vital component Kavatron from the Groven Institute, the doctor can create an invincible race of humanoids. Kraspin begins by transforming Inspector Golob of the Metropolis Colony into a humanoid. Golob runs amok in Metropolis, tearing through the wobbly sets, but eventually sides with Earth's defenders against the invaders.

Golob was played by Richard Kiel (wearing a WWI flying helmet), who also played Jaws in the James Bond films, *The Spy Who Loved Me* and *Moonraker*. He'd appeared earlier in his career in the US-Italian sci-fi movie *The Human Duplicators* (1965), as the giant alien Kolos. Mystical Tibetan child Tom Tom (Marco Yeh) and Earth leader the Great Brother (Massimo Serato) are key good guys. Graal's cohort, Lady Agatha (Bond girl Barbara Bach, looking like a startled Siamese cat), is kept eternally youthful with serum injections from Dr Kraspin.

In *Humanoid* no *Star Wars* cliché is left unexploited, from the scrolling, starfield titles, to the laser beam shootout finale. Heroic Nick (Leonard Mann) is Luke Skywalker, imperilled Barbara Gibson (Corrine Clery) subs for Princess Leia Organa and cute robots are represented by Golob's sidekick Kip the robot space dog, who resembles a paper shredder on wheels. Morricone's score is partly a synthesiser rehash of his theme from *Burn!* (1969). When Golob is transformed into a humanoid the process also strangely zaps off his beard; Nick is lumbered with exclamations such as 'Well I'll be disintegrated!' and Kennedy appears to be taking the enterprise seriously. *The Humanoid* is a little-seen classic that deserves its place in sci-fi cult history.

Michele Lupo's **The Sheriff and the Satellite Kid** (1979) cleverly casts Cary Guffey, who had played the child abducted by aliens in Steven Spielberg's *Close Encounters of the Third Kind* (1977). Bud Spencer starred as Hall, the ambling sheriff of Newnan City, Georgia, which is in the grip of UFO-fever. The sheriff saves stranded H7–25 (Guffey) – an extraterrestrial child with incredible powers – from capture by the National Guard, led by Captain Briggs (Raimund Harmstorf). The film was shot on location in Georgia, in Newnan itself, at the Warner Robins and Dobbins Air Force Bases, and at the Confederate Civil War monument which is carved into Stone Mountain. Gigi Bonos appeared as Deputy Allen, Joe Bugner was resourceful jailbird Brennan and stuntmen Riccardo Pizzuti, Claudio Ruffini and Giovanni Cianfriglia appeared as National Guardsmen. The special effects depicting H7–25's feats included talking animals, and much footage sped-up, slowed-down and played backwards. 'Sheriff', the pounding disco pop theme by G & M De Angelis, will drive you right up the wall but the film is a well-made, charming comedy-fantasy that cleverly exploited the children's market during the 1970s sci-fi vogue.

Lupo's sequel, **Why Did You Pick on Me?** (1980), was a sorry addition to the saga, with Spencer and Guffey reprising their roles. The sheriff and his young companion (who calls himself 'Charlie Warren') are on the run. Hall becomes sheriff of Monroe, Georgia, and battles local hoodlums and a squad of extraterrestrial robots (led by Robert Hundar) who seek H7–25. Eventually the local ruffians (including stuntmen Riccardo Pizzuti and Lorenzo Fineschi) take on the police force (who have been brainwashed by the aliens) during a massed punch-up at the town's Eldorado Day festivities, which was filmed in the Six Flags amusement park in Atlanta. G & M De Angelis provided a less-than-memorable score, the troublemaking biker gang is straight out of Clint Eastwood's *Every Which Way But Loose* (1978) and the whole venture smacks of opportunism by producer Elio Scardamaglia, who did such a fine job on the first film. This poor sequel barely features Guffey and his special powers and ends with a homage to *Chitty Chitty Bang Bang*. Hall and H7–25 fly into space in a yellow vintage car, providing reason enough to keep watching the skies.

Chapter Six

Vita All'Italiana
Love and Death

In addition to muscleman epics and science fiction, Italian cinema occasionally wandered into the realms of reality. Rome has provided the setting for many great Hollywood films, including romances such as *Roman Holiday* (1953), *Three Coins in the Fountain* (1954) and *Seven Hills of Rome* (1958). When depicting their own country on screen, Italian filmmakers have often surprised international audiences with their dramas of life and love, which are swelled with optimism but riven with pessimism. In the 1960s, directors such as Federico Fellini, Vittorio De Sica and Michelangelo Antonioni created a new cinema, one which met with great international success. Italian cinema found its voice with stories ranging from filmmaking, celebrity and war atrocities, to slum life, murder and mental breakdowns. Drama All'Italiana never delivered the expected and was rarely mellow-drama.

Roma Therapy: Antonioni

Michelangelo Antonioni's ***L'avventura*** (1960 – *The Adventure*) begins with a yachting party cruising the volcanic Aeolian Islands in the Tyrrhenian Sea, north of Sicily: on board are Sandro (Gabriele Ferzetti), his fiancée Anna (Lea Massari), her friend Claudia (Monica Vitti), husband and wife Giulia (Dominique Blanchar) and Corrado (James Addams), and Raimondo (Lelio Luttazi) and Patrizia (Esmeralda Ruspoli). On Lisca Bianca, Anna vanishes and following an extensive search of the island she remains missing. Sandro and Claudia continue their investigation on Sicily, but they begin an affair, with Sandro eventually asking Claudia to marry him. In a hotel near Messina, Claudia discovers Sandro sleeping with a prostitute and Anna is never found.

L'avventura made Monica Vitti a star and gained Antonioni international recognition. The tension of the early scenes, particularly of Anna's sudden disappearance after she has told Sandro that she needs a break from their relationship, gradually fades from the story. Claudia's search for Anna becomes her affair with Sandro, though neither seems capable of emotional involvement. Sandro is an architect struggling with the artless boredom of life, while Claudia 'becomes' Anna, his lost fiancée. Their relationship is a strange *ménage à trois*, between Sandro, Claudia and the constant, ghostly presence of Anna. Through exemplary use of monochrome photography (by Aldo Scavarda), Antonioni depicts the gulf between Sandro and Claudia, emotionally distant and alienated, even if spatially close. One of Claudia's comments to Sandro, 'Say you want to kiss my shadow on the wall', is typical of Antonioni's abstract vision. Antonioni filmed on location in Sicily, including Lisca Bianca. This part of the shoot was dangerous, with the crew ferried from the island of Panarea to the remote location by fishing boat. Sandro and Claudia's search takes them around Sicily: Milazzo (the train station), Messina, Palermo, Noto and finally to a hotel near Messina. Now Claudia alone searches for Sandro in the vast, deserted luxury hotel and worries that Anna has returned. After spending so much time searching for her friend, Claudia now wonders: 'I fear she may be alive'. Initially greeted with boos and yawns at Cannes, the film went on to international success, heralding a new style of cinematic language. The director's style, with long dialogue-free passages and meaningful stares into the distance by the actors, was dubbed 'Antonioniennui'. At 143 minutes, the mystery unfolds very slowly and Antonioni offers no conventional resolution, leaving the question without an answer.

Antonioni continued in a similar vein with his next films, *La notte* (1961 – starring Marcello Mastroianni, Jeanne Moreau and Monica Vitti) and *The Eclipse* (1962), confounding audiences with narrative titbits and resolutions. The latter starred Alain Delon as stockbroker Piero, who has a relationship with Vittoria (Vitti), and the film concludes depressingly with an appointment that neither of them keeps. In **Red Desert** (1964), Antonioni's first colour feature, Vitti played mentally fragile Giuliana. While recovering from a car accident she falls in love with Corrado Zeller (a miscast and dubbed-in-Italian Richard Harris). The film is notable for its Eastmancolor photography (the images appear hand-tinted), the avant-garde soundtrack mix of musical score and whining, screeching electronica, and Antonioni's impressive deployment of the concrete and steel industrial landscape of foggy Ravenna in northern Italy – pylons, belching chimneys, a radio telescope, cargo freighters – as a barren backdrop to Giuliana's disintegration.

If *Red Desert* introduced colour to Antonioni's world, **Blowup** (1966) introduced commercial success – it remains the director's only box-office hit. *Blowup* was based on 'Las Babas Del Diablo' [The Devil's Drool], a short story by Argentinian Julio Cortázar, and starred David Hemmings as Thomas, an impatient, selfishly cold London fashion photographer. When taking shots in Maryon Park, Charlton, Thomas snaps a couple embracing. The woman (Vanessa Redgrave) angrily demands that Thomas hands over the film, but he refuses. Thomas develops the pictures and realises that he has prevented a murder: when he blows the images up, he discovers a gunman lurking in the bushes behind a fence, about to shoot the woman's lover.

Mystery and Murder: Thomas (David Hemmings) snaps model Veruschka in an international poster for Michelangelo Antonioni's abstract *Blowup* (1966).

Only later does Thomas realise, through further 'blowups', that her lover was, in fact, killed – his corpse can be seen in one of the enlargements. Thomas revisits the park at night and finds the man's body, but when he returns to his studio all evidence pertaining to the murder has been stolen. Now the crime exists only in Thomas' mind. The film ends with Thomas, back at Maryon Park, watching two people mime a game of tennis. When the ball 'lands' near him, Thomas 'throws' it back, before vanishing into thin air, a figment of the audiences' imagination.

Blowup is a desolate, cold film, as Antonioni looks at London with the same inscrutable gaze he cast over his Italian urban landscapes. He depicts a tense London that's barely moving, let alone 'swinging'. Even a rock gig (when Thomas sees the Jimmy Page-era Yardbirds) ends edgily with a guitarist having amp problems and smashing up his guitar. Antonioni digresses, stalling the mystery – Thomas rattily snaps hung-over 'dolly birds', purchases a propeller from an antiques shop, discusses a book he's putting together with his business partner Ron (Peter Bowles), visits his lover Patricia (Sarah Miles) and her artist husband (John Castle) and romps with two perky teenage models (Gillian Hills and Jane Birkin). There's also a photo shoot with German fashion model Veruschka. *Blowup*'s mystery survives such ramblings. The eerie park murder, the trees in full leaf rustling in the blustery wind, is one of Antonioni's finest sequences. When Thomas reconstructs the sequence of murder in a series of monochrome stills, hung throughout his studio, the scene is Godardian in its imagery of cinema taken back to its simplest form. The couple embrace; a man lurks in the bushes; a corpse lies in the undergrowth. Thomas shoots a picture and the assassin shoots his victim, while Antonioni shoots them both. Hemmings later puzzled his way through Dario Argento's murder mystery *Deep Red* (1975).

Blowup was produced by Carlo Ponti and MGM and shot in MGM's Borehamwood Studio and on location in London. It was the first film to feature full-frontal female nudity, which no doubt helped its box office but garnered an X certificate. Herbie Hancock provided the jazzy score, including the classic instrumental theme tune, which was covered to great success by the James Taylor Quartet in 1985 (as 'Blow Up') and provided the distinctive bouncing bassline for the 1990 pop hit 'Groove is the Heart' by Deee-Lite. *Blowup* won the Palme d'Or at Cannes, Antonioni won a Silver Ribbon in Italy and was nominated for Best Director and Screenplay at the Oscars. Antonioni's first American film, the counterculture disaster *Zabriskie Point* (1970), bombed spectacularly. His best 1970s work was *The Passenger* (1974), which starred Jack Nicholson in what many believe to be his finest role, as reporter David Locke. He exchanges identities with a dead man, whom he later discovers to be an endangered gunrunner. It was shot on location in Africa and Almeria by Luciano Tovoli.

Two Women: Loren, Bardot and Art Cinema

Federico Fellini won the first ever Best Foreign Language Film Oscar for *La strada* (1954 – starring Anthony Quinn as a travelling strongman) in 1956 and won again the following year for *Nights of Cabiria* (which became the musical *Sweet Charity*). Anna Magnani won a Best Actress Academy Award for her performance in the US film *The Rose Tattoo* (1955) and Italian actors Rossano Brazzi and Gina Lollobrigida were becoming international stars in such films as *South Pacific* (1958) and *Solomon and Sheba* (1959). Director Vittorio De Sica was well-known internationally for his neorealist treatment of sentimental, primal drama. In *The Bicycle Thieves* (1947 – *The Bicycle Thief* in the US) Antonio Ricci (Lamberto Maggiorani) takes a job pasting billposters of Rita Hayworth's *Gilda* around Rome, to feed his poverty-stricken family. When his 'Fides' bike is stolen, he and his little son Bruno (Enzo Staiola) vainly search the city until, driven to despair, Antonio stoops to steal one himself.

Sophia Loren and Brigitte Bardot, two of the biggest stars of European cinema, were often better known for frothy fare – light comedy and romance – than for visceral drama. But at the start of the 1960s, both made films in Italy that would demonstrate their formidable acting credentials. De Sica's **Two Women** (1960), based on a 1957 novel by Alberto Moravia, was produced by Carlo Ponti and starred Ponti's wife, Loren. The wartime story details the relationship between a widowed mother and her daughter, who become refugees when they flee Rome to avoid the Allied bombing. Loren, then aged 26, was originally to play the daughter, with 52-year-old Anna Magnani as her mother. Magnani, who once called Loren 'a Neapolitan giraffe', balked: 'I'm too young to play Loren's mother. Let her play the part herself'. De Sica then cast Eleanora Brown as Rosetta, the daughter, and lowered her age to 12, so Loren could play Cesira, her mother. They leave their grocery shop in Rome in the care of Cesira's lover, Giovanni (Raf Vallone), and head to the mountains to live with relatives. They settle into country life and meet political intellectual Michele (Jean-Paul Belmondo). News arrives that Mussolini is in jail and the Americans have invaded. With liberation at hand, Cesira and Rosetta head for home, but while they shelter in a ruined church, Moroccan auxiliaries (who are fighting alongside the Allies) savagely assault both women.

Gabor Pagany's monochrome cinematography makes *Two Women* one of the most strikingly shot Italian films, a neorealist document of rural Italy. Interiors were filmed at Titanus Studios, with location scenes at Saracinesco, to the east of Rome, and Itri, to the south. Andrea Checchi played a fascist official, Renato Salvatori was a peasant boy who takes Rosetta dancing (angering her mother) and Luciano Pigozzi was an Italian soldier forcing peasant lads to enlist. *Two Women* is a one-woman show – it is Loren's greatest film and her most convincing performance. Loren could play street girls or princesses – here she's working class and strong, a refugee striving to give her daughter the best. The scenes of Loren carrying a suitcase balanced on her head along dusty country tracks or lying slumped, tearfully destroyed, in the road following her assault are iconic images.

Two Women is concerned with the horrific human cost of war. A US soldier snapping photos with his camera wants starving Cesira to show some leg, when all she wants is food, and marker flares for the bombing raids are watched by the peasants like a firework display. It is the allies of the Americans, not the enemy, who assault Cesira and Rosetta, leaving their lives changed in an instant; Rosetta's youth is torn from her and she is left catatonic, while Cesira is unable to protect her daughter, something she has somehow managed for the entire war. The film's dark side is exemplified by the fate of Michele. He is taken away by a retreating German patrol (led by Franco Balducci) to guide them to safety through the mountains. Cesira later discovers that his murdered body has been found in the hills. Up against Audrey Hepburn (for *Breakfast at Tiffany's*), Piper Laurie, Geraldine Page and Natalie Wood, Loren won Best Actress at the 1961 Oscars – the first time a foreign language film actress had won for a foreign language film, although an English-dubbed version was also prepared, with Loren voicing herself. 'Before I made *Two Women* I had been a performer', Loren remembered, 'Afterward, I was an actress'.

Produced by Carlo Ponti and inspired by a book by Moravia (*Il disprezzo* or 'A Ghost at Noon'), Jean-Luc Godard directed **Contempt** (1963 – *Le Mépris*) at Cinecittà. In Rome, following the success of his script for *Totò against Hercules*, playwright Paul Javal (Michel Piccoli) is commissioned by US producer Jerry Prokosh (Jack Palance) to rewrite a script based on Homer's *The Odyssey* which is about to shoot on Capri. Paul deliberates about taking the assignment but the $10,000 fee will pay off his Rome apartment. Paul's wife, Camille (Brigitte Bardot), suspects that Paul is having an affair with Prokosh's secretary and translator, Francesca Vanini (Georgia Moll), and Paul suspects that Camille no longer loves him and has been unfaithful with Prokosh.

Contempt is one of the great works of international cinema. For its title sequence, a camera slowly dollies forward, while the credits are spoken aloud. As the camera swivels down to face the audience, the voiceover continues, 'For what we see, Bazin said, the cinema substitutes a world that conforms to our desires – *Le Mépris* is the story of that world'. *Contempt* is a send-up of itself: an international co-production with a multinational cast which parodies such co-productions. *The Odyssey* is being directed by Austrian émigré Fritz Lang (playing himself), Godard plays Lang's assistant (screening rushes at Cinecittà) and Lang's cinematographer is Raoul Coutard (*Contempt*'s director of photography). Godard wanted Frank Sinatra and Kim Novak in the leads, while Ponti envisioned Marcello Mastroianni and Sophia Loren. 'C'est formidable!' enthused Bardot when she was cast, 'I've joined the new wave now!' She received her highest fee to date – $510,000. Too often wasted in second-rate vehicles, Bardot gave her best performance as Camille. She has never looked better, her tousled blonde hair held in place with a headband, her eyes and pout reproachful and contemptuous of her sell-out husband.

Prokosh is based on *Contempt*'s producers: Joseph E. Levine (of *Hercules* fame) and Carlo Ponti. Levine released *Contempt* internationally. Prokosh sells off part of his studio to become a shopping precinct. He needs a commercial film

Ghost at Noon: Brigitte Bardot as adulterous Camille in French artwork for Jean-Luc Godard's *Contempt* (1963), a tragic story filmed in fabulous settings at Cinecittà Studios and on the island of Capri.

and encourages Lang to include more nudity. Godard draws parallels between the heroes of *The Odyssey* and his characters, with Camille subbing for Penelope. 'I like gods, I like them very much', says Prokosh, 'I know exactly how they feel'. During footage of a naked siren (Linda Veras) swimming in the water, Prokosh visibly livens up. He lends Paul a book of Roman paintings to inspire his writing, even though *The Odyssey* is Greek. 'Whenever I hear the word culture', says the producer, 'I bring out my chequebook'. He has a little book of idioms which he quotes, making himself feel more intelligent. Lang and Paul casually quote philosophy, poetry and literature classics by heart. The 'B.B.' here is Bertolt Brecht, whom Lang memorably cites to describe Hollywood: 'Each morning to earn my bread I go the market where they buy lies and hopefully line up with the vendors'.

Godard shot on location on Capri, the azure ocean, white cliffs and verdant vegetation captured by Raoul Coutard in widescreen Franscope. Prokosh's island villa perched on a rock outcrop (with its huge ramped staircase ascending to a rooftop sundeck) was Curzio Malaparte's villa (now called Villa Malaparte). Georges Delerue composed the moving score – one of cinema's greatest. The rolling, dramatic strings of 'Camille', 'Générique' and 'Capri', tugging and languorous, complement the haunting story. The finale is worthy of Greek tragedy. Camille departs with Prokosh, leaving Paul a note. En route to Rome they stop for petrol, but as they pull off, Prokosh's red Alfa Romeo convertible collides with a tanker truck, killing them both. The words of Camille's letter fill the widescreen: 'I kiss you, goodbye... Camille'.

The film was released as *Le Mépris* in France, with the actors speaking their own languages (Piccoli and Bardot French, Lang German and French, Palance English) and with Prokosh's translator Francesca translating for us. It was released as *Il disprezzo* in Italy (cut to 84 minutes and with a new score by Piero Piccioni) and as *Contempt* in the US (at 103 minutes). The producers wanted more nudity from Bardot, so a scene was added with Paul and Camille lying on a bed – her nude – where they discusses the finer points of Bardot's anatomy (Bardot received an extra $20,300 to film this scene). *Contempt* wasn't released in the UK until 1970, dubbed entirely into English, which renders Francesca's role obsolete. The misleading tagline ran: 'Bardot at her Bold, Bare and Brazen Best! Revelling in Rome... Cavorting in Capri... Jolting even the jaded international jet-set in her pursuit of love!' The film's French language trailer is a work of art: 'The woman... the man... Italy... the cinema... a tragic story in a fabulous setting, a fabulous story in a tragic setting'. *Contempt* is visually beautiful, thematically rich and powerfully tragic. It is the greatest film about film, and also one of the greatest about trust and love, and the betrayal and disintegration of both.

Sophia Loren went on to further Oscar success with De Sica's three-part sex comedy **Yesterday, Today, and Tomorrow** (1963), which won the 1964 Best Foreign Film Oscar. Loren played 'Adelina of Naples', a black market cigarette girl who avoids a prison sentence when she discovers a loophole in the law. She can't be imprisoned when she's pregnant, so she has seven children, until her husband, Carmine (Marcello Mastroianni), has a nervous breakdown and she goes to jail. In 'Anna of Milan', Loren was at her most beautiful, dressed by Christian Dior, as rich, shallow socialite Anna, who falls out with her lover Renzo (Mastroianni) when he prangs her Rolls Royce on a tractor. In 'Mara of Rome', Loren played a prostitute who is the obsession of trainee priest Umberto (Giovanni Ridolfi). It is here that Loren performed her famous striptease, while her client, Augusto Rusconi (Mastroianni), howls like a wolf. The lush score was by Armando Trovajoli; the film was shot at Titanus Appia Studios and on location in Naples, and Mara's apartment overlooks the Piazza Navona in Rome. The English dubbed version presented by Joseph Levine is inferior to the original Italian language version.

Mastroianni also starred in **Divorce – Italian Style** (1962), which won the Best Original Screenplay Oscar for Ennio De Concini, Alfredo Gianetti and Pietro Germi. Carlo Rustichelli provided the music and Germi directed. Mastroianni was nominated for Best Actor for his role as Baron Ferdinando Cefalù who decides to murder, rather than divorce, his sex-crazed wife, Rosalia (Daniela Rocca), so that he can marry his young lover, Angela (Stefania Sandrelli). Set in Agromonte in Sicily, the baron times his deed with a showing of *La dolce vita* at the local cinema. Mastroianni followed *Divorce* with De Sica's *Marriage, Italian Style* (1964), for which Loren was again nominated for a Best Actress Oscar. She starred as Filumena who tries to cajole, convince and hoodwink her lover Domenico Soriano (Mastroianni) into marriage.

Fellini's Roma

The spirit of the eternal city during the early 1960s was captured in Federico Fellini's **La dolce vita** (1960). Journalist Marcello Rubini (Marcello Mastroianni) and his photographer sidekick, Paparazzo (Walter Santesso), lurk in the Via Veneto and its nightspots, snapping celebs and unearthing lurid gossip. Fellini depicts the indulgent world of high-flyers in Rome's playground and also Marcello's life refracted through his relationships with his jealous fiancée Emma (Yvonne Furneaux), Maddalena (Anouk Aimee), his lover with whom he shares a shallow, indulgent nature, and Sylvia Rank (Anita Ekberg), an American movie star visiting Rome with her drunken fiancé, Robert (Lex Barker), to star in a Cinecittà spectacular for producer Toto Scalise (Carlo Di Maggio).

Marcello and Maddalena make love in a prostitute's flooded apartment (its exteriors were Tor Di Schiavi) and Marcello's fiancée attempts suicide. Marcello covers the arrival of Sylvia at Ciampino Airport and attends her press conference at the Excelsior Hotel. She visits St Peter's and the Quirinal Palace, climbing the spiral stairs to the dome. Sylvia and Marcello slip away from a party at a nightclub (the ruined baths at Terme Di Caracalla) and wander the silent streets. Sylvia finds a stray kitten and sends Marcello to find some milk. While he searches, she bathes in the Trevi Fountain, in her scoop-necked black gown, a moment which was used extensively in the film's advertising. This was based on an incident

Life is a Party: Sylvia dances and Marcello smokes in Federico Fellini's *La dolce vita* (1960). Anita Ekberg and Marcello Mastroianni in an Italian poster, courtesy Ian Caunce Collection.

in Ekberg's life, though she took the dip in August and Fellini filmed in freezing March. Marcello wades in after her – Mastroianni wore a wetsuit under his clothes and was 'insulated' with vodka. Marcello covers a 'field of miracles' in the provinces (filmed at Bagni Di Tivoli) where two children (Massimo and Giovanni Busetti) claim to have seen the Madonna. The press converge and the infirm are stretchered out to be cured. Marcello and Emma attend a soiree at the house of Steiner, a depressive intellectual (Alain Cuny) who tries to convince Marcello to leave tabloid journalism and become a proper writer. When Marcello's father (Annibale Ninchi) visits from the provinces and hooks up with showgirl Fanny (Magali Noël), his taste of the hectic 'sweet life' almost kills him.

Marcello's life spirals ever downwards. He attends an aristocrats' party in a castle at Bassano Di Sutri (filmed at Livio Odescalchi's sixteenth-century villa at Bassano Romano, Viterbo). Their decadence is contrasted with the grand surroundings and the guests, gothic in their attire and manner, resemble the cast of a horror movie. The hosts are Don Giulio (Giulio Questi, later the director of *Django, Kill!*) and his fianceé, Nicolina (model and future Velvet Underground singer Nico). Ida Galli appeared as Irene, debutant of the year, and Audrey McDonald played Jane, an English painter. Steiner then shoots his two children and himself, and the press hyenas wait for the return of Steiner's unsuspecting wife (Renée Longarini), to snap her reaction. At a party at the beachside pad of Riccardo (Riccardo Garrone) to celebrate Nadia's divorce (in Fellini's cynical world, something to be celebrated), Nadia (Nadia Gray) performs a striptease as the gathering descends into bacchanalia, with Marcello riding drunken Cara (Franca Pasut), then covering her in feathers. Jacques Sernas appeared as a matinee idol and Laura Betti was a partygoer. Riccardo throws them out and they walk into the cold dawn. Fishermen are landing the rotting corpse of a giant ray on the beach (filmed at Passo Oscura) and the revellers gather around. Marcello encounters Umbrian girl Paula (Valeria Ciangottini), whom he met earlier in a café. She tries to call to him across the beach, but he can't hear her, wandering away to his aimless 'sweet life'.

Fellini lensed the film (with the working title *Via veneto*) on location and in Cinecittà from March to May 1959. A stretch of the Via Veneto outside Café De Paris was built in the studio. It was shot in monochrome 2.35:1 Totalscope by Otello Martelli, who had lensed Fellini's *La strada* (1954), *The Swindle* (1955) and *Nights of Cabiria* (1957). *La dolce vita* features one of Nino Rota's most beautiful scores. A delicate harp shimmers as Sylvia bathes in the Trevi. The producers couldn't clear the rights to use 'Mack the Knife', so Rota copied the melody into his own composition for the castle party. The rousing, burping organ of 'Patricia' by Perez Prado accompanies Nadia's strip and wafts from Paola's beachside café jukebox. Rock 'n' roll at Caracalla's features pop singer Adriano Celentano and Fellini's beloved circus is represented by Polidor, the sad old clown trumpeter, and his performing balloons in the old-fashioned Cha-Cha Club.

US poster for the three-part portmanteau film *Boccaccio 70* (1962), starring Sophia Loren, Anita Ekberg and Romy Schneider. Vittorio De Sica directed 'The Raffle', Federico Fellini 'The Temptation of Dr Antonio' and Luchino Visconti 'The Job'. Poster courtesy Ian Caunce Collection.

Fellini's producers wanted Paul Newman as Marcello, but Fellini refused; Mastroianni is excellent in the role. We first meet Marcello flying over Rome in a helicopter pursuing a statue of Christ (suspended from another chopper) that is being airlifted into the Vatican. Suave, chain-smoking Marcello wears shades at night and drives a Triumph Spider convertible. He's shallow, a creep who lives only for his own indulgence. He winds up working as a publicity agent, but in reality he's like the big fish on the beach: washed up and rotten on the inside, despite appearances.

Sylvia was originally to have been named 'Anita', but Ekberg found the role too autobiographical. Sylvia's fiancé was modelled on Ekberg's husband of the time, Anthony Steel. The former Miss Malmoe based her character on Ava Gardner (the 'Barefoot Contessa') and Rita Hayworth as *Gilda*. Fellini cast Ekberg again in *The Temptation of Doctor Antonio*, his episode of the portmanteau film **Boccaccio 70** (1962). Anita played 'Anita', the voluptuous image on a giant billboard provocatively advertising milk. Prudish Antonio Mazzuolo (Peppino De Filippo) fantasises that colossal Anita comes to life.

La dolce vita was released into a storm of scandal in Italy – one patron spat at the director – but it made a fortune and was awarded the Palme d'Or at Cannes. Fellini was nominated as Best Director at the Oscars and it was the film that cemented his international popularity. A dubbed version of the film was released in the US in 1966. Fellini's tale of idlers and idolaters is still powerful and remains his finest work.

Fellini's *8½* (1963) was his most autobiographical film. Marcello Mastroianni played Fellini's alter ego, director Guido Anselmi. At a health spa Guido is under pressure to begin his next project, a sci-fi film. The expensive sets are already under construction – a towering rocket and launch pad – for a sequence involving thousands of extras. Earth has been destroyed by nuclear war and the survivors board the rocket to escape an atomic plague. Guido's financiers and the cast are causing him problems, so he escapes into flights of fancy and nostalgic reveries. Matters are further complicated when Guido's mistress Carla (Sandra Milo) and his wife, Louisa (Anouk Aimee), arrive at the spa. This juxtaposition of Guido's real life and his fantasy world becomes Fellini's film.

Fellini egotistically wallows in his role as 'artist' and in the creative process. Guido is selfish and a liar – his every action is self-serving. He can't make sense of the 'shambles in my head' and Fellini depicts this shambles on film – Guido imagines he's floating like a balloon on a string, remembers his parents and moments from his childhood, and fantasises about women. He can't decide whether to start the film or shoot himself. The climax of *8½* is a parade around a circus ring by the entire cast, orchestrated by Guido. 'Life is a party', he tells Louisa, 'Let's live it together'. The musical accompaniment is a four-man clown band, with 'Guido as a child' on flute. This was originally shot as a trailer for the film, but it replaced Fellini's planned ending. A scene of Guido and Louisa travelling on a train back to Rome with the cast was shot but later axed.

8½ was photographed in monochrome by Gianni Di Venanzo on location at the beach at Ostia (where the 'rocket' was constructed), Tivoli, Filacciano, Viterbo and a wood in EUR was the spa. The film's dreamlike visual style recalled Alain Resnais' *Last Year in Marienbad* (1960), his haunting story of a half-imagined

Italian poster for Fellini's Oscar-winning *8½* (1963) depicting film director Guido Anselmi (Marcello Mastroianni) and the women in his fantasy life: Sandra Milo, Anouk Aimee, Claudia Cardinale, Rosella Falk and Barbara Steele. Poster courtesy Ian Caunce Collection.

affair. Nino Rota wrote *8½*'s bittersweet score. The famous Cordovox organ theme was used when busty, raven-haired La Saraghina (Edra Gale) dances on the beach for schoolboy Guido and his friends. The spa sequences are populated by Fellini's living portraits of those in need of recuperation. Rosella Falk played Rosella, Louisa's spiritualist sister, Guido Alberti played producer Pace and Jean Rougeul was critic Fabrizio Carini. Producer Mario Mezzabotta (Mario Pisu) and his young fiancée, budding actress Gloria Morin (Barbara Steele), imitated Carlo Ponti and Sophia Loren. Aimee lost 15 pounds to play long-suffering Louisa and Milo gained 15 to play Carla. When Guido and the film's producers watch screen tests to decide who will play who, we see alternative choices for the cast. Each woman Guido meets becomes part of his imagined 'harem'. In the film's most famous sequence Guido – 'The Emir' – 'lays down the law' to his harem with a whip, like a circus ringmaster, to Wagner's *Ride of the Valkyries*. The only women who aren't treated in this manner are Guido's mother and Claudia (Claudia Cardinale), Guido's ideal. He imagines casting Claudia in his film (she appears as a nurse at the spa) until he realises there's 'no part' as there's 'no film'. But what is *8½*? Are we viewing 'the film' or is the entire movie Guido's daydream while he's bored, trapped in a traffic jam? The title refers to the number of films Fellini had made up to 1963 – seven features (including *8½*), plus a co-directed film (*Lights of Variety* [1950]) and two shorts, each of which count 'half'. *8½* was a great success, both in Italy and abroad, and won the Best Foreign Film Oscar in 1963.

Mastroianni parodied his performance as Guido in Mario Monicelli's glossy **Casanova '70** (1965), an episodic farce set throughout Europe, including Paris, Sicily and Naples. Mastroianni played Major Andrea Rossi-Colombotti, an amorous NATO liaison officer who becomes sexually aroused only when there's an element of danger to the encounter. Andrea romances the cream of European female beauty: Virna Lisi, Michele Mercer, Rosemary Dexter, Margaret Lee, Marisa Mell, Moira and Liana Orfei, Senya Seyn and Jolanda Modio. Enrico Maria Salerno played a psychiatrist who attempts to cure Andrea and Memmo Carotenuto had a humorous cameo as an art forger, who announces, 'A pair of Baroque-style Angels. Late eighteenth century. Just out the kiln. Hot as pizza'. Armando Travajoli and the Cantori Moderni contributed the up-tempo score. *Casanova '70* ends with a trial where Andrea's 'harem' turn up in court as condemning character witnesses. Mastroianni noted that the film was 'built around the attempt – close to my heart – to destroy the image of the Italian Latin-lover stud, a label which is far from flattering'.

Fellini's **Juliet of the Spirits** (1965) was his first full-length colour film. Giulietta Masina (Fellini's wife) starred as Juliet (Giulietta in the Italian print), who suspects her vain husband Giorgio (Mario Pisu) is having an affair. She hires the Eagle Eye private detective agency and discovers that Giorgio is seeing a 24-year-old model, Gabriella Olson. Eventually the man whom Juliet sees as 'husband, lover, father, friend...my home' leaves her for his mistress. This relationship breakdown is offset by Fellini's extravagant style. Her fragile mental state fractured by her husband's indiscretions – mysterious phone calls, late nights at the office – emotional Juliet experiences surreal visions. She remembers the time when her grandfather (Lou Gilbert) eloped with a circus dancer, Iris (Sandra Milo), flying away in a contraption which appears to have been constructed by the Wright Brothers. Juliet visits a seer, a guru man-woman named Bishma (Valeska Gert), who promotes the Universal Spirit of 'Love is a religion'. Juliet remembers that as a child she was cast as a Christian martyr in a theatre production staged by nuns, which ended with Juliet being executed by the Romans, 'burning' on a griddle. This martyrdom is recreated, with leaping flames and a hideous, staring victim clad in white dress and bonnet.

Fellini had visited several mediums and had experimented with LSD, both of which infused his work on *Juliet of the Spirits*. It is most memorable for its Technicolor cinematography by Gianni Di Venanzo, for the colour-coded sets, stylised costumes and huge hats, and for Fellini's depiction of Juliet's flights of fantasy. Fellini filmed on location at his coastal villa in Fregene, north of Fiumicino, with interiors shot at Safa-Palatino and Cinecittà. Next door to Juliet lives exotic, erotic Susy (Sandra Milo), whose orgies are attended by way-out guests who resemble Juliet's apparitions. Nino Rota's jazzy, carnivalesque music provides the ideal complement to these rich, often perversely sacrilegious images – a party at Susy's deploys a percussive, Eastern arrangement, with a sinuous vocal by Gianna Spagnolo.

Sylva Koscina played Juliet's sister, flowery model Sylva; Luisa Della Noce was Juliet's practical sister, Adele; and Caterina Boratto was their patrician mother. Fellini had Susy's entourage arrive on the beach by barge, like Cleopatra, while Juliet imagines emaciated horses drifting on a raft and a primitive ramped galley, which anticipates *Fellini Satyricon*. Juliet's visions include talking flowers, Iris dressed as a bride on a swing, and rows of bowed and shrouded nuns – visions which become her waking nightmares. At a garden party, Juliet sees a burning martyr, Botticelli's *Birth of Venus*, a naked woman sitting beside a tree (enveloped in the slithery coils of an immense snake) and a hearse carrying Juliet's childhood friend Laura, a suicide. When Giorgio departs, so do the spirits – they pack up and leave en masse on a rickety cart. Fellini's imagery here resembles Mario Bava at his most outré, but Fellini tends to be more psychoanalytical of his subjects, while Bava strives for the supernatural.

Fellini's fragmented narratives became ever more distorted in **Roma** (1972), which contrasted ancient and modern Rome. The trailer, a barrage of powerful, memorable images, promised, 'Fellini examines the Fall of the Roman Empire: 1931–1972'. The film follows Fellini (Peter Gonzales) – a young journalist who arrives from the northern provinces at Termini station in Rome – and his impressions of the fascist city in wartime. These depictions of boisterous Italian family life, variety shows, brothels and air raid shelters are interspersed with vignettes of modern Rome, a city overrun with hippies. Fellini constructed an entire Roman street, Via Albalonga, in Cinecittà's Studio 5, complete with trams. There are numerous scenes filmed at the city's monuments (the Colosseum, the Trevi Fountain, Sant'Angelo Bridge and Castel Sant'Angelo) but the Spanish Steps are covered with lounging longhairs and the police move student demonstrators on from a fountain in Piazza Santa Maria. Fellini himself appears onscreen at various moments, directing the action. Cameos from Marcello Mastroianni and Alberto Sordi were omitted from the final cut, though Anna Magnani – from *Rome, Open City* – makes her last film appearance here. In the climax, massed bikers speed through the city at night, in scenes which wouldn't be out of place in *1990: The Bronx Warriors* or other 1980s Italian exploitation.

Roma is wildly incoherent Fellini, episodic and exuberant. The surreal journey along Rome's traffic-jammed ring road (Raccordo Anulare) in the pelting rain, which climaxes with a horrific accident involving a toppled cattle truck, recalls Toby Dammit's arrival in *Histoires Extraordinaire*. A family visit the cinema to see a stagy gladiator movie, which is followed by fascist newsreels. In a vast subterranean construction tunnel moling beneath the city, the engineers discover a fabulous Roman house, but almost immediately the colourful, perfectly preserved ancient frescos fade to grey. A theatre patron describes vaudeville as a combination of 'circus and brothel', which also sums up Fellini's cinema. At the 'Festa De Noantri', Gore Vidal chats with journalist John Francis Lane. Vidal comments that Rome is 'a city after all of the church, of government, of the movies…they're all makers of illusion'. The film's most famous and elaborate sequence is an ecclesiastic fashion show, with models strutting the catwalk in outlandish outfits designed by Danilo Donati – flapping gull-like nuns' cowls, roller-skating and bicycling priests, neon 'stained glass' designs, and Vegas cardinals in flashing mitres, glittering capes and surpluses. *Roma* didn't travel well in Italy and it was popular only in Milan and Rome. The film's distinctive poster featured a naked woman with three breasts, bent on all fours, resembling Romulus and Remus' suckling she-wolf.

Set in the Adriatic coastal resort of Rimini in north-eastern Italy (Fellini's birthplace), **Amarcord** (1973 – Italian dialect for 'I Remember') wistfully excavates Fellini's past. His depiction of Italy, in what many believe to be his best film, is a rose-tinted regression to his adolescence in the mid-1930s. A lawyer (Luigi Rossi) is our onscreen guide, providing historical context to events. *Amarcord* depicts one year, beginning in the spring with the arrival of the 'Fairy Fluff', drifting windblown white spores. The end of winter is marked by the burning of an effigy of the Old Witch of Winter. The central protagonists are young Titta Biondi (Bruno Zanin) and his extended family – including his mother, Miranda (Pupella Maggio), and father, Aurelio (Armando Brancia), a building foreman – plus Ninola (Magali Noël), a glamorous local hairdresser known as 'Gradisca', whose movie star good looks are a focal point for the town's men.

Amarcord is Fellini's most coherent, accessible work. It boasts a bittersweet romantic score from Nino Rota and rich cinematography by Giuseppe Rotunno. There are episodes of Titta and his classmates at school and play – chubby Ciccio

Marconi (Fernando De Felice) attempts to date uninterested Aldina Cordini (Donatella Gambini), while Titta watches westerns at the Fulgor Cinema and pisses off the balcony on his father's friend's hat. Gradisca enjoys a tryst at the Grand Hotel (the exterior of which was filmed in Anzio) with a visiting prince and dreams of meeting the right man. The 'VII Mille Miglia' car rally speeds through town and a fascist rally is held to welcome the provincial party secretary. The entire populace take to the sea in a flotilla of small boats to see the ocean liner *Rex* ('The government's greatest achievement') return from a transatlantic voyage. There's an immense, flower-decorated talking Mussolini and when winter arrives the town suffers a blizzard, with the metre-deep snow transforming the streets into a picturesque labyrinth.

Fellini's female characters are bawdily clichéd. Slavering blonde nymphomaniac Volpina (Josiane Tanzili) appears to have strayed in from *Satyricon* and Luccia (Maria Antonietta Beluzzi), the town's busty, lusty tobacconist, demands that awestruck Titta suck her enormous breasts. Adolescent sexual fantasies permeate the film – a Victory Monument is admired only because of its shapely rear and a lowly street vendor tells tall tales of having been invited into the Grand Hotel suite of a visiting emir's 30 concubines. Ciccio Ingrassia played Teo, Titta's mad uncle, who on a family outing climbs a tree and demands, 'I want a woman', until he's coxed down by a midget nun. Such grotesque comedy is undercut by the death of Titta's mother during the winter and the undercurrent of fascist oppression. Most of the town are party members, but Aurelio is a Socialist and is tortured by being forced to drink castor oil. The film ends with Gradisca finding love and marrying Matteo, a policeman ('her Gary Cooper'). The Fairy Fluff blows in and life goes on in the sunny seaside town. *Amarcord* deservedly won Best Foreign Language Film at the 1974 Oscars.

Giuseppe Tornatore's **Cinema paradiso** (1988) – another Best Foreign Film Oscar winner – nostalgically harked back to the cinema of youth, in much the same way that Fellini distilled his Rimini past, through the relationship between Sicilian projectionist Alfredo (Philippe Noiret) and young Salvatore Di Vita called 'Toto' (Salvatore Cascio) and their shared love of cinema. They watch John Wayne in *Stagecoach* (1939), Kirk Douglas in Mario Camerini's early peplum *Ulysses* (1954), Silvana Mangano, Vittorio Gassman, and comedian Totò on the flickering silver screen. This sentimental story, with its wonderful, bittersweet Morricone score, is essentially 'Fellini-Lite' aimed squarely at an international audience.

The Outsiders: Visconti, Delon, Bellocchio and Pasolini

In contrast to Fellini's Rimini reminiscences, filmmakers such as Luchino Visconti, Marco Bellocchio and Pier Paolo Pasolini depicted a different Italy, an Italy riven with alienation, poverty and violence. Visconti first made his mark with a neorealist portrait of Sicilian fishermen, *La terra trema* (1948 – *The Earth Trembles*). Visconti's *Rocco and his Brothers* (1960) was based on Giovanni

Testori's novel *The Bridge of Ghisolfa*. It depicts the five Parondi brothers and their widowed mother Rosaria (Katina Paxinou), who move from Sicily to Milan. Two of the brothers, Rocco (Alain Delon) and Simone (Renato Salvatori), share a lover, prostitute Nadia (Annie Girardot), who Simone brutally stabs to death. The supporting cast included Paolo Stoppa, Roger Hanin and Claudia Cardinale. Nino Rota supplied the score to this controversial epic drama, which was photographed in monochrome by Giuseppe Rotunno.

Often seen by critics as a pretty boy pin-up rather than an actor, Alain Delon was cast in some of the finest European films of the 1960s, including *Rocco*, *The Eclipse*, *The Leopard* and *Le Samouraï*. In René Clément's **Purple Noon** (1960 – *Plein Soleil*, *Lust for Evil* and *Blazing Sun*) – an Italian-shot adaptation of Patricia Highsmith's 1955 murder mystery *The Talented Mr Ripley* – Delon played Tom Ripley. In Rome, Tom befriends Philippe Greenleaf (Maurice Ronet) and his fiancée, Marge (Marie Laforet). As they cruise around the Tyrrhenian Sea, Tom causes friction and Marge disembarks on Taormina, Sicily. Tom knifes Philippe, trusses him up with cable, weighs him down with an anchor and throws him overboard. Tom impersonates Philippe and sends letters to Marge, making it appear their affair is over. Philippe's American friend Freddy Miles (Bill Kearns) arrives in Rome and finds Tom impersonating Philippe: when a landlady addresses Tom as 'Greenleaf', Tom kills Freddy. Inspector Riccordi (Erno Crisa) suspects missing Philippe of the murder. In Mongibello, Sicily, Tom engineers Philippe's suicide: Philippe has conveniently 'bequeathed' his entire fortune to Marge, whom Tom now plans to seduce.

Clément's film is a Hitchcockian blend of suspense, romance and murder. The animated title sequence – with tinted travelogue shots of Rome and a dramatic score by Nino Rota (billed as 'Rotta') – establishes an intensity in imitation of Hitchcock. The Italian locations were photographed in Eastmancolor by Henri Decaë. *Purple Noon* was filmed in Rome (the Colosseum, the Piazza Del Popolo and Piazza Navona), with footage lensed in the Bay of Naples, in the 'old town' of Naples itself, on Ischia and the waterfront of Procida, with its quaint harbour and pastel buildings. Much of the action was set in Sicily, at Mongibello (the Italian name for Mount Etna) and Taormina. The azure blue of the Tyrrhenian Sea contrasts with the sleek yacht, also called *Marge*. As the yacht is dry-docked in the harbour, *Marge* tows in one final secret. Dapper Delon is convincing as the cold-hearted, calculating double-murderer. Tom's a weakling, both physically and mentally, and a fantasist, living a lie and thriving on deception and forgery. Philippe picks on Tom during the cruise and maroons him in a dinghy for several hours in the hot sun, causing Tom's back to become badly burnt. When Tom impersonates Philippe, Clément peels away the blistered layers of Tom's 'sunburn', until the impostor and murderer is revealed.

Writer-director Marco Bellocchio's debut, **Fists in the Pocket** (1965 – *Fist in His Pocket* in the US), depicted a dysfunctional family in a secluded provincial villa in the mountains: brothers Augusto (Marino Masé), Alessandro ('Sandro', played by Lou Castel) and Leone (Pier Luigi Troglio), their sister Giulia (Paola Pitagora) and their blind mother (Liliana Gerace). Alessandro, Leone and Giulia are epileptic, and Giulia incestuously loves Alessandro and Augusto, the family's sole breadwinner. Alessandro, an indolent, childlike misfit, plots to free Augusto of his hideous relatives. He resolves to kill the rest of the family, so that Augusto can move into town with his lover, Lucia (Jennie MacNeil).

The film is filled with beautiful, disturbing imagery – funerals, snowfall, bonfires and familial quarrelling – creating a strange mix of drama, horror and even black humour. Alessandro lies that he has passed his driving test – he plans to drive the entire family off a cliff on their way to the cemetery to visit their father's grave but becomes distracted and forgets to. When Alessandro attempts to start a chinchilla-breeding business, he needs 3 million lire to bankroll the project – exactly the amount they spend each year to care for their mother. Alessandro pushes his mother off a cliff and then drowns Leone in the bath, which results in Giulia falling down the stairs, leaving her injured but alive. When Alessandro suffers an epileptic seizure, thrashing like a speared fish, recuperating Giulia doesn't rise to help him even though she is able. Castel is excellent as Sandro, an angry young man, his fists clenched in his pocket. Giulia has a postcard of Marlon Brando on her bedstead and intense Castel resembles Brando's petulant little brother. It's a mesmerising performance by the 23-year-old. In an unsettling scene, Alessandro reads the newspaper to his mother, eventually abandoning the real headlines and concocting his own: 'Premeditated matricide', he intones, 'Son kills mother. She forced him to take a bath'. 'That sounds good', his mother enthuses. Alessandro continues, 'Husband and wife pensioners gas themselves. He was 68, she was 53'. 'My age', notes mother, 'Isn't there any cheerful news?' Shot in bleak monochrome by Alberto Marrama, *Fists in the Pocket* anticipates the giallo cycle of psycho thrillers. This resemblance is accentuated by Ennio Morricone's avant-garde score, a dissonant music box of tolling bells, wailing soprano and eerily beautiful strings.

In 'The Witch Burned Alive', Luchino Visconti's segment of the five-part film **The Witches** (1966), superstar actress Gloria (Silvana Mangano), who is apparently on the brink of a nervous breakdown, arrives at an alpine chalet in Kitzbühel, to stay with her friend Valeria (Annie Girardot). Gloria is the centre of attention with the chalet's male guests, but when she faints jealous women guests unmask her – removing her false eyelashes, her gold, Cleopatra-like headdress and her taped eye-slanters – revealing Gloria's beauty to be false. Gloria discovers that she is pregnant but Antonio, her producer husband, on the phone from New York, suggests an abortion. The photograph of 'Antonio' beside Gloria's bed is Mangano's husband, producer Dino De Laurentiis. Paparazzi gather and Gloria appears on the verge of collapse, until a mysterious helicopter arrives with stylists on board. They prepare Gloria to face the press's flash bulbs, cloaking her in a hooded leopardskin coat and shades, before whisking her away. 'The Witch Burned Alive' deals with the fragility of stardom and its psychological pressures.

Accattone (1961), novelist and poet Pier Paolo Pasolini's directorial debut, starred Franco Citti as Vittorio Accattone, a petty criminal and pimp in Rome's slums. Silvia Corsini played his prostitute earner, Maddalena. It was based on Pasolini's novel of the same name and shocked audiences in Italy with its realism. In one scene, Vittorio steals from his own son to buy shoes for his lover Stella (Franca Pasut). Citti was excellent as the hard-faced 'accattone' [beggar or scrounger]. Bernardo Bertolucci was the assistant director, Tonino Delli Colli photographed the film in grimy sunlit monochrome and the music was the serene 'Matthew's Passion' by Bach (as orchestrated by Carlo Rustichelli). Pasolini remained in this slum netherworld for *Mamma Roma* (1962), which cast Anna Magnani in the title role, another prostitute, and Ettore Garofalo as her son, Ettore. Delli Colli again provided the gritty monochrome cinematography and Rustichelli penned the score.

Theorem (1968) – a hybrid of Pasolini's slum fairytales and the religious and mythical themes he'd explored in *The Gospel according to St Matthew* and *Oedipus Rex* – depicts the empty lives of a bourgeois Milanese family: Paolo (Massimo Girotti), a factory owner, his wife, Lucia (Silvana Mangano), their children Odetta (Anne Wiazemsky) and Pietro (Andres Jose Cruz Soublette) and maid Emilia (Laura Betti). They are visited by a mysterious houseguest (Terence Stamp), who seduces each of them, beginning with Emilia. On his departure, the family is destroyed. Odetta become catatonic, baffling doctors, and is taken away to an institution. Pietro, an artist, hates his work and urinates over his canvasses. Lucia drives the city streets in her Mini, searching for her lost lover through casual sex. Paolo strips himself of his assets (including his factory) and disrobes on the platform of Milan station. He wanders, morally and financially bankrupt, naked and screaming, through a smoking desert wilderness. Only Emilia benefits from her contact with their visitor. She returns to her village where she becomes a nettle-eating rural saint, performing healing miracles for the locals. She levitates above the village and is buried alive on a building site, her tears forming a puddle which becomes a holy water spring.

Theorem was lensed in spring 1968 on location in Lombardia, in Milan, and at Elios Studios by Giuseppe Ruzzolini. Pasolini deployed Mozart – the 'Requiem' performed by the Russian Academy Chorus and the Moscow Philharmonic – and cues by Ennio Morricone. Pasolini published a novelisation of the film prior to its release. When *Theorem* premiered at the 29th Venice Film Festival in September 1968, Betti won Best Actress for her role. As Pasolini's angelic visitor, Stamp appeared naked in the first instance of full-frontal male nudity in mainstream cinema. *Theorem* was confiscated and Pasolini was tried for obscenity in November 1968 in Venice but was acquitted.

Pasolini enjoyed his greatest commercial successes in Italy with his medieval 'Trilogy of Life'. All were produced by Alberto Grimaldi's PEA, featured costumes designed by Danilo Donati and were scored by Pasolini and Morricone. ***The Decameron*** (1970) was adapted from Giovanni Boccaccio's stories. Pasolini appeared as the artist Giotto, who is seen on a scaffolding painting a church fresco. The most effective tale is one which also inspired poet John Keats's 'Isabella: or The Pot of Basil'. Isabella discovers her dead lover concealed in a shallow woodland grave (buried by her murderous brothers) and beheads the corpse, planting the head in a basil pot. Pasolini's other episodes feature oversexed nuns, clandestine sex, serenades and weddings. Tonino Delli Colli lensed the film on beautiful locations across Italy. Copious onscreen nudity (and the scandal it caused) plus the great production design ensured its colossal success in Italy, inspiring many bogus sequels including *Decameroticus* (1972). As Enzo Siciliano put it, 'Art triumphed over pornography'. In the finale – a depiction of Heaven and Hell in a quarry – Silvana Mangano appeared briefly as the giant Madonna presiding over the anarchic scene, as the naked damned are thrown into Hell.

Based on the writings of Geoffrey Chaucer, **The Canterbury Tales** (1971) was shot in England with an Italo-British cast. Pasolini, his cinematographer Delli Colli and costumier Donati created a memorable 'Olde Englande' (of half-timbered buildings, shacks, gothic churches and taverns) filmed in authentic settings – Cambridge, Bath, Canterbury, Chipping Campden, Warwick, Rye, Maidstone, Rolvenden, Laverham, Wells and Hastings (the ruins of Battle Abbey). There were featured roles for Laura Betti and Franco Citti, and Hugh Griffith, Josephine Chaplin, Michael Balfour and Jenny Runacre also appeared. Ninetto Davoli played a Chaplinesque rogue in a comedy segment. The film also features future *Doctor Who* Tom Baker in the nude and Robin Asquith (later of the UK 'Confessions' sex comedies) urinating on ale house patrons from a balcony. Pasolini played Chaucer, working at his ornate writing desk. Characters are executed and blinded; one has a red hot poker shoved up his backside. In the film's most controversial scene, Pasolini staged a visit to Hell, filmed on grey, misty Mount Etna, among gibbets and other torturous ephemera. Hideous winged demons torture the naked souls, as Morricone's tolling bells and church organ mingle with the screams of purgatory. There was copious nudity and the film's massive success in Italy inspired several rip-offs, including *More Sexy Tales from Canterbury*, *The Other Canterbury Tales* and *The Lusty Wives of Canterbury* (all 1972).

Pasolini's **Arabian Nights** (1973) was more exotically erotic than its predecessors. It was photographed by Giuseppe Ruzzolini in Ethiopia, Yemen, Iran and Nepal. The loose story features Ines Pelligrini as a slave girl who impersonates a man and is crowned 'king'. Davoli and Citti both appeared, the latter as a red-haired flying wizard who turns a man into a chimpanzee. The chimp is then made king when people see that the animal can write. There's a beautiful harp and strings theme from Morricone which accompanies Pasolini's tales of love, magical illusion, shipwrecks, desert caravans, betrayal and sex. *Arabian Nights* is easily the most sexually explicit of the trilogy and most of the 'One Thousand and One Nights' seem to have been spent fornicating. Pasolini made only one more film, the outrageous, repulsive *Salo, or the 120 Days of Sodom* (1975), before his untimely death, aged 53. He was battered to death by a male prostitute in November 1975 near the seaside at Ostia.

Morto All'Italiana

Often a pessimistic, visionary director, Luchino Visconti surpassed himself with **Death in Venice** (1971), his adaptation of Thomas Mann's 1912 German novella, which recounted the death of an artist (in the book a novelist, in the film a composer). Professor Gustav Von Aschenbach (Dirk Bogarde), a composer and conductor based on Austrian Gustav Mahler, arrives in Venice to convalesce following a breakdown. He stays at the Grand Hotel De Bains on the Lido and spends his days on the beach, observing life. He becomes distracted and then transfixed and obsessed by one of the young guests, Tadzio (Bjorn Andresen), a handsome blond Polish teenager on vacation with his mother, Mrs Mause (Silvana Mangano), his three sisters and their governess (Nora Ricci). Tadzio seems to reciprocate Gustav's interest, with lingering glances and provocative behaviour, but they are destined to remain apart. Venice isn't the haven Gustav had hoped it to be, as the city is wracked by a cholera epidemic.

Death in Venice is the kind of movie Visconti excels at – a slow-paced 'art film' with sumptuous, authentic period production design and a great score. Piero Tosi designed the film's costumes and Ferdinando Scarfiotti was the art director. Visconti used Mahler's Third and Fifth Symphonies, played by the National Academy Orchestra of Santa Cecilia conducted by Franco Mannino and featuring alto soloist Lucrezia West. These looming compositions, epically mournful, aptly complement Pasqualino De Santis' Panavision cinematography. Interiors were filmed at Cinecittà, with the steamer wharf, the lagoon, the beach and the street scenes lensed in Venice. As the plague spreads, the streets are sluiced with reeking white disinfectant, decontamination fires burn and the once-beautiful city resembles a slum – Visconti also depicts the 'Death of Venice'.

Visconti intercuts flashbacks to Gustav's life in Munich – intellectual theorising and arguments with his colleague Alfred (Mark Burns); the death of his daughter; the disastrous booing and catcalling reception to his latest work; Gustav's relationship with his wife (Marisa Berensen); and his clandestine visits to prostitute Esmeralda (Carole Andre). *Death in Venice* is a stately work of art, rather like one of Mahler's compositions. Bogarde is brilliantly cast as Gustav. Bogarde's finely observed details of the frustrated composer, which were shaped by Visconti, add to his interpretation. Gustav arrives in Venice confronted by his own mortality and feels displaced among the bourgeois hotel patrons. He's never satisfied, which aggravates the polite hotel manager (Romolo Valli). Gustav visits a barber, who transforms him – he dyes Gustav's hair and eyebrows black, trims his moustache, and applies thick white foundation and red lipstick. This façade becomes Gustav's death mask. Perhaps the loneliest protagonist in Italian cinema, Gustav sits on the beach in a deckchair in the burnished evening sun and watches Tadzio – his unattainable love – at the dappled water's edge. Hair dye begins to trickle down Gustav's cheek, a black tear. He slips away and slumps in his seat, as Mahler's music movingly underscores the scene. Art remains but death comes to us all.

Chapter Seven

Shoot, Gringo...Shoot!
Italian Westerns

Of all the Italian film crazes, 'spaghetti' westerns are the most famous, influential and continually popular in cult circles. During each Italian genre cycle, sets and locations were redressed and reused from film to film – this is in addition to the recycling of plots, costumes and actors. Spaghetti westerns demonstrate this endless mix-and-match more than any other Italian genre and also created their own roster of heroes, with Django, Ringo, Sartana, Sabata and Trinity the most popular. The genre's production design is one of its major advantages and spaghetti westerns were predominantly shot in Italy and Spain. The Italian locations are often betrayed by the distinctive, spear-like Italian Cypress trees – fine for pepla, not so good for westerns – and the green pastures of Lazio often looked more like Wales than the American southwest, but the arid Spanish landscapes around Madrid and in Almeria convincingly resembled the Tex-Mex borderlands.

The Far West, Italian Style

Ricardo Blasco's ***Duello nel Texas*** (1963) was a popular early entry, with Richard Harrison avenging his father's death at the hands of three gold-hungry killers (Giacomo Rossi-Stuart, Barta Barry and Aldo Sambrell). It was released as *Gringo* in Spain, *Gunfight at Red Sands* in the US and *Gunfight in the Red Sands* in the UK. The UK and US versions have different dubbing tracks and scripts, and the music was by a young composer named 'Dan Savio' (Ennio Morricone).

Most of the early Italian westerns were 'Cowboy and Indian' adventures. ***Buffalo Bill, Hero of the Far West*** (1964) is an archetypal example, lumbering under the twin influences of pepla and Hollywood westerns. Mario Costa directed as 'John W. Fordson'. Gordon Scott starred as Colonel Bill Cody, 'The Paleface Buffalo Hunter', who is sent to Fort Adams in Indian Creek Territory to quell a Sioux uprising. Cody discovers that Gold Dust Saloon proprietor Jack

Monroe (Jan Hendriks), his sidekick Red (Piero Lulli) and emporium owner Big Sam (Mario Brega) are selling renegade Yellow Hand (Mirko Ellis) Winchester repeaters and hard liquor. Love story subplots involve Cody's affair with Sioux maiden Silver Moon Ray (Catherine Ribeiro), and Captain George Hunter (Hans Von Borsody) courts the colonel's daughter Mary (Ingeborg Schöner). Ugo Sasso played Cody's scout, Snack, and Carlo Rustichelli's score trotted out traditional western cues. As telegraphed by the casting of muscleman Scott, Cody often indulges in wrestling and fisticuffs, shredding his costume. The film was shot in Italy and Spain. The Monte Gelato waterfalls was Yellow Hand's camp, Cody plummets off the Marmore Falls in Umbria, the gorge at Tolfa was used for an ambush, the Grotte Di Salone became a disused mine, and US Fort Adams was a set in Lazio. The town of Indian Creek was a western set at Elios Film Studios, Rome. There are also several scenes filmed in the vicinity of Manzanares El Real, near Madrid, including the mountainous rock formations at La Pedriza (as the Sioux's Sacred Mountain) and the picturesque Santillana Reservoir.

Joaquin Romero Marchent's **Seven Hours of Gunfire** (1965) cast Rik Van Nutter as Buffalo Bill. Nutter appeared under the pseudonym 'Clyde Rogers'. Adrian Hoven played drunken brawler Wild Bill Hickok who works for the 'Poney Express', Gloria Milland was feisty Calamity Jane and Elga Sommerfeld was Ethel – the daughter of missionary Padre Norman (Paco Sanz) – who falls for Cody. The plot tells of how Cody and Hickok, with help from Frank North (Mariano Vidal Molina), the white chief of the Pawnee, foils a band of gun traffickers trading with Red Cloud's on-the-warpath Sioux. *Seven Hours* opens with a patriotic march from Angelo Francesco Lavagnino and an introductory scrawl praises the heroes: 'To them and all those who, like them, made the young American Nation great, this film is dedicated'. This is comic strip American history, with real events and characters blended into a largely fictitious 'greatest hits' biopic in the manner of Cecil B. De Mille's *The Plainsman* (1936). The film was shot in the vicinity of Madrid, including a western town set at Colmenar Viejo, a US Cavalry stockade (Fort Fletcher), La Pedriza (the half-built settlement of Leavensworth) and Golden City, a wild west town at Hojo De Manzanares (as the town of Custer). The arms peddlers were played by Lorenzo Robledo (Charlie), Alvaro De Luna (Utter) and Antonio Molino Rojo (their boss, Mr Deedle), while Alfonso Rojas played the commander of Fort Fletcher and Raf Baldassarre was the padre's Sioux companion, William. The film's colourful western outfits resemble a children's dressing up box: Buffalo Bill wears fringed buckskins, a red neckerchief, black hat and knee-high buckled boots, which is complete historical fiction but looks great.

Pistols and Fistfuls: Eastwood and Leone

In 1964, two westerns were shot back-to-back in Spain, on many of the same locations, using some of the same crew – *Pistols Don't Argue* and *A Fistful of Dollars*. Jolly Film (Italy) and Constantin (West Germany) co-produced both films – with Ocean Film as the Spanish backers of *Fistful* and Trio Film owning the Spanish interest in *Pistols*. Both films cast six-feet four-inch stars as their heroes, though their heights were where any similarity ended, as the stars were at opposite ends of their careers. *Pistols* headlined 54-year-old Canadian cowboy star Rod Cameron, famous in 1960 for divorcing his wife to marry her mother, while *Fistful* cast 33-year-old Californian Clint Eastwood, then a co-star in US western TV series *Rawhide*.

Mario Caiano's **Pistols Don't Argue** (or *Bullets Don't Argue*) cast Cameron as Sheriff Pat Garrett of Rivertown. On Garrett's wedding day the Clanton brothers – Bible-reading Billy (Horst Frank) and easily-led George (Angel Aranda) – clean out the Rivertown bank of $30,000 and head for Mexico, so Garrett spends his honeymoon tracking them down. He apprehends them in the town of Corona and brings them back across Devil's Valley. They are tracked by a band of Mexican bandits led by Santero (Mimmo Palmera) – there may be no Indians in this movie, but the US Cavalry still arrive to save the day. Caiano filmed his western north of Madrid: Rivertown was the Golden City set. The Colmenar Viejo set appeared as a ghost town and the Rio Grande was the river Alberche at Aldea Del Fresno. Further scenes were filmed in Almeria, southern Spain – Lucainena De La Torres played the Mexican pueblo of Corona. The mountainous Sierra Alhamilla (with its Aztec-like 'Balneario' structure) appeared, as did the sand dunes at Cabo De Gata as Devil's Valley. Jose Manuel Martin played Santero's lieutenant Miguel. Perhaps the most significant aspect of this rather ordinary western was the score by 'Savio'/Morricone. The film begins with 'Lonesome Billy' (a loping traditional ballad crooned by Peter Tevis) and includes a riding theme, with a French horn carrying the simple melody backed by incessant syncopated strings. This piece enjoyed particular longevity, reappearing uncredited in many westerns including *Seven Women for the MacGregors* and *Viva Django!*

Morricone also worked on Sergio Leone's **A Fistful of Dollars**, but their collaboration was a major departure for western film music. Leone and Morricone had attended school together and their rapport led to one of the most significant director-composer collaborations in cinema. For *Fistful*, Morricone composed a distinctive whistled theme tune (performed by Alessandro Alessandroni) which became as renowned as the film itself. *Fistful* was Leone's remake of Akira Kurosawa's *Yojimbo* (1961). In *Fistful* Clint Eastwood played gringo 'The Man With No Name' who drifts into the Mexican border town of San Miguel. The town is home to two squabbling gangs: the gringo Baxters and Mexican Rojos, who run guns and liquor to Indians across the frontier. The stranger sets the two gangs at each other's throats – working as a hired gun for the Rojos, then the Baxters – until both clans reside in Boot Hill and San Miguel is peaceful once more.

Leone used Golden City as San Miguel and staged a massacre beside the river at Aldea Del Fresno. *Fistful*'s desert and pueblo scenes were filmed in

Original US poster artwork for Sergio Leone's *A Fistful of Dollars* (1964) introduced Clint Eastwood's Man With No Name and a new style of western to filmgoers. Poster courtesy Ian Caunce Collection.

Almeria, at El Sotillo near San Jose, and in the village of Los Albaricoques. The Techniscope cinematography by Massimo Dallamano captured these locations in vivid Technicolor and the film resembled a comic book western, with the beatings and gunplay heavily stylised. Eastwood, cloaked in mystique, swathed in a Mexican poncho and scowling over a cheroot, was ideal as the brutal anti-hero. In the finale he goads bandit chief Ramon Rojo (Gian Maria Volonté) to 'aim for the heart' but wins the duel by cheating – he's wearing an improvised bulletproof vest under his poncho. In the Italian print, Eastwood's voice was dubbed by Enrico Maria Salerno, who had also dubbed Enrique Irazoqui in Pasolini's *The Gospel According to St Matthew*. In Italy the avenging 'Man With No Name' had the same voice as Jesus.

In 1964 *Fistful* was the highest-grossing film ever released in Italy, making Eastwood a star. Leone's sequel ***For a Few Dollars More*** (1965) again teamed him with Morricone and Dallamano. Eastwood returned as the hero, now named Manco, who joins forces with Colonel Douglas Mortimer (Lee Van Cleef), a heavily armed bounty hunter. They are on the trail of El Indio (Volonté) and his bank-robbing bandits, who steal the El Paso safe which is disguised as a drinks cabinet. *For a Few* was an Italian-Spanish-West German co-production, shot in Almeria and Madrid, with interiors at Cinecittà. El Paso was a set built for the film near Tabernas in Almeria – it's still open to tourists as 'Mini Hollywood'.

For a Few provides an interesting demonstration of how these multinational westerns were shot. Lensed between April and July 1965, *For a Few* was filmed with no sound, so that the international cast could speak their lines with ease in their own language. In addition to English-speaking Eastwood and Van Cleef, there were Austrian Josef Egger, Germans Klaus Kinski, Werner Abrolat, Mara Krup and Kurt Zipps, Italians Mario Brega, Roberto Camardiel, Luigi Pistilli and Benito Stefanelli, Spaniards Aldo Sambrell, Jesus Guzman, Riccardo Palacios and Antonio Ruiz, and Greek Panos Papadopoulos – playing everything from put-upon hoteliers and carpetbaggers, to corrupt sheriffs and quick-tempered hunchbacks. This way of filming allowed five different prints of the film to be prepared in the dubbing studio – English, French, Spanish, German and Italian – with the film's title sequence and publicity showcasing different actors for different markets. Morricone began to expand on his style, mixing usual sound effects (twangs and whistles) with direct melodic 'quotes' from classical pieces by Beethoven, Bach and Wagner.

For a Few wasn't particularly well received by international critics. 'From the first whining bullet to the last this film is a prodigious, straight-faced hoax', wrote Penelope Mortimer in the *Observer*, which was typical of the film's reception. It was the highest-grossing film in Italy in 1965 and propelled Van Cleef to stardom. United Artists were so impressed with Leone's two westerns that they bought the rights to distribute them internationally and both were substantial hits. Two of Van Cleef's subsequent successes – Giulio Petroni's *Death Rides a Horse* and Tonino Valerii's *Day of Anger* (both 1967) – cast him opposite young gunmen (John Phillip Law and Giuliano Gemma respectively), who learn from old master Van Cleef.

By the time Leone directed **The Good, the Bad and the Ugly** (1966), he attracted a co-production deal with United Artists and Alberto Grimaldi's PEA, who each provided half the $1.2 million budget. It would be easily spent, as Leone planned an epic story of the American Civil War, with the three title characters seeking a cashbox of stolen gold as Union and Confederate forces wrestle for control of New Mexico. Eastwood played The Good, a bounty hunter named Blondy, Van Cleef was The Bad, an icy-eyed hired killer called Angel Eyes, and Eli Wallach was The Ugly, raucous Mexican bandit Tuco Ramirez. Leone filmed their adventures in locations scattered across Italy and Spain, including the Almerian desert, at Manzanares El Real near Madrid, and in the lush greenery and impressive rolling hill country in Castilla-León, between Madrid and Burgos. Town sets at Elios Studios, Colmenar Viejo and Tabernas played Leone's desolate, clapboard settlements, ravaged by war and deprivation. The sand dunes at Cabo De Gata in desiccated Almeria were the baking Jornada Del Muerto (the 'Day's Journey of the Dead Man'); the Union railroad was the Almeria-Guadix line; and a mission hospital run by monks at San Antonio was filmed at Cortijo De Los Frailes in Almeria and inside the Monastery of San Pedro de Arlanza, north of Madrid.

The Good, the Bad and the Ugly is an imaginative, comic book historical adventure which has become one of the world's most popular westerns. Morricone's one-off theme tune – a howling, panicked coyote caught in a cavalry charge – would have assured the film cult status, but the unholy trinity of Eastwood, Van Cleef and Wallach are formidable antagonists. In addition to Morricone's trademark whistles, he also composed elegiac cues for the Civil War scenes. In a Union prison camp, Confederate inmates are beaten and robbed – there's no honour in defeat, but an unequivocal, Romanesque to the victor the spoils. The final three-way shootout, in the centre of a sprawling circular cemetery at Sad Hill ringed by hundreds of war graves, is gladiatorial spectacle relocated to the Civil War west. Leone studied archives of war photographs and his anarchic adventurers' escapades unfold in an authentic representation of the period, with the Spanish army dressed as Yankees and Johnny Rebs. Leone's attention to detail in his depiction of historical period has much in common with meticulous Italian filmmakers such as Visconti (*The Leopard*) and Pasolini (*The Gospel According to St Matthew*). Carlo Simi designed *The Good*'s sets and costumes, as he had on the previous 'Dollars' films.

The supporting cast included Luigi Pistilli (Tuco's brother, friar Pablo), Mario Brega (Unionist corporal Wallace), Chelo Alonso (a Mexican peasant) and Rada Rassimov (prostitute Maria), with stuntmen Romano Puppo, Benito Stefanelli, Lorenzo Robledo, Frank Braña and Aldo Sambrell as heavies. Leone's visual style – the huge close-ups, the long duels, the milieu of dust and sun – reached its apogee here, as his iconic gunslingers fought to the last man in an unforgiving land-without-hope. Tonino Delli Colli's Technicolor cinematography (in widescreen Techniscope) reduced figures to tiny flyspecks in these vast desert vistas, as the long and level sands stretched far away. 'Il deserto', the echoing, bone-dry landscape of Leone's westerns – where even the trees seem to be clinging onto life – has never looked more magnificent and fills the screen with its emptiness. It was the most successful film in Italy in 1966, outgrossing De Laurentiis' megahit *The Bible... in the Beginning* and was also a smash internationally when released in 1968.

Stranger and Stranger

Eastwood's 'Man With No Name' stranger spawned many imitators. Enterprising Italian companies attempted to release old episodes of *Rawhide* on an unsuspecting public as new Eastwood vehicles titled *Il magnifico straniero*, *El maladetto gringo* and *El gringhero*. Mickey Hargitay starred as Mike Jordan in Sergio Bergonzelli's **A Stranger in Sacramento** (1965). Jordan's father and brothers are murdered and their cattle rustled by Barnett (Mario Lanfranchi). The film resembles a Hollywood western, even down to its chequered-shirt costuming for the cowboys. Sacramento was the Elios western set and the Lazio landscape around Manziana stood in for California. Muscleman Hargitay predictably loses his shirt (he makes it into hoof-mufflers for his horse), villain Barnett has an artificial, leather-gloved hand and the film features some genuinely disconcerting moments, as when Jordan and a posse search for the buried bodies of his siblings and unearth the corpse of a cow.

The 'Stranger' films starring Tony Anthony demonstrate how a western formula could mutate from something reasonably close to its inspiration, to something outlandishly dislocated. Luigi Vanzi's **A Stranger in Town** (1967 – *For a Dollar in the Teeth*) was an Italian-US remake of *Fistful*. A poncho-clad Stranger (Anthony) arrives in the Mexican border town of Cerro Gordo (Cinecittà's western set) and helps Mexican bandit Aguila (Frank Wolff) to steal a shipment of US army gold. Aguila refuses to pay the Stranger his share, so he steals it all. Brief sojourns into the Mexican desert were filmed in a Lazio quarry and the film's stumbling block is its interminable noodling guitar score by Benedetto Ghiglia. It was a big hit in US drive-ins and made Anthony a minor star.

The Stranger Returns (1967 – *A Man, A Horse, A Gun* and *Shoot First, Laugh Last*) had outlaw gang 'The Treasure of the Border' led by En Plein (Dan Vadis) steal a solid gold stagecoach worth $200,000 and hide out in Santo Spirito (Elios Studio's Mexican set). The Stranger, with help from the Prophet (Marco Gugliemi), wipes out the bandits with his four-barrelled sawn-off shotgun at can't-miss, point-blank range. Ettore Manni played US army lieutenant Stafford. Stelvio Cipriani's score (much recycled in later westerns) drives the film along with bells, flutes, electric guitar licks, trumpet flourishes and agonising screams. Anthony's Eastwood homage is acknowledged onscreen: having passed himself of as 'Postal Inspector Ross' to the US army, the Stranger notes, 'In this day and age, everybody's walking around trying to be somebody else'.

Vanzi's *The Silent Stranger* (1968 – *The Stranger in Japan*) was a west-goes-eastern, which transported the Stranger to Japan into a *Yojimbo*-style scenario. In Ferdinando Baldi's **Get Mean** (1976) the Stranger is hired to escort Princess Elizabeth Maria De Burgos (Diana Lorys) to her homeland of Spain. The film was shot amid the beautiful castles of Granada, the rock formations at La Pedriza and Cuidad Encantada, and the dunes and beach at Cabo Da Gata. An impressive set in the Almerian desert (Fortress El Condor) was used as the Fortress of Rodrigo and Bixio-Frizzi-Tempera provided the catchy score. *Get Mean* is another reworking of *Fistful*, with Spain engulfed in a civil war between Princess Maria's turbaned Moors and the Barbarian invaders (whose horned helmets, crazy beards, moustaches and pigtails resemble Vikings). Who cares if Granada, the Moors' last refuge in Spain, fell in 1492? The Stranger's nemeses are barbarian chief Diego (Raf Baldassarre) – who the Stranger kills by dropping scorpions down his armour – and hunchbacked, Richard III-lookalike Sombra (Lloyd Battista, who co-scripted the movie). The Stranger arrives for the final showdown at Fortress Rodrigo armed to the teeth, draped in dynamite and packing bow and arrow, a six-shooter and a four-barrelled shotgun, to face Sombra, who deploys a revolving cannon. *Get Mean* is the epitome of Italian cult cinema, a wildly imaginative blend of unrelated genres which curdle onscreen to entertaining effect.

They Called Him Ringo

Competing with Eastwood and Van Cleef at the Italian box office as top draw was Giuliano Gemma. In his western breakthrough, Duccio Tessari's **A Pistol for Ringo** (1965), Gemma (billed as 'Montgomery Wood') played mercenary gunman Ringo, known as 'Angel Face'. Following a hold-up of the Quemado bank during Christmas 1894, Mexican bandit Sancho (Fernando Sancho) and his gang hide out at the ranch of Major Clyde (Antonio Casas), a Texan aristocrat, and his daughter, Ruby (Tessari's wife, Lorella De Luca). Ruby's fiancé, Sheriff Ben (George Martin), lays siege to the ranch and sends in Ringo to free the captives. Gemma gives his best western performance as the cocky gunfighter and the supporting cast includes Jose Manuel Martin as Sancho's lieutenant Pedro, Nieves Navarro as Sancho's lover, *bandida* Dolores, and Pajarito as deputy Tim. Major Clyde's ranch was filmed at a *finca* (country house) nestled in the valley at El Romeral in Almeria. The pueblo of San Jose, where Ringo guns down the Benson brothers was filmed in the Almerian town of San Jose. Quemado was 'Esplugas City', the PC Balcazar Studios' western set called Esplugas De Llobregat, near Barcelona. Morricone's scoring is traditional, with the lilting title song, 'Angel Face', sung in wholesome fashion by Maurizio Graf. Incidental cues incorporated the carol 'Silent Night' and the galloping 'Messico Eroica' recalled the horn theme from *Pistols Don't Argue*. *A Pistol for Ringo* was a smash in Italy and the song 'Angel Face' went to number one in the Italian charts.

It didn't take long for the Ringo imitations to surface, with Alberto De Martino's **$100,000 for Ringo** quickest on the draw, though Richard Harrison's

Italian poster artwork for Duccio Tessari's *A Pistol for Ringo* (1965) starring Giuliano Gemma as the wisecracking gunslinger 'Angel Face'. Poster courtesy Ian Caunce Collection.

hero wasn't actually called Ringo. Returning from the Civil War to the town of Rainbow Valley, Lee Burton (Harrison) is mistaken for Ward Kluster. Kluster's wife, Rose (Monica Randall), has been killed by landgrabber Tom Cherry (Gerard Tichy) and Kluster's son, Sean (Loris Loddi), has been raised by Apaches. Cherry is smuggling guns to the Mexican army for $200,000. At a rendezvous at the church of Todo Santos, Ringo, with help from bounty hunter Chuck (Fernando Sancho), routs the soldiers and discovers the money concealed in a bell tower. *$100,000 for Ringo*, like *The Texican*, *A Dollar of Fire* and *Five Dollars for Ringo* (all 1966), is an archetypal Barcelona-shot 'Buttifarra' (Catalan sausage) western. Rainbow Valley was the Esplugas City western set and desert location footage was shot at Fraga and Candasnos, Huesca (in Aragon) and Castelldefels (in Catalonia) near Barcelona, amid the ziggurat-type hills. The film benefits from a Bruno Nicolai score and the title song, 'Ringo Came to Fight', is sung in an Elvis quiver by Bobby Solo. Rafael Albacin played Apache chief Grey Bear, Luis Induni portrayed Rainbow Valley's ineffectual sheriff, Massimo Serato (under the dynamic pseudonym 'John Barracuda') played Ives, a redeemed drunk, and Eleonora Bianchi was his tolerant lover, Deborah. The film opens with a violent surprise: Rose, her baby son in a papoose, is cornered by a band of Apaches. Cherry guns down her assailants and then skewers her with a war lance. *$100,000 for Ringo* throws everything at the audience, but its combination of Ringo, Indians, bounty hunting, robbery, gunrunners and revenge proved to be a winning one – it was the seventh most popular film in Italy in 1965.

The real Ringo star returned in Tessari's **The Return of Ringo**, which was released in Italy in time for Christmas 1965. Italian posters warned, 'Beware of fake guns – this is the one and only true Ringo!' Two months after the end of the Civil War, Captain Montgomery Brown (Giuliano Gemma) returns to his home town of Mimbres to find his father dead and his wife, Hally (Lorella De Luca), and daughter, Elizabeth (Monica Sugranes), held hostage in their villa. The villains are two Mexican brothers, Paco and Esteban Fuentes (George Martin and Fernando Sancho). Antonio Casas played Carson, the powerless alcoholic sheriff of Mimbres. Pajarito was florist Morning Glory and Nieves Navarro played gypsy fortune-teller Rosita. The film was shot at Esplugas City (as straw-blown Mimbres) and in the desert of Fraga, Huesca. *Return* is a well-plotted retelling of Homer's *The Odyssey* as a western and demonstrates the different trail Tessari took to Leone – this feels more like a Hollywood western in the classic tradition. Morricone contributed a moody score, with the title song again crooned by Graf, and the film was the third biggest grosser in Italy in 1965. Gemma also enjoyed great box office with *One Silver Dollar* (1965), *Adios Gringo* (1965), *Fort Yuma Gold* (1966), *The Long Days of Vengeance* (1966), *Day of Anger* (1967) and *Wanted* (1967), which made him a superstar in Italy, but his popularity didn't transfer to the US or UK. Giorgio Ferroni's *Fort Yuma Gold* was a 'sword and sandal' Civil War western which pitted Gemma against fellow peplum stars Dan Vadis and Jacques Sernas.

Shot in 1965 but released in Italy in 1966, Sergio Corbucci's *Johnny Oro* was retitled **Ringo and his Golden Pistol** for international release. Mark Damon starred as Jonathan Gonzales, called 'Johnny Ringo', a Mexican bounty hunter with a solid gold pistol. Mexican bandit Juanito Perez (Franco De Rosa) swears revenge on Ringo when his brothers are killed and teams up with Apache war chief Sebastian (Giovanni Cianfriglia). The Apaches attack the town of Coldstone (the Elios set), where Ringo has been jailed by Sheriff Bill Norton (Ettore Manni). Sebastian kills gunrunning saloon owner Gilmore (Andrea Aureli) with a tomahawk through the skull and Juanito shoots Ringo's girl Margie (Valeria Fabrizi), before the hero blows the Apaches and Coldstone to smithereens with dynamite. With some second unit riding scenes shot at the reservoir at La Pedriza, Manzanares El Real in Spain, most of the location footage was filmed at Tor Caldara. Carlo Savina provided the flavourful trumpet and whistling score.

Mud and Blood: Corbucci's West

Like Leone, Sergio Corbucci remade *Yojimbo*, as **Minnesota Clay** (1964) on location near Madrid. Cameron Mitchell starred as gunfighter Clay Mullighan, who escapes from Drunner forced labour camp and resolves a gang war in Mesa Encantada (the *Fistful* western set) between self-appointed sheriff 'Five Aces' Fox (Georges Riviere) and Mexican general Domingo Ortiz (Fernando Sancho), even though Clay is losing his eyesight.

Also using *Yojimbo* as inspiration, Corbucci's ***Django*** (1966) was as influential in Italy as Leone's 'Dollars' films. Franco Nero played gravedigger Django, the mud-splattered hero of this blood-splattered cult classic. He's a Union soldier who returns from the war to take revenge for the death of his wife. The ghost town is run by red-hooded Confederate fanatics led by Major Jackson (Eduardo Fajardo) and a band of Mexican cutthroats headed by General Hugo Rodriguez (Jose Bodalo). Corbucci filmed on location in Italy and Spain in the winter of 1965. The disintegrating, quagmired town was filmed at Elios Studios' weathered set, redressed as a pigsty. The town's Tombstone Cemetery, the mud flats and a rope bridge were at Tor Caldara, Lazio, which is unrecognisable from peplum days. 'Riding' exteriors were filmed at La Pedriza, Spain.

Django's grisly highlights include a fanatic sucked into a quicksand pit, prostitutes mud wrestling, Brother Jonathan (Gino Pernice), a Confederate priest, eating his own ear, and Django having his gun hand pulped with a Winchester butt and the Mexicans riding their horses over his hands. Django mows down the fanatics with a machine-gun fired from the hip, when in reality the immense recoil would have driven him into the mud. Virtually the entire cast is killed, including the ghost town's genial bartender Nathaniel (Angel Alvarez). Stuntman Remo De Angelis played Hugo's lieutenant Riccardo, with Simon Arriaga, Lucio De Santis, Jose Canalejas and Raphael Albacin as the cackling Mexican renegades. The major's Ku Klux Klansmen deployed Ivan Scratuglia, Luciano Rossi and Jose Terron, the latter as a scar-faced, snaggletoothed backshooter named Ringo. Loredana Nusciak played Django's battered love interest, Maria, who in the film's opening sequence is savagely flogged. Luis Enriquez Bacalov provided the doom-laden score, with the title song, 'Django', crooned lustily by 'Rocky Roberts' (Roberto Fia). Argentine Bacalov later won an Oscar for his score to

Mud and Blood: Franco Nero as avenging gunrunner Django, on set at Elios Studios, Rome, for Sergio Corbucci's *Django* (1966). Lobby card courtesy William Connolly Archive.

Michael Radford's *Il Postino* (1994). Nero was voiced in the English language version by Tony Russel, but the Italian dub is far superior. The English language *Django* cult has grown via home video, as it was never exhibited theatrically in the US or UK. Forget about pristine DVD releases – *Django* is best viewed in the grimiest, most scratched print possible, preferably on battered VHS (Inter-Ocean Video released it in the UK), which accentuates Enzo Barboni's gritty Eastmancolor cinematography. The rotten town swimming in mud, the desolate crosses of the Tombstone bone yard and Django's tatty rags contribute to the film's atmospheric decrepitude.

Corbucci didn't make another 'Django' film, but he did rehash the plot for **The Big Silence** (1967 – *The Great Silence*). Corbucci filmed in snowbound Cortina D'Ampezzo in the Dolomites. The town of Snow Hill was the Elios set, given an alpine makeover with shaving foam and swirling fog. French star Jean-Louis Trintignant played mute avenger Silence and Vonetta McGee was Pauline Middleton, who hires Silence to kill her husband's murderer, Loco (Klaus Kinski). Frank Wolff played Gideon Burnett, the Snow Hill sheriff, and Luigi Pistilli, Bruno Corazzari, Raf Baldassarre, Remo De Angelis and Mario Brega were the bad guys. Kinski's cowled villain was called Tigrero [The Tiger] in the Italian version and is described by Burnett as the 'Clever one with a priest's hat and a woman's fur coat'. With spectacular whiteout photography by Silvano Ippoliti and a moving, poetic score by Morricone (notably the aching, shimmering 'E L'Amore Verrà'), *Silence* is Euro action-drama of the highest order, though it failed to find a distributor in the US and UK. If Corbucci were a cocktail maker, he'd serve them with an ironic twist. The nihilistic finale of *The Big Silence* boasts the cruellest twist of all: Loco pitilessly shoots incapacitant Silence through the head.

A Bastard Called Django

Django was the most resilient and popular of all the Italian western heroes, surviving from 1966 into the 1980s. In Leon Klimovsky's ***A Few Dollars for Django*** (1966) bounty hunter Regan (Anthony Steffen) is hired by the Denver Mining Company to track down the perpetrators of a robbery. In Miles City, Montana, Regan poses as 'Sheriff Coleman'. Montana is divided by a range war between the ranchers, led by Amos Brandsbury (Alfonso Rojas), and the farmers, led by Trevor Norton (Frank Wolff), who is the outlaw Regan seeks. Enio Girolami (billed as 'Thomas Moore') and Jose Luis Lluch played Sam Lister and Buck Dago, Brandsbury's hired guns. Gloria Osuña played Norton's niece, Sally, Joe Kamel was farmer's spokesman, Graham, and Angel Ter was jumpy deputy Smitty. The film's interiors were shot at Incir-De Paolis Studios, with location footage lensed north of Madrid: Miles City was the Colmenar Viejo western set and Rancho Galicia-Cubero appeared as Norton's farm. Carlo Savina's score included the title song 'There Will Come a Morning' sung by Don Powell. Action footage from this film was reused in Enzo Castellari's *Seven Winchesters for a Massacre* (1967), as the Confederate guerrilla exploits of Colonel Blake (Guy Madison).

Negotiating a labyrinth of pseudonyms, audiences discovered that it was Dutch actor Roel Bos (billed as 'Glenn Saxson' or 'Glenn Saxon') who played Glenn Garvin (known in Mexico as Django) in Alberto De Martino's jokey ***Django Shoots First*** (1966 – *He Who Shoots First*). Django arrives in Silver Creek (the Elios set) to find that his father, Thomas Garvin, now deceased, shares half-ownership of the town with crooked banker Ken Kluster (Nando Gazzolo). Kluster framed Thomas, but Django, with help from layabout Gordon (Fernando Sancho) and mysterious stranger Doc (Alberto Lupo), clears Thomas' name. Django kills Kluster in a cemetery duel, but Kluster's son Jesse (Luigi Montefiori) shows up to claim his father's wealth. Bruno Nicolai provided the memorable title song, 'Dance of Danger (Bolero)', sung by Dino. Location scenes were shot in Italy and Spain – Django is ambushed by Kluster's men in a cemetery (at Tor Caldara, Lazio) and is chased on horseback to Embalse De Santillana (Santillana Reservoir) at Manzanares El Real, near Madrid. Saxson rides a horse like a sack of potatoes and Lupo's Doc is dressed like Lee Van Cleef: he carries a switchblade in his cane and is in town to take revenge on his bigamous wife, Jessica ('Evelyn Stewart'/Ida Galli), now married to Kluster. Erika Blanc played Django's love interest (saloon owner Miss Lucy), Valentino Macchi was Hicks, Silver Creek's bumbling sheriff, and Guido Lollobrigida played Kluster's black-clad henchman, Ward. The film's best moments are its pretitle sequence, filmed in the high sierras of Almeria. Django encounters bounty hunter Ringo (Jose Manuel Martin) and the mercenary hero kills Ringo and carts his own father's body into town to collect the reward.

The next instalment of the Django saga was Romolo Guerrieri's ***$10,000 Blood Money*** (1967). Mexican outlaw Manuel Vasquez (Claudio Camaso, Gian Maria Volonté's brother) is released after four years in prison and kidnaps Dolores (Adriana Ambesi), rich landowner Mendoza's daughter. Mendoza approaches bounty hunter Django (Gianni Garko billed as 'Gary Hudson') to get her back, but Django refuses until Manuel's reward reaches $10,000. He infiltrates the kidnappers and helps them attack a stagecoach carrying gold (filmed in the valley at Tolfa, Italy). Django tracks Manuel to the pueblo of Tampa (Elios Studios' Mexican village) and gets his man. From its lyrical seaside opening scene (filmed on the sunny Mediterranean coast of Almeria) with Django sunbathing on a beach, *Blood Money* is a surprisingly powerful western. Nora Orlandi's emotive score deploys descending strings, tolling bells and a virtuoso trumpet solo by Athos Martin, mixed with Spanish guitar themes and an eerie theramin. The film was largely shot on location in Lazio, Italy, with occasional shots of the grand sierras of Almeria adding an epic backdrop. Fernando Sancho had a cameo as Manuel's father, Stardust. When Django is bushwhacked by Manuel's men, he's badly wounded. Saloon owner Mijanou (Loredana Nusciak) helps him recuperate and tries to convince him to give up bounty hunting. When she leaves on the stagecoach to Frisco, she is killed in Manuel's ambush. Nusciak and Garko's love scenes are believably moving, making her futile death more effective.

Made under the shooting title *Oro Hondo*, Giulio Questi's *Se Sei Vivo, Spara!* (1967 – 'If You Live, Shoot!') was retitled ***Django, Kill! (If You Live Shoot!)*** for international release and has since blurred into the 'Django' series by reputation. Tomas Milian starred as a nameless stranger in Questi's vigorous *Fistful of Dollars* remake, with the hero sandwiched between a band of sadistic rancheros ramrodded by landowner Zorro (Roberto Camardiel) and the lynch-simple yokels, led by zealot Hagerman (Paco Sanz) and saloonkeeper Templer (Milo Quesada). Questi reused Leone's set at Hojo De Manzanares as his clapboard town where he staged hangings, tortures and scalpings. Glowering Milian made an excellent hero, Frank Braña was Templer's henchman and Ray Lovelock played Templer's son, Evan. Marilu Tolo appeared as Flory, the worst-dubbed saloon singer in the genre. Patrizia Valturri played Elizabeth, Hagerman's pyromaniac wife, who causes the fiery 'Fall of the House of Hagerman' finale – her husband is scalded by a death mask of molten gold.

Artful Techniscope cinematography by Franco Delli Colli makes *Django, Kill!* one of the best-looking Italian westerns. A sun-bleached desert massacre by outlaw Oaks (Piero Lulli) was filmed on a building site near Madrid and the stranger ropes wild horses at Caldara Di Manziana in Lazio. A graveyard was filmed near Hojo De Manzanares and Zorro's rancho – where Zorro chats with his psychic parrot – was the walled house and stables of Villa Mussolini, Lazio.

The fully restored version of *Django, Kill!* (rated 15 in the UK) runs 112 minutes and includes a scalping, a disembowelling and additional dialogues between the stranger and two Indian medicine men, which slows the film down. The cut 94-minute print is the finest version, never losing its nightmarish, comic-strip momentum. It was this frantic version that was released in the UK by Golden Era in 1969 (rated X, the same year that Corbucci's *Django* was rejected) and by Fletcher Video in the 1980s. UK pressbooks identified Milian as Barney and Lulli as Hoaks. *Django, Kill!* is a cult classic tale of blackmail, deviance and murder, drenched in sweaty Latin machismo.

Django next appeared in Ferdinando Baldi's **Rita of the West** (1967 – *Little Rita of the West* and *Rita the Kid*), starring 22-year-old Italian pop singer Rita Pavone as Little Rita, 'the famousest gunfighter of the west'. Rita, with her German sidekick, Fritz Frankfurter (Italian singer-songwriter Lucio Dalla), shoots it out with 'super bounty hunter' Ringo (Kirk Morris, dressed as 'The Man With No Name') in the main street at Elios Studios. Ringo opens his saddle-cloth to reveal a long-range pistol with detachable shoulder stock, but Rita dispatches him with a golden grenade. She then faces Django (Lucio Rosato, with broken hands and a coffin in tow) in Boot Hill at Tor Caldara, the shooting location from Corbucci's original. Rita also faces a Mexican bandit gang led by Fernando Sancho and falls for charming outlaw Black Stan (Terence Hill). Gordon Mitchell clearly enjoys himself as Big Chief Silly Bull ('How! Big Little Rita!'). The 41-year-old singer Teddy Reno appeared as a cowardly sheriff – Pavone married him the following year, causing a scandal in Italy due to their age difference.

During the western boom in Italy, there were comedy westerns (*Seven Guns for the MacGregors*), murder mystery westerns (*Death at Owell Rock*), convoluted spy movie westerns (*Gatling Gun*) and gothic horror-westerns (*And God Said to Cain*). *Rita of the West* is that deadliest of hybrids: a musical spaghetti western. Having dispatched outlaw Cassidy (Remo De Angelis), Rita and Fritz launch into the up-tempo 'Piruliruli'. In Silly Bull's camp Rita rattles through the thumping 'Ma Che Te Ne Fai' (as the Indians join the hoedown). In town Rita sings 'Rita sei tutti noi', a lively duet with Teddy Reno, and having fallen for Black Stan, she performs 'Tu Sei Come', a delicate love song. For 'Ma Che Te Ne Fai' (and its reprise in the finale), dancing girls and prancing cowboys are deployed, choreographed by Gino Landi. Not since Django massacred Major Jackson's Klan had the Elios western set seen such carnage.

Hollywood Romes the Range

During the spaghetti western boom, many Hollywood stars roamed the Italian west. Joseph Cotten starred as Colonel Jonas, a Confederate renegade who tries to restart the Civil War with a coffin full of stolen cash hidden in a hearse, in Corbucci's *The Hellbenders* (1967). Burt Reynolds played tomahawk-hurling Native American hero *Navajo Joe* (1966), also for Corbucci. Dan Duryea and Henry Silva appeared in Carlo Lizzani's *The Hills Run Red* (1966) – leathery

Duryea had been a stalwart of 1950s Hollywood westerns and *Hills* was one of his last films. Prolific Morricone scored all three films as 'Leo Nichols'.

Sergio Leone assembled the most prestigious Italian western cast for **Once Upon a Time in the West** (1968), his epic railroad western shot on location in Almeria, Utah and Arizona. Leone filmed some sequences amidst the cathedral rocks of Monument Valley, Utah. Frank (Henry Fonda), a hired regulator, is working for crippled railroad tycoon Morton (Gabriele Ferzetti), who is trying to run widow Jill McBain (Claudia Cardinale) off her Sweetwater ranch. The railroad needs water to continue its progress across the desert towards the Pacific. The Almeria-Guadix railway line stood in for the A & PH Morton rail line (modelled on the Union Pacific company) and boomtown Flagstone City was constructed in Almeria at La Calahorra station. Charles Bronson played Harmonica, a gunman seeking revenge on Frank for the lynching of his brother. Jason Robards was wanted outlaw Cheyenne Gutierrez, who is framed for Jill's husband's murder. Cardinale, a cascade of copper hair framing her beautiful face and dressed in authentic frontier apparel, has never been better. Frank is one of the western genre's great sadists, whether gunning down children or leaving his former employer Morton to die alone in the waterless desert. Frank Wolff played Jill's husband, Brett, and Lionel Stander, Keenan Wynne and Paolo Stoppa contributed cameos. Frank's gang included Italian western heavies Benito Stefanelli, Antonio Molino Rojo, Frank Braña, Fabio Testi and Spartaco Conversi, and Cheyenne's henchmen featured Aldo Sambrell and Lorenzo Robledo.

By now Leone deemed himself an oater auteur and *Once Upon a Time* is a beautifully shot, meticulously designed period drama: as though Visconti had directed a western epic. Ennio Morricone's score, incorporating sweeping orchestrations, lacerating electric guitars, wailing harmonicas and soprano Edda Dell'Orso, is one of his most popular. The burnished Italian print accentuates the ochre deserts and brown costuming (resembling sepia photographs), a palette which is lost in remastered English language DVD releases. This Italian print runs 170 minutes, while the English language version is 12 minutes shorter. The opening sequence at Cattle Corner railway station, where three of Frank's hired regulators (Jack Elam, Woody Strode and Al Mulock) lurk in wait for Harmonica, lasts 14 languorous minutes in the Italian print, but 12-and-a-half in the English version. The Italian version's pacing is slower, delivering 'Leone Deluxe'. *Once Upon a Time* was a great success in Europe but failed in the US when cut to an almost incomprehensible 148 minutes. Since its restoration on video and DVD, it is now regarded as one of the great westerns.

The mere presence of William Shatner (*Star Trek*'s Captain Kirk) in **White Comanche** (1968) would have assured its notoriety. The fact that he plays half-breed twins doubles the 'Shatner' value of this shot-in-Spain cult item. 'White Eyes' gunman Johnny Moon (Shatner) is trying to track down his twin brother Notah Moon (Shatner again), the renegade 'White Comanche'. Johnny is mistaken for his murderous brother and wants to settle accounts with Notah. The action is set around Rio Hondo (the Colmenar Viejo western set) and Notah's camp. The location scenes were filmed near Madrid, mostly beneath the mountain at La Pedriza, Manzanares El Real. A subplot has a range war brewing between saloon owner Jed Grimes (Luis Prendes) and a landowner, General Garcia (Mariano Vidal Molina), that culminates in a massed shootout in a sandstorm. Rosanna Yanni played Kelly, a woman raped by Notah during a stage hold-up, who blames Johnny for the crime. Aged Joseph Cotten played Logan, the Rio Hondo sheriff, though he appears to be struggling with the Spanish heat. Perla Cristal was Notah's squaw White Fawn and Luis Rivera played traitorous Comanche Kah To.

As Johnny Moon, Shatner delivers lines such as, 'Eat your Peyote, drug of the devil, dream your dreams of hate!' and 'It's between the two of us...Me and myself, you might say'. But it's his hammy turn as Notah that gives the film its cult status. His booming voice apparently relayed through a tannoy, Notah delivers his rousing 'sermon on the mount' to his followers prior to attacking Rio Hondo: 'I have seen in the dream that does not lie that White Fawn and Kah To have warned the whitefaces!' He tells his people that after years of reservation life, the Comanche will be great once more: 'Greater than the Pawneeeeeee! Greater than the Apacheeeeeeee!' Shatner clearly enjoys himself in this larger-than-life role. *White Comanche* also features an inappropriate jazz-fusion score with high hat, brushed snare, bass and brass, by Jean Ledrut. This cult classic is a must-see – it's cinema, but not as we know it.

The Specialists: Sartana and Sabata

Gianfranco Parolini's *If You Meet Sartana...Pray for Your Death* (1968) launched a series of 'Sartana' films which rivalled the popularity of Ringo and Django. Sartana is a conjurer, dressed in a black suit, and the red lining in his cape recalls Mandrake the Magician. Gianni Garko, cast in the heroic title role, is spectrally invincible. 'I am your pallbearer' is his ominous catchphrase and his presence is heralded by a ghostly whistling wind and the tinkling carillon of a pocket watch. As Garko said of the character, 'Sartana is like a bat flying through the night sky. He shifts shape like Dracula. His cultural roots lie in the comic strips'.

A stagecoach gold shipment from Gold Spring to Green Hill is stolen by Mexican bandit Miguel El Moreno (Sal Borgese), who has the gold taken from him by Lasky (William Berger). The shipment is a ruse by Gold Spring bankers Jeff Stewell (Sydney Chaplin, Charlie's son) and Al Holman (Gianni Rizzo) to claim the insurance money. Sartana discovers that the gold is to be shipped to Tucson, Arizona, in a judge's coffin. Others after the cache include knife-throwing outlaw Morgan (Klaus Kinski, with bells on his spurs) and a Mexican bandito, General El Tampico (Fernando Sancho). Snowy-haired Franco Pesce played elderly undertaker Dusty and Piero Piccioni's score was more akin to honky-tonk saloon music, though moments of tension were eerily scored, horror movie style, as in the final duel between Lasky and Sartana in coffin maker Dusty's 'vestibule of the beyond'. Gold Spring and Green Hill were the Elios and SCO (Studi Cinematografica Ostia) western sets; Green Wells (where Lasky massacres his own men with a Gatling gun) was a Magliana quarry sump near Rome; and Tampico's ranch was Villa Mussolini. The distinctive white road and rocky outcrops of Monti Simbruini were used for the gold robbery and the opening stagecoach ambush at White Canyon was a quarry at Magliana.

Parolini then cast Lee Van Cleef as **Sabata** (1969). Gadgets featured heavily in the film (including a Winchester hidden in a banjo), but Parolini also added a liberal dose of acrobatics, as three nefarious businessmen hatch a plan to clean out the bank of Daugherty City (the Elios Studios set). With William Berger as deadly minstrel Banjo, Linda Veras as Banjo's lover Jane and Franco Ressel as Hardy Stengel, the chief baddie, *Sabata* was a big hit. Parolini filmed on location in Lazio and Almeria, and Marcello Giombini's bouncy score has become a classic. Parolini helmed a sequel with Van Cleef, *Return of Sabata* (1971), which was wackier but less successful. He also directed *Adios Sabata* (1970 – *The Bounty Hunters*), with Yul Brynner. Gianni Rizzo appeared as a villain in all three 'Sabata' films, and Pedro Sanchez was thrice the heroes' sidekick – a blustering Mexican rogue, always out for gain and self-preservation.

Though *Sabata* sired few unofficial sequels – for example, Tullio Demichelli's *Sabata the Killer* (1970 – *Viva Sabata!*), starring Anthony Steffen, who had a go at impersonating everyone – Sartana was more imitated. George Hilton starred in the lively *I Am Sartana...Trade Your Pistol for a Coffin* (1970 – *Fistful of Lead*) and William Berger donned the hero's mantle in the shoddily incoherent *Sartana in the Valley of Death* (1970). Garko reprised the hero in *Sartana the Gravedigger* (1969 – *I Am Sartana...Your Angel of Death*, again with Kinski), *Have a Good Funeral, Amigo...Sartana Will Pay* (1970 – Parolini's *Sabata* in all but name) and *Light the Fuse...Sartana's Coming* (1970 – *Run Man Run...Sartana's in Town!*), all of which were directed by 'Anthony Ascott'/Giuliano Carnimeo. Garko also played Sartana-like gunman Silver in the western whodunit *Price of Death* (1971).

In **Light the Fuse...Sartana's Coming**, the best of the series, Sartana frees outlaw Grand Full (Piero Lulli) from arid Everglades Jail, to locate $2 million in counterfeit cash and half a million dollars in real cash. Sartana arrives in Mansfield (Elios' western set) and finds himself up against crooked sheriff Manassas Jim (Massimo Serato), widow Belle (Nieves Navarro), federal agent Sam Puttnam (Frank Braña) and General Monk (Jose Jaspe) and his renegade army. Carnimeo filmed on location near Madrid, which gives the film more grandeur than its Italian-shot predecessors. Jose Pesce played Sartana's friend, Pom-pom and the spectral gunman deploys 'Alfie', a clockwork toy Indian which appears to be a cigar lighter but is actually a bomb. The finale sees Sartana facing Monk's army in the main street of Mansfield. Sartana mows down the villains with a church organ which conceals cannons and machine guns. Bruno Nicolai composed the score, which were re-orchestrations of *Adios Sabata*.

Italian Westerns 161

'I Am Your Pallbearer': Gianni Garko as spectral shootist Sartana in Giuliano Carnimeo's *Have a Good Funeral, Amigo... Sartana Will Pay* (1970). Italian poster courtesy Ian Caunce Collection.

Django Rides Again

In 1968 the 'Django' series got back on track with Ferdinando Baldi's ***Viva Django!***, which was photographed by Enzo Barboni in the gritty style of Corbucci's original. Terence Hill was cast as cider-drinking Django, the bodyguard of ambitious politician David Barry (Horst Frank). Django is wounded by Barry and his henchman Lucas (George Eastman) during a gold shipment robbery that leaves Django's wife dead. Five years later Django is back, posing as the local hangman. Django frees condemned convicts he's supposed to have hanged, using them to steal Barry's gold bound for Santa Fe. Jose Torres was Mexican knifethrower Garcia, Barbara Simon was his wife, Mercedes, and Lee Burton, Luciano Rossi, Spartaco Conversi, Ivan Scratuglia and Lucio De Santis played Django's 'phantom' gang. Pinuccio Ardia appeared as telegrapher Horace, who owns a talking parrot (recalling *Django, Kill!*).

The muddy town of Altus was the Elios western set, the setting for a virtuoso shootout: having received a rib-kicking he won't forget from Barry's men, Django sets fire to Barry's saloon. Django's hideout at Mendez Ford was filmed on the River Treja near Monte Gelato falls and much location footage was lensed at Camposecco, near Camerata Nuovo, in the Parco Naturale Dei Monti Simbruini, Lazio – grassy valleys and woods littered with jutting outcrops – where Django faces Barry and his gang in the Altus cemetery. *Viva Django!*'s alternative title is *Django Get a Coffin Ready* and here we discover why. Django is forced to unearth what Barry thinks is a gold cache. Django shovels until he exhumes a casket which he buried earlier with his machine gun hidden inside and trademark mayhem ensues. Gianfranco Riverberi's punchy 'You'd Better Smile' is sung by Nicola Di Bari and the film's downbeat 'Deguello' (with plodding guitar, mournful chorus and trumpet) became famous in 2006 when it was sampled by duo Gnarls Barkley as the looped backing track for their global pop hit 'Crazy'.

Sergio Garrone's violent ***No Room to Die*** (1969) was retitled *A Noose for Django* for some markets and became a Django-versus-Sartana movie in Germany. It's a wintry reworking of *For a Few Dollars More* shot in Italy, with an atmospheric score by Vasco and Mancuso. Anthony Steffen and William Berger played two bounty hunters, Johnny Brandon and Avert Murdock, who team up to track down slave trafficker Fargo (director Garrone's brother Riccardo). Murdock is a fine creation, a bible-reading preacherman with an arsenal that includes a seven-barrelled shotgun.

Garrone and Steffen reunited on ***Django the Bastard*** (1969 – *The Stranger's Gundown*) which Steffen co-wrote with Garrone under his real name Antonio De Teffé. In 1881, Django (Steffen) tracks down the three Confederate officers who betrayed his regiment during the Civil War. Django kills Lieutenant Sam Hawkins (Fred Robsahn), then Captain Ross Howard (Jean Louis), before going after Major Rod Murdok (Paolo Gozlino). In Desert City, Murdok surrounds himself with a gang of mercenaries. Django seems to be supernaturally indestructible and with the help of Alida (Rada Rassimov), Murdok's traitorous sister-in-law, the avenger prevails. *Bastard* showcases Steffen's best work, as he stalks the streets of Desert City, a spindly, spectral killer: 'a devil from Hell'. He sports a bat-like black poncho and announces the death of each villain with crosses marked with the day's date. Luciano Rossi (billed as 'Lu Kamante') was cast as Murdok's brother, epileptic albino Luke. Teodoro Corra played Murdok's accountant, William, and Furio Meniconi was Desert City's sheriff. Carlo Gaddi played Murdok's hollow-eyed henchman, Brett, Tomas Rudi appeared as hired gun Roland and Osiride and Renzo Pevarello, Bruno Ukmar, Angelo Susani, Mimmo Maggio, Alberto Dell'Aqua, Remo Capitani and Claudio Ruffini cropped up amongst the bad guys. The deserts were filmed in a Magliana quarry, southwest of Rome. Desert City was the Cinecittà western set and Murdok's ranch was Villa Mussolini. The gothic, nocturnal action was enhanced by Vasco and Mancuso's dissonant score, deploying flutes and a ghostly soprano soloist. The supernatural element is ambiguously played by Garrone – when shot, Django bleeds, but he can materialise at will. After Django has killed Murdok, Alida says, 'We'll be rich forever'. 'We won't live forever', answers the spectre, and when she looks again, he's gone. The action-packed finale of Steffen's jokier *A Man Called Apocalypse Joe* (1970) parodies its equivalent in *Bastard*.

Django the Bastard was the last hurrah of the solo Django outings, as most subsequent entries yoked the hero to Sartana, as in 'William Redford'/Pasquale Squitieri's *Django against Sartana* (1970) and Demofilio Fidani's *One Damn Day at Dawn...Django Meets Sartana!* (1970). As the titles became longer, the audiences got smaller. In **Django against Sartana**, the bank at Tombstone is robbed, its manager Philip Singer (Bernard Faber) murdered and his niece kidnapped. Django's brother Steve (John Alvar) and gunman Sartana (George Ardisson) are blamed and Steve is lynched. Django (Tony Kendall) catches up with Sartana but discovers that the culprit is Singer, now living in Vera Cruz as rancher 'Don Felipe'. Set in 1871 (though the fashions and haircuts look like 1971) and shot entirely in Italy (in the Magliana quarry and at Tiburtina), *Django against Sartana*'s shoestring budget is readily apparent. The Elios set (as Tombstone) is falling to pieces and few townsfolk roam its streets. Rick Boyd and Salvatore Billa had cameos as Singer's gunmen, Teodoro Corra played bandit Juan Corvo, Fulvio Mingozzi appeared as the Tombstone sheriff, and Jose Torres played mute Mexican knife-throwing peon Loco. Singer's memorable demise, with a set of trophy antlers attached to his head, is a first for the genre. The film deploys Piero Umiliani's score from *Son of Django* (1967 – which starred Gabriele Tinti as Clint, Django's son) despite an incongruous lyrical reference to Django as 'He was my father'.

Demofilio Fidani directed **One Damn Day at Dawn...Django Meets Sartana!** as 'Miles Deem'. He helmed other efforts as 'Slim Alone', 'Sean O'Neal' and 'Dick Spitfire' and looking at his work it's easy to see why. This film is a plotless meander made on the cheap in familiar Lazio quarries. Jack Ronson, the new sheriff of Black City (Fabio Testi, in coat, hat and a ten-foot-long scarf) finds that his star is a nice big shiny target for smugglers Bud Wheeler (Dean Stratford) and Sanchez (Dennis Colt). Django (Hunt Powers) helps Ronson, who is actually famed gunman Sartana. Fidani's style – from casting to set furnishing – is minimalist and he deploys a supporting cast even the most seasoned Italian western fans won't recognise. Fidani's westerns, particularly this one, are notable for their stunt performers' twitching deaths, which more closely resemble electrocution or gymnastics. Noteworthy aspects of this wintry western are the windy Elios set as dank Black City, and a Lallo Gori score that's superior to the film it accompanies. The same year that Testi played Sartana he also appeared in Vittorio De Sica's *The Garden of the Finzi-Continis*, the 1971 Best Foreign Film Oscar winner.

Fidani has been compared to an Italian western Ed Wood and you can't fault him on titles, which are always more imaginative than the bargain basement films they publicise. He directed *The Django Story* (1971 – *Reach You Bastard!*) as 'Lucky Dickerson', with Django (Hunt Powers) reminiscing with Wild Bill Hickok (Dean Stratford) in a saloon about Django's most famous adventures, which are illustrated via stock footage from Fidani's ropy back catalogue, including *The Stranger that Kneels Beside the Shadow of a Corpse* and *Sartana, If Your Left Arm Offends, Cut It Off* – also known as *Django and Sartana Are Coming…It's the End.* After this travesty, it soon was.

It was 21 years after Corbucci's original that Franco Nero resurrected Django in an official sequel, **Django Strikes Again** (1987 – *Django 2:Il Grande Ritorno*), directed by 'Ted Archer'/Nello Rossati. Exasperated Nero once observed that nearly all his westerns were retitled in Germany as 'Django' movies, so he might as well make one himself. Django is now a monk, Brother Ignatius, ensconced in the Santo Domingo monastery. When his daughter, Marisol, is taken prisoner by a slaver, Django comes out of retirement. Django's adversary is Prince Orlowsky (Christopher Connelly), a lepidopterist, and his white-uniformed Hungarian mercenaries. They traverse the river in their armoured steamboat – *Mariposa Negra*, named after a mythical black butterfly which the prince seeks – attacking villages and dooming the locals to forced labour. Django is captured and put to work in a silver mine but breaks out. In a fitting sequence, he digs up his machine gun from a grave marked 'Django': 'You could use a little oil', he tells his old companion, 'You've got more to do'.

Django Strikes Again is a brutal, pretentious film that has its moments, mostly of action. Django impersonates an undertaker, travelling incognito in a hearse, and kills the bad guys with bolas, throwing axe, dynamite, pistol and his trusty machine gun in a series of well-staged shootouts. Sandro Mancori's Eastmancolor cinematography is a plus and the biblical score by Giovanni Plenizio evokes Morricone, with a soprano, plush orchestration, percussion and hollow tolling bells. The mine sequence – involving hundreds of extras – resembles outtakes from *Barabbas*. It was filmed in Colombia and the atmosphere resembles a jungle adventure (a bank Orlowsky plans to rob is the 'Banco

Tropical'). Donald Pleasence played Gunn, a Scottish butterfly expert imprisoned by Orlowsky, Consuelo Reina was Django's lover, Dona Gabriela, and tall actress Licinia Lentini played Orlowsky's lover, the Contessa. She is eventually stabbed by her love rival, a statuesque black slave trader dressed in a leopardskin bikini and draped in gold chains. As Django rides away, he assures, 'I'll be back', though Nero hasn't surfaced since.

A Pair of Aces: Hill and Spencer

Before they became an internationally successful comedy double act, Terence Hill and Bud Spencer rocketed to stardom in a trio of action westerns directed by Leone's friend Giuseppe Colizzi: *God Forgives... I Don't* (1967), *Ace High* (1968) and *Boot Hill* (1969). ***God Forgives... I Don't*** was prepared under the working title 'The Dog, the Cat and the Fox'. The Dog was Hutch Bessy (Spencer), an insurance agent working for the Harold Bank in El Paso, who is on the trail of a missing $100,000 gold shipment. The Fox was outlaw Bill San Antonio (Frank Wolff), who has faked his own death and is in cahoots with the bank's president, Mr Harold. The Cat was gunman Cat Stevens (Hill) who teams with Hutch to track down the haul. Bill is hiding out in Mexico near Puntal, so Cat and Hutch steal the strongbox and bury it in the desert. A duel between Bill and Cat ends with Bill being blown to smithereens with dynamite.

God Forgives... I Don't was shot on location in Almeria, with interiors at Elios Studios, Rome. The Almeria-Guadix railway line stood in for the El Paso-Canyon City route: the film opens with the driverless MK&T train arriving in Canyon City with all on board dead. Hammy Wolff grandstands as Bill San Antonio, his sickly charm giving way to explosive, needless violence. Perennial sidekick Jose Manuel Martin played Bill's chump henchman, Bud. The contrast between graceful, acrobatic Hill and hulk Spencer subtly undercuts the serious story: Hill is obviously 'doing' Clint Eastwood while bearded Spencer is more original, in his huge shaggy goatskin jacket. The violent action sees Cat and Hutch beaten and tortured at regular intervals, with Cat being repeatedly tossed down a well (cats hate water) and Hutch branded with hot irons. Hill is really put through the mill in this one, either dangling upside down in a mantrap or led at rope's length through the scorching Almerian desert. Cat and Hutch are called Cat 'Doc' Stevens and Hutch Earp in the Italian print and Django and Dan in the German version (which was retitled 'God Forgives... Django Doesn't'). The grandiose, operatic score was by Carlo Rustichelli, with his choir chanting a 'Dies Irae' pastiche at full volume. *God Forgives... I Don't* (released in the UK as *Blood River*) was the most successful film in Italy in 1967.

In ***Ace High*** (1968) Cat and Hutch return the stolen treasure to El Paso (the Mini Hollywood set in Almeria) and claim the reward for Bill. The bank president, Mr Harold (Steffan Zacharias), hires condemned killer Cacopoulos (Eli Wallach) to steal Cat and Hutch's reward money. Caco wants revenge on the three men who double-crossed him 15 years ago: Mexican regulare Paco Rosa

(Livio Lorenzon), proprietor Drake (Kevin McCarthy) and Harold, so Cat and Hutch agree to help Caco. He kills Harold and tracks Paco to his fortress stronghold near the Mexican village of Tula. With the help of revolutionaries led by Canganciero (Remo Capitani), Paco is killed. Caco and company head for Fair City, near Memphis, where Drake runs a crooked casino and plan a heist on his establishment.

Sluggishly paced, *Ace High* isn't up to the standard of *God Forgives*, as Colizzi introduces more comedy into the violent mix, including the first of Hill and Spencer's many knockout fistfights. Carlo Rustichelli again provided the score and the desert action was filmed in Almeria, with interiors at Elios. Wallach, fresh from his success in *The Good, the Bad and the Ugly*, played Caco, a 'lice-infected jailbird' of Greek descent. Brock Peters was black trapeze artist and tightrope walker Thomas, who joins the heroes for the heist. The final duel in Drake's posh casino is well staged: Cat, Hutch, Thomas and Caco face Drake and four henchmen, as the well-heeled punters hit the floor. Caco orders the casino's orchestra to play 'a slow, sweet waltz' as a roulette ball whizzes around the wheel. When the wheel stops, the shooting starts. The film was partly financed by production company San Marco, one of the backers of *Once Upon a Time in the West*, and the hefty budget ensured that the film was a success at the Italian box office: it was the second most successful western of 1968 in Italy, after *Once Upon a Time*. *Ace High* was retitled *Revenge at El Paso* in the UK, though the final revenge takes place in Fair City and revolves around a roulette wheel, not poker.

Boot Hill has Cat and Hutch team up once more to help Sharp (Enzo Fiermonte), an old acquaintance in Libertyville. Corpulent town tyrant Honey Fisher (Victor Buono) is exploiting the miners. Wounded by Fisher's gunmen, Cat convalesces in a travelling circus and, with Hutch and his deaf-mute partner Baby Doll (George Eastman), sets about defeating Fisher. *Boot Hill* has the shortest running time of the trilogy (92 minutes), though it feels like the longest, with Hill and Spencer hardly onscreen. The travelling circus is a novel idea, but Colizzi dwells on its performances, with trapeze artists, can-can girls and a dwarf orchestra. Woody Strode (or 'Stroode' as he's billed) played gunfighter-turned-trapeze artist Thomas (recreating Brock Peters' role) and Lionel Stander played ringmaster and fortune-teller Mami. Rustichelli again supplied the score, which redeploys themes from the earlier movies, and the film contrasts sweaty frontier faces and dusty range clothes with the grease-painted circus folk. Exteriors were again filmed in Almeria (the Libertyville shootout occurs at night on the Mini Hollywood set) and the interiors were lensed at De Laurentiis Studios and Elios. The actual English title according to the film's credit sequence is *Boots Hill*, a mistranslation of the original Italian title *La Collina Degli Stivali*: 'The Hill of Boots'. *Boot Hill* was the least successful of the trilogy, but Hill and Spencer were still immensely popular and it was the highest earning western in Italy in 1969. Colizzi's trilogy was the catalyst for the transition in Italian westerns in the early 1970s from violence to slapstick humour, via the forging of the Hill-Spencer partnership.

Chapter Eight

Passports to Hell
Euro Crime and Crimebusters

Italian crime cinema has taken many forms, from imitations of James Bondian global supercrime to caped superheroes and elaborate, meticulous heist movies. Crime became the singularly most popular subject in world cinema in the late 1960s and early 1970s. This was assured by the popularity of Mafia movies (following the hefty box office and Oscar triumphs of the 'Godfather' films), rogue cops in the person of Clint Eastwood's *Dirty Harry* (1971), drug trafficking and car chase action in *The French Connection* (1971) and vigilantism inspired by *Death Wish* (1974). As to be expected, Italian filmmakers approached these genres in their own distinctive manner, which led to some big box office hits and the creation of the ultraviolent 'poliziotteschi' police films.

Unlicensed to Kill: Spy Movies

The James Bond films were the most successful film series of the 1960s and were massively influential on worldwide popular cinema. The codename 007 was out-of-bounds for Italian copyists. United Artists grew tired of filmmakers alluding to 007 and cautioned, 'Only James Bond…can be agent 007. Warning is given to all Italian companies which, exploiting the success achieved by agent 007, have distinguished the leading figures by the same numerals'. This didn't deter enterprising Italian productions and many coded agents interpreted thinly veiled variations on Ian Fleming's hero.

Ken Clark played Dick Malloy – CIA Agent 077 – in *Mission Bloody Mary* (1965), *From the Orient with Fury* (1965 – rather than *From Russia with Love*) and *Special Mission Lady Chaplin* (1966). Directed by Alberto De Martino, with action sequences staged by Giorgio Ubaldi and future director Enzo G. Castellari, **Special Mission Lady Chaplin** is the finest example of Italian 'Bondage'. Malloy is on the trail of 16 Polaris nuclear missiles which have been stolen from the wreck of *USS Thresher*, an atomic submarine. In Spain Malloy investigates wealthy salvager Ken 'Kobre' Zoltan (Jacques Bergerac) and encounters a sexy French assassin, Lady Arabella Chaplin (Daniela Bianchi). Arabella, ostensibly a high fashion designer, is a master of disguise. She's introduced as a machine gun–toting nun, shooting it out with two industrial spies (posing as monks), and later appears as an elderly countess who assassinates a witness with guns concealed in her wheelchair. Arabella's partner-in-crime is Constance Day ('Evelyn Stewart'/Ida Galli). Zoltan uses a newly developed expanding rubber to steal the missiles, which he plans to sell to enemy agent Hilde (Helga Line) for $5 million in diamonds. Eventually Arabella falls for Malloy and works as a double agent, scuppering Zoltan's scheme.

All three Malloy films were produced by Edmondo Amati for his Fida Cinematografica. *Special Mission*'s globetrotting story was filmed on location in Spain, the UK, the US and France. Malloy is dispatched from New York by his boss at the Secret Service, Commander Heston (Philippe Hersent). Much of the action was shot in Madrid (including the Hotel Luz Palacio) and in southern Spain: the port at Escombreras, a power station at Cartagena, San Pedro De Pinatar, Cabo De Palos, plus locations in Murcia, Malaga and Marbella. On London locations (including Tower Bridge, Trafalgar Square and Big Ben) Lady Chaplin steals the missile propellant from a military train en route to Dover. A diversion to Paris climaxes with Malloy electrocuting Ivan (Peter Blades), Zoltan's metal-clawed henchman, following a fight at the funicular railway at Sacré-Coeur. When Malloy trails Zoltan and Arabella to the missiles' hiding place it's supposed to be Morocco, but is more of Spain's Mediterranean coast. Tomas Blanco played Spanish policeman Soler and Alfred Mayo played Sir Hillary, the traitorous head of British missile research. Goffredo Unger, Joaquin Parra and Enzo Castellari crop up as Zoltan's henchmen in a shootout with Malloy in a bullring.

Lady Chaplin benefits from great production design, with outré costumes for Bianchi, Galli and Line. Bruno Nicolai's score is brassy spy fodder and the dramatic title song, 'Lady Chaplin', is sung by Bobby Solo (presumably UNCLE agent Napoleon's brother). Throughout the trilogy, 077 is a good agent but 'woman crazy' though this third instalment concentrates on plot and action. Two helicopters attack a ship, while Malloy examines the *Thresher* in a bathyscaphe submersible. Other action highlights include Malloy's escape from his car when a digger bucket crushes its roof (an ejector seat fires Malloy through the boot); Lady Chaplin's escape from a plane in a parachuting dress; a shootout on a beach where Malloy deploys an explosive harpoon; and the final fight between Zoltan and Malloy in a burning missile storeroom, which ends with Zoltan stung to death by his own fighting scorpions. Arabella chemically converts the volatile propellant into red material and weaves it into a collection of dresses and when undercover CIA agent Jacqueline (Mabel Karr) is shot whilst wearing one of them, she explodes.

Greg Tallas's Italian-Spanish ***Espionage in Tangiers*** (1965) starred Luis Davila as smarmy Mike Murphy, Agent S.077, who seductively topples women with unconvincing ease and whose deadpan wisecracks thud to earth, thanks to the inept English dubbing. He's dispatched on the trail of a ray gun invented by Professor Greff (Tomas Blanco) which atomises its targets, resulting in cliff-hanging shenanigans. Set in Tangiers and Nice (but looking like Spain), this fast-moving film benefits from a whistled theme (composed by Benedetto Ghiglia) and the glamorous presence of Jose Greci and Perla Cristal, though the mediocre cinematography makes it resemble a made-for-TV movie.

Silvio Amadio's ***Assassination in Rome*** (1967) had journalist Dick Sherman (Hugh O'Brien), the editor of Rome's *American Daily*, investigate the disappearance of William North, the husband of his old flame, Shelley (Cyd Charisse). When it's revealed that William was involved with heroine smugglers, Dick questions the 'narcotics crowd' of Rome's sleazy underbelly, including an artist (Antonio Casas), a jazz trumpeter and a peplum actor at Cinecittà, which offers a behind-the-scenes glimpse at moviemaking, with a grand exterior set littered with peplum extras for a Cleopatra epic. 'Where's Richard Burton?' asks Dick when he passes Cleo and her entourage. The best reasons for viewing *Assassination* are the magnificent location shots of Rome and Venice, in Eastmancolor and Totalscope. The story opens with the discovery of a corpse near the Trevi Fountain. The film's exteriors include the Arch of Constantine, the Colosseum and Fiumicino Airport. The film is an old-style Hollywood melodrama crossbred with a giallo thriller, essentially 'Three Corpses in the Fountain'.

In Antonio Margheriti's ***Lightning Bolt*** (1965 – *Operation Goldman*), Professor Rooney (Paco Sanz) discovers excessive radioactivity off Cape Kennedy but goes missing. Captain Pat Flanagan (Diana Lorys) and Lieutenant Harry Sennett (Anthony Eisley) of Section S investigate. The culprit is smiling beer baron Rehte (Folco Lulli), the head of REHTE BEER – 'The long life beer' claims its tagline – who is using laser beams fired from beer delivery trucks to destroy NASA rockets. His long-term plan is to site a laser beam on the moon. Margheriti blends sci-fi with Bondian espionage: Rehte operates from an underwater city (interiors constructed at De Paolis Studios) and Harry and Pat are almost drowned in a giant beer vat. Lulli is nondescript as the German-accented, beer-swigging villain, though the female characters – Pat, enemy agent Ursula (Luisa Rivelli) and Rehte's hostage Carrie (Wandisa Guida) – are more prominent than in usual spy fare. Though the film is supposedly set in Florida, Harry speeds towards the rocket launch site and passes ANZIO painted in large white letters on the tarmac at a road junction. Rehte's underwater complex is 'fully automated' – Margheriti's excuse for Rehte's few henchmen, who in their black bodysuits and masks resemble Diabolik. Margheriti makes good use of stock footage, including that of a NASA control room and rockets taking off from Cape Kennedy. When Rehte's base floods with lava, Margheriti reuses the climax from his own *Wild, Wild Planet*. The villain's 'hibernation chamber', with imprisoned victims suspended in limbo, is also inspired by *Wild Planet*. While Harry Sennett is no James Bond, *Lighting Bolt* was cheekily advertised as 'Strikes Like a Ball of Thunder'.

Sergio Sollima directed two secret agent movies under the pseudonym 'Simon Sterling': *Passport to Hell* (1965) and *Hunter of the Unknown* (1966), both starring George Ardisson as karate-chopping Walter Ross, Agent 3S3 – agent number three of the US Third Special Division. **Passport to Hell** sent Ross after Mr A, a master criminal. Following the murder of agent Elisa Van Sloot (Beatrice Altariba) in Holland, Ross contacts Mr A's daughter, Jasmine Von Wittheim (Barbara Simons), in snowbound Vienna and then travels with her to Lebanon to locate her father, whom they discover long dead in his villa on Rapid Island. The real villain is Mr B, Professor Steve Dickson (Georges Riviere), who plans to kill both Ross and Jasmine. Ardisson's agent deploys a combination of panache and ruthlessness and carries a golden bullet inscribed with an 'A' as his good luck charm. His opponents include henchman Gutierrez (wrestler Dakar), Bel Ami (Frank Andrews), Arabian temptress Fawzia (Leontine May) and nefarious Jackie Yen (Senya Seyn). Two of Mr A's hitmen, bespectacled Nobel (Paco Sanz) and mute Salkoff (Calisto Calisti), discuss their mission on the Vienna Ferris wheel from *The Third Man*. Ahmed, Ross' ally in Beirut, was played by Jose Marco, the Russian ambassador Doliukin was Fernando Sancho, and Major Taylor and Captain Moran, Ross's superiors, were Tom Felleghy and Anthony Gradwell. With stock footage inserts evoking foreign locations, *Passport to Hell* is an archetypal Italian spy movie. In a memorable scene, Ross fights a gang of leather-jacketed thugs (including Federico Boido, Sal Borgese, Pietro Torrisi and Gino Barbicane) in a bar, while a jukebox blasts out The Kinks' 'Everybody's Going to be Happy' and 'Tired of Waiting'. Piero Umiliani provided the jazzy score and the Shirley Bassey-ish title song, 'Let Me Free', was sung by Edith Peters.

In **Hunter of the Unknown** (also released as *Agent 3S3: Massacre in the Sun*), Ross is sent to the Caribbean island of San Felipe – the dictatorship of General Siqueiros (Fernando Sancho), who is working with uranium expert Karleston (Eduardo Fajardo). Ross infiltrates the island posing as a gunrunner to search for Agent 3S4 (Luis Induni), who has gone missing. Frank Wolff (with dyed blond hair) played Russian agent Ivan Terenczhov, dispatched to the island by his Kremlin boss (John Karlsen). Umiliani again supplied the score and the apt title song, 'Trouble Galore', was performed by Orietta Berti.

The UK-financed **Deadlier than the Male** (1966) exhibited a strong Italo-spy influence, due to its cast and scenery. Elke Somer and Sylva Koscina played Irma and Penelope, two sexy female assassins in the mould of Lady Chaplin. They emerge from the sea wearing skimpy bikinis to spear investigator Wyngarde with harpoons at Villa Erix on the Italian coast. Their deadly arsenal features bullet-loaded cigars, bombs, dart guns and poison, and they are eventually blown to pieces by an exploding hairpiece. The megalomaniac villain (Nigel Green) lives in a castle above the picturesque village harbour of Castelmare (filmed at Lerici on the Gulf of Poets in north-western Italy) and Chang, his bulldog henchman, was played by peplum wrestler Milton Reid, who also appeared in *Dr No* (1962) and *The Spy Who Loved Me* (1977).

A less outlandish Italian stab at espionage was Sergio Corbucci's convoluted **Moving Target** (1967 – *Death on the Run*). US actor Ty Hardin starred as Jason, a 'Houdini' thief on the run in Athens. Of all the actors who used pseudonyms, Hardin had the best justification: his real name was Orson Whipple Hungerford II. Jason finds himself blackmailed into stealing a valuable microfilm from the corpse of an agent who has recently died in prison; the microfilm, containing a list of important agents working in the East and West, is concealed in the cadaver's tooth filling which Jason must extract from the corpse's jaw. Jason is pursued through Athens by two rival mobster gangs and the Greek police, led by Inspector Starkis (Nando Poggi). With help from his old friend Pizza (Vittorio Caprioli), the Italian owner of the Gold Star striptease club, and Greta (Paola Pitagora), a tour guide who works at the Acropolis, he evades capture, eventually delivering the microfilm to the authorities in exchange for Greta's sister's child, held hostage by the Communist villains. *Moving Target* was shot on location in Greece, with the famous hilltop ruins of the Acropolis and numerous backstreet scenes adding local colour. Ivan Vandor's jazzy score reinforces the spy movie milieu. The complicated plot is saved by several shootouts and punch ups, lensed with Corbucci's customary élan: Greta is killed and both her eyes are shot out, fitting 'eye for an eye' vengeance for the missing tooth. Gordon Mitchell was cold mobster the Albanian, while Vassili Karis and Corbucci's stunt supervisor Remo De Angelis appeared as henchmen to rival mobster Dimitrios. Graziella Granata played stripper Rumba and Michael Rennie was Major Worthington Clark, an agent working on Her Majesty's Secret Service who is a double agent.

Laugh Laugh...Bang Bang: Spy Spoofs

Following their 'Ringo' westerns, Duccio Tessari cast Giuliano Gemma as Englishman Kirk Warren in **Kiss Kiss Bang Bang** (1966). Having been accused of high treason and theft, Warren is spared from the gallows by the British Secret Service. They recruit him to steal the secret formula for a new alloy with a high melting point for use in jets and spacecraft. Mr X is also after the formula, which is contained in a Swiss safe 'only Ali Baba can open'. Kirk assembles a crack team: circus acrobat Chico Perez (George Martin), safecracker Dupont (Pajarito) and electronics expert Padereski, a professor known as 'Radar the Blip' (Antonio Casas). They are successful and teach talking circus parrot Socrates the formula, but unfortunately the bird gets shot.

Tessari's film is often too clever for its own good. There are numerous references to the 'double-o' designation, and when Kirk watches film footage of the Swiss installation they have to break into, he comments that it's 'better than James Bond'. Gemma is dubbed with a cut-glass English accent, which doesn't suit his screen persona and wears glasses in the style of Harry Palmer. He's great in the action scenes, but the story rambles from London and Switzerland, to Italy (Cortina D'Ampezzo and Venice) and Spain. The heist is well staged, with the incompetent crooks negotiating electric fences, armed guards, TV monitors and a death ray. There are plenty of sight gags (there's a running joke about spies hidden in dustbins) and gadgets, including laughing gas pills, an amphibicar on the canals of Venice and a talking pigeon in St Mark's Square. The ending, a fistfight in a fairground and a castle, degenerates into the kind of self-indulgent silliness that blighted so much of 1960s cinema – or perhaps Tessari is parodying that too, you can never tell.

Lorella De Luca (Tessari's wife) played Kirk's love interest, ditzy Fanny. Antonio Molino Rojo was her oil baron fiancé, Nieves Navarro was Hilary Shakespeare (a double-agent), Daniele Vargas played a Chinese judo expert villain, Nazzareno Zamperla was his chauffeur and Jose Manuel Martin was prisoner Jamaica. George Rigaud played Sir Sebastian Wilcox (aka Mr X), an agent working on counter-espionage in the armaments industry. Bruno Nicolai composed the Bondesque score and 'Love Love... Bang Bang', the memorably swinging title song, was sung by Nancy Cuomo. Following this novel diversion, Gemma mostly made westerns for the remainder of the 1960s.

In the Bond film *Thunderball* (1965 – *Agente 007: Thunderball* in Italy), Adolfo Celi enjoyed great success playing SPECTRE No2 Emilio Largo, who lives on his Palmyra estate in Nassau and aboard a luxury hydrofoil yacht, the *Disco Volante*. Celi then played Beta, the second-in-command of the powerful global crime organisation Thanatos (the Greek god of Death), in Alberto De Martino's **OK Connery** (1967), the most blatant of the Italian Bond rip-offs. It was also known as *Operation Double 007* and *Operation Kid Brother*. All titles refer to the presence of Neil Connery (Sean's younger brother) as plastic surgeon Neil Connery, the brother of 'Allied Counter-espionage's top agent'. Producer Dario Sabatello hired several Bond regulars: Lois Maxwell (Bond's Miss Moneypenny), Bernard Lee (Bond's boss 'M'), Daniela Bianchi (Corporal Tatiana Romanov in *From Russia With Love*) and Anthony Dawson (Professor Dent, a villain in *Dr No*). Dawson played Thanatos' top man, Alpha, and Bianchi was Maya, an enemy agent who helps Connery. At Malaga Airport, Ward Jones (Nando Angelini) is killed when a remote-controlled car crashes into his plane. Ward's lover Yashuko (Yachuko Yama) is being treated in Monte Carlo by a world-famous plastic surgeon, Dr Connery, who is also expert at karate, hypnotism and lip reading. Ward has used Yashuko as a 'human electronic brain', hypnotising her with secret information about Thanatos' scheme. Via Operation Blackmail, Alpha and Beta plan to control the world's gold reserves by stealing an atomic nucleus, generating an ultra-high-frequency magnetic wave which will fuse metal. The Allied Counter-espionage boss, Commander Cunningham (Bernard Lee), and his secretary, Miss Maxwell (Lois Maxwell), employ Connery to track down Yashuko. The assignment flies him from Monte Carlo and Malaga, to Tétouan, Morocco, and finally to Thanatos' HQ, a cave lair beneath a castle near Munich. The surreal finale has Maya leading a party of archers on horseback into the HQ and the adversaries shooting it out with bows and arrows, and harpoons.

OK Connery is tangentially way-out, a splendidly offbeat pastiche packed with invention and cinematic theft. A subplot has Thanatos employing blind Moroccan weavers to craft radioactive rugs, and Connery plays mind control games with his adversaries with his hypnotic stare. The supporting cast includes Guido Lollobrigida (as Beta's henchman Kurt), Antonio Gradoli (as Monte Carlo's police inspector) and Agata Flori (as Thanatos assassin Mildred). Anna Maria Noe's torturer Lotte Krayendorf closely resembles Lotte Lenya's Rosa Klebb in *From Russia with Love*. The film's title song, 'Man for Me', is voiced in ear-piercing style by Christy (billed as 'Khristy') to music co-composed by Ennio Morricone and Bruno Nicolai. Bianchi, Flori and Celi wear some colourful 1960s attire, ranging from black and red leather fetish gear, to impractical pink feathered creations and gold kaftans, and Beta has a yacht moored in Monte Carlo harbour with an all-woman crew. Disguised as can-can girls, Maya's female gang steal the atomic nucleus by waylaying an army convoy and escape dressed as 'cat women' hostesses of 'The Wild Pussy Club', a mobile casino. When Connery suspects that Beta is planning to blow up Maya's crew on the yacht, she smiles, 'You read too many novels by Fleming'. Having defeated the villains and saved the world, Cunningham tells Dr Connery, 'You should have seen your brother's face when he heard of it'. Neil Connery was working as a plasterer before he was cast and as a screen superspy he achieved a smooth finish when he coolly obliterated Thanatos' HQ with a time bomb, in trademark Bondian fashion.

Caped Crusaders and Masked Avengers, Italian Style

Just as America had its crime-fighting heroes – Batman, Superman and Spiderman – so did Italy. In *The Witches* (1966) a fantasy sequence featuring Clint Eastwood depicts the Italian comic book icons Diabolik, Mandrake the Magician, Flash Gordon, Batman, Sadik and Nembo Kid (the Italian name for Superman), while elsewhere several caped crusaders careered across the screen in the best tradition of Italian exploitation movies and 'fumetti' comic strips.

The most famous of the Italian crime-fighters was Superargo, a wrestler in the mould of Mexican film institutions' Santo and Blue Demon. In Nick Nostro's pacy ***Superago against Diabolicus*** (1966), champion wrestler Superargo was played by rock-jawed stuntman Giovanni Cianfriglia (alias 'Ken Wood'), his hulking frame constrained by a bright-red bullet-proof bodysuit. When he accidentally kills opponent El Tigre in a world championship bout, Superargo retires from the ring and is employed by Colonel Kenton (Francisco Castillo Escalo), the head of the Secret Service, to investigate cargo ship hijacks in which uranium and mercury have been stolen. Superargo tracks the culprits to an island, using cocktail olives containing tiny Geiger counters. There he faces villain Diabolicus (Gerard Tichy) – 'The Future Ruler of the Universe' – and his sadistic partner (Loredana Nusciak) in their subterranean hideout. Alchemist Diabolicus has discovered the secret of turning base metals into gold using nuclear power and he plans to flood the world's gold supply. Monica Randall played Superargo's lover, Lydia, who is kidnapped by Conrad (Geoffrey Copplestone), Diabolicus' ally in the Secret Service.

Superargo was a key influence on Mario Bava's *Danger: Diabolik*. Indestructible Superargo drives a white E-type Jaguar, which is bullet-proof and loaded with gadgets. The scenes in the island grottos and Diabolicus' lair as well as Franco Pisano's trumpet score and atmospheric flute cues also pre-empt *Diabolik*. *Superargo* was stylishly filmed in Eastmancolor and Cromoscope, with interiors at Estudios Balcazar (Barcelona) and De Paolis (Rome). Superargo deploys numerous ridiculous gadgets and takes on Diabolicus' goons armed with a machine gun, a flamethrower, a fire extinguisher and dynamite. He wears a wrestling mask (concealing his identity) and is able to withstand extremes of temperature and breathe underwater. As Diabolicus tries to escape in a one-man rocket, Superargo closes the launch pad doors so the rocket can't take off, destroying the island.

It the sequel, Paolo Bianchini's **Superargo** (1968 – *Superargo and the Faceless Giants* and *The King of Criminals*), Superargo (Wood) is now teamed with Kamir (Aldo Sambrell) a guru-like Hindu who has trained Superargo in psychic mind manipulation and mysticism. Superargo attempts to solve 'The Case of the Missing Champions' – 16 top athletes have gone missing in the last two years. The last abductee is wrestler Joe Brand. Superargo guards Brand's sister, Claire (Luisa Baratto), but she is kidnapped by tall, blank-faced robots wearing metal helmets, shoulder pads and gauntlets. Eventually the trail leads to the castle lair of mad professor Wond (Guy Madison) and his lover, Gloria Devon (Diana Lorys), the daughter of an eminent scientist who is creating human organs. Wond has created an army of remote-controlled androids. *Superargo* is enjoyable hokum. Franco Pisano again wrote the saxy theme tune, which resembles Henry Mancini's 'Pink Panther' theme. Wood acquits himself well in the fight sequences and, even though he's retired from the ring, still wears his conspicuous red bodysuit, black pants, gloves and eye mask – it brings him good luck. In addition to his Jag he drives a station wagon with blades on the bonnet. When trapped in a cell filling with poisonous gas, Superargo and Kamir levitate above the noxious cloud. They zap the robot army with ray guns and callous Superargo throws Wond into a pool of quicksand and lets him sink – 'It's all he deserves'.

Patterned on the Superargo movies, Gianfranco Parolini's **The Fantastic Three** (1967 – *Three Fantastic Supermen*) initiated an acrobatic series. The heroes, Tony, Brad and Nick, were played by Tony Kendall, Brad Harris and Nick Jordan, dressed in red bullet-proof suits, masks and capes. Sequels included *Three Supermen in Tokyo* (1968) and *Three Supermen in the West* (1973). Alfonso Brescia's surreal *Super Stooges Versus the Wonder Women* (1973) reuses sets, costumes and actors from Brescia's own *The Beauty of the Barbarian*, with three superheroes (a warrior, a kung fu expert and a black strongman) up against the Amazons.

The Fantastic Argoman (1966), directed by 'Terence Hathaway'/Sergio Grieco, was a spoof, with Roger Browne playing both Sir Reginald Hoover and his alter ego, Argoman, a yellow-suited, red-cloaked, black-masked crimebuster who is able to move objects and control pliant minds with 'telekenetics' thought control. He's called in by Inspector Lawrence (Dario De Grassi) of Scotland Yard to battle sexy superthief Jenabell (Dominique Boschero), the self-proclaimed Queen of the World, who steals the Muradoff A-4, a massive diamond. She aims to take over the world with the aid of her army of black-suited henchmen and a robot. Filmed on location in London and Paris, *Fantastic Argoman* never quite fulfils the promise of its surreal opening sequence, when the hero is put before a Chinese firing squad. He utters his snappy catchphrase in a Dalek-like monotone ('Kill each other, kill each other') and his captors do just that. Eduardo Fajardo played Sir Reginald's Indian butler, Chandra, Nadia Marlowa was Reginald's girlfriend Samantha, and Mimmo Palmera played Jenabell's beefy henchman Kurt. The interior of her headquarters, a space-age maze of steel corridors and chambers, was created at Cinecittà. Jenabell travels by hovercraft (a credit thanks 'Hovercraft England' on the Isle of Wight) and fools Argoman with a series of doppelgangers. 'She tricked me with these doubles', says Argoman, like a drunk in an expensive nightclub. Piero Umiliani provided the jazz score. For a somewhat patchy superhero, it seems appropriate that the less-than-fantastic Argoman's symbol is a turd-like red spiral on his forehead.

Alberto De Martino's **Puma Man** (1980 – *The Pumaman*) is notorious as one of the worst superhero movies of all – it's right down there with *Rat Pfink a Boo Boo* (1966) and *Condorman* (1981). The opening scrawl informs us, 'An ancient Aztec legend tells of a God who descends to Earth from the stars at the dawn of time and became the father of the first Puma Man'. In London, Professor Tony Farms (Walter George Alton), an American dinosaur expert, meets Aztec Vadinho (Miguelangel Fuentes) who has the wordy job title 'High Priest of the Temple of the God who Came from Other Worlds'. Vadinho knows that Tony is Puma Man, the possessor of a multitude of Puma-inspired special abilities. Once Tony dons a magic belt he can sense impending danger, land safely when dropped from a great height, claw through metal, see in the dark and, bizarrely, even fly. Puma Man later discovers that he can walk through walls, teleport to any location and stop his heartbeat to appear dead. At this last skill, Alton is most convincing.

Garbed in tan slacks and a brown cape, Puma Man doesn't exactly look the part, but fortunately his adversaries are even more ridiculously dressed. Puma Man searches for an Aztec mask that has special mind-controlling powers. Sydne Rome is Jane Dobson (an Aztec expert and Tony's love interest) and Silvano Tranquilli is her ambassador father. The mask has been stolen by Kobras (Donald Pleasence, his name misspelt 'Pleasance' in the titles) and his henchman Rankor (Benito Stefanelli), both of whom model shiny PVC outfits. Nello Pazzafini, Giovanni Cianfriglia and Guido Lollobrigida are among Kobras' toughs. The bad guys control Jane's mind, hypnotise a summit of international generals and steal Puma Man's powers. Everyone except Pleasence pronounces the hero's name as 'Poo-ma Man', which enlivens the awful script. De Martino shot on location in London, with interiors at Incir-De Paolis, Rome. The music by Renato Serio is mostly inappropriately jovial synthesiser cues and funky disco. Bland Alton is no actor, nor is he particularly proficient at the action scenes – he's certainly not the epitome of someone who has 'the powers of a man-god, the powers of a Poo-ma Man'. The film is amateurish in all departments, but the flying sequences stand out, as becaped Puma Man is suspended, flailing, by the seat of his pants from wires. This humiliation is performed in front of rear-projected aerial shots of London apparently shot on wobbly Super-8. There's little pretence of an effect, special or otherwise. Needless to say, Poo-ma Man continues to find a cult audience among those who are also mystically protected and immune to poor dubbing and special effects.

Crime Does Pay: Heists

During the 1960s, international heist films allowed enterprising producers to blend big-name international casts, glamour, sex and exotic locales, in a variation on the Bond cocktail, with the thieving villains now the heroes. The best Italian caper movie was Giuliano Montaldo's **Grand Slam** (1967), originally titled *Ad Ogni Costo* [At All Costs]. In the third Bond film, Goldfinger's plan to destroy Fort Knox's gold reserve was 'Operation Grand Slam'. Professor James Anders (*Little Caesar* himself, Edward G. Robinson), a retired schoolteacher, hatches a plan to steal $10 million in diamonds during the February carnival in Rio De Janeiro. With help from New York crime lord Mark Milford (Adolfo Celi), Anders recruits electronic technician Agostino Rossi (Riccardo Cucciolla), dapper French gigolo Robert Brissac alias 'Jean Paul Audry' (Robert Hoffman), aristocratic English safecracker Gregg (George Rigaud) and syndicate killer Erich Weiss (Klaus Kinski). Brissac befriends Mary Ann Davis (Janet Leigh), the diamond company's secretary, who holds the vault key. Though the safe, a Royal 1964, has been installed with a state-of-the-art sonic security system, the Grand Slam 70, the gang pull the job off. Only Weiss escapes and he is killed by Milford, who discovers the diamond case is empty. The plan has been an elaborate, intricately engineered ruse by the professor and his real partner, Mary Ann.

Made on a big budget, *Grand Slam* blends the international aspects of heist films with the meticulous robbery of *Rififi* (1955) and the tragic dénouement of *The Asphalt Jungle* (1950). Montaldo shot on location at Westminster Bridge, Big Ben and the Houses of Parliament in London, the Spanish Steps and Colosseum in Rome, and the Statue of Liberty and the Pan Am Building in New York. Most of the action is set in Rio during the 1967 carnival and many of the city's landmarks appear, including the beaches at Copacabana, Ipanema and Botafofo, Sugar Loaf mountain in Guanabara Bay and the statue of Christ the Redeemer atop Corcovado mountain. The robbers prepare for their heist on a yacht in the harbour and the Rio backdrop gives the film an added visual dimension. Interiors were shot at DEAR Cinestudi in Rome, with additional footage lensed in Madrid. Montaldo pays minute detail to the heist's planning and execution: Weiss climbs into the sewers under the bank, Rossi and Gregg access the vault by abseiling across a street packed with Rio revellers, while Brissac seduces Mary Ann and steals the vault key. The vault is criss-crossed with laser beams and rigged with sound-sensitive alarms. Ennio Morricone supplied the inventive score, which features a jaunty Euro-pop trumpet theme and an angelic children's choir. The samba music used for the carnival scenes was the LP 'Bafo Da Onca', released by Rozenblit Mocambo records. Setuaca (played by Jussara), a girl living on a boat in Rio harbour, sings 'Go Away Melancholy' and 'He and I' (actually voiced by Brazilian bossa nova singer Maysa Matarazzo). Produced by Jolly Film, *Grand Slam* was touted as a possible Sergio Leone film and enjoyed great success on its international release.

Montaldo assembled another international cast for the explosive **Machine Gun McCain** (1969), based on Ovid Demaris' novel *Candyleg*. Hank McCain (John Cassavetes) is pardoned having served 12 years of a life sentence for armed robbery, but his release from San Quentin has been engineered by New York mobster Charlie Adamo (Peter Falk). McCain is to rob the Royal Hotel in Las Vegas, a prestigious new casino owned by the Family, headed by Don Francesco DeMarco (Gabriele Ferzetti) and Don Salvatore (Salvo Randone). With help from Irene Tucker (Britt Ekland), McCain plants bombs in the hotel and poses as a fire-fighter to lift $2 million. The Mafia discover Adamo's involvement – executing the traitor and his lieutenant Duke Mazzanga (Luigi Pistilli) – and mobilise hitman Pete (Tony Kendall) to track the fugitives down.

McCain is a slow-burner, which builds to a frantic last half-hour as Hank and Irene – the Bonnie and Clyde of Italian crime films – have nowhere to hide. Cassavetes makes a fine stroppy hero and Falk's gravelly delivery is perfect for tough mob movies. The film's highpoint is Hank's incredible, random act of selfish terrorism, when a series of bombs devastate the hotel. The strong supporting cast includes Pierluigi Apra as McCain's traitorous son, Jack (a small-time hood), Florinda Bolkan as Adamo's wife, Joni (who is having an affair with Don Francesco) and Steffen Zacharias as casino manager Abe Stilberman. Gena Rowlands (Cassavetes' wife) contributed a fine cameo as McCain's ex-partner in crime, Rosemary Scott – they were once known as 'The Machine Gun Lovers'. When captured by mobster Pete, Rosemary shoots herself rather than disclosing McCain's hiding place. *McCain* was photographed in Techniscope by Enrico Menczer at De Paolis and DEAR Studios, and on location in San Francisco Bay and Las Vegas, including neon-lit Sunset Strip. Morricone provided the theme music, a frantic, dissonant jazz cue. Hank's languorous theme is played on trumpet, a 'love theme' for Hank and Irene is familiarly lush, and Morricone's song 'Belinda May' can be heard on the car radio as Hank leaves San Quentin. Fans of Morricone's 'Ballad of Hank McCain' (sung by Jackie Lynton), which features prominently on the soundtrack album, needn't get excited. In the 96-minute English language print this cue is reduced to a fragment played over the end titles. The full version of the song is used more extensively in the 115-minute Italian print, *Gli intoccabili* (The Untouchables).

The Hit Parade: Mobsters and Killers

If they weren't knocking off banks and casinos, Italian crime villains were mobsters, hitmen and small-time crooks. Sergio Sollima's **Violent City** (1970) was typical of Charles Bronson's international stardom. It was an outright smash in Europe at 105 minutes; however, the US print, cut to 92 minutes, fared badly. Bronson had to wait until *Death Wish* (1974) to have a blockbusting hit in the US, whereupon *Violent City* was re-released, retitled *The Family*. Jeff Heston (Bronson), a professional hitman, is commissioned to assassinate Coogan's rich uncle in the US Virgin Islands. Having gained his inheritance, Coogan ambushes Jeff, leaving him for dead. Jeff goes after Coogan and Coogan's lover – also once Jeff's girl – Vanessa Sheldon (Jill Ireland). With old friend Killain (Michel Constantin), a heroin addict, Jeff tracks Coogan to the Michigan International Speedway and kills him. Jeff then locates Vanessa in New Orleans, where he discovers she is – and always has been – married to crime kingpin Al Weber (Telly Savalas), head of the billion-dollar 'Organisation'. Weber, Killain, Coogan and even Jeff are pawns in Vanessa's game. Jeff is duped into killing Killain and Weber and is later framed by crooked attorney Steve (Umberto Orsini) and Vanessa. They learn that Jeff has fled Louisiana and is fighting as a mercenary in Africa, but on the day the couple arrive at the Organisation's skyscraper for Vanessa to take her place as majority shareholder, Jeff lies in wait.

Hit Man: Jeff Heston takes aim at the Michigan International Speedway track in Sergio Sollima's *Violent City* (1970). Charles Bronson pictured on the sleeve of Ennio Morricone's original soundtrack.

Violent City sees athletic, muscle-bound Bronson at his Euro peak. It is certainly the best of the films in which he appeared with his wife, Ireland, though their many costume changes seem excessive – incognito Jeff apparently travels light, when in reality he would need a trailer-sized suitcase. *Violent City* was co-scripted by future director Lina Wertmüller, to whom it probably owes Vanessa's prominence in the narrative, charting her rise from fashion model to godmother. With the working title *Final Shot*, *Violent City* was to have starred Tony Musante and Florinda Bolkan, but Universal became involved and upped the budget. Sollima filmed interiors at Cinecittà and exteriors on the island of St Thomas in the US Virgin Islands; in New Orleans (the International Airport, the Louisiana bayous and plantations hung with Spanish Moss and the French Quarter where Jeff stays at the Cornstalk Fence Hotel); and the Michigan International Speedway track at Irish Hills. Jeff poses as a picnicker, with his precision rifle hidden in a wicker hamper. He lies in wait for Coogan's racing car, to make Coogan's death appear to be a tyre blow-out. The Can-Am racing was filmed during an actual meet – Sterling Moss and other drivers make cameo appearances.

The film's opening scenes in the Virgin Islands are devoid of dialogue, as Jeff and Vanessa are snapped by an unseen photographer, freeze-framing the images. Not simply a stylistic device by Sollima, this is one of Weber's cronies keeping track of Vanessa. On St George, the couple are chased by thugs – this frantic, dusty car chase was staged by stunt driver Remy Julienne, from *The Italian Job* (1969). Jeff drives a white Mustang and Sollima deploys many classic American cars throughout the film, the boxy, shiny autos' shape and elegance emphasised by the letterbox Techniscope frame. Aldo Tonti's glossy cinematography is completely lost in panned-and-scanned prints of the movie. In the finale, the 'Widow Weber' and Steve take the external glass elevator up to the board meeting. Halfway up, bullets shatter the glass and Steve falls dead. Jeff, hidden on the flat roof of I.L. Lyons & Co. across the street, takes aim at Vanessa. The whole scene is played out in silence and Vanessa mouths, 'Please don't make me suffer', as Jeff puts a well-aimed bullet though her head. *Violent City* also benefits from a powerful Morricone theme, a popular choice with soundtrack buyers, which is re-orchestrated throughout the action to menacing effect. The title theme begins with doom-laden chords and feedback, then the melody is picked up by jagged guitars and syncopated strings, driven by a drum kit and pulsing bass. A pop version of his giallo themes, this is maestro Morricone at his best.

Sollima then made **Revolver** (1973). Vito Cipriani (Oliver Reed), the vice-governor of Monza Prison, is forced to release small-time thief Milo Ruiz (Fabio Testi) when Vito's wife, Anna (Agostino Belli), is kidnapped by mobsters. Ruiz agrees to help Cipriani and the trail leads to Paris to drug-addled hippy pop star Al Niko (Daniel Beretta). Cipriani realises that the mobsters want to kill Ruiz: he can prove the innocence of a man accused of murdering a rich capitalist. In order to save his wife, Cipriani guns down Ruiz and then deliberately fails to identify the corpse of the chief kidnapper. Rather like Reed's foul-mouthed Cipriani,

Revolver is one mean bastard of a film, its dark subject matter accentuated by the miserable grey, wintry atmosphere. Sollima filmed in Milan, with interiors at ICET De Paolis Studios. Parisian-shot footage includes the narrow streets of Montmartre, Notre Dame Cathedral on Ile de la Cité (where Niko films a pop video) and Niko's apartment overlooking the Eiffel Tower. In a snowbound interlude, Cipriani and Ruiz sneak into France across the Alps. Morricone provides one of his least-heard scores, featuring the sweeping, stately main theme which is a re-orchestration of the song 'Un Amico' as performed by Beretta (as Christ-like pin-up boy Niko). The supporting cast features Frederic De Pasquale as kidnapper and heroin trafficker Michel Granier, Steffen Zacharias as Joe Lacour (Granier's associate), Paola Pitagora as Ruiz's love interest, Carlotta, Marc Mazza as a duplicitous French police inspector, and Calisto Calisti as Monza Prison guard Maresciallo Fantuzzi, who is run over by Granier's Sicilian henchmen. Rene Kolldehoff played the lawyer who tells Cipriani that society has many ways of defending itself: 'Red tape, prison bars and the revolver'. It is this reasoning that convinces Cipriani that there is no moral contest between saving his innocent wife and executing crook Ruiz. Largely ignored outside Europe at the time of its release, it was exhibited in the US as *Blood in the Streets* with the tagline 'Makes *Death Wish* look like wishful thinking'.

Lee Van Cleef's contribution to Italian crime movies was Michele Lupo's **Mean Frank and Crazy Tony** (1973). Ageing, pipe-smoking Chicago crime kingpin Frank Diomedes, known as 'Frankie Dio' (Van Cleef), arrives in Italy to kill Giuseppe 'Joe' Sciti (Mario Erpichini). Rival crime boss Louis Annunziata (Jean Rochefort), a Marseille heroin smuggler, is determined to put Frankie away for good and has his hoods kill Frankie's associate Massara (Fausto Tozzi) and Frankie's brother, Sylvester (Silvano Tranquilli), a doctor who has nothing to do with organised crime. Frankie and young hood Tony Breda (Tony LoBianco) steal an ESSO oil truck and drive to Marseille where they attack Annunziata's heroin operation in a fortified frozen fish factory. *Mean Frank and Crazy Tony* was also released in a severely truncated 79-minute version as *Escape from Death Row*, which lost 18 minutes of footage, toning down the violence but reducing the plot to incomprehensibility.

The film's powerful score was penned by Riz Ortolani and many cult movie regulars propped up the supporting cast: Edwige Fenech played Tony's long-suffering girlfriend, Orchid, Steffen Zacharias was Tony's lawyer, Jess Hahn was Frankie's contact Jeannot, and Claudio Ruffini and Gilberto Galimberti were ESSO drivers. Romano Puppo played an assassin who attempts to shoot Frankie while he's relaxing in the prison yard and also doubled Van Cleef in the action sequences (Puppo dons a flesh-coloured swimming cap to appear bald). Stuntmen Nello Pazzafini and Osiride Pevarello played bullying jailbirds and Annunziata's gang features Adolfo Lastretti, Goffredo Unger, Giovanni Cianfriglia and Robert Hundar. The latter stabs Frankie's brother to death in a photo booth and then sneers when the developed photos emerge. Frankie kills Hundar with an electric drill and electrocutes Lastretti in a bath with a hairdryer. Frankie speeds the truck along the Marseille waterfront pursued by French border police and the fish factory shootout ends with Annunziata locked in an industrial refrigerator, which Frankie turns down to –60º to deep freeze the villain.

Many Italian crime films of the period capitalised on the newfound box office popularity of the Mafia. In Alberto De Martino's *Crime Boss* (1972) Sicilian Antonio Mancuso (Antonio Sabato) arrives in Milan to take revenge for his father's death on godfather Don Vincenzo (Telly Savalas). Nardo Bonomi's ***The Long Arm of the Godfather*** (1972) cast Peter Lee Lawrence as Vincenzo, a cowardly little thug who purloins a truckload of stolen armaments from his boss, Don Carmelo (Adolfo Celi). Vincenzo flees to North Africa with his lover Sabina (Erika Blanc), but when he tries to sell the guns to an Arab prince, the godfather and his hoods show up. The ending sees Vincenzo and Sabina, who is mortally wounded, attempting to escape with their money in a rapidly sinking motorboat.

Duccio Tessari's international gangster hit ***Tony Arzenta*** (1973 – *Big Guns*) cast Alain Delon in one of his finest vehicles as Tony, a hitman who plans to retire. Tony is a distant cousin of Delon's iconic Jef Costello in *Le Samouraï* (1967). When his four Mafia bosses (including Richard Conte and Anton Diffring) try to rub Tony out, they accidentally blow up his wife, Anna (Nicoletta Machiavelli), and little son, Carlo, with a car bomb, which catapults Tony on a brutal vendetta. Excellently shot across Europe by Silvano Ippoliti and with a fine Gianni Ferrio score, *Tony Arzenta* deployed Carla Gravina, Marc Porel, Roger Hanin, Erika Blanc, Rosalba Neri, Umberto Orsini, Claudio Ruffini, Ettore Manni and Loredana Nusciak in supporting roles. Silvano Tranquilli played an Interpol agent who allows Tony his revenge – as he's doing the law a favour – but during a Mafia wedding in Sicily, Tony finds that it is he who has become the target.

Fernando Di Leo's ***Milan Calibre 9*** (1972) saw Ugo Piazza, known as 'Potatohead' (Gastone Moschin in a stoic performance), released from prison after three years. Money-laundering godfather 'The Mikado' (Lionel Stander) wants to know where Ugo's hidden the $300,000 he has stolen from the mob, but despite beatings and torture Ugo remains silent. The hoods on his trail include Mario Adorf as greasy, sadistic blabbermouth Rocco Musco, with Angelo Infanti and Giuseppe Castellano as his henchmen. Philippe Leroy played Ugo's ally, Kino, Ivo Garrani was blind ex-mob boss Don Vincenzo and Barbara Bouchet was Ugo's lover, go-go dancer Nelly. Frank Wolf and Luigi Pistilli played the cops out to get the Mikado, who bicker about the north-south/rich-poor divide in Italy. Based on the novel by Giorgio Scerbanenco, *Milan Calibre 9* was photographed by Franco Villa and boasts a powerful score by Luis Enriquez Bacalov and prog-rock band Osanna. The gripping, labyrinthine plot builds to one terrible, violent final act worthy of Jacobean tragedy.

In Di Leo's ***Manhunt*** (1972) two New York hitmen (Henry Silva and Woody Strode) arrive in Milan to rub out a small-time pimp, Luca Canali (Adorf). In a horrific scene, Canali's wife (Sylva Koscina) and daughter are deliberately run down in the street and during the incredible ensuing chase, Canali head-butts the windscreen of the speeding van, smashing through the glass and attacking the driver. The manhunt for Luca is actually a diversionary ploy by sadistic mobster boss Adolfo Celi, which leads to a confrontation between the hitmen and Canali in a junk yard.

Set in Sicily, Di Leo's **The Boss** (1973) cast Henry Silva as Lanzetta, a Mafia hitman who in the film's opening scene obliterates a rival don and his crew in a cinema with a grenade launcher. In retribution, Lanzetta's boss's daughter is kidnapped by hoods disguised as student radicals, which escalates the gang war. Gianni Garko was the bemused police commissioner caught in the crossfire and Marino Masé played Lanzetta's cohort. Di Leo's high-calibre trilogy is defined by car chases, explosions, sleazy nightclubs, parcel bombings, groovy fashions, murders, very cruel beatings, excessive violence, excellent production values and unpredictable, engrossing stories – as to be expected from the proficient screenwriter-turned-director.

There was a host of loony psychopaths in Italian crime movies – conscienceless thrill-killers who perpetrated kidnappings involving strong violence and sadistic sexual humiliation. Mario Bava's **Rabid Dogs** (1974 – *Kidnapped*) had bystanders Maria (Lea Lander), Riccardo (Riccardo Cucciolla) and his gravely ailing infant son (who Riccardo is speeding to hospital) taken hostage by three payroll thieves: Blade (Aldo Caponi), Doc (Maurice Poli) and Thirty-two (Luigi Montefiori). After a horrific roadtrip, Riccardo finally rids himself of his captors, but the twist is that he is also a kidnapper and the child is his victim. In **Redneck** (1973), Telly Savalas and Franco Nero played Memphis and Dino 'Mosquito' Bianco, two hoods on the run following a jewellery robbery, who inadvertently kidnap 13-year-old Lennox Duncan (Mark Lester), a UN diplomat's son. Memphis is a madcap villain, a sadistic, dope-smoking, hymn-singing fanatic, with Savalas shouting most of his dialogue in a thick Alabaman accent. This nasty little film is notable for the horrific scene when Memphis pushes a family of German campers locked inside their caravan into a river.

In Pasquale Festa Campanile's **Hitch-hike** (1976) alcoholic reporter Walter Mancini (Nero) and his wife, Eve (Corrine Clery), are returning to Los Angeles from a hunting vacation, when they are taken hostage by lunatic Adam Collins (David Hess), who is on the run following a $2 million robbery. Based on Peter Kane's book *The Violence and the Fury*, *Hitch-hike* is grim entertainment. The sexual humiliation of Eve by Adam is voyeuristic and only Morricone's creepy, twanging score and the magnificent mountain scenery are of note. Though set in the US, the film was shot in the Abruzzo National Park and the falls at Monte Gelato, Lazio.

Umberto Lenzi's **Almost Human** (1974) headlined Tomas Milian as triggerhappy psychopath Giulio Sacchi, who kidnaps a rich heiress. Raymond Lovelock played Giulio's sidekick, Carmine, and Henry Silva was Inspector Walter Grandi.

The film, supported by a strident Morricone score, features some particularly unpleasant violence – at one point Giulio machine-guns a house-full of hostages and kills his lover Iola (Anita Strindberg) by driving her Mini off a cliff. When it appears that Giulio, having killed the heiress, has got away with the money, Grandi executes Giulio himself.

When Michele Placido directed **Romanzo criminale** [Crime Novel] in 2005, he welded Quentin Tarantino and Martin Scorsese's brand of movie gangsterism to its Italian crime movie equivalent. Placido depicted the rise of underworld kidnappers Dandy (Claudio Santamaria), Lebanese (Pier Francesco Favino) and Ice (Kim Rossi Stuart) against a backdrop of Rome's drug trade from the 1970s through to the 1990s. The visuals, kinetic action and costumery are clearly based on films such as Lenzi's. *Romanzo criminale* has since spawned a miniseries of the same title, directed by Sergio Sollima's son, Stefano.

Top of the Cops: Italian Poliziotteschi

The shift in audience preference from Italian westerns to crime movies in the early 1970s was a reflection of the times. Westerns were now laughing at their heroes in spoofs and parodies, so crime film 'poliziotteschi' moved spaghetti western-style violence onto the streets of Italy, where the fantasy violence of the far west was replaced by convincing mean street brutality. Poliziotteschi were often set in northern Italy – within the industrial triangle of Milan, Genoa and Turin – and were Italian political films reinvented as reactionary action cinema.

The most influential of the 'poliziotteschi' was Enzo G. Castellari's ***The Marseilles Connection*** (1973 – *High Crime*). The Italian title translates as 'The Police Indicts, The Law Acquits'. A new gang have muscled in on the Marseilles-Genoa drug trade and their calling card is castration. Trafficker 'The Lebanese' is killed by a car bomb, so Vice-Commissioner Belli (Franco Nero) of the Squadra Volante (Flying Squad) asks for help from gangster Cafiero (Fernando Rey, from *The French Connection*). Belli's boss, Chief Commissioner Aldo Scavino (James Whitmore, from *The Asphalt Jungle*), has compiled a dossier on those he thinks responsible but is murdered in the street when he tries to deliver it to the DA. Belli reconstructs the missing dossier, but as he inches closer to severing the Marseille Connection, his loved ones stray into the firing line.

This is the best Nero-Castellari collaboration. Amid the colourful 1970s décor and fashions, Castellari isn't concerned with the story's political agenda (strikers demonstrate briefly outside a factory) and concentrates instead on the corrupting social issues, with heroin smuggled from Beirut in children's toy cement mixers and crates of oranges. Commissioner Scavino's patience is contrasted with cop Nero's overzealous behaviour, though the latter needs and finally learns to be patient. To Scavino there are 'no heroes, no crusaders...we are only policemen'. On-location filming in Genoa and Marseille added authenticity to what was already a gritty story, and Castellari revelled in the gleeful depiction of stylised slow-motion slaughter. Industrialist Rivalta (Mario Erpichini) is

High Crime: Vice-Commissioner Belli (Franco Nero) takes on a ruthless gang of drug traffickers in Enzo G. Castellari's 1973 cop classic *The Marseilles Connection*. Artwork for the film's UK home video release.

run over while playing golf by motorcyclist Rico (Daniel Martin), who is himself murdered in the docks, torn apart by meat-hook wielding thugs. Umberto Griva (Duilio Del Prete), a gadabout playboy – the embarrassing brother of wealthy DUNANCO industrialist Franco Griva (Silvano Tranquilli) – is machine-gunned through a glass door. This violence is matched by tough-talking dialogue: 'There's someone spitting in our soup', notes Cafiero of their rival traffickers. A foot pursuit through the backstreets of Genoa and a screeching car chase opens the film with a blast. Guido and Maurizio De Angelis' funky car chase music was entitled 'Gangster Story'. Their urban score, with rattling percussion, electric piano, echoing voices and flute blasts, is one of the film's main attractions. The street killing of Scavino, shot down at point-blank range by a hood (Bruno Corazzari), wouldn't have such impact without the De Angelis' searing accompaniment.

Eventually Belli's closest relationships are endangered. Belli's lover, Mirella (Delia Boccardo), receives threatening phone calls and is beaten up by two of Griva's thugs (Nello Pazzafini and Giovanni Cianfriglia). Belli's young daughter, Annie (Stefania Castellari, the director's daughter), arrives in Genoa and nervous Belli sends her to the countryside into hiding. The traffickers trace her, fatally running her over. When the case appears cracked and the drug dealers have been defeated in a wild west gun battle in a Marseilles boatyard, Belli is felled by an assassin in the pay of untouchable industrialist Franco Griva. Director Castellari had one of his many 'Hitchcock moments' in *Marseilles Connection* (a cameo as a TV reporter) and Natasha Richardson appeared as a little girl playing hopscotch – Richardson was the daughter of Vanessa Redgrave, Nero's offscreen lover and later wife. Nero was in top athletic form as Belli in this massive box office hit – even the film's trailer is more entertaining than most cop thrillers. A typical Castellari electrocardio-drama, it kick-started poliziotteschi in style.

Steno's **Flatfoot** (1973) headlined Bud Spencer as Inspector Rizzo, aka 'Flatfoot' (slang for detective), an unorthodox cop in Spencer's hometown of Naples, who has a reputation for using his fists to solve cases. He finds himself up against the Baron (Angelo Infanti), who is smuggling drugs from Marseilles. With the death of Flatfoot's hunchback informant, Peppino, Flatfoot's investigation becomes a personal matter, bringing him into conflict with his new superior, Commissioner Tabassi (Adalberto Maria Merli). Flatfoot unites the crime factions in Naples against the Marseilles interlopers.

As in Spencer's comedies, there's a massed fistfight (here in a fish freighter's refrigeration room) but *Flatfoot* is mainly a well-plotted, violent cop movie. Spencer gives one of his best performances as the moseying cop who always gets his man and the blows that rain on him during the fight scenes actually seem to hurt him, rather than bouncing off his ursine frame. It was shot on location in sunny Naples, in the backstreets and dock waterfront of this beautiful city, including the port and the Hotel Excelsior (where the Baron meets his drug cartel superiors). Juliette Mayniel played Flatfoot's landlady, Maria, Jho Jekins was a US sailor involved in the trafficking, Enzo Cannavale was Deputy Inspector Caputo (Flatfoot's sidekick) and Dominic Barto was drug dealer Tom Ferramenti. Mario Pilar played digitally challenged 'Two-fingered Tony' (called Manomozza in the Italian print), the mobster behind Peppino's death and the drug operation. A funky score by G & M De Angelis livened up the action, and the jaunty 'Piedone Lo Sbirro' [Flatfoot's Theme] was played on Hank Marvin-style guitar by 'Santo and Johnny'. Three more 'Flatfoots' followed, seeing the hero … *in Hong Kong* (1975), … *in Africa* (1978) and … *in Egypt* (1980), all directed by Steno and starring Spencer.

In Franco Prosperi's **Risking** (1976), imprisoned jewel thief Massimo Salvatore (Raymond Lovelock) befriends mob boss Giulianelli (Martin Balsam) and with Giulianelli's henchman Piero (Heinz Domez) they break out. Salvatore is actually an undercover cop, Sergeant Massimo Turlani, who plans to destroy the drug rings running dope from France into San Remo and Genoa. He also has a personal score to settle with the traffickers – three years ago, two of mobster Marti's men paralysed Massimo's mother with a shotgun blast. Working for drugs baron Perrone (Ettore Manni), Massimo drives a Fiat lorry across the border. Gangly Lovelock was on top form as Massimo, Elke Sommer played Perrone's secretary (who knows he's a cop) and Riccardo Cucciolla was Commissioner Sacchi. Interiors were filmed at DEAR Studios, with location footage in Rome, San Remo and Genoa. Ubaldo Continiello's bouncy theme song jars with the film's violence. In jail, new arrival Massimo is subjected to arena combat in the Colosseum-like prison yard, a football match erupts into violence, and numerous shootings deploy the expected slo-mo blood splatters.

Bruno Corbucci, a journeyman writer-director and younger brother of Sergio, hit pay dirt with **The Cop in Blue Jeans**, the third most popular film in Italy in 1976. Tomas Milian played rampant special agent Nico Giraldi, battling purse snatchers in Roma. A gang of thieves led by the Baron (Guido Mannari) get more than they bargain for when they steal a briefcase containing $5 million in mob money from American businessman Norman Shelley (Jack Palance). This was the first time that Tomas Milian played unconventional cop Giraldi, a terrific creation based in part on Al Pacino's shaggy *Serpico* (1973). In Milian's high-octane interpretation, Giraldi rides a motorbike like Evel Knievel and apprehends criminals by kicking them in the groin. Nico wears shades, a woolly hat, extra-long scarf, sneakers, a bomber jacket and denims. Giraldi used to be a thief himself (The Pirate) and uses his connections to his advantage. He has a pet bird called Lieutenant Callahan (after 'Dirty' Harry) and a pet mouse named Serpico. Roberto Messina appeared as Giraldi's boss, Commissioner Tozzi, Raf Luca and Marcello Martana were cops Gargiulo and Trentini, and Maria Rosario Omaggio was Milian's love interest, literary agent Signorina Cattanio.

Cop in Blue Jeans was shot on location in Rome, at Fiumicino Airport, the football stadium (for a match between Lazio and Roma) and at Elios Studios. The film depicts the seedy underbelly of Rome – a murder occurs in the 'Carambola' pool hall, Giraldi impersonates a pimp in the 'Crocodile Club' disco, and Shelley's mobsters (headed by Benito Stefanelli) handcuff an enemy operative inside a car and feed the exhaust pipe through the window. The stunts are excitingly staged – Giraldi rides his bike up the staircase of a tenement block and destroys a fruit market. G & M De Angelis' catchy theme tune sounds more appropriate for a comedy, but the incidental cues hark back to their work on *Marseilles Connection*. Shelley poses as embassy official Richard J. Russo to smuggle laundered money back to the US and Palance steals the film with his croc-eyed villainy. He also played Manzari, a drug trafficker who clashes with rival Edmond Purdom, in Fernando Di Leo's revenger *Rulers of the City* (1976 – *Mister Scarface*).

Such was Milian's popularity as Nico Giraldi that a 10-film series followed. Each episode was directed by Corbucci and the last movie was released in 1984. Milian always displayed extravagant dress sense and Nico gained an expectant wife, Angela (Olimpia Di Nardo), and later a son, as ever more convoluted scenarios whisked him from Rome and Milan, to San Francisco, New York's 'Little Italy' and Miami. Milian also starred as vengeful cop Ravelli in Stelvio Massi's *Emergency Squad* (1974), who is on the trail of murderous criminals Marseillaise (Gaston Moschin) and Rino (Raymond Lovelock). The soundtrack foregrounds funky 'wacka-chacka' guitar, courtesy of Stelvio Cipriani.

Italian cinema didn't just reinvent film genres. If an actor became popular, then look-alikes would be employed in similar vehicles. Such was the case with Maurizio Merli, a dead-ringer for Franco Nero, who rose to stardom in a series of cop movies, Klondike adventures and westerns, though he was an excellent actor in his own right. Merli's finest film remains the massively popular **Violent Rome** (1976 – *Forced Impact*), directed by Enzo Castellari's father, Marino Girolami (as 'Franco Martinelli'), and scored by the De Angelis brothers. Inspector Bettini (Merli) and Rome's Special Squad take on the violent street scum who snatch bags and rob supermarkets. Cockney mobster Frank 'English' Spadoni (John Steiner) is behind the crime spree. During a bank hold-up Bettini's partner, undercover agent Biondi (Raymond Lovelock), is paralysed, leaving him confined to a wheelchair. Merli kills Spadoni but is prosecuted. He resigns from the force and joins the private 'vigilante committee' law enforcers of lawyer Giorgio Sartori (Richard Conte).

Violent Rome lives up to its title. When two hoods break into Sartori's villa and savagely assault his daughter, Sartori's retribution has the culprits thrashed to a pulp by his vigilantes. Even convalescing Biondi is beaten up in his wheelchair. Stunt coordinator Benito Stefanelli played one of Spadoni's balaclava-clad henchmen, Giovanni Cianfriglia was a hoodlum and Luciano Rossi played a rapist. Silvano Tranquilli was the police chief who lives by the credo 'Freedom through Law', Mimmo Palmera played Bettini's superior and Daniela Giordano was Bettini's hotellier lover, Erika. The film was shot on interiors at Incir-De Paolis with exteriors at many tourist spots in Rome and was a worldwide hit. Its highlight is an extended, tyre-screeching car chase cut to the De Angelis brothers' 'Gangster Story' cue, as Bettini pursues Frank Spadoni following a bungled hold-up. This is the most exciting, violent car chase in poliziotteschi, as Bettini kicks out his shattered windscreen and zooms after Spadoni, who machine-guns three innocent children in an effort to waylay his pursuer. If Eastwood's Dirty Harry Callahan was accused in the US of being fascist, then Bettini is Il Duce. Bettini's brother was killed during a robbery two years before and Merli's hard-line cop – and borderline vigilante – uses unorthodox methods. Biondi gleans information by bribing informants with drugs, while Bettini beats up suspects during interrogations and tells criminals the names of those who grassed on them. Merli is a fine hero in the Nero mould (he even runs like Nero) and *Violent Rome* closely resembles *Marseilles Connection*, down to its downbeat ending, as Bettini is machine-gunned as part of the ongoing vendetta between criminals and vigilantes.

In a spurt of prolificacy, Merli capitalised on his popularity with vehicles such as *A Special Cop in Action* (1976), *Tough Ones* (1976 – *Rome Armed to the Teeth*), *Violent Naples* (1976), *Magnum Cop* (1977 – with Joan Collins), *The Cynic, the Rat and the Fist* (1977) and *Convoy Busters* (1978). Giuseppe Rosati's **Fear in the City** (1976) is typical of such fare. Retired inspector Mario Murri (Merli) is happily trout fishing in the mountains until he's reinstated on the force by the commissioner (James Mason) to recapture Alberto Lettieri (Raymond Pellegrin). Cyril Cusack played Lettieri's cohort, Giacomo Masoni. Murri reassembles his old squad, Sergeants Esposito (Fausto Tozzi) and Neri (Giovanni Elsner), and begins to investigate in his own inimitable way, which involves gunfights, car chases and black eyes – the assistant prosecutor (Franco Ressel) tells Murri, 'This is not the far west, inspector'. Murri befriends Masoni's niece Laura (Silvia Dionisio), a vice girl, and eventually discovers that the hoods plan to steal a million-lira shipment of out-of-circulation cash being shipped from Milan to Rome. Shot on location in Rome (including Fiumicino Airport and Luna Park fairground), *Fear* is memorable for its action. Murri pursues two robbers in a tense motorbike chase and foils a robbery of the Agricultural Bank. Merli was excellent as the cool, Marlboro-smoking hero, cursed with a death wish since the murder of his wife and daughter in a car bomb explosion planned by Lettieri. Murri buys flowers and visits their grave, where he is set upon in a machine gun ambush by two of Lettieri's thugs, resulting in a cemetery shootout.

For a period in the mid-1970s it was tight as to who was top of the cops: Maurizio Merli, Franco Nero, Tomas Milian or Fabio Testi. Luc Merenda joined the fray with *The Violent Professionals* (1973), in which Merenda's police lieutenant is suspended from the force for callously shooting two escaped convicts (Antonio Casale and Luciano Rossi). Richard Conte was Merenda's adversary, crime boss Billion. Castellari and Nero reteamed on *Street Law* (1974), which was *Death Wish*, Italian style. Fabio Testi starred in Castellari's **The Big Racket** (1976), one of the fastest-paced and most excessively violent poliziotteschi. Rome storekeepers, merchants, club owners and restaurateurs are being made to pay protection to racketeers led by Rudy (Gianni Loffredo), who is also trafficking heroin. When Inspector Nicola 'Nico' Palmieri (Testi) uses unauthorised police procedural methods to combat these preying thugs he's thrown off the force. To take revenge he assembles a group of specialist killers to attack Rudy's warehouse stronghold.

Big Racket was shot on location in Rome (Piazza Navona, the Colosseum, the Arch of Constantine and the ruins of the Roman Forum) but is certainly not a tourist guide image of the city. Castellari depicts a Rome of discos, flared fashion disasters and fast cars, where 'pure snow' heroin mingles with the blood of the innocent. There are car chases and some impressive explosions – no other director orchestrates violent mayhem quite like Castellari. It is easily his most brutal, frightening film, mixing action with extremist politics, and was condemned by many in Italy as too reactionary. It was banned in the UK for many years, not only for its bloody thuggery but also for two rape scenes. Restaurateur Luigi Giulti (Renzo Palmer) agrees to help the police, but the mobsters kidnap his teenage daughter, Stefania (Stefania Girolami), and savagely assault her. Giulti guns the culprits down and is imprisoned, thus the innocent and law-abiding are dragged down to the level of scum.

Castellari stages a succession of violent set pieces in comic-book manner. The opening scenes depict the racketeer thugs, including Giovanni Cianfriglia, Roberto Dell'Aqua, Massimo Vanni and Marcella Michelangeli (as the sadistic Marcy), smashing up stores and restaurants in slow motion, cut to G & M De Angelis' deafening, frantic score. These neon-lit images of the motorcycle gang anticipate Castellari's post-apocalypse films, such as *1990: The Bronx Warriors*. Nico's car is rolled downhill by the mobsters, with the camera providing a view from inside the vehicle as it tumbles down the slope, a cascade of broken glass exploding across the screen. When the police think they are about to ambush the hoods at a deposit box robbery in Tiburtina, they are ambushed – Rudy's crew attack the cops' rearguard and massacre them. Nico's partner, Sergeant Salvatore Valesci (Sal Borgese), is killed and Giovanni Rossetti (Orso Maria Guerrini), a professional hunter who has just returned from a skiing holiday, helps the police rout the mobsters. Rossetti's apartment is later torched and his wife raped and killed.

Nico's vengeful 'Magnificent Five' comprises Rossetti; wronged nightclub owner Piero Mazzarelli (Glauco Onorato), now wearing a neck brace following a beating; jailbird hitman Doringo (Romano Puppo); pickpocket Pepe (Vincent Gardenia); and restaurateur Giulti, now a psychopath. They wait in ambush at an agricultural tools plant for a summit meeting of top mobsters: Rudy, his attorney Giovanni Giuni (Antonio Marsina), and crime bosses Fabrizi (Salvatore Billa), Cuomo (Giovanni Bonadonna), Arresti Siccla (Franco Borelli) and Luigi Mayer (Pietro Ceccarelli). This bushwhack results in a pitched battle of slow-motion violence. Nico ends the film captured in freeze-frame – smashing his shotgun in a raging fit – having incinerated Rudy's car. Castellari followed this with the lesser *The Heroin Busters* (1978), with Testi and David Hemmings, but *Racket* remains his cop masterpiece – its raw energy and unleashed savagery still powerful. Let's hear it for vigilantism!

Chapter Nine

Anarchy and Allegory
Political Cinema

Italy was at the forefront of political cinema in the 1960s, though its preoccupation with matters Italian – Fascism, Communism, 'strategies of tension', student revolts and terrorism – often proved too parochial for international audiences. The internal politics of Italy held little interest for audiences with scant understanding of the political system and few reference points. But some Italian political films – directed by Francesco Rosi, Damiano Damiani, Elio Petri, Gillo Pontecorvo and Bernardo Bertolucci – did find international success, disguised as historical adventures, westerns and thrillers, or as biographies of rebel bandit Salvatore Giuliano, mercenary William Walker and gangster Charles 'Lucky' Luciano.

Moral Victories: Gillo Pontecorvo

Gillo Pontecorvo's ***Battle of Algiers*** (1966), written by Franco Solinas from a story by Solinas and Pontecorvo, was based on historical fact. It recounts the Algerian peoples' struggle to rid themselves of French occupation, through revolt and terrorism: Pontecorvo and Solinas drew on 10,000 eyewitness accounts. In 1954, criminal Omar Ali, alias 'Ali La Pointe' (Brahim Haggiag) joins the National Liberation Front (FNL), a Muslim movement which plans its revolution from the Casbah district, an impenetrable warren of narrow streets and alleys. In 1956 the FNL clean up the Casbah, cracking down on drug traffickers and banning alcohol, prostitution and other iniquities blamed on colonialism. They begin 'direct action', shooting police officers in the streets, which leads the French to seal off the Casbah with checkpoints. The attacks continue and French extremists detonate bombs in the Casbah while the inhabitants sleep. In revenge, women of the FNL dress in western garb to blow up the offices of Air France, a mambo milk bar on Rue D'Isly, a café on Rue Michelot, and later a racetrack, causing many civilian casualties. On 10 January 1957, the French

UK poster for Gillo Pontecorvo's revolutionary docu-drama *Battle of Algiers* (1966), which depicted the Algerian National Liberation Front's (FNL) insurgence against French colonial rule.

Tenth Paratroop Division led by Colonel Philippe Mathieu (Jean Martin) arrive and resolve to break up the FNL.

Battle of Algiers opens with Ali La Pointe trapped in hiding by Mathieu's paratroops and then flashes back to tell his story, in grainy monochrome footage which resembles newsreels. The docu-realism is apparent in the aftermath of the FNL's bombing campaign, as Pontecorvo films the dead and walking wounded. Pontecorvo and his nine-man Italian crew (including cinematographer Marcello Gatti) filmed in Algiers, using actual locations. The film was a co-production between Igor Films (Rome) and Casbah Films (Algeria). It was the country's first film since its independence and almost the entire cast were non-actors. Mohamed Ben Kassen played FNL boy soldier Little Omar and Yacef Saadi (an actual leader of the FNL and the producer of the film) played himself, renamed 'Jaffar'. Pontecorvo doesn't take sides and with the arrival of the French paratroopers, the colonel is given his voice, notably in a press conference where he explains their swift, ruthless stratagem in dismantling the FNL cell structure. They torture FNL suspects, administering blowtorches, beatings, drownings and electrodes. Ennio Morricone, in collaboration with Pontecorvo, wrote an edifying theme which intensifies the film's power. The simple four-note flute cue, backed by swelling, ominous strings, scores the aftermath of bomb blasts, or Pontecorvo's sweeping pans across Algiers from the rich European City to the labyrinthine Casbah. This theme becomes the revolution's anthem. Morricone also deploys an organ fugue (for the harrowing torture scenes); throbbing, chugging percussion (for the rebels' bomb preparations and during demonstrations); and the brisk snare drum, staccato piano and brass of 'Algeri: 1 Novembre 1954' for the paratroops' storming the Casbah.

Mark Robson's *Lost Command* (1966) was a Hollywood treatment of the same subject. Anthony Quinn starred as a French Paratroop commander, Lt. Col. Raspeguy, and Alain Delon was his subordinate, Captain Esclavier. Footage of the Algerian War was filmed in Almeria and at La Pedriza, Madrid. A miscast George Segal played Algerian freedom fighter Mahidi, with Aldo Sambrell as his sidekick. Claudia Cardinale played Aicha, a glamorous freedom fighter, who sneaks detonators through checkpoints into the Casbah and dates Esclavier. The action scenes are re-enacted on a grand scale by the Spanish army, but in *Lost Command* the heroic paratroopers win the final confrontation. In *Battle of Algiers*, Ali is killed by Mathieu in late 1957, having been given the chance to surrender. The rebellion is smashed, but the film ends on an optimistic note. In December 1960, the Muslim populace of Algiers rises up in mass demonstrations which descend into riots and in July 1962 the country is granted independence. *Battle of Algiers* won the 1966 Golden Lion at the Venice Film Festival and a glance at the news will confirm that its subject matter is equally relevant even today. In 2003, after the US occupied Iraq, *Battle of Algiers* was screened in the Pentagon. The scene where three women FNL bombers plant charges at their crowded targets and watch the customers (who are blissfully unaware of the horror in their midst) is not easily forgotten.

Pontecorvo then made ***Burn!*** (1968), written by Solinas and Giorgio Arlorio. In 1838, mercenary Sir William Walker, a British Admiralty agent, travels to the island of Queimada, a Portuguese colony in the Lesser Antilles. The island's chief export is sugar cane, grown on slave plantations, and Santiago, the rebellious slaves' leader, is beheaded. Walker convinces dock porter Josè Dolores to rob the Bank of the Holy Spirit in Queimada of 100 million gold Reales. The troops dispatched to apprehend Josè are massacred and he is soon a revolutionary hero. Walker convinces politician Teddy Sanchez (Renato Salvatori) to assassinate the Portuguese governor, during a coup d'état led by rich landowners Prada (Thomas Lyons) and Shelton (Norman Hill). The new government can't agree on a constitution with rebel general Josè: the slave army lays down its arms and Walker leaves for Indochina. In 1848 Walker returns to Queimada, as the British government's military advisor to the Antilles Royal Sugar Company. He must help President Sanchez and General Prada put down a wildfire revolt. As captured rebel Masina (Joseph Persaud) informs Walker, 'Josè Dolores says that we must cut heads instead of cane'. The guerrillas are in the Sierra Nevada. Walker's scorched earth policy destroys the network of rebel villages deep in the jungle and smokes Josè out. Sanchez tries to sack Walker, but Prada seizes power and has the president executed. Walker doesn't want Josè to be hanged, reasoning the hero will become a martyr, then a myth, with songs praising his memory. 'Better songs than armies', says Shelton; 'Better silence than songs', replies Walker.

With the casting of Marlon Brando as Walker, Pontecorvo's cinema vérité style is dissipated and *Burn!* resembles a Hollywood colonial adventure. With United Artists bankrolling two-thirds of the $3 million budget, Pontecorvo stages some impressive scenes, accompanied by one of Morricone's finest scores. The swelling, anthemic 'Titoli', with religious chanting by I Cantori Moderni, is powered along by percussion and a throbbing, sinuous Thomas 900 organ. This theme is also used when Walker meets the vast rebel army (armed to the teeth with looted Portuguese hardware) on a beach, en route to Queimada City. The lush organ and strings of 'Josè Dolores – Revolutionary' and 'William and Josè' score the pair's relationship; the jarring discords, chorus and pounding percussion of 'The Battle of Queimada' accompanies Walker's regulars mowing down guerrillas as they emerge from the burning cane; and the harsh, choral requiem 'Dies Irae' underscores Walker's murder. After Josè's execution, a dock porter stabs Walker on the quayside as he's about to depart.

Burn! was made in Cartagena, Colombia, but the soaring temperatures and noisy sets irritated Brando, who wore wax earplugs to concentrate. The ramshackle settings suit the story and most of the cast were non-professionals, including Evaristo Marquez as Josè Dolores, in a role originally slated for Sydney Poitier. When Pontecorvo took 40 takes to shoot a scene in a burning cane field, Brando left and producer Alberto Grimaldi sued Brando for $750,000. The film was eventually completed at Cinecittà and in Marrakech, Morocco. Despite the troubled production, Brando is excellent as the manipulative, dandyish fop – Brando maintained that Walker was the best performance of his career. *Burn!* was a financial flop in the US in 1970. The English language print ran 106 minutes (20 minutes less than the Italian cut) and was released on UK video as *Battle of the Antilles*.

Viva La Revolucion!: Political Westerns

If political dramas had trouble finding an international audience, then westerns didn't. Set in Mexico, circa 1915, Damiano Damiani's **A Bullet for the General** (1966) featured El Chuncho (Gian Maria Volonté), a Mexican gunrunner who works for General Elias (Jaime Fernandez), a rebel. Yankee Bill Tate (Lou Castel) joins their band and is revealed to be a government-sponsored assassin. His hit is to kill the general, an intention which he conceals from Chuncho until they reach Elias' HQ in the Grande Sierras. *A Bullet for the General* (originally titled *El Chuncho: quien sabe?*) is a highly politicised 'western' (though Damiani hated the term) which conveys its message succinctly. Franco Solinas contributed to the script. The revolution is justified, the poor shouldn't be exploited, all land shouldn't be owned by a few rich men and in times of rebellion bread is sometimes worth more than dynamite.

Bullet is an arid film – few movies have captured the bone-dry atmosphere of Almeria so convincingly. Damiani planned to film in Mexico, but dusty Almeria is a convincing substitute. The monastery at Cortijo De Los Frailes appeared as an army outpost and the whitewashed country house at El Romeral (from *A Pistol for Ringo*) was rich landowner Don Filipe's hacienda. Cuidad Juarez station was actually Guadix station, with the Guadix-Almeria railway line transformed into the Nacionale De Mexico. Luis Bacalov's Mexican-flavoured score is one of his best. Klaus Kinski played shaggy zealot El Santo [The Saint], Chuncho's half-brother, a revolutionary priest who is 'On the side of God and the people', using the Devil's money to do God's work. Castel gives a good performance as the smartly suited Yankee who carries a high-precision rifle and a golden bullet. Bond girl Martine Beswick played bandita Adelita, with Guy Heroni as her lover, Pedrito. Joaquin Parra, Spartaco Conversi and Santiago Santos played Chuncho's gunrunners. Jose Manuel Martin was cast against type as Raimundo, the one-armed spokesman for the dirt-farming peons of San Miguel. Andrea Checchi played their oppressor, Don Filipe, with Carla Gravina (Volonté's wife) playing Filipe's wife, Rosario. Aldo Sambrell had a cameo as a Mexican lieutenant whose armaments train is ransacked by Chuncho.

The first half of the film is an adventure movie, with train hold-ups and fort attacks, as the gunrunners gather stock to sell to Elias. The second half, as Chuncho discovers his conscience, is more interesting – his band liberates the town of San Miguel and Chuncho becomes a rebel hero to the populace. For his golden shot, Tate receives 100,000 pesos in blood money, which he splits with his unwitting accomplice, Chuncho, but Tate is murdered by the Mexican as he's boarding a train back to 'Los Estados Unidos'. Yankees who stick their noses into Latin American country's affairs are not welcome: the general may have caught a bullet, but courtesy of Chuncho, the government assassin gets one too.

Director Sergio Sollima made two politically flavoured westerns detailing the adventures of persecuted peon Manuel 'Cuchillo' Sanchez (Tomas Milian): the cat-and-rat manhunt western *The Big Gundown* (1967), co-starring Lee Van Cleef, and its Mexican Revolution sequel, *Run, Man, Run* (1968). Between the 'Cuchillo' films, Sollima also made *Face to Face* in 1967, which dissected the relationship between a hunted outlaw (Milian again) and Boston professor Brad Fletcher (Gian Maria Volonté). Tonino Valerii's *The Price of Power* (1969) was an allegory of the Civil Rights movement and a comment on the assassination of John F. Kennedy in Dallas, through the murder of President James Garfield (Van Johnson) in 1881. Sergio Leone made *Duck You Sucker* (1971 – *A Fistful of Dynamite*), which teamed IRA demolition expert James Coburn and Mexican highway robber Rod Steiger. Sergio Corbucci directed a trilogy of Mexican Revolution-set political westerns, all of which were scored by Ennio Morricone – *A Professional Gun* (1968 – *The Mercenary*) starred Franco Nero, Tony Musante and Jack Palance, *Compañeros* (1970) headlined Nero, Palance and Tomas Milian, and *What Am I Doing in the Middle of a Revolution?* (1972), starred Vittorio

Gassman and Paolo Villagio. Their violent action-comedy resembled a hybrid of *The Good, the Bad and the Ugly* and *Burn!*

Giulio Petroni's **Tepepa** (1969) is set in the aftermath of Francisco Madero's Mexican rebellion which installed him as El Presidente. One-man guerrilla army Tepepa (Tomas Milian) feels betrayed by Madero (Paco Sanz) and sees the whiplash brutality of Cascorro, a Rurale colonel, as indicative of the new regime – promised land reforms haven't materialised and the political process is moving at a snail's pace. Meanwhile English doctor Henry Price (John Steiner) seeks revenge on Tepepa for the rape of his fiancée Consuela De Coruña (Paloma Cela). *Tepepa* is beautifully photographed by Francisco Marin on location in Almeria (including the hacienda at El Romeral) and the city of Guadix. Jose Torres played El Piojo [The Louse], a Mexican peon who has had his hands chopped off by the Rurales for thievery. Piojo's son Paquito (Luciano Casamonica) joins Tepepa's revolutionary band after Piojo betrays Tepepa to Cascorro; in an ambush on the road to Toluca, Tepepa is almost riddled by a machine gun. One set-piece illustrates the ingenuity typical of a peasant revolt. Tepepa's army ambush Cascorro's column in a valley, halting the troops with exploding goats rigged with dynamite. Orson Welles, the film's lumbering, sweaty guest star, is ideal as Cascorro. Tepepa's full name is 'Jesus Maria Moran Tepepa Tierra e Libertad' – 'Quite a name, Chico', sneers Cascorro. Morricone wisely avoids the fiesta clichés of the sub-genre: the theme tune, 'Viva la revolucion', builds to a majestic national anthem, while the gloomy piano and flamenco guitar of 'Tradimento primo' is Cascorro's theme. The song 'Al Messico che vorrei' by Christy doesn't appear in the truncated English language print, *Blood and Guns*, but is present in the uncut Italian version. Solinas again worked on the screenplay. In the downbeat ending, Price murders wounded Tepepa with a scalpel. Price is then shot dead by Paquito with Price's Mauser automatic pistol – again the anglo interloper has been slain by a peasant who is on the road to revolutionary self-awareness.

Non-conformist Cinema: Damiani and Bertolucci

Damiano Damiani followed *Quien sabe?* with *The Day of the Owl* (1968 – *Mafia*), an adaptation of Leonardo Sciascia's 1961 novel. Franco Nero played Captain Bellodi, who in his investigation of a shotgun murder in Sicily encounters a conspiracy of silence. Claudia Cardinale played the presumed culprit's wife and Lee J. Cobb was a Mafia boss. Damiani then directed **Confessions of a Police Captain** (1970), a lucrative box office hit in Italy, with Nero cast as incorruptible district attorney Traini in Palermo, Sicily. He investigates the attempted murder of Ferdinando Dobrosio (Luciano Catenacci), a building magnet and known mobster. The trail leads back to Captain Giacomo Bonavia (Martin Balsam), who released deranged crook LiPuma (Adolfo Lastretti) from a mental hospital. LiPuma wanted to settle a score with Dobrosio over LiPuma's sister, Serena (Marilu Tolo), who is also Dobrosio's mistress. Crazed LiPuma arrives at Dobrosio's office disguised as a policeman and opens fire with a machine gun.

Bonavia has been trying to nail Dobrosio for years, but the wily crook always evades capture. Traini discovers widespread corruption in the construction business and shady civic figures in league with the mob. Eventually Bonavia loses patience with the law, shooting Dobrosio dead, and is arrested. In prison he's stabbed to death by two prisoners at the very moment Traini has enough evidence to expose those in power.

Beginning with the disclaimer 'The events of this film are imaginary', *Police Captain* is heavily political but retains a thriller's pace and drama. With the casting of American Balsam, it travelled well internationally when it was released in 1971. Dobrosio is protected from the law by his lawyer Cannestallo (Arturo Dominici) and is in league with key public figures, including the Palermo mayor, councillors and the building commission. Attorney General Malta (Claudio Gora), Traini's superior, is involved. Captain Bonavia, an idealist, has sought Dobrosio since the murder of union organiser Rizzo (Franco De Rosa) ten years ago. Rizzo's corpse was buried under rocks and had to be excavated by diggers, while a shepherd boy who witnessed the crime was thrown off a cliff. In Damiani's world no one can be trusted, with bribery, backhanders and phone taps rife – even Traini is approached with the keys to a luxury penthouse apartment to keep him sweet – and the attorney general instructs Traini to dig to 'the bottom', not the top. But Traini doesn't dance to his masters' tune, so Dobrosio dispatches his henchmen (led by Calisto Calisti) to dispose of key witness Serena – they kill her, hiding her body in a crate and cast her corpse in the reinforced concrete stanchion of a construction project. Riz Ortolani's jarring electric guitar theme adds intensity to proceedings, with Damiani shooting on location in Palermo (including the Basile Rooms of the Grand-Hotel Villa Igiea) and at Incir-De Paolis Studios. Damiani also directed the highly rated Mafia TV mini-series *La piovra* (*The Octopus*) in 1984, which to date has spawned seven sequels. *Confessions of a Police Captain* is his best political thriller and one of the most resonant films detailing Italian corruption and the power of land and lira over life itself.

Having worked as the assistant director of Pasolini's *Accattone* (1961) and on the story treatment of *Once Upon a Time in the West* – in addition to directing *Before the Revolution* (1964) and *Partner* (1968) – Bernardo Bertolucci made **The Conformist** (1970), a cerebral, multi-layered film masquerading on the simplest level as a 'hitman' thriller. Marcello Clerici (Jean-Louis Trintignant) is a fascist who works for OVRA, tracking down anti-fascist subversives. In 1938, Clerici marries middle-class Giulia (Stefania Sandrelli) and uses their honeymoon in Paris to spy on his old philosophy professor, Luca Quadri (Enzo Tarascio), an anti-fascist living in exile. Clerici falls in love with Quadri's beautiful wife, Anna, who also has a liaison with Giulia. With fascist special agent Manganiello (Gastone Moschin), Clerici is assigned to liquidate Quadri. Clerici discovers that Quadri is driving alone to his country villa in Savoy and arranges an ambush, but Anna unexpectedly accompanies her husband on the fateful trip.

French poster for Bernardo Bertolucci's Oscar-nominated *The Conformist* (1970), which starred Jean-Louis Trintignant as fascist agent Marcello Clerici.

Told via flashback fragments in archaic style by editor Franco Arcalli, *The Conformist* is Bertolucci's masterpiece. Trintignant is ideal as the rigid, formal Clerici, dressed in a long black coat and Borsalino. He strives to blend into 'normal life' – this is his main reason for marrying airy Giulia, with whom he has little in common. His behaviour is traced to a childhood trauma in 1917. When he was thirteen, Clerici (played by Pasquale Fortunato) had shot the family's chauffeur, Pasqualino 'Lino' Semirama (Pierre Clémenti), who tried to sexually assault him. After the overthrow of Mussolini in 1943, Clerici spots Lino – who has miraculously survived – picking up a male street hustler. Clerici brands him 'a pederast, a fascist' and accuses him of the murders of Quadri and Anna on 15 October 1938. Clerici and Giulia now have their normal life with a daughter (Marta Lado), but Giulia worries of fascist reprisals for Clerici's OVRA past.

Conformist was sumptuously photographed in Technicolor by Vittorio Storaro on location in Rome – the Sant'Angelo Bridge and Castel Sant'Angelo – and a wintry Paris, including the Eiffel Tower, the Palais de Chaillot plaza and Gare D'Orsay (as the honeymooners' 'Hotel Palais D'Orsay'). Storaro's cinematography bathes the film in a surreal colour scheme – for example, in the luminous blue Parisian night scenes. Its rich visual design is complemented by elegant costuming (by Gitt Magrini and Tirelli) and period art direction and sets (by Nedo Azzini and Fernando Scarfiatti), seen to best advantage in the Hotel Palais D'Orsay interiors and during Anna and Giulia's sexy tango in Joinville. French actress Dominique Sanda burst onto the international scene as cool Anna, the bisexual ballet teacher, and Sandrelli, Moschin and Tarascio are excellent in complex roles. Sanda and Sandrelli went on to appear in Bertolucci's lengthy pastoral period epic *1900* (1976), co-starring Robert De Niro, Gérard Depardieu, Donald Sutherland, Alida Valli, Sterling Hayden and Burt Lancaster. In *Conformist*, Milly Monti played Clerici's morphine addict mother, Giuseppe Addobatti was his insane father, Yvonne Sanson was Giulia's mother and Jose Quaglio played Clerici's blind fascist friend, Italo. Rustling autumn leaves fluttering in the wind take on an added, threatening dimension when cut to Georges Delerue's haunting score – the romantic cues recall the composer's work on Godard's *Contempt*, and *Conformist* shares its pervading sense of doomed love. *Conformist* was also based on an Alberto Moravia novel. Quadri's address in Paris (17 rue Saint-Jacques) and telephone number were actually Godard's and Bertolucci has said that *The Conformist* 'is a story about me and Godard ... I'm Marcello and I make fascist movies and I want to kill Godard (who) makes revolutionary movies and is my teacher'.

Throughout the film Bertolucci cuts back to Manganiello and Clerici in a car speeding through a frozen landscape, as they pursue Quadri and Anna. A faked car accident waylays Quadri, as a fascist hit squad in long coats (Carlo Gaddi, Umberto Silvestri, Furio Pellerani and Claudio Cappeli) emerge from the mist. This set piece is chillingly staged in a silent pine forest wreathed in snow. The hitmen stab Quadri to death and Anna runs to Clerici's car, screaming for her lover to save her. Clerici is emotionless as she's chased into the woods and shot dead, her blood-smeared death throes cut to Delerue's 'love theme'. *The Conformist* is available in both Italian and English language dubs and was Bertolucci's international breakthrough in 1970, even garnering an Oscar nomination for Best Adapted Screenplay.

Before moving away from political cinema to make *Last Tango in Paris* (1972), which concentrated on erotic themes he'd explored in *Conformist*, Bertolucci directed **The Spider's Stratagem** (1970) for Italian television. Athos Magnani (Giulio Brogi) arrives in the town of Tara to investigate the murder of his father (also called Athos Magnani) but is treated with hostility by the locals, despite their mantra 'We're all friends here'. His father, a heroic anti-fascist, was shot in the back on 15 June 1936 during a theatre performance of *Rigoletto*. Athos interviews his father's mistress, Draifa (Alida Valli), and his father's three trusted anti-fascist compatriots: Costa (Tino Scotti), the cinema owner; Rasori (Franco Giovanelli), a teacher; and Gaibazzi (Pippo Campanini), a salami taster. They tell Athos that they planned to blow up Mussolini during the theatre's inauguration, but the plot was discovered. Shortly afterwards Athos' father had received a warning letter not to go to the theatre and a fortune teller had read death in his palm. He was killed as part of a political vendetta and a motorcyclist, an outsider, was seen in the area. As the mystery deepens, Athos begins to doubt the trio's story.

Spider's Stratagem has little of *Conformist*'s scope and international appeal, but the mystery is still engaging. It was based on a short story by Jorge Luis Borges and the colour photography was by Storaro. Dusty Tara and its environs, draped in exotic foliage and trailing creepers, were filmed at Sabbioneta, Mantua in Lombardia. The film is set in the early 1960s – the local cinema advertises *The Last Sunset* (1961) and Mina sings 'Il conformista' on the soundtrack – though there are frequent flashbacks to Athos' father and his companions in 1936. Both Athos's were played by Brogi, who gives fine performances as the resolute opponent of the Black Shirts and his mystified son. Athos' father wasn't a hero and his 'murder' was a myth concocted by his three comrades. Athos had betrayed the anti-fascist cause and was executed in 'a hero's legendary death...a theatrical spectacle', which the populace of Tara unknowingly participated in. He should have been exposed as a traitor, but sometimes 'a hero is more useful'.

Political Icons: Rosi and Volonté

Francesco Rosi has worked almost exclusively in political cinema throughout his career. **Salvatore Giuliano** (1962), co-written by Franco Solinas, established his name internationally. Filmed on interiors at Incir-De Paolis and on location, Rosi told the life and death of Sicilian bandit Salvatore Giuliano (Pietro Cammarata). The film opens with the discovery of Giuliano's bullet-riddled corpse face down in a sunlit courtyard in Castelvetrano in July 1950. Rosi then rewinds to show Giuliano's rise to prominence in the early 1940s as the leader of a band of separatist freedom fighters. They hide in the hills around the town of Montelepre, Giuliano's birthplace, and ambush the army. This leads to government reprisals, including a garrison occupation of Montelepre, curfews, water rationing and the confiscation of supplies being smuggled to Giuliano. Rosi also depicts events after Giuliano's death – this non-linear structure was a signature of Solinas' work. Giuliano is eventually betrayed by his lieutenant Gaspare Pisciotta (Frank Wolff) and shot dead in bed, but the authorities arrange the scene in Castelvetrano to imply Giuliano was killed in a shootout. The film ends in 1960 with the murder of Benedetto Minasola, the collaborator who sold Pisciotta to the authorities.

Salvatore Giuliano questioned cinema's depiction of heroic rebels – were they freedom fighters or terrorists? The narrative veers from documentary-style newsreel footage and war movie action, to courtroom drama and biopic. The film depicts the trial held in the Viterbo Assizes Court (presided over by judge Salvo Randone) of Pisciotta and Giuliano's gang for the infamous massacre at Portella Della Ginestra on 1 May 1947, when they opened fire on a Communist parade. Other scenes depict the media harassing Giuliano's mother when she arrives to identify her son's body (which is packed in ice) and the freedom fighters' guerrilla raids. Rosi filmed on location in Sicily, in the actual towns of Montelepre and Castelvetrano, and cast locals as extras. Gianni Di Venanzo's monochrome cinematography captures the Sicilian landscapes' grandeur – sunlight floods the rolling hill country and whitewashed streets – which contrasts with dark figures (usually the bandits) picked out in the topography by the roving camera. Rosi's documentarist approach is underscored by his sparing use of music. Piero Piccioni's ominous title music bodes ill and his later themes are similarly atmospheric: a twanging maranzano (a Sicilian folk instrument) is augmented with deathly strings and drums, as in the aftermath of the Portella Della Ginestra massacre.

Rosi uses Giuliano as a symbol of revolt, to depict how post-war Sicilian banditry became infused with gangsterism: the Onorata Società (the Mafia). The film doesn't feature any close-ups of Pietro Cammarata's face as Giuliano (though we see a photograph of the actual Giuliano) and the hero is depicted at distance in his distinctive long white coat, directing his men in the mountains. Stuntman Bruno Ukmar played a spy who infiltrates Giuliano's band and identifies its members to the authorities and the film's nominal star is San Francisco–born Frank Wolff who worked with Roger Corman prior to moving to Italy, where he achieved stardom in spaghetti westerns. Wolff's Italian career started on a high working with Rosi and ended on a nadir: by the time his caveman comedy *When Women Lost Their Tails* was released, Wolff had committed suicide in 1971. In *Salvatore Giuliano* traitorous Pisciotta dies in jail, screaming and dribbling. He's poisoned by Antonino Terranova, one of Giuliano's cohorts, with strychnine-laced tea – such is the price of betrayal in Sicily.

Rosi followed *Salvatore Giuliano* with *Hands over the City* (1963), casting Rod Steiger as a corrupt politician involved in Neapolitan corruption in the building industry. In Rosi's *The Mattei Affair* (1972), Gian Maria Volonté played global magnet Enrico Mattei, the head of oil company AGIP, who died in a plane 'accident' in 1962 – some say at the hands of the Mafia, though Mattei's list of enemies was long. Volonté became the most prominent actor in Italian political cinema – he was a fervent left-winger – through his work for Rosi and others, who used Volonté's powerful screen image to convey their political agenda to an international audience. Volonté also played anti-fascist novelist Carlo Levi in Rosi's *Christ Stopped at Eboli* (1979), factory worker Lulu in Elio Petri's *The Working Class Go to Heaven* (1971 – *Lulu the Tool*) and fishmonger Bartolomeo Vanzetti in Giuliano Montaldo's well-received *Sacco and Vanzetti* (1971), the true story of the trial and execution of two men accused of a payroll robbery in Bridgewater, Massachusetts. Riccardo Cucciolla played his co-accused, shoemaker Nicola Sacco. The film is best remembered for Joan Baez's powerful rendition of Morricone's 'The Ballad of Sacco and Vanzetti'.

In Elio Petri's **Investigation of a Citizen above Suspicion** (1970), Volonté gave the performance of his career – he won Best Actor and the film Best Picture at the David Di Donatello Awards, Italy's Oscars. A nameless police inspector (Volonté), the head of Rome's Sezione Omicidi (Murder Squad), is promoted to chief of political intelligence. On the inspector's last day on homicide, he murders his lover Augusta Terzi (Florinda Bolkan) in her apartment on Via Del Tempio. During intercourse he slits her throat with a razor blade. The fascist inspector knows that he's above suspicion, above the law. Despite copious evidence suggesting that he is the murderer, his former colleagues won't arrest him, instead focussing on Augusta's ex-husband. The inspector uses his position to

A Man to Respect: Poster for the English language release of Elio Petri's Oscar-winning *Investigation of a Citizen above Suspicion* (1970). Gian Maria Volonté plays the head of Rome's Sezione Omicidi, who tries to get away with murder.

implicate anarchist revolutionary Antonio Pace (Sergio Tramonti), with whom Augusta had begun an affair. Eventually the inspector confesses and waits at his home for the police commissioner (Gianni Santuccio) and his entourage.

Set against the backdrop of political unrest in late-1960s Rome – with demonstrations and bombings by student radicals – *Investigation* also resembles a giallo thriller. The paranoid atmosphere reflects the fantasist inspector's mental disintegration and Petri's treatment of time resembles gialli's dreamlike imagery. Flashbacks depict the inspector and Augusta's strange relationship, via their 'murder games'. He photographs her in a series of lurid poses, re-creations of sex murder slayings which he has investigated. She mocks the inspector's sexual immaturity and begins a relationship with Antonio. When the inspector threatens Augusta ('I could murder you') she muses, 'Who would catch you? You'd have the investigation'. The inspector's sexual frustration manifests itself in political anger; thus his arrest of Antonio and his fellow radicals appears politically motivated. The inspector believes that there's no distinction between criminal and political acts – his scheme backfires when Pace refuses to identify the inspector as the murderer. It is useful to have a blackmailed ally 'in their pocket' as the chief of political intelligence. The premise of the inspector's aims ('To prove the case that I am completely beyond suspicion') is a better idea on paper than on film. *Investigation* works perfectly as a labyrinthine thriller, but as a polemic, it's a political struggle.

The inspector fantasises that his superiors won't accept the overwhelming evidence against him. He 'arranges' obvious clues around Augusta's apartment for the homicide squad to find, including a thread from his blue silk tie snagged on her fingernail, footprints in blood and dozens of his fingerprints. Only Inspector Biglia (Orazio Orlando) suspects that his ex-chief may be the culprit. Arturo Dominici played Mangani, the new head of homicide, and Fulvio Grimaldi was a journalist on *Paese sera* to whom the inspector feeds leads. *Investigation* was released in both Italian and English language versions. In its original version, it won the Best Foreign Language Film Oscar. 'When you're a big man in the big city', ran the tagline, 'can you get away with murder?' Ennio Morricone's wheezing, clockwork score – augmented by twangs, boings and quirks from his Italian western music – with avant-garde gialli stylings creates a memorably eccentric backdrop to Volonté's equally eccentric performance.

At one point in *Investigation*, Volonté's inspector convinces a janitor (Salvo Randone) to buy two dozen blue ties and take them to homicide, but when the janitor discovers the inspector's position, he denies knowing the policeman. Thus an innocent 'man in the street' becomes an accessory to murder. The Russo-Italian thriller **Betrayed** (1979) developed this theme. Through his love for waitress Maria (Ornella Muti), taxi driver Antonio Morio (Giancarlo Gianni) becomes involved in a terrorist cell plotting to assassinate the president. Here the secret police are the villains and Antonio is imprisoned and tortured, before engineering a breakout in an armoured-plated bullet-proof car. Well-plotted and acted, with some genuine surprises, *Betrayed* features an effective score by Armando Travajoli. The terrorist organisation's credo is 'Life is beautiful' and the original Italian title was *La vita è bella*.

Francesco Rosi's gangster biopic **Lucky Luciano** (1973) starred Volonté as Sicilian mobster Salvatore Lucania, alias Charles 'Lucky' Luciano, who in 1931 became the 'Boss of Bosses' when 40 old-line Mafia heads were murdered on the Night of the Sicilian Vespers. Rosi's film is not particularly well constructed and mainly depicts Luciano's enforced exile from the US in Naples through to his death, when he keels over from a heart attack as he meets a screenwriter at Naples airport who is to script his life story. The film also charts the attempts by US Bureau of Narcotics agent in Rome, Charles Siracusa (Siracusa himself), to nail Luciano for his involvement in the international heroin trade. Edmond O'Brien appeared as Commissioner Harry J. Anslinger, present at the UN International Conference on Drug Traffic and a fervent anti-Mafia investigator. Magda Konopka had a brief role as a contessa who beds Luciano. Rod Steiger played foul-mouthed gangster Eugenio Giannini alias 'Gene Pellegrino', who attempts to use his relationship with Luciano as a bargaining chip when he's imprisoned – Giannini is later shot dead, clattering into trash cans outside a New York gambling joint. The film has a good period atmosphere and was shot on location in Naples, the ruins at Pompeii, in New York, Rome and Sicily – a reunion banquet of US- and Italian-based Mafiosi was filmed in the sumptuous Hotel Delle Palme in Palermo (from Visconti's *The Leopard*). The Night of the Sicilian Vespers (a montage of very brutal machine gun killings) and other bloody mob hits pepper the film like buckshot. Most interesting is Rosi's depiction of how the Mafia aided the US occupying forces in the immediate aftermath of Italy's liberation: in particular the easily bribed Charles Poletti (Vincent Gardenia), the US colonel who filters goods into the Italian black market in return for a flashy yellow Packard automobile.

The Valachi Papers (1972), which exposed the workings of the Cosa Nostra in simpler terms, enjoyed greater international success. Helmed by Terence Young, the film starred Charles Bronson as New York informer Joseph M. Valachi, one of few gangsters to break their 'omerta' code of silence. In 1963, incarcerated Valachi agrees to testify to the Senate Permanent Investigations Subcommittee, which is televised. He seeks to bring down his former employer, Don Vito Genovese, who in turn puts a $100,000 contract on Valachi's head. Valachi died naturally in jail in 1971, outliving Genovese by six months.

The film, produced by Dino De Laurentiis and based on Peter Maas' bestseller of the same name, takes place in flashback, as Valachi recounts his life of crime to an FBI special agent, Ryan (Gerald S. O'Loughlin). He began as a small-time hood in 1929 working as a driver for 'Boss of Bosses' Salvatore Maranzano (Joseph Wiseman). Lino Ventura played Genovese, Fausto Tozzi was volatile assassin Albert Anastasia ('Double A'), the chief executioner of 'Murder Inc.', Alessandro Sperli was Giuseppe Masseria ('Joe the Boss') and Angelo Infanti played Lucky Luciano ('Charlie Luck'). Anthony Dawson appeared as an FBI narc, Franco Borelli was hitman 'Buster from Chicago', and Guido Leontini and Walter Chiari were mobsters Tony Bender and Dominick 'The Gap' Petrilli. Jill Ireland (Bronson's wife) played Valachi's wife, Maria, and Jason McCallum, Ireland's son with David McCallum, played the Valachis' son, Donald. Young laced the biopic with sadistic violence to please Bronson fans – there are shoot-outs, drive-bys, garrottings, stabbings and a castration (the film is still an 18 on UK video). *Valachi Papers* was shot on location in New York (though modern cars can be seen in the background of many period street scenes) and at De Laurentiis Studios, Rome. Though Bronson was the biggest box office draw in the world, this was his first big hit in the US, where it was released in the wake of *The Godfather*.

Francesco Rosi followed *Lucky Luciano* with **Illustrious Corpses** (1975), his masterpiece. Inspector Amerigo Rogas (Lino Ventura) investigates the murders of prominent judges, all of whom have been shot by the same .22 rifle. District Attorney Varga is shot in the street after visiting the catacombs; Judge Sanza (Francesco Callari) is discovered lying on the side of the freeway and Chief Judge Calamo is assassinated in the Banca Nazionale. Rogas suspects this is a vendetta following a miscarriage of justice. He interviews a vagrant (Marcel Buzzuffi) and a gay mechanic (Mario Meniconi), both of whom were wrongly sentenced, but can't locate Cres, a chemist, who is thus deemed responsible. Judge Rasto (Alain Cuny) is shot dead in his home and Judge Perro is killed in the street – a prostitute (Tina Aumont) reports that she saw a white Mercedes with Swiss plates at the scene. Rogas is encouraged by his bosses to find a political angle for the crimes – Communist Party demonstrations blight the city. Rogas doubts his 'sniper' theory when he finds that his chief of police (Tino Carraro) is lying to him and that General De Sarmiento (Claudio Nicastro) has been appointed supreme commander of the armed forces. Chief Magistrate Richès (Max Von Sydow) is killed and Rogas' phone is tapped, so he sleeps in his car. Rogas realises that the government is planning a coup d'état, or at least military retaliation against demonstrating Communists, to relieve the political situation (a 'strategy of tension') using the judges' murders as the catalyst.

Illustrious Corpses is based on Leonardo Sciascia's 1971 novel *Il contesto* (*Equal Danger* in its English language translation). The film version is part whodunit giallo, part political polemic. It begins as a *Dirty Harry* procedural – a hunt for a rogue sniper – but having engaged his audience with Rogas' investigation, Rosi hits them with his political message, as stealthily as a sniper's bullet. Rosi claimed the film is a 'philosophical and political thriller which could be set in England, but is perhaps more like Italy'. Rosi shot on location in Agrigento and Palermo in Sicily, in Naples and Rome, with interiors at Cinecittà. Piero Piccioni contributed the atmospheric score, which mixed discords of a gathering storm with traditional arrangements (the tango 'Jeanne y Paul' by Astor Piazzolla and a dirge-like funeral march). Few political films look as beautiful as *Illustrious*

UK poster for Francesco Rosi's *Illustrious Corpses* (1975). Lino Ventura stars as Inspector Amerigo Rogas who is on the trail of a vengeful sniper targeting prominent members of the judiciary.

Corpses, from the dusty streets of Sicily, to the grand architecture of Rome. The art direction was by Andrea Crisanti, costumes were by Enrico Sabbatini and the cinematography was by Pasquale De Santis. Renato Salvatori played a surveillance specialist who helps Rogas and Fernando Rey was the duplicitous minister of justice, who carouses at a Leftist party with rich shipping magnate Pattos (Alexandre Mnouchkine) and party representative Galano (Paolo Graziosi). Rosi cleverly cast Ventura, the anti-hero of many a French *policier*, as Rogas. As Rogas, Ventura wears the same style of tan mac he donned as wily inspector Le Goff in *The Sicilian Clan* (1969), a highly commercial depiction of Mafia politics co-starring Alain Delon and Jean Gabin. Ventura's presence brings with it the iconography of such films, making *Illustrious Corpses* internationally accessible: audiences who cared little for Italian politics could identify with Ventura's dogged screen persona.

Corpses was a massive success in Italy, though its topical, reactionary politics provoked much debate. It is filled with strange moments – the state funeral of Judge Varga, his hearse pulled by eight coal black horses; paranoid, chain-smoking Rogas hearing the ominous rumble of tanks trundling through the city in the middle of the night; and a blind man's guide dog fitted with a bug to eavesdrop on Rogas' conversation in a park. Most effective is the opening sequence, with wrinkled Charles Vanel (as Varga) staring at rows of skeletal, decomposing mummifications in the catacombs of the Convento Dei Cappuccini in Palermo.

'He'd make the dead reveal the secrets of the living', notes a Capuchin monk (Enrico Ragusa) of Varga. Varga emerges into the sunlit street and dies clutching a jasmine blossom he has just plucked.

Luigi Pistilli played Rogas' friend Cusani, a Communist journalist who tells Rogas, 'One judge is a police matter, but kill four and it's political'. Cusani arranges a meeting between Rogas and Communist Party leader Amar (Giorgio Zampa) in the National Gallery, but Rogas and Amar are both shot. Rosi provides us with an assassin's-eye-view of the proceedings, in slow motion, as bullets punch two holes through a window. A pistol is planted in Rogas' hand and it is announced that Rogas, in a fragile mental state following the lengthy investigation, shot Amar and then himself. Cusani and Amar's successor (played by film director Florestano Vancini) decide that 'truth is not always revolutionary' and don't reveal what really happened, as tanks are poised on the streets to attack the demonstrators. Cres may have begun the murders of the judiciary, but the government escalated them to their own political advantage. It doesn't matter who pulls the trigger, as long as the 'right people' – for the governing party at least – get shot.

Chapter Ten

Mission Improbable
World War II Movies

Inspired by the success of Hollywood movies *The Dirty Dozen* (the highest-grossing film of 1967) and *Tobruk* (1967), all-action Italian war cinema (dubbed 'macaroni combat' films) enjoyed a spurt of popularity from 1967 to 1971. *Dirty Dozen* featured Charles Bronson, Telly Savalas, Jim Brown and John Cassavetes as condemned prisoners offered pardons if they'll undertake a mission to assassinate Nazi officers in a chateau in Brittany. *Tobruk* (starring Rock Hudson and George Peppard) sent its Allies on a mission to destroy a fuel dump and fortifications in North Africa. *The Secret Invasion* (1964), colourfully shot in Yugoslavia, was also a key influence. British major Stewart Granger led a group of ex-convicts on an operation to free Italian general Quadri (Enzo Fiermonte) from the Nazi fortress in Dubrovnik, with the aid of Balkan partisans. The all-star *Von Ryan's Express* (1965) was shot in Italy on the Capranica and Viterbo railroad. Frank Sinatra and Trevor Howard were among 400 British and America POWs careering through occupied Italy in a stolen train. Sergio Fantoni played a sympathetic Italian officer, William Berger was a delving Gestapo agent, Adolfo Celi was the prison camp's commandant, and stuntman Remo De Angelis was the train's fireman.

Desert Rats: North Africa

The Italian 'mission' film's main variables were the objective, the theatre of war and the specialists who made up the group: all three were highly dependant on budget. In Umberto Lenzi's **Desert Commandos** (1967), Captain Fritz Schöeller (Ken Clark) leads four German commandos to assassinate 'The Big Three' – Churchill, Stalin and Roosevelt – amid tight security in Casablanca in January 1943. Parachuted into the desert disguised as allied commandos, the unit – Lieutenant Wolf (Horst Frank), Sergeant Huber (Carlo Hinterman), Willy Mainz (Howard Ross) and Corporal Ludwig (Hardy Reichelt) – rendezvous at an oasis

War Games: GI Lieutenant Clem Hoffman (John Garko) attempts to steal 'Plan K' from SS Colonel Hans Muller (Klaus Kinski) in Gianfranco Parolini's lively *Dirty Dozen* derivative *Five for Hell* (1969). Original UK video box artwork.

with their Moroccan contact, Faddja Hassan (Jeanne Valerie) and take French bar owner Simone (Fabienne Dali) hostage. When they reach Casablanca they discover Faddja is a double-agent. Schöeller and Huber overhear Churchill and burst into his hotel room, only to find a gramophone playing one of the prime minister's speeches and a military police reception committee. Co-produced by Alberto Grimaldi's PEA, *Desert Commandos* was filmed in North Africa and the sidewinding plot makes this one of Lenzi's superior efforts. Gianni Rizzo was the commandos' kasbah contact Perrier and spy star Clark was at home in such exotic action fare. Frank was good as Wolf, the German forced to fight for something he doesn't believe in, for a dictator he doesn't care about. The African-flavoured score was by Angelo Francesco Lavagnino. Lenzi includes the expected desert drama clichés: the squad negotiate a minefield and the desert offers only dust storms, rotting sun-bleached carcasses, windblown ruins, dry wells, scorpions and the Tuareg: fearsome camel-mounted nomads.

Armando Crispino's **Commandos** (1968) was one of few Italian war movies to depict Italian combatants. Lee Van Cleef headlined as Sergeant Sullivan, a crack US commando. His unit are assigned an inexperienced commander, Captain Valli (Jack Kelly), and dispatched on 'Operation Torch' in October 1942, on the eve of the US landings in North Africa, to take an Italian-held oasis equipped with a water-pumping station. Parachuting into the desert disguised as Italians, they take over the depot and imprison the garrison. The raiders are informed that Operation Torch has been aborted and Italian commander Tomassini (Marino Masé) alerts a nearby Panzer unit of German Afrika Korps.

Shot from July to August 1968, the film was made on location in Sardinia, with interiors at Incir-De Paolis Studios. Van Cleef makes a fine commando, embittered and unbalanced. Sullivan suffers nerve-shredding flashbacks to his time in Bataan, when his unit was massacred by the Japanese. Giampiero Albertini and Van Cleef's stunt double Romano Puppo played commandos Aldo and Dino – Italian actors playing US soldiers playing Italian soldiers. A strong German contingent, including Götz George and Joachim Fuchsberger, played the Afrika Korps. Mario Nascimbene's epic score – an oscillating haze of feedback and a slow, anti-heroic dirge – gave the film added edge. In the actionful climax, the Italian prisoners escape in a truck but are obliterated by a minefield. The US commandos fight it out in an explosive pitched battle with the German armour, as Sullivan wields a mean bazooka and his unit is annihilated. The engagement's only survivors, an American and a German, decide to call a truce, as blood and oil mingle amid the smoking ruins.

Further North African-set movies included Mino Loy's *Desert Battle* (1969 – *Desert Assault* or *Battle in the Desert*), with Robert Hossein, George Hilton and Frank Wolff. *Heroes without Glory* (1971) saw martinet Britisher major Briggs (Isarco Ravaioli) clash with US lieutenant Billings (Jeff Cameron) during a mission to blow up an Axis fuel dump – they are sidetracked by a treasure map and hunt for the ancient tombs of the pharaohs. *Desert Tigers* (1977) wheeled musclemen Gordon Mitchell and Richard Harrison into action for a raid on an oil depot in North Africa.

What a Guy!: Madison's War

If the sub-genre had a signature star it was Guy Madison, who made a series of Italian war movies in rapid succession – as though he was petrified the craze would peter out. They took him to almost every theatre of combat, with mixed results. *Hell in Normandy* (1968) was made on a shoestring by Alfonso Brescia, a journeyman director whose talent is hard to estimate. On Omaha beach, Normandy, in late May 1944, Lieutenant Strobel (Peter Lee Lawrence), an ex-actor, impersonates a German officer to infiltrate See Herr (Sea Lord), a German bunker. Part of the Western Wall defences, the beach is heavily mined and a sophisticated defence system pumps gasoline into the sea which creates a wall of fire. Captain Jack Murphy (Guy Madison) leads a squad of US commandos on Operation Gambit to knock out the bunker. Although the commandos are under-equipped and their mission is aborted due to bad weather, they decide to go ahead, rendezvousing with Strobel and attacking on the eve of D-Day. The Omaha bunker was filmed on Tor Caldara beach, Anzio Cape, while Murphy's commandos train by attacking an 'exact replica' of the bunker – so exact that it was also filmed at Tor Caldara. French Resistance contact Denise (Erika Blanc) wearing a beret and scarf and toting a machine gun appears to have stepped out of *Bonnie and Clyde*.

Jose Merino shot two war movies starring Madison and 'Stan Cooper'/Stelvio Rosi on interiors at YSA Film, Milan and exteriors near Madrid. In ***The Battle of the Last Panzer*** (1968), US officer Lofty (Madison) hunts for rogue Panzer 71 commanded by German lieutenant Hunter (Cooper) through a highly unconvincing post D-Day 'France'. Location footage was shot in the rolling hills of Guadalajara, Castilla-La Mancha and at the River Alberche. In the battered French town of 'Villebois' (the wild west town set at Colmenar Viejo) the Germans take three French locals prisoner and try to evade a squad of Spanish-looking partisans led by 'Rene' (spaghetti western bandido Riccardo Palacios). The film opens with a well-staged ambush by US troops on the squad of Panzers and the finale is also effective. The US soldiers disguise a look-alike Panzer 71 and infiltrate the German frontline as the real Panzer 71 attempts the same manoeuvre: Lieutenant Hunter is shot by his own troops mistaking him for a US impostor.

Hell Commandos (1969) has Major Carter (Madison) leading US marines disguised as Germans to free Professor Van Kolstrom (Alfredo Mayo) and his daughter, Sara (Raffaella Carra), from the clutches of the SS – commanded by Colonel Krautzfeld (Piero Lulli) – in a fortified villa at Truniger, Germany, in 1945. Hitler has ordered the professor to develop germ warfare which causes blindness. Carter's squad are killed in error by US marines led by Sergeant Arthur Nolan (Stan Cooper) and Carter convinces them to carry out the dead soldiers' mission. To explain the budget-pared lack of SS guards around the villa, the building is protected by automatic machine guns and dogs and has gates and fences with 10,000 volts running through them. Nolan's squad includes a knife-throwing Cheyenne warrior named Geronimo Lightcloud. The nihilistic finale (in which virtually no one survives) has the US soldiers drop the toxin into the villa's water supply and the Germans die horribly. Colonel Krautzfeld releases the SS Alsatians, so Carter throws a stick of dynamite and the dogs, ever obedient, retrieve it and take it back to the colonel, who is blown to smithereens.

Bitto Albertini's *The War Devils* (1969) opened in Tunisia 1943, as US paratroopers led by Captain George Vincent (Madison) carry out Operation Red Devil, blowing up an Axis gun emplacement (M Battery) with help from Sheik Faisal (Raf Baldassarre). During the subsequent engagement, Vincent and his men are captured by Captain Heintich Meinike (Venantino Venantini, billed as 'Van Tenney'). Vincent escapes and a year later in France he and Meinike find themselves face to face. When Colonel James Steel (Anthony Steel), a British secret weapon's expert, is captured by Meinike, Vincent and his US Rangers are sent to rescue him. *War Devils* stages some convincing tank battles and contrasts combat in sweltering North Africa with that in snowbound France. The supporting cast included diminutive French actress Pascale Petit as French resistance contact Jeanine Raush. John Ireland guest starred as Captain Jennings, a US commander, and stuntmen Frank Braña, Giuseppe Castellano, Federico Boido, Massimo Righi and Julio Perez Taberno played assorted US and German troops.

A Place in Hell (1969 – *Commando Attack*) directed by Giuseppe Vari was a sweaty jungle adventure set in the Philippines. Major Mac Graves (Madison), an alcoholic Pulitzer Prize–winning journalist, escapes from Manila with jazz club hostess Betsy and Italian-American marine Mario Petrello (Maurice Poli). They arrive at the US marine base on Lubang, but the garrison has been massacred. They encounter six US marine survivors, two Filipino freedom fighters and a British naval officer, who aim to blow up the captured US experimental radio station transmitters at Surigao. Its Manila interiors were filmed at Tirrenia Studios and the film relies almost totally on ambushes to create its tension, punctuated by much jungle trudging. Fabio Testi played a marine and Lilia Neyung was Filipino rebel Esperanza. Helene Chanel – as peroxide blonde pin-up Betsy, in an eye-catching backless, almost frontless, dress – looks too contemporary for the period by 20 years. Concealing a lack of Japanese extras, much of the action takes place at night or in dense undergrowth. Roberto Pregadio's intrusive score is a blend of marches and sentimentality, and the jingoistic title song was performed by the Folkstudio Singers.

Frederick the Great: Stafford's War Efforts

Madison's main competition in the war movie stakes was Austrian actor Frederick Stafford (real name Friedrich Strobel Von Stein), who appeared in spy films as agents OSS 117 and Agent 505 and was the lead in Hitchcock's *Topaz* (1969). The Edmondo Amati-produced, Alberto De Martino-directed ***The Dirty Heroes***

(1967) is the most overlooked war movie of the 1960s. Set in Holland during the last days of the war, it told the story of a gang of Chicago crooks who team up with the Dutch underground to steal diamonds from the Wehrmacht HQ in Amsterdam. The robbers include safecracker Joe Mortimer, known as Sesame (Stafford); US air force captain O'Connor, known as Lawyer (John Ireland); Sesame's fellow escapee from a POW camp, Randall (Renato Rossini); German sergeant Rudolph Petrowsky, another gangster (Michel Constantin); and Dutch partisans Marta Van Staten (Faida Nichols) and Luc Rollman, the 'Fox of Amsterdam' (Adolfo Celi). They blackmail Kristina Von Keist (Daniela Bianchi), the wife of a German commander, General Edwin Von Keist (Curd Jürgens), into helping them. She is a Jew, Hanna Goldschmidt, who has concealed her identity from her husband to avoid the concentration camps. Sesame and his crew plan to keep the diamonds for themselves, but conscienceless SS general Hassler (Helmut Schneider) is determined to track them down.

The elaborate story – shot on location in Italy and Holland amid canals, dykes and windmills – rockets along at breakneck pace. De Martino handled the set pieces with aplomb and the film is given extra power by an Ennio Morricone-Bruno Nicolai score, which contrasts a menacing choral march title cue with subtler love themes for Kristina and Sesame. The elaborate heist on Von Keist ends with the robbers escaping in a tugboat and being pursued by Hassler and his men in a heavily armed river cruiser. There's a pitched battle between German tanks and US paratroopers (filmed at Caldara Di Manziana, Lazio) amid sandbagged bunkers, trenches, barbed wire and plane wreckage. The diamond heist includes a scene where Sesame, Rollman and Randall drive their car at the Germans like Chicago gangsters and then steer into the canal, enabling them to gain access to the basement in diving suits. The film's ending, as the gang try to smuggle the diamonds out of Holland in a war hero's coffin, seems tacked-on. The film predates Clint Eastwood's *Kelly's Heroes* by two years and is its obvious inspiration, with seemingly selfless heroic acts masking selfish personal gain.

The Battle of El Alamein (1968) was directed by Giorgio Ferroni as 'Calvin Jackson Padget', with interiors at Cinecittà and a score by Carlo Rustichelli. The film concentrates on the Italian contribution to the two battles of El Alamein in Egypt during 1942, via a company of Folgore paratroopers commanded by Lieutenant Giorgio Bori (Stafford) and his infantryman brother, Sergeant-Major Fabio Bori (Enrico Maria Salerno). The Germans and Italians are allies – though it's made clear that Hitler's orders are morally abhorrent to the Italian troops – and the 'limeys' are the villains. Michael Rennie played General Montgomery as the bad guy and British troops mercilessly execute unarmed German prisoners with grenades. Robert Hossein played Erwin Rommel, the Desert Fox, and Argentinian George Hilton appeared as English lieutenant Graham. Massimo Righi, Nello Pazzafini, Riccardo Pizzuti, Giuseppe Castellano, Ettore Manni and Sal Borgese played Italian troops, Marco Guglielmi, Gerard Herter, Tom Felleghi, Andrea Fantasia and Giuseppe Addobatti played Germans and Max Lawrence and Renato Romano appeared as Brits. The depiction of these nationalities is sometimes clichéd – 'Mamma Mia! A million tanks!' exclaims Pazzafini as British armour appears on the horizon – but the dusty, explosive action scenes, convincingly staged with the co-operation of the Italian army, lift the film and transform it into above-average fare. The Italian rearguard, hidden in foxholes, attempt to slow the British offensive with mines, dynamite, homemade Molotov cocktails and individual heroics, allowing Rommel's main forces to retreat safely to Tobruk. The Axis defeat is thus depicted as Rommel's 'real victory', with Hitler to blame for sacrificing their Italian rearguard.

Stafford's best war movie was Enzo G. Castellari's ***Eagles over London*** (1969), also produced by Amati. During Operation Dynamo (the Allied retreat from France at Dunkirk), a squad of German SS commandos disguise themselves as British soldiers and arrive in Dover in rescue boats. Led by Major Krueger (Luigi Pistilli), the commandos assemble in London, rendezvousing with Sheila (Teresa Gimpera), a German agent who works in a forces pub. Their objective is to knock out key radar installations, enabling the Luftwaffe to cross the English Channel undetected, but British captain Paul Stevens (Frederick Stafford) is on to them. Stevens organises Operation Valiant to track down the commandos, while in the skies above, the Battle of Britain rages between the RAF and the Luftwaffe. The original Italian title translated as 'The Battle of England' to cash in on the UK production *Battle of Britain* (1969).

Eagles slickly combines the mission combat movie with elements of espionage, RAF aerial combat dramas and even murder mysteries. To conceal their identities, Krueger's commandos murder Allied soldiers, stealing their identities, so bodies stripped of their uniforms turn up around London. A shootout between a trapped German commando and British troops through bombed-out houses resembles a spaghetti western gunfight. The twist-riddled plot is the epitome of 'Careless Talk Costs Lives' and Castellari cross-cuts several subplots, including a love story between Stevens and RAF lieutenant Meg Jones ('Evelyn Stewart'/Ida Galli). Shot in Italy, Spain and on location in London (Tower Bridge, the Houses of Parliament and London Transport buses appear), the film uses split-screen images which are lost in cropped TV prints. Renzo Palmer played Sergeant Donald Mulligan (dubbed in the English language version with an abrasive cockney accent), Luis Davila and Christian Hay were two womanising Free French pilots enrolled in the RAF, Van Johnson played the RAF's Air Marshal George Taylor, and Eduardo Fajardo was the German commander overseeing Operation Marine Lion, the invasion of Britain. The film hits the mark with its trademark 'war movie' score from Francesco De Masi and the action sequences, including German fighters attacking convoys of Allied troops, the evacuation of Dunkirk, the evacuees' arrival in Dover, the German commandos' attempts to blow up radar installations (they become human bombs, with knapsacks packed with dynamite), and several impressive aerial dogfights staged by Emilio Ruiz Del Rio.

D-Daze: The Battle for Europe

The most internationally successful Italian war movie was ***Anzio*** (1968 – originally *Lo sbarco di Anzio*: 'The Anzio Landing'), a US-Italian co-production between Columbia Pictures and Dino De Laurentiis. It was co-directed by Edward Dmytryk and Duilio Coletti and was scored by Riz Ortolani. Robert Mitchum starred as philosophical US war correspondent Dick Ennis. His assignment is to cover the Allied landings at Anzio (codenamed Operation Shingle) on 22 January 1944. Having witnessed the Germans building concrete pillboxes and artillery emplacements with forced Italian labour, Mitchum and seven US rangers have to fight their way back to enemy lines after their battalion is massacred. Peter Falk, Earl Holliman, Mark Damon, Reni Santoni, Thomas Hunter and Giancarlo Gianni played US rangers, Anthony Steel, Wayde Preston, Venantino Venantini, Arthur Kennedy and Robert Ryan were the Allied top brass, and Wolfgang Preiss was their opponent, Field Marshal Kesselring. *Anzio* resembles a big budget B-movie, with hundreds of extras and some impressive battle scenes. Riddled with 'war is hell' clichés, an overly wordy script and an awful title song ('This World Is Yours' belted out by Jack Jones), *Anzio* recreates the Italian campaign. Location footage was filmed in Naples harbour (the embarkation scenes), on Anzio Cape and in the Eternal City, for the Allies' triumphant arrival at the Colosseum as conquering heroes.

1969 was the peak year for Italian war movies, with Gianfranco Parolini's ***Five for Hell*** an archetypal example of an Italianate *Dirty Dozen*. In Occupied Italy, 1944, Lieutenant Clem Hoffman (John Garko) assembles a crack team of GI's to attack Villa Verdi, a heavily fortified chateau near the village of Corigliano, to steal 'Plan K', the Germans' stratagem to destroy the Allies. Hoffman recruits acrobat Nick Amadori (Nick Jordan), safecracker Al Siracusa (Sal Borgese), muscular knifethrower Sergeant Sam McCarthy (Samson Burke) and sharpshooting explosives expert Johnny 'Chicken' White (Luciano Rossi). Athlete Hoffman's strength lies in his accuracy at pitching baseballs to silently knock out guards. Parolini mixed elements of war movies with a crime story heist and Klaus Kinski played SS colonel Hans Muller at Villa Verdi. Parolini staged the action – which is outlandish even by his own implausible standards – on location in north-west Italy and at Elios Studios. Acrobat Amadori bounces over Villa Verdi's electric fence using a portable trampoline and the machine-gun shootouts and motorbike chases propel the film along at breakneck pace, accompanied by Vasco and Mancuso's jaunty score. The film ends with Muller's twitching death throes, when he is electrocuted on his own electric fence, as Amadori escapes with the microfilm of 'Plan K' concealed in a baseball.

In Tonino Ricci's ***Salt in the Wound*** (1969 – *The Liberators*, *War Fever* and *The Dirty Two*) during the battle for Italy, Corporal Brian Haskins (Klaus Kinski) and Private John Grayson (Ray Saunders) are sentenced to death for looting and murder. Rookie lieutenant Michael Sheppard (George Hilton) is assigned their execution, but a German ambush kills the firing squad. Haskins and Grayson escape, with Sheppard in tow. They encounter a massacred US patrol – Haskins and Grayson steal dog tags from two of the dead and become 'Norman Carr' and 'Calvin Malloy'. Hiding out in the hilltop town of San Michele, the trio are greeted as liberators and the two convicts learn a little humility: Haskins falls for refugee Daniela (Betsy Bell) and Grayson befriends a young orphan, Michele (Roberto Pagano). Haskins discovers that the church contains valuable relics and attempts to steal them.

Salt in the Wound is a rain-drenched, grimy war movie – even the daylight scenes have a watery, bleak sunlight – made even gloomier by Riz Ortolani's atonal score. San Michele was the Tuscan medieval hilltop town of Montecarlo, Lucca (with its distinctive church bell tower and narrow streets), with interiors at Tirrenia Studios. As German armour attacks San Michele, ploughing through woodland and interrupting a celebration of the town's patron saint, Haskins, Grayson and Sheppard defend the town. Michele is wounded and Daniela is mown down in the crossfire. Grayson is killed and Haskins runs amok, screaming Daniela's name and suicidally charging headlong at a tank. The film's *Dirty Two* re-titling presented Haskins and Grayson as redeemed convicts. At 'The End', Sheppard salutes their graves in a vast military cemetery, highlighting the film's message of bad men made good.

Jack Palance shot two combat films in 1969: *The Battle Giants* (*The Fall of the Giants* and *Attack Force Normandy*) and *The Battle of the Commandos* (*The Legion of the Damned*). In 'Henry Manckiewicz'/Leon Klimovsky's **The Battle Giants**, Major John Heston (Palance) is assigned by General Moore (Giuseppe Addobatti) to assemble a team of US officers to contact Field Marshall Rommel (Manuel Collardo). Rommel is under house arrest in a villa on the Rhine. Heston's hand-picked group comprises a pilot, Lieutenant Steve Bloom (John Gramack); a civil engineer, Captain Stuart Latimore (Carlos Estrada); a professional baseball player, Lieutenant Thomas Mulligan (Antonio Pica), and an improbably named medical officer, Captain Agamemnon Geeves (Andrea Bosić). 'They're tops', assures Heston. The squad are accompanied by Herman Truniger (Alberto De Mendoza), a turncoat SS major. Each member of the party has a microfilm embedded in his shoulder and has his own individual instructions. The party's real objective is the Kesselberg Emplacement, a fortified bridge with concrete defence works. Their task is to distract as many German troops as possible, enabling the US army to launch an offensive through the Zella Pass.

Battle Giants was filmed near Madrid, including the railway line through the pinewooded Guardarrama Mountains. The German assault on the concrete sandbagged bunker at the Kesselberg Emplacement ends the film with a bang: the Second Panzer Division, with assault troop support, advance up the valley into a firestorm unleashed by Heston and his men. Palance fires a variety of German hardware, including a Panzerschreck, the German anti-tank bazooka. Good performances by Jesus Puente as Colonel Wolf and Gerard Tichy as General Von Grüber gave the Axis fans something to cheer, while the budget provided much army surplus hardware, including staff cars, half-tracks and the column of Panzers. Despite the mission's risible call-sign ('Kangaroo Calling Swordfish') and German paratrooper helmets for the US commandos that are a size too small, chain-smoking Palance adds gravitas as driven Heston. The film is a slick, successful star vehicle which benefited from a suspenseful Armando Travajoli score.

In Umberto Lenzi's similarly styled **The Battle of the Commandos**, co-starring Curd Jürgens, Thomas Hunter, Robert Hundar, Aldo Sambrell, Antonio Molino Rojo, Wolfgang Preiss and Diana Lorys, Palance played Colonel Charlie MacPherson, who must destroy a railway-mounted long-range Nazi cannon in France (though it was again filmed in Spain).

Giuliano Montaldo's **The Fifth Day of Peace** (1969) was a departure for the Italian war genre – an antiwar movie set in dank Emmen prisoner of war camp in Holland. In the last days of the war, Canadian captain John Miller (Richard Johnson) and his assistant, Lieutenant Romney (Relja Basic), are instructed to set up a POW camp in an abandoned stockade to house over 2,000 German inmates. Colonel Von Bleicher (Helmut Schneider) and the prisoners rigidly stick to their military discipline, sentencing to death two deserters: Ensign Bruno Grauber (Franco Nero) and Corporal Reiner Schultz (Larry Aubrey). The battle of wills between Miller and Von Bleicher comes to a head when Miller refuses to arm Von Bleicher's firing squad. The prisoners demonstrate and Miller calls out the guard to disperse the prisoners. When Miller asks his superior, General Snow (Michael Goodliffe), what the relationship with his German prisoners should be, Snow is blunt ('They've lost the war – don't let 'em forget it') and advises Miller to pass the buck. Canadian troops escort Grauber and Schultz outside the camp and supervise a German firing squad, which execute the deserters. The camp's equilibrium restored, Miller, now promoted to major, has a clear conscience. *Fifth Day* is superior drama, well acted by an interesting cast, including British actors Johnson and Goodliffe. Renato Romano played Miller's batman, Sergeant O'Mally, and Bud Spencer was Corporal Jelenek, a supplies officer who shelters the German deserters. The film benefits from muddy Eastmancolor cinematography by Silvano Ippoliti, the eerie camp towers and the gate sign 'Arbeit Mein Frei' chillingly silhouetted. The film was known by various titles, including *Crime of Defeat* and *Gott Mit Uns*: the slogan that appears on German military belt buckles. The sinister score by Ennio Morricone includes 'Gott Mit Uns' [God With Us], a haunting echo of *Once Upon a Time in the West*'s theme.

Many big Hollywood stars gravitated towards Italian war movies. Rock Hudson led a party of street urchins to blow up an Italian dam in *Hornets' Nest* (1970), which featured Sylva Koscina, Sergio Fantoni, Jacques Sernas and Giacomo Rossi-Stuart. **The Battle of Neretva** (1969) was a $12 million Yugoslavian-Italian-US-German co-production which detailed the German offensive against Yugoslav partisans in 1943. The film was nominated for a Best Foreign Film Oscar but was later cut and dubbed for US distribution, from 175 minutes to 102. Even this cut version boasted international talent: Yul Brynner, Sylva Koscina, Franco Nero, Hardy Kruger, Curd Jürgens and Orson Welles. The UK print, titled *The Battle on the River Neretva*, is a 126-minute compromise.

Battle Fatigue: The 1970s

The 1970s saw the Italian combat craze quickly die out, as gialli and comedy caught audience attention. Carlo Lizzani's *Mussolini: The Last Days* (1974 – *The Last Four Days*) starred Rod Steiger as Il Duce. George Pan Cosmatos's **Massacre in Rome** (1973 – *Rappresaglia*) starred an international cast – Richard Burton, Marcello Mastroianni, Leo McKern, Anthony Steel and John Steiner – and deployed a dissonant Morricone score. Based on Robert Katz's novel *Death in Rome*, it told the true story of the Ardeatine Caves massacre, an atrocity perpetrated by the Nazis beneath Rome on 24 March 1944. In retaliation for the ambush of an SS patrol by partisans (who detonated a roadside bomb hidden in a dust cart in Via Rasella), 10 Italians were executed for every German soldier killed. Lieutenant Colonel Hubert Kappler of the Gestapo (Burton) is assigned the grisly task of rounding up the victims and overseeing their executions: 330 Italian men are trucked over to the grotto, which becomes their death chamber. In an administrative error, 335 are killed – each is shot in the head with a pistol – then the caves are sealed with explosives. Filmed on location in the capital, *Massacre in Rome* is a powerful, suspenseful film. It features one of Burton's best performances, with Mastroianni equally good as Father Pietro Antonelli, who opposes Kappler and the Gestapo and finds himself in the caves in the film's horrible shock ending. At the time of the film's release, Kappler was still in an Italian prison serving his life sentence.

The Biggest Battle (1978 – *The Greatest Battle, The Great Battle, Battle Force* and *Battle of Mereth*) was directed by 'Humphrey Longan' (Umberto Lenzi). It starred Henry Fonda, Samantha Egger, Helmut Berger, Stacy Keach, John Huston and Giuliano Gemma, intercut with newsreel footage narrated by Orson Welles. Directed, or rather assembled, by 'Hank Milestone' (Lenzi again), **From Hell to Victory** (1979) was passable war fare. This was a soap opera war movie, telling of multinational friends, whose relationships are redefined and destroyed by war. The friends agree to rendezvous annually on 24 August at a café by the Seine, but few of them appear for the final reunion. George Peppard played American OSS agent Brett, Raymond Lovelock was his estranged son Jim, Horst Buchholz was cast as Nazi tank commander Jürgen, Sam Wanamaker played US war correspondent Ray and Anny Duperey was French Resistance fighter Fabienne. French actor Jean-Pierre Cassel played English Spitfire pilot Dick and suntanned George Hamilton appeared, unconvincingly, as French Resistance fighter Maurice (sample line, while on a nighttime raid: 'Do not wake ze Bosch'). Peppard is sent to Holland to destroy a facility making V-2 rocket propellant. The film is a whistle-stop tour of the Battle for France – from the German invasion, Dunkirk and

Battle of Britain, to D-Day and the liberation of Paris – mostly via stock footage from *The Dirty Heroes* and *Eagles over London*.

Tinto Brass' fleshy **Salon Kitty** (1976) depicted the depravity of the Third Reich. Helmut Wallenberg (Helmut Berger) sets up a brothel for German officers run by Madame Kitty Kellermann (Ingrid Thulin) but falls for Margherita (Teresa Ann Savoy), one of the prostitutes. Brass equated the Third Reich with the Roman Empire (his next film was the infamous *Caligula*) and deployed decadent sets (created at DEAR Studios by Ken Adam) and risqué musical numbers in the style of *Cabaret*. The supporting cast included cult movie stalwarts Luciano Rossi, John Ireland, John Steiner and Dan Van Husen. It resulted in a short-lived craze for unpleasant Nazi-ploitation potboilers, which depicted forced prostitution to serve the German army (the so-called Joy Division), or else vile tortures inflicted in Nazi experimental camps. They boasted bleak titles – *SS Experiment Love Camp* (1976), *SS Girls* (1977), *Red Nights of the Gestapo*, *SS Extermination Love Camp* and *Gestapo's Last Orgy* (all 1977) – and were helmed by schlock directors such as Sergio Garrone and Bruno Mattei.

A belated addition to the Italian combat cycle was Enzo G. Castellari's **The Inglorious Bastards** (1977 – *The Counterfeit Commandos*), which thrashed the *Dirty Dozen* formula to its ridiculous conclusion. In France 1944, five misfit US army convicts, deserters, murderers and thieves are being transported by MPs to a stockade when a German air attack allows them to escape. The escapees – Tony (Peter Hooten), Fred Canfield (Fred Williamson), Nick (Michael Perglani), Berle (Jackie Constantin) and Lieutenant Robert Yeager (Bo Svenson), a pilot – decide to head for neutral Switzerland. They accidentally massacre a squad of American soldiers who are disguised as Germans – as in *Hell Commandos*, Yeager and company undertake the deceased commandos' special mission. Briefed by Colonel Buckner (Ian Bannen), they waylay an armoured train carrying a V-2 rocket warhead prototype and steal the device's gyroscope guidance system. The train is halted when the French Resistance demolish the Saint Dru Bridge and force the locomotive to detour to Pont Mosson station, but a German military train arrives. Buckner removes the gyroscope and escapes, Nick and Berle are killed, and Yeager, with the warhead's self-destruct mechanism set to blow, drives the train straight into the station.

Bastards was filmed in Italy and at Cinecittà and Vides Studios. One scene depicts a group of female German soldiers skinny dipping in Monte Gelato Falls and the railway sequences were filmed between Capranica and Viterbo. Raimund Harmstorf appeared as German prisoner Adolf and Debra Berger, as French Resistance nurse Nicole, is lumbered with lines such as, 'Age is not important when you fight for something in which you believe, n'est pas?' With his chiselled granite features and broken nose, towering Svenson plays the tongue-in-cheek action straight. Scrounging 'Mr Fix-it' Perglani (sporting long hippy hair and a bushy moustache) and blaxpoitation star Williamson (with cigar and *Superfly* 'tache) lend excellent support. Perglani rides a mean motorbike, Steve McQueen style – when a bullet punctures his gas tank, he seals the hole with chewing gum. Hooten's flaky portrayal of needling 'white trash' Tony is memorable and it is he who survives, embracing fellow survivor Nicole on the railroad tracks.

The most macho, daft and cynically un-PC war movie, *Inglorious Bastards* is never dull and from its colourful title sequence (accompanied by Francesco De Masi's rip-roaring march) to its explosive conclusion, it doesn't hang around. Castellari's gleeful mayhem, choreographed by stunt coordinator Rocco Lerro, features the same German extras being repeatedly killed and the same vehicles being blown up, often in Castellari's trademark slow motion. Castellari, who would have made a fine action hero himself, appears as various German soldiers (he dies at least half a dozen times) and as the commander of a German mortar detachment. Optical effects and miniatures are deployed – for example, the US army depot and a bombed-out town – which increases the film's sense of scale.

It is a mark of the continued popularity of films such as *The Inglorious Bastards* on DVD that cult film aficionado Quentin Tarantino misspelt Castellari's title for his 2009 war movie *Inglourious Basterds*, which depicted a mission by commandos to blow up Hitler at a film premiere in Paris. Tarantino namechecked Antonio Margheriti and Edwige Fenech, thanked in his acknowledgements Castellari, Bo Svenson and Sergio Sollima, and deployed Ennio Morricone cues from *Battle of Algiers*, *The Return of Ringo*, *The Big Gundown*, *Death Rides a Horse*, *A Professional Gun* and, most effectively, 'Un Amico' from *Revolver*.

Chapter Eleven

Knives in the Dark
Gialli Thrillers

Italian 'gialli' psycho-thrillers were named after a series of crime thrillers published in Italy with yellow covers ('giallo' in Italian). Their protagonists were often American nationals working or vacationing in Italy, who become sleuths to solve a murder which they have inadvertently witnessed – this enables the casting of an American or British star in the principal role. The investigating police officers often have quirks – for example, they're trying to quit smoking or have a passion for ornithology or philately – and their specialist knowledge helps them to solve the case. The films' stylised visuals are defined by roving point-of-view camerawork and the killers are often dressed in brimmed hats, long coats and leather gloves. Gialli have been accused of misogyny in their presentation of the bloody murders of often naked, always beautiful, women, though the killer is often revealed to be a disturbed woman, when all clues infer a male aggressor. The musical scores are a key ingredient in the films' effectiveness. Gialli deployed the breathy orgasms of Edda Dell'Orso, the whining feedback of Ennio Morricone or the thumping heavy metal of Goblin, though their ear-splitting rock left some audiences with 'metal fatigue'.

Black Lace, Blood and Bava

The Girl Who Knew Too Much (1963) was Mario Bava's homage to Hitchcock's thriller *The Man Who Knew Too Much* (1956). New Yorker Nora Davis (Leticia Roman), an impressionable reader of murder mystery novels, arrives in Rome to visit her ailing aunt, Ethel Widnell Batocci (Chana Coubert). Ethel suffers a fatal heart attack soon afterwards. On her way to fetch Dr Marcello Bassi (John Saxon), her aunt's physician, Nora witnesses a woman being stabbed. With no evidence to prove her story, Nora turns amateur sleuth to identify the perpetrator of the 'Alphabet Murders', which after three victims are up to the letter D.

A mediocre murder mystery, *Girl* is of note mainly for its monochrome cinematography. This is the Rome of *La dolce vita*, a tourist book version of the city. Nora visits the Colosseum, the Garden of Venus, the Sant'Angelo Bridge and Castel Sant'Angelo, and the Stadio Dei Marmi at the Foro Italico (a running track ringed by 60 statues). Nora's aunt lives in a house in the Piazza Di Spagna and Nora witnesses the murder on the Spanish Steps, the cascade of three flights of stairs which is dominated by the Trinità Dei Monti Church. Bava shot on location in Rome, with interiors at Titanus. The theme song, 'Furore', was sung by Adriano Celentano. For the US release by AIP, *Girl* was rescored by Les Baxter (replacing Roberto Nicolosi's jazzy cues) and retitled *Evil Eye*. The US version accentuated the film's comedic aspects, with jokier scenes inserted (Bava appears at one point in a portrait), and all reference to marijuana-laced Kent cigarettes was removed – it's hinted in the Italian version that the Spanish Steps murder could have been Nora's hallucination. John Saxon described *Evil Eye* as a *giallo brillante*, a spoof thriller, but it is the more serious Italian print that influenced later gialli.

Bava's **Blood and Black Lace** (1964) was his most violent film of the 1960s and the proto-giallo. Model Isabella (Francesca Ungaro) is murdered in the Christian Haute Couture fashion house run by manager Max Morlan (Cameron Mitchell) and the recently widowed owner, Countess Christina Como (Eva Bartok). Inspector Sylvester (Thomas Reiner) discovers that the world of high fashion conceals a tangled web of narcotics, infidelity, murder and blackmail. The list of suspects includes Morlan himself, his employees – nervous epileptic Marco (Massimo Righi) and creepy dress designer Cesar Lazar ('Alan Collins'/Luciano Pigozzi) – antiques dealer Frank Scalo (Dante Di Paolo) and Marquis Richard Morell (Franco Ressel), both of whom are dating models. With the discovery of Isabella's diary, everyone is edgy. The killer slays Scalo's girlfriend Nicole (Arianni Gorrini) with a taloned gauntlet in Scalo's antiques shop. Model Peggy (Mary Arden) is tortured by the killer – her hand and face pressed against a hot stove – and the marquis' lover, Greta (Lea Kruger), is suffocated with a cushion. It is revealed that Max is the culprit, and Christina his accomplice: they are having an affair and her husband didn't die in an accident. Max convinces Christina to kill one last time – she drowns model Tao-Lin (Claude Dantes) in her bath, but Max double-crosses Christina, hoping to implicate his lover.

Bava filmed during the winter of 1963–64 in six weeks. The fashion house's exterior was filmed at Villa Pamphili, Rome (with its fountain and squeaky sign), with interiors at ATC Studios. The scenes at Scalo's antiques shop were filmed courtesy of La Società DEDALO. The nocturnal exteriors, with foggy streets and windblown leaves, create a milieu worthy of Jack the Ripper. While the English language title is darkly poetic – the victim's blood spilled on the fashion house's garments – the original Italian title, *6 donne per l'assassino* [Six Women for the Murderer], is more representative: Max and his six victims. The incriminating red leather diary links the killings with the flimsiest of pretexts. Bava's film

Fashion Victims: Lurid Italian poster for Mario Bava's *Blood and Black Lace* (1964) depicting the blank-masked killer and four slain models.

closely resembles the 'krimi' thrillers made in West Germany, which were based on the works of Edgar Wallace. *Black Lace* boasts Carlo Rustichelli's finest score, with its percussive bossa nova trumpet theme and threatening, descending cues. The killer's outfit, a long black-belted mac, black gloves and brimmed hat, was highly influential on gialli, as was the faceless white mask which shields the killer's identity. The killer (as played by stunt double Goffredo Unger) goes berserk in the murder scenes. Lifeless, bloodied women's corpses, their clothes torn, their faces disfigured, are manhandled, shoved in car boots and dragged around, as bodies begin literally to stack up. The camera takes perverse pleasure stalking its victims in gliding movements – gaudily lit and elegantly shot – as befits a film set in a chic fashion house. Bartok's classy black mourning attire was designed by Eleanora Garnett.

In the UK *Black Lace* was X-rated in 1965, following a plethora of cuts. The US version released in 1966 by Woolner Brothers used a slower Rustichelli cue as the title music and replaced Bava's original title sequence (with the cast photographed as though they were wax dummies amid garishly lit mannequins) with wicker tailor's dummies, skulls, and bloody gunshot wounds, designed by Filmation Associates. Lurid posters promised 'Guaranteed! The 8 Greatest Shocks Ever Filmed!' starring '30 of the most Glamorous Girls in the world!' – six of whom don't survive the movie.

Bava's next giallo was a warning to all newlyweds. Stephen Forsyth starred as bride-killer John Harrington in **Hatchet for the Honeymoon** (1969 – *Blood Brides*), which was set in Paris but mostly filmed in Barcelona and Villa Frascati outside Rome (with interiors at Frascati and Balcazar Studios, Barcelona). John is the head of a bridalwear fashion house where he lures his victims. He butchers them with a gleaming meat cleaver, buries their remains in his plant hothouse and disposes of the bodies in an incinerator. When John falls for model Helen Woolett (Dagmar Lassander), he kills his wife Mildred (Laura Betti) whilst wearing lipstick and a veil and then burns her. Mildred returns and haunts her husband – everyone can see her spectre except John. Betti's ghostly countenance is effective in these scenes. The murders are investigated by Inspector Russell (Jesus Puente), Femi Benussi played victim Alice Norton and 'Alan Collins'/Luciano Pigozzi was designer Vences. With its romantic score by Sante Romitelli, *Hatchet* is an insipid psycho thriller, with few Bava flourishes in evidence, though the opening train-bound murder (as John kills two newlyweds) and Mildred's manifestations are well handled. In an in-joke, John watches Bava's *Black Sabbath* on late-night TV. John's flashbacks reveal that when he was a child (Guido Barlocci), he murdered his own mother and her lover.

Bava's next thriller, **Five Dolls for an August Moon** (1970), stranded its cast on a secluded island. Seven guests are invited to the luxury pad of businessman George Stark (Teodoro Corra) and his wife, Jill (Edith Meloni): Professor Jerry Farrell (William Berger), his wife, Trudy (Ira Fürstenberg), mysterious Isabel (Justine Gall), and businessmen Jack Davidson (Renato Rossini) and Nick Chaney (Maurice Poli) and their wives, Peggy (Héléna Ronée) and Marie (Edwige Fenech). The businessmen want to buy Farrell's invention – a formula for industrial resin – but he refuses to sell. In the boozed-up, decadent atmosphere of Stark's retreat, murder games, marital infidelity and jealousy thrive – Marie begins an affair with the Starks' houseboy Charles (Mauro Bosco), who is soon found murdered. The islanders begin to die one by one, until by the film's twist dénouement, the killers are revealed in the formulaic plot's saving grace.

Five Dolls resembles Agatha Christie's *Ten Little Indians* and the black humour of the piece surfaces in a macabre running gag: each corpse is put on ice and hung in polythene body bags in Stark's walk-in deepfreeze. Bava shot the film in 19 days in October 1969. The beach footage of the island was Tor Caldara, Anzio. The female cast of Euro stars – the 'five dolls' of the title – add glamour, though for the most part they are mannequin set dressing. The film's best feature is the interior production design shot at DEAR Studios, Rome, its chintz worthy of *Diabolik* – in fact, Diabolik's revolving bed reappears here. The cast are decked out in campy outfits at the outré end of 1970s style. The film is an exercise in groovy stylistics, highlighted by Bava's always-interesting camerawork and complemented by a trademark lounge score by Piero Umiliani and hazy prog-rock tracks – including 'Neve calda' [Hot Snow] – performed by Italian experimental band Il Balletto Di Bronzo (The Ballet of Bronze).

If *Hatchet for the Honeymoon* and *Five Dolls for an August Moon* had been relatively bloodless in their carnage, Bava made amends with **A Bay of Blood** (1971). Filmed during January and February 1971 at Sabaudia on the Lazio coast, with interiors at Villa Frascati and Elios Studios, the film has architect Frank Ventura (Chris Avram) attempting to develop a quiet seaside bay into a tourist resort. The present owners, Countess Federica Donati (Isa Miranda) and her husband, Count Filipo (Giovanni Nuvoletti), are murdered. Their daughter, Renata (Claudine Auger), and her husband, Albert (Luigi Pistilli), arrive to claim their inheritance and discover that the countess had an illegitimate son, Simon (Claudio Volonté), who lives in a shack on the bay. Ventura and his lover, Laura (Anna Maria Rosati), have a villa on the bay, as does ecologically minded insect collector Paul Foscari (Leopold Trieste) and his wife, Anna (Laura Betti), who is a medium. Four giggling, idiot teenagers – Brunhilde (Brigitte Skay), Bobby (Roberto Bonanni), Denise (Paola Rubens) and Duke (Guido Boccaccini) – arrive in a yellow beach buggy and are caught in the crossfire, their bloody bodies dumped in a bath. As the film progresses, a murderous chain of events dispatches the entire cast. The film was released in Italy as *Reazione a catena* [Chain Reaction].

Bay of Blood is notable for its 13 brutal murders, convincingly staged by Carlo Rambaldi. The countess is hanged when someone nooses her and kicks away her wheelchair; her husband is stabbed; Brunhilde goes skinny dipping and has her throat slashed with a machete; Bobby (Roberto Bonanni) has his face split with the machete and Denise (Paola Rubens) and Duke (Guido Boccaccini) are skewered on a spear as they make love; Renata stabs Ventura with scissors; Albert strangles Paul with a telephone cord and Renata beheads Anna with an axe; Simon strangles Laura and is then killed himself, when he's speared by Albert. Now the sole owners of the real estate, Renata and Albert return to their bayside caravan, where they've been camping with their children (Renato Cestie and

Nicoletta Elmi). In a shock payoff, the children find a shotgun and accidentally blast their parents: 'Gee, they're good at playing dead, aren't they?'

Backed by a suspensefully groovy percussive bossa nova by Stelvio Cipriani, *Bay* delivers shocks and style in equal measure. Bava is in fine form with this gruesome effort – he was also the cinematographer and the prowling camerawork on the eerie wooded bay, an ominous twilight perpetually dispersing the light, is the director at his best. In a memorably unpleasant scene, the body of the count is discovered on Simon's fishing boat with a squid hideously squirming on the corpse's decomposing face. The bloody killings are highly convincing and have been cut or abridged in all UK releases of the film. *Bay of Blood* was refused a certificate by the BBFC in 1972, then released in truncated form in 1980 as *Blood Bath* (rated X) and banned on home video as a 'Video Nasty'. In the US it initially appeared in 1972 as *Carnage*, then as *Twitch of the Death Nerve* and as *Last House – Part II*. *Bay of Blood* is now available uncut on DVD. It was hugely influential on US horror movies such as *Halloween* (1978) and *Friday the 13th* (1980) and remains Bava's most controversial film.

Murder All'Argento

Though Bava was a giallo pioneer, Dario Argento remains the genre's maestro. The son of producer Salvatore Argento and Brazilian photographer Elda Luxardo, Argento began as a film critic on *Paese sera*. He collaborated with Sergio Leone on the original treatment of *Once Upon a Time in the West* and co-scripted several war movies (*Commandos, Probability Zero, The Battle of the Commandos*) and spaghetti westerns (*Today It's Me…Tomorrow You!, The Five Man Army*). His directorial debut, the murder mystery **The Bird with the Crystal Plumage** (1970), welded the shock 'slash and hack' of the shower murder in Hitchcock's *Psycho* (1960) to the prowling menace of Bava.

American writer Sam Dalmas (Tony Musante) witnesses the attempted murder of Monica Ranieri (Eva Renzi) in a Rome art gallery. Her husband, Alberto (Umberto Raho), is the chief suspect. Inspector Morosini (Enrico Maria Salerno) is investigating a series of murders that have already claimed three female victims. Grounded by Morosini as the gallery murder's chief witness, Sam begins to delve, until the killer threatens his girlfriend, Julia. Two more women are killed and the police go to Alberto's apartment, where he's about to kill Monica. Alberto falls from a high window and confesses to the crimes before he dies, but when Julia goes missing, the trail leads Sam back to the gallery.

Crystal Plumage was shot on location in Rome and at Incir-De Paolis Studios from August to October 1969, with Argento's father, Salvatore, producing. Fulvio Mingozzi played a police inspector, Werner Peters was an effeminate antiques dealer and Gildo Di Marco was the stuttering pimp 'So Long' Garullo. Reggie Nalder (the assassin from Hitchcock's *The Man Who Knew Too Much*) played yellow-jacketed marksman Needles (named Siringa in the Italian print) hired by the killer to liquidate Sam. Suzy Kendall played Julia and went on to appear

Original Italian 'locandina' poster for Dario Argento's trendsetting giallo thriller *The Bird with the Crystal Plumage* (1970).

in several gialli, including Sergio Martino's *Torso* (1973), where she was one of several art students stalked by a killer. A voyeuristic blend of titillation and mutilation backed by a wilted giallo score by G & M De Angelis, *Torso* was made interesting by its locations: the rural villa of Castello Di Corcolle; the Monte Gelato Falls, the ancient town of Tagliacozzo, L'Aquila, and the splendid Fontana Maggiore in Piazza IV November in Perugia, Umbria.

Argento's cinematographer was Vittorio Storaro, who went on to win Oscars for his work on *Apocalypse Now*, *Reds* and *The Last Emperor*. Storaro's

Eastmancolor Cromoscoped images bathe the screen in colour-coded symbolism, usually involving lurid reds or bright whites. A pursuit through the foggy streets of Rome resembles Bava's approach, but Storaro's command of light and shade and his manipulation of angles, juxtapositions and unexpected camera movements updated Bava's gothic style to a neon-lit modern world of concrete and glass. Storaro's style is best demonstrated when Julia is trapped: the killer plunges her apartment into darkness, then chisels a hole in her wooden front door with a knife and peers through it.

The archetypal giallo killer – dressed in a black leather mac, black gloves, scarf and hat – stalks and photographs potential victims before lacerating them with knives or cut-throat razors. Sam is walking home one night when he sees Monica's attempted murder. When he tries to help her, he is trapped between the sliding automatic glass doors – like a fly twixt double-glazing – as she claws towards him, crying for help. When he returns to the darkened gallery, searching for Julia at the film's climax, he is again trapped, this time deliberately by the killer, and pinned to the ground beneath a heavy spiked frieze. Such moments of terror are scored by Ennio Morricone's jangling cues. It was with gialli that his avant-garde style broke into mainstream film scoring. In this period Morricone collaborated with experimental group Nuova Consananza. Together they constructed an atonal, clattering score for Elio Petri's psychosexual ghost story *A Quiet Place in the Country* (1968) starring Franco Nero and Vanessa Redgrave, which was abstract filmmaking at its most interesting and incomprehensible. *Crystal Plumage*'s main theme is a lilting lullaby, with a folksy acoustic guitar, twinkling music box and a 'la la' vocal line sung by Edda Dell'Orso and the Cantori. Her breathy vocals are used to menacing effect (in 'Silenzio nel caos'), while the score fractures with the tolling bells, whining strings and stuttering cornet of 'La citta si risveglia' [The City Wakes Up].

The killer's motivation is explained via a Naif painting that depicts a grotesque stabbing of a little girl in a snowy meadow. When Sam visits its artist, Berto Consalvi (Mario Adorf), a cat-eating rural hermit who lurks in a bricked-up house, he discovers that the painting is based on an attempted murder in the village of Aviano 10 years ago. The riddle's resolution hinges on a threatening phone call from the killer, which features a screeching noise in the background. Professor Carlo Dover (Renato Romano), Sam's ornithologist friend, recognises it as the cry of the Hornitus Nevalis, an exotic bird with white, glass-like plumage and native only to Northern Siberia; there's one in Rome's zoo which is near Ranieri's apartment. The film was released in the US as *The Bird with the Crystal Plumage* and *The Phantom of Terror*. In the UK it was retitled *The Gallery Murders* and rated X. *Crystal Plumage* remains Argento's most suspenseful, artful giallo and it was a massive, unexpected hit in Italy on its release in February 1970.

With his horror-thriller formula firmly established, Argento directed **The Cat O'Nine Tails** (1971). Blind ex-journalist and enigmatographer (puzzle fanatic) Franco 'Cookie' Arno (Karl Malden) and his niece Lori (Cinzia De Carolis) team up with reporter Carlo Giordani (James Franciscus) to solve a mystery linked to the Terzi Institute of Genetic Research. Dr Calabresi (Carlo Alighiero) falls in front of a train and Righetto (Vittorio Congia), a photographer who snaps his death, is garrotted when his negatives reveal a hand pushing the doctor. Calabresi's lover, Bianca Merusi (Rada Rassimov), is also garrotted and the killer is interested in the institute's programme which researches criminal tendencies via their 'xyy' genetic formula. Suspects include Dr Braun (Horst Frank), his lover Manuel (Werner Pochath), Professor Fulvio Terzi (Tino Carraro) and his daughter, Anna (Catherine Spaak, modelling voluminously coiffured hair). The killer tries to poison Carlo's milk delivery and gas Arno and then stabs Braun and kidnaps Lori.

Drawing on Henry Hathaway's *23 Paces to Baker Street* (1956), where blind playwright Van Johnson investigates a kidnap plot, *Cat* demonstrates Argento's style already overtaking content. The set piece murders are violent, but only Calabresi's decapitation under a train shows any imagination. *Cat* is predominantly an industrial espionage thriller – the 'cat o'nine tails' are Carlo and Arno's nine leads, rather than an implement of torture. Pier Paolo Capponi played investigating officer Spimi and Ugo Fangareggi was hopeless criminal Gigi the Loser, whom Carlo recruits to break into Terzi's villa. Morricone's score ranges from the melancholic main theme, 'Ninna nanna in blu' [Lullaby in Blue] – with strummed guitar, flute, strings, chimes and Edda Dell'Orso's soothing vocal – to the jazz percussion, animal cries and strangled cornet for 'Placcaggio'. Filmed from September to October 1970 on city locations in Rome, Turin and West Berlin (with interiors at Cinecittà), *Cat* was the ninth most successful film in Italy in 1971.

Four Flies on Grey Velvet (1971), the third of Argento's Animal Trilogy, was an opportunity for Morricone to foreground his jazz-rock jams. The story focuses on rock band drummer Roberto Tobias (Michael Brandon, pre-*Dempsey and Makepeace*) and his wife, Nina (Mimsy Farmer). Morricone's title music, when Roberto rehearses with his band in the studio, is a fuzzy Hammond organ groove, with strangled wordless vocals. The film's most famous composition – the ghostly 'Come un madrigale' [Like a Madrigal] – resembles Morricone's hit 'Chi mai'. The score's best cue is the twinkling theme (deploying acoustic guitar and Edda Dell'Orso's vocal) used in the bath-time love scene between Roberto and Nina's cousin, Dalia (Francine Racette).

Four Flies finds Roberto falsely accused of stabbing to death Carlo Marosi (Calisto Calisti). Someone wearing a doll-faced mask snaps the murder, a set-up, in an empty theatre. Carlo isn't actually dead, but a web of blackmail and murder envelopes the Tobias household. Their maid Maria (Costanza Spada) is stabbed in a park; Carlo himself is bludgeoned and garrotted; Gianni Arrosio (Jean-Pierre Marielle), a private investigator working for Roberto, is killed by lethal syringe injection in a subway lavatory cubicle; and Dalia is stabbed to death. These murders are presented by Argento as lengthy set-pieces, with the build-up to each crime reaching a crescendo at the moment of death. They resemble ritualised spaghetti western gunfights, or the cymbal crash at the climax of a drum solo. Noteworthy features include Roberto's recurring nightmare of a Middle Eastern beheading, an odd cameo by Bud Spencer as Roberto's friend Godfrey and a slow-motion special effect of a bullet flying through the air.

Argento commenced filming in July 1971, on location in Turin, Rome and Milan, with interiors at Incir-De Paolis. As expected in gialli, light switches never work when characters are home alone and the twist dénouement is especially well handled. The poetic title refers to the human retina retaining the last image it sees at the moment of death – here a victim's eyeball reveals that the last thing she saw was four flies. Roberto realises that Nina's necklace features a fly in amber, which has been 'photographed' swinging four times by the retina. Nina jumps into her car to escape, but in an impressive, slow-motion windscreen-shattering set piece (cut to the hymnal 'Come un madrigale'), she crashes into the back of a truck and is decapitated.

Flashing Blades: Gialli Fever

In the wake of Argento's success, gialli fleetingly became the most popular genre at the Italian box office. Franco Nero played investigative reporter Andrea Bild in Luigi Bazzoni's **The Fifth Cord** (1971), which benefited from another Morricone score, including the Hammond organ lounge groove theme tune 'Giocoso, giocoso' and the quivering love theme 'Voce secondo'. John Lubbock survives an attack on his way home from a New Year's Eve party. Four subsequent killings claim people who were present at the party: Sophia Bini (Rossella Falk), the invalid wife of Dr Richard Bini (Renato Romano), is strangled and thrown down a stairwell; newspaper editor Traversi (Guido Alberti) suffers a heart attack as he walks home through a park; Isabel Lancia (Ira Von Fürstenberg), the fiancée of Eduardo Vermont (Edmund Purdom), is found drowned in a hotel bath; and hooker Giulia Suave (Agostina Belli) is murdered in a motorway underpass. A black glove is found at each murder scene – firstly with one finger missing, then another, suggesting there will be five victims. Reporter Andrea is a suspect, but the killer attacks his little son, Toni, at home. Andrea deduces that the culprit is Lubbock, a native of Aries – the Italian title was *Gionata nera per l'Ariete* [Black Day for Aries] – for reasons that are only partially explained, involving perversion, blackmail and Lubbock's love for Vermont. Alcoholic Andrea's relationship with his estranged wife, Helene (Silvia Monti), is well handled. Interiors were lensed at Incir-De Paolis, with location work in Rome. Wolfgang Preiss played the investigating police inspector and Pamela Tiffin was Andrea's mistress, Lu. What sets *Fifth Cord* apart from other gialli is Vittorio Storaro's consummate cinematography, with shards of light slicing through the darkness. He also photographed Bazzoni's unfathomable mystery *Footprints* (1975), starring Florinda Bolkan.

Giuliano Carnimeo's **The Case of the Bloody Iris** (1971) was as convoluted as its alternative title – *What Are Those Strange Drops of Blood on the Body of*

Jennifer? Someone is killing glamorous women in a Genovese apartment block and Commissioner Enci and his homicide team are on the case. High-class prostitute Lola (Evi Farinelli) has had her throat slit in the elevator and exotic nightclub performer Mizar Harrington (Carla Brait) is trussed up and drowned in her bath. Two glamour models, Marilyn Ricci (Paola Quattrini) and Jennifer Landsbury (Edwige Fenech), move into Mizar's apartment, which is loaned to them by smoothy architect Andrea Barto (George Hilton). When Marilyn is stabbed in broad daylight in a crowded street, suspicion falls on Andrea, who is pathologically scared of the sight of blood and has knowledge of the apartment block's layout. As in all gialli, the roster of suspects lengthens to include Jennifer's unhinged ex-husband, Adam (Ben Carra), a weird old neighbour, Mrs Moss (Maria Tedeschi), who appears to live alone (she shelters her deformed son, who has a passion for horror comics) and Sheila Isaacs (Annabella Incontrera) and her violin-playing father, Professor Isaacs (George Rigaud). Giampiero Albertini's Commissioner Enci is a philatelist, enthusing over rare stamps, and Luciano Pigozzi appeared as Fanelli, a seedy nightclub owner. The killer models a black facemask, hat, overcoat and surgical gloves and packs chloroform and a scalpel. Carnimeo is aided by Bruno Nicolai's trademark Euro score, some colourfully 1970s fashions, hip interiors (filmed at Elios Studios), kaleidoscopic flashbacks and plenty of roving, handheld camerawork. The main clue to the killer's identity, a white iris flower found near the victims, was the symbol of a 'free love' cult to which Jennifer belonged with Adam, though he is wiped from the suspect list when he falls out of cupboard with a flick-knife in his guts.

Following Argento's lead, many gialli filmmakers incorporated numbers, animals or flowers in their titles. Sergio Martino's ***The Case of the Scorpion's Tail*** (1971) was a good example of the genre, shot on location in London (Trafalgar Square, Buckingham Palace and Westminster), Athens (the Parthenon) and at Elios Studios. Lisa Baumer (Ida Galli) collects the $1 million life insurance policy on her pilot husband, Kurt (Fulvio Mingozzi), when he's killed in a plane crash. Insurance investigator Peter Lynch (George Hilton) is assigned to track her to Greece, but shortly afterwards Lisa is murdered and the money vanishes. More victims die – slain by a maniac dressed in a Diabolik-style bodysuit – and Greek police inspector Stavros (Luigi Pistilli) and Interpol agent John Stanley (Alberto De Mendoza) investigate. Anita Strindberg played photographer Cleo Dupont (Peter's love interest), Janine Reynaud was Kurt's Greek lover, Lara Florakis, and Luis Barboo was her henchman, Sharif. Martino can certainly stage gory action – in one scene, a victim has his eye gouged out – and deploys some Bavaesque lighting effects. There's also a jagged trademark giallo score courtesy of Bruno Nicolai. The key lead is a blown-up photograph depicting Kurt wearing distinctive golden scorpion cufflinks, which are found at a crime scene, implying he's still alive and collected his own life insurance.

Maurizio Lucidi's ***The Designated Victim*** (1971) was a giallo remake of Hitchcock's *Strangers on a Train* (1951). Milan advertising executive Stefano

Argenti (Tomas Milian) has an affair with Fabienne Berongé (Katia Kristine) and plans to take her to Venezuela, but his wife, Louisa (Marisa Bartoli), refuses to sell him her share of their ad company. In Venice, Stefano encounters Count Matteo Tiepolo (Pierre Clémenti) and their idle chat soon turns to murder. Matteo wants to rid himself of his abusive brother and proposes that Stefano kill him, while Matteo will kill Louisa. Stefano doesn't take Matteo seriously but Louisa is found strangled in her apartment. Police commissioner Finzi (Luigi Casellato) investigates, with Stefano the chief suspect. Matteo continues to contact Stefano, blackmailing him with incriminating evidence, so Stefano travels to Venice to carry out his part of their 'pact'. As instructed by Matteo, Stefano climbs the roof of the Basilica Di Santa Maria Della Salute: when the clock strikes 12, he takes aim at a window across the canal with a precision rifle and shoots.

Lucidi makes the most of his locations in foggy Venice and Milan and filmed the Argentis' holiday villa at Moltrasio, on Lake Como. Luis Bacalov wrote the romantic score, with fuzz guitar cues from prog-rock band New Trolls. Milian himself crooned the melancholic title ballad, 'My Shadow in the Dark'. Sandra Cardini played Kristina Muller, the count's mysterious accomplice. Confezioni San Remo provided Milian's stylish wardrobe and Mayer of Rome furnished Clémenti's. Clean-shaven Milian looks rather tidier than he does in his westerns and cop movies. He's upstaged by Clémenti as Matteo, whose gaunt, pale face is framed by long, black hair. Modelling hippy regalia and a cape or long coat, Matteo is a prowling Dracula, haunting Vienna's foggy byways and stalking Stefano's every move as his new best friend.

Lucio Fulci contributed some interesting additions to the gialli trend. *One on Top of the Other* (1969) starred Marisa Mell and Jean Sorel in a San Francisco-set tale of doppelgangers influenced by *Vertigo*. *A Lizard in a Woman's Skin* (1971) was a hallucinogenic London-set murder mystery which featured Florinda Bolkan, Stanley Baker, Jean Sorel and Leo Genn, grotesque special effects by Carlo Rambaldi and a beautiful soundtrack by Morricone-Dell'Orso. Fulci also made an effective adaptation of Edgar Allan Poe's *The Black Cat* (1981 – with Patrick Magee, Mimsy Farmer and David Warbeck) and the repellent, infamous slasher film *The New York Ripper* (1982), which was banned in the UK.

Don't Torture a Duckling (1972) is a strong candidate for Fulci's best film, due to its sustained tension, ultra-weird atmosphere and troubling subject matter. It was set in the fictional southern Italian village of Accendura but was filmed on location in Monte Sant'Angelo in the National Park of Gargano (on the 'spur' of Puglia) and in Matera, Basilicata (from *The Gospel According to St Matthew*). The local police are hunting a child killer. Andrea Martelli (Tomas Milian), a journalist for Milan's *The Standard*, investigates with help from Patrizia (Barbara Bouchet), a city woman who has moved to the countryside, only to be ostracised by the insular locals. Giuseppe Borra (Vito Passeri), the village idiot, is initially blamed for the crimes, but his innocence is soon established, leaving the police commissioner (Virginio Gazzolo) and the chief-of-police (John Bartho) stumped.

Fulci's giallo killer is no longer a shadowy, caped phantom stalking city streets, but a lunatic roaming a rural landscape. One of the murders occurs beside the Monte Gelato falls and the finale – when Andrea wrestles with the culprit atop a cliff – ends with the murderer plunging down a spectacular gorge. The rock promontories, mountains, pastures and woodland are handsomely photographed in widescreen Techniscope by Sergio D'Offizi. Fulci mixes references to voodoo with superstition, shallow graves and the dark arts. At the centre of the community is its young priest, Don Alberto Avallone (Marc Porel) – who encourages the local boys to stay on the straight and narrow via his soccer school – his mother Dona Aurelia (Irene Papas) and Malvina his deaf-mute sister. Little Malvina witnesses the crimes and imitates the killings by pulling the heads off her dolls, which provides Andrea and Patrizia with a clue to the killer's identity.

Whitewashed Accendura resembles Kernigan in *Kill, Baby...Kill!*, a place where the community's minds are as narrow as its streets. The contrasts between city life and provincial prejudice and superstition are delineated unsubtly by Fulci. Patrizia drives a bright red dune buggy, smokes marijuana, lives in an ultramodern pad on the outskirts of town and dresses less-than-conservatively, which incites the locals. The community tensions caused by the killings erupt when the young victims' fathers brutally beat local woman Maciara (Florinda Bolkan) to death with chains. Maciara practiced black magic with her mentor, Old Francesco (George Wilson). When the killings continue even after her death, the stony-faced locals show no remorse. Her horribly drawn-out murder (cut to a blaring car radio) is one of the most sickeningly brutal in Fulci's oeuvre. This scene apart, *Duckling* is eerily disturbing rather than graphically violent and is enhanced by Riz Ortolani's subdued, Morriconesque string and flute cues. Fulci's condemnation of small-town mentalities, the pious church and the inept police ensured it was a massive success in Italy. It failed to gain cinema release in the US or UK and remains a controversial film.

The killer in Paolo Cavara's ***The Black Belly of the Tarantula*** (1971) deploys gialli's most sadistic modus operandi. Someone is killing the female staff and clients of a Rome beauty salon, injecting them in the back of the neck with an acupuncture needle dosed with a paralysing serum, so they remain conscious as the killer disembowels them with a knife, which are depicted in grisly, unflinchingly filmed eviscerations. This method is derived from the manner in which a wasp kills a tarantula and then lays its eggs in the spider's belly, so the larvae can feast on the still-living host. Victims include nymphomaniac Maria Zani (Barbara Bouchet), cocaine dealer Mirta Ricci (Annabella Incontrera), blackmail victim Franca Valentino (Rosella Falk), receptionist Jenny (future Bond girl Barbara Bach) and Laura (ex-Bond girl Claudine Auger), the blackmailing owner of the spa. Tellini (Giancarlo Gianni), a young officer on the Flying Squad, investigates. Maria's husband, Paolo (Silvano Tranquilli), is the chief suspect, until he falls from a building while chasing photographer Mario (Giancarlo Prete). Mario is working with Laura to blackmail her clients with compromising photos.

Mario is run over by his own sports car and the killer targets Tellini's wife, Anna (Stefania Sandrelli). In the dénouement, scientific and psychological flimflam explains how the salon's blind masseur (Ezio Marano) became a maniac. Filmed on location in Rome in kaleidoscopic 1970s style by Marcello Gatti, *Black Belly* is an effective, by-the-numbers giallo, which benefits from a Morricone-Dell'Orso soundtrack.

Cold Eyes of Fear (1971 – *Desperate Moments*) was Enzo G. Castellari's contribution to the gialli cycle, shot on location in a seedy, neon-lit 'London by Night' of strip clubs, cabarets and amusement arcades. Pistol-packing ruffian Quill (Julian Matteos) and Arthur Welt (Frank Wolff – disguised as a policeman) take solicitor Peter Badel (Gianni Garko) and his Italian lover, Anna (Giavanna Ralli, sporting a bubble perm), hostage in 336 Kensington Road, the house of Peter's uncle, Judge Horatio Badel (Fernando Rey). Robber Welt, imprisoned by Badel 15 years before, searches for the evidence that put him away. The judge is working late at court and Welt has rigged his office door with a bomb. *Cold Eyes* is a bad film – badly acted (by a cast of usually reliable performers), badly photographed (on familiar interior sets at Cinecittà), badly written (with a dearth of tension and menace, essentials for any giallo) and very badly dubbed. The film's saving grace is Morricone's score, especially the title sequence's jazzy jam session (with wailing cornet, pumping double bass and growling feedback), which accompanies Welt driving through night-time London. The opening scene depicts Karin Schubert menaced in her boudoir by a flick-knife-wielding assailant, whom she stabs (accompanied by Morricone's whirs and whines on the soundtrack). An archetypal giallo tableau, this murder is revealed to be a nightclub act in the *The Carousel – Ooh La La!*, which is watched lasciviously by Anna and Peter.

Fernando Di Leo's **Asylum Erotica** (1972) was an updated gothic 'old dark house' scenario set in a secluded women's 'loony bin' run by Professor Osterman (John Karlsen). Amongst the inmates are sex addict Ann Palmieri (Rosalba Neri), suicidal Cheryl Hume (Margaret Lee), psychotic Ruth (Gioia Desideri) and Mara (Jane Garret), who is having a clandestine affair with a nurse (Monica Strebel). All except the nurse are brutally killed by a black-caped murderer who uses medieval weapons (axe, dagger, crossbow and Iron Maiden) to dispatch his victims. The police chase the killer, who breaks into the nurses' quarters and in a frenzy bludgeons them with a mace. Only the presence of Klaus Kinski as Dr Francis Clay and the score (by Silvano Spadaccino) add gravitas, while the copious nudity defines the film as the worst in trashy sexploitation. It was released in the US as *Slaughter Hotel*, with a tasteless tagline: 'Carved out of today's headlines – see the slashing massacre of 8 innocent nurses!'

What Have They Done?: Lado and Dallamano

Aldo Lado's **Who Saw Her Die?** (1971) was highly influential on Nicolas Roeg's *Don't Look Now* (1973 – *A Venezia un Dicembre rosso* in Italy). Both are set in Venice, deal with parents coming to terms with their child's death and include flashback inserts which juggle the narrative. In *Who Saw Her Die?* sculptor Franco Serpieri (George Lazenby) lives in Venice. His little daughter, Roberta (Nicoletta Elmi), arrives from London but is kidnapped and found by market traders floating in a canal. Franco and his wife, Elizabeth (Anita Strindberg), blame themselves for her death – Franco was seeing his mistress, Gabriella (Rosemarie Lindt), when Roberta was abducted. A journalist (Piero Vida) establishes a link with another disappearance a year previously. An array of suspects confuse the audience – Bonaiuti (Jose Quaglia), a rich lawyer and child molester; his employees Philip Vernon (Peter Chatel) and blackmailing Ginevra Storelli (Dominique Boschero); art dealer Serafian (Adolfo Celi); and Father James (Alessandro Haber) – and predictably the suspect list is whittled down via killings.

Lado, who had worked as Bertolucci's assistant director on *The Conformist*, shot the film on location in wintry Venice, with interiors at De Paolis. The film is red-haired Elmi's finest film – she also appeared to menacing effect in *Baron Blood*, *A Bay of Blood*, *Footprints* and *Deep Red*. Moustachioed one-time James Bond Lazenby is excellent too. What makes *Who Saw Her Die?* work is the creepy Venetian atmosphere – it may be one of the most romantic cities in the world, but on a foggy night it is also one of the most menacing. This is accentuated by Ennio Morricone's score. A children's choir (conducted by Bruno Samale) chant jagged, syncopated 'la-la-la's', the volume and intensity of which ebb like the psycho's killing urges. The opening scene, accompanied by Morricone's intimidating choristers, is one of the most disturbing in gialli. A little red-haired girl and her nurse are playing in the snow. They are stalked by a weird woman – a black widow in veil and hat – who snatches the little girl, kills her with a rock and buries her in the snow.

Massimo Dallamano directed two of the finest gialli, *What Have You Done to Solange?* (1972) and *What Have They Done to Your Daughters?* (1974). **What Have You Done to Solange?** begins with the discovery beside the River Thames of schoolgirl Hilda Erikson, who has been savagely stabbed. She was a pupil at St Mary's School for Girls, where married Italian PE teacher Enrico Rossini (Fabio Testi) is having an affair with one of his pupils, Elizabeth Seckles (Cristina Galbo). Elizabeth thinks she glimpsed the killing and that the murderer was dressed as a priest. Enrico is implicated when his silver pen is found at the crime scene and his wife, Herta (Karin Baal), begins to suspect him. Inspector Bart (Joachim Fuchsberger) of Scotland Yard interviews the school staff, including two tutors: Professor Bascombe (Gunther Stoll) and peeping tom pervert Newton (Antonio Casale). More schoolgirls are killed: Janet Bryant is abducted and found dead in a field and Elizabeth is drowned in her bath. The key to the murders is Ruth Holden, an ex-nanny, but when Enrico arrives at her cottage he finds her dog bludgeoned and Ruth killed with a sickle. The schoolgirls were part of a secret society. When one of the girls, Solange Beauregard (Camille Keaton), became pregnant, Ruth and the others performed a harrowing abortion, which has left Solange in a state of infantile regression. Waiflike Solange's first appearance in the film – during Enrico and Herta's parkland picnic, as she's pursued by her carer – is particularly unsettling.

What Have You Done to Solange? is a disturbing experience. Dallamano filmed on location in London, including Kensington, Buckingham Palace and Westminster Bridge, during autumn 1971. The burnished cinematography was by Aristide Massaccesi in short-lived 2.35:1 Reversalscope. Ennio Morricone's famous romantic title music, 'Cosa avete fatto a Solange?' gives no indication of the film's dark subject matter. Its delicate descending piano motif, flute, measured strings and Edda Dell'Orso's floating vocal suggest a love story. *Solange* doesn't pull its punches in its depiction of distressing, violent murder. It was severely cut in the UK, with good reason, and was also abridged in the US for its 1976 release by AIP/Newport as *Terror in the Woods*.

What Have They Done to Your Daughters? is no less lurid than its predecessor. In Brescia, pregnant schoolgirl Sylvia Polvesi (Cheryl Lee Buchanan) is discovered hanged – a murder made to appear a suicide. On her first case, the assistant DA, Dr Vittoria Stori (Giovanna Ralli), investigates with inspectors Silvestri (Claudio Cassinelli) and Valentini (Mario Adorf). They uncover teenage prostitution rackets, corruption of minors, and drugs. The vital clue is a sex tape recording of the prostitutes' encounters. Meanwhile, a cleaver-wielding psychopath is stalking Brescia by motorbike. A private investigator is found dismembered in his car boot and the killer takes a swing at Vittoria in her apartment's underground car park.

Daughters was shot on location in Brescia in Techniscope by Franco Delli Colli, with interiors at DEAR Studios. Ralli is well cast as the female investigator, negotiating a particularly nasty case, and Adorf is good as the cop who finds his daughter, Patricia, has been corrupted too. Steffen Zacharias played Dr Beltrami, the prostitution racket's ringleader, Franco Fabrizi was sleazy photographer Bruno Paglia, and Farley Granger and Maria Berti were Sylvia's distraught parents. After a promising opening, Dallamano becomes less concerned with the film's horror and concentrates on the police investigation; the film closely resembles a cop thriller: Dallamano even stages a street chase, when the Polizia pursue the cleaver-wielding killer. Stelvio Cipriani's pulsating score is one of his best. The title music is mediocre Euro-pop (with its 'la la' refrain mimicking Argento's movies), but the incidental themes – especially a rolling, purposeful cue with brass and syncopated drums (later reused in the regatta scene of *Tentacles*) – power along the investigation with style. Dallamano manages a couple of good shocks, but *Daughters* is a bloody, unsavoury film, in the mould of *Solange*, and like its predecessor, it leaves a bitter aftertaste.

The City Runs Red

After birds, cats and flies, Dario Argento signalled a bold new direction with the garishly titled **Deep Red** (1975), the longest, most convoluted and most brutally violent Italian giallo. Jazz pianist Marcus Daly (David Hemmings) witnesses the murder of mind reader Helga Ulmann (Macha Meril). Investigating officer Calcabrini (Eros Pagni) presses Marc for evidence, but the musician can't recall one vital detail. In contrast to the tenuous links and scant, implausible explanations of most gialli, *Deep Red* is very well constructed. To solve the mystery, Marc teams up with reporter Gianna Brezzi (Daria Nicolodi, Argento's partner).

Argento filmed *Deep Red* on location in Turin and Rome, with interiors at De Paolis Studios, in autumn 1974. The supporting cast features Gabriele Lavia as Carlo, a drunken, self-destructive pianist in the Blue Bar. Clara Calamai played his mother, ex-actress Martha. Calamai had been the most popular Italian actress during World War II, most famously starring opposite Massimo Girotti in Luchino Visconti's *Ossessione* (1942 – *Obsession*), his lustful adaptation of *The Postman Always Rings Twice*. Furio Meniconi played the caretaker of a decrepit villa at 24 Via Susa which conceals a hideous fresco and a long-dead cadaver and Nicoletta Elmi was his creepy daughter, Olga, a 'little witch' who tortures writhing lizards with pins (a shot missing from most prints of the film). At a public appearance, psychic Helga senses a murderous presence in the audience and soon afterwards is attacked with a meat cleaver and has her throat slit as she crashes through a window (a signature Argento demise). Amanda Righetti, the author of *Ghosts and Black of Modern Times*, is scalded to death in her bathtub. Her story 'La Villa Del Bambino Urlante' [The House of the Screaming Child] holds a vital clue. Professor of psychiatry Giordani (Glauco Mauri) has his teeth bashed out on a mantelpiece and the corner of a table and is knifed in the neck. Other deaths include a man being dragged behind a refuse cart by a hook in his leg (he's dashed against a pavement and has his head squashed by a car) and a decapitation involving an entangled necklace and an elevator. These convincing special effects were staged by Germano Natali and Carlo Rambaldi. The killer's gloved hands are those of Argento himself.

Luigi Kuveiller's widescreen cinematography was among the most innovative of the 1970s and the film's visual code is black, white and red. The funk-rock of *Four Flies on Grey Velvet* is replaced here by a score written by Giorgio Gaslini and performed by rock trio Goblin. The score's recurrent theme is a syncopated bassline, glacial arpeggios, synthesizer flourishes and discordant blasts of church organ. During the title sequence this is displaced by a child's lullaby, for a jarring scene depicting a stabbing in a dining room beside a Christmas tree (the trigger for the killer's psychosis). Later murders are accompanied by a pulsing bassline, synthesizer squeals and pops, and funky drumming – the adrenalin rush of blood pumping through the killer's veins.

Profondo rosso, the Italian version of the film released in 1975, is 126 minutes long. It includes many extra scenes of Mark and Gianna's bickering investigation and the unexpurgated murders. The US cut, entitled *Deep Red*, ran a tighter 98 minutes for release in 1976. It was also re-released in 1980 as *The Hatchet Murders*. The shorter version's narrative benefits from truncation, but the murders are abridged and a shot of two dogs fighting is missing from many prints of the film. *Deep Red*'s climax springs a surprise which is superior to anything Hitchcock concocted – it's a killer twist.

Argento's ***Tenebrae*** (1982) had New York horror fiction writer Peter Neal (Anthony Franciosa) arrive in Rome on a promotional tour for his new bestseller, *Tenebrae*. Captain Germani (Giuliano Gemma) is investigating the murder of shoplifter Elsa Manni (Ania Pieroni), who was killed with a cutthroat razor and had her mouth stuffed with pages from Neal's novel. Tilde, a journalist critical of Neal's 'sexist bullshit' horror stories, and her lover, Marion (Mirella Banti), are butchered in their apartment block with a razor, a modus operandi inspired by Neal's book. Eventually the culprit is identified as Neal's superfan, daytime TV talk show host Cristiano Berti (John Steiner), but the murders continue, even after Berti has an axe planted in his skull.

Argento made *Tenebrae* on location in Rome, at Elios Studios and at Kennedy Airport in New York. With its over-the-top bloodletting and stylised choreography, this is comic-book Argento. John Saxon played Neal's agent Bulmer, Daria Nicolodi was Neal's PA Anne, Enio Girolami played a store detective, Fulvio Mingozzi was a hotel porter and Veronica Lario was Neal's estranged wife, Jane McKarrow, who's having an affair with Bulmer. In the preamble to Tilde and Marion's murders, the camera glides up the outside of the apartment building, peeping through windows, then sweeps up over the roof and swoops down to the block's landing, in an impressively intricate take that was inspired by Sergio Leone's gliding Chapman crane shot at the railway station in *Once Upon a Time in the West*. Maria (Lara Wendel) is chased through a park in a terrifying sequence, which ends with her stumbling on the killer's basement lair. Bulmer is stabbed in broad daylight in a busy municipal square – a most un-giallo setting for a murder. The killings, involving razors, knives and axes, were staged by Giovanni Corridori, and Lamberto Bava, Mario's son was the film's first assistant director. Flashbacks from the killer's perspective depict the traumatic beach murder of a beautiful woman (played by transsexual 'Evan Robins'/Roberto Coatti) wearing a white dress and red high heels. The film's punchy rock-style synthesizer fugues were provided by Claudio Simonetti, Massimo Mornate and Fabio Pignatelli, the members of Goblin. *Tenebrae* was released cut in the US as *Unsane* in 1987, but the bloody, uncut print now available on DVD is Italian axe-ploitation at its best.

Magic and Murder: The Three Mothers

Between *Deep Red* and *Tenebrae*, Argento made two horror films that interwove gialli with the supernatural. In ***Suspiria*** (1977), American student Susy Banyon (Jessica Harper) attends the Tanz (Dance) Academy near Freiburg in southern Germany's Black Forest; the academy is run by Madame Blanc (Joan Bennett) and her tutors, including strict Miss Tanner (Alida Valli). Two students are killed in hideous fashion the night of Susy's arrival. Susy realises that the staff of the school are a coven ruled by the Black Queen, Helena Markos, an age-old sorceress.

Iconic artwork by 'Almos' (Antonio Mos) for Dario Argento's supernatural tale of witchery in the Freiburg Tanz Academy: *Suspiria* (1977).

Suspiria was written by Daria Nicolodi and was based on occult literature and recollections of her grandmother, who when she was 15 years old discovered that the music school she was attending was a coven. The title is taken from Thomas De Quincey's 'Suspiria De Profundis' in *Confessions of an English*

Opium-Eater. Nicolodi planned to play Susy, but Argento cast Jessica Harper in the lead. Nicolodi was offered the supporting role of Susy's friend Sara but dislocated her ankle during rehearsals for the ballet scenes and left the production. Stefania Casini was cast as Sara instead. Hollywood star Joan Bennett had recently appeared in US TV's *Dark Shadows* (1966–71) and the movie spin-off *House of Dark Shadows* (1970). Susy's fellow students included Olga (Barbara Magnolfi) and Mark (Miguel Bose). Udo Kier played psychiatrist Frank Mandel, Fulvio Mingozzi appeared as a cabbie and Giuseppe Transocchi was Pavlo, the school's Lurch-like handyman. Flavio Bucci played Daniel, the school's blind pianist, who has his throat ripped out by his wolfhound guide dog.

Suspiria is the ultimate Argento horror movie and the film for which he will be remembered. In its updating of Bava and Freda's fantasy horror, it is an inferno of swirling, vibrant imagery. Argento filmed the stylised interiors of his Black Forest chateau at De Paolis Studios, from July 1976 for 16 weeks, and in Munich, Bavaria and Rome. The school exterior was in Freiburg and the swimming pool, where Argento's camera seemingly glides across the surface of the water, was Munich's public baths. Argento used intricate camera movements, wire-guided cameras and complicated lighting rigs to achieve extraordinary effects. Luciano Tovoli shot *Suspiria* in garish widescreen Technovision. Blocks of colour – predominantly red, black and white, occasionally icy blue or green – dominate the screen, suggesting the malingering witchery lurking in the school. When the practice hall is hastily converted into a dormitory with suspended sheets (following an attic infestation of maggots) the room is bathed in throbbing reds and dark shadows. For a film set in a ballet school attended by young, attractive women, Argento resists the usual sexploitation angle of Italian horror and shuns voyeuristic nudity.

The killings are staged for maximum shock effect by Germano Natali. The opening double murder of Pat Hingle (Eva Axen) and her friend Sonia (Susanna Javicoli) may be the most elaborately choreographed murder in cinema history. Pat is pulled though a glass window by a hairy arm, is stabbed in her still-beating heart (shown in close-up) and left lying on a stained glass ceiling decoration. Pat's weight eventually causes her to plunge through the pane – as she drops, a noose around her neck pulls tight, hanging her. Down below Sonia has been skewered by part of the window frame and her face bisected by a huge shard of glass. Sara later suffers a lacerated, barbed wire death when she falls into a room full of iron coils and has her throat slit (actually a close-up of a razor slitting a fish). The murderer's gloved hand in this scene is again Argento's. When Susy infiltrates the witches' lair, Sara, now reanimated, attacks her with a butcher's knife. Susy stabs Helena, a hag, through the throat with a sculptured peacock's tail made of ornate, crystalline pins. Helena's death destroys the coven's power and causes the kinetic whirlwind destruction of the school. Susy had arrived during a storm and escapes into one in the finale, as Poe's burning mansions are eviscerated by Argento's pyrotechnic paroxysm.

Suspiria's deafening score is again by Goblin (here billed as 'The Goblins'), in collaboration with Argento. It is one of the great horror scores, a web of sound – at one moment delicate folk music, the next a clattering dustbin lid din. It is used not only as the trigger to a shock effect, but as the shock effect itself, its sudden presence intensifying Argento's images. The glistening, twinkling music box of 'Suspiria' is gradually permeated with atonal washes of sound effects. Synths glide and echo, and spiteful voices spit 'Witch!', as Susy arrives at the airport and steps into a maelstrom of black magic. Thudding heartbeat drums back the screaming damned (as on the track 'Witch'), hisses and moans suggest dark malevolence and scenes of tension are abruptly sliced by jangling steel wires of sound (as on 'Sighs'). It is a kaleidoscopic, cacophonous sound collage, resembling the depths of a torture chamber set to music.

Suspiria was the seventh most successful film in Italy in 1977. Its iconic poster, depicting a bloodstained pirouetting ballerina with her throat slit, was designed by Antonio Mos ('Almos'). *Suspiria* was also a hit in the US (rated R) for Twentieth Century-Fox and in the UK (rated X) in 1977, when advertised with the wholly truthful tagline 'The Most Frightening Film You'll Ever See!'

Argento's **Inferno** (1980) continued the story of 'The Three Mothers', a fictional book by architect E. Varelli, who designed houses for each of the witches. In New York, Rose Elliot (Irene Miracle) buys the book from Mr Kazanian (Sacha Pitoeff) in an antique shop and discovers that the Three Mothers reside in Freiburg ('Mater Suspirorum', the Mother of Sighs from *Suspiria*), Rome ('Mater Lachrymarum', the Mother of Tears) and New York ('Mater Tenebrarum', the Mother of Darkness) – the latter is in Rose's apartment building. She writes to her brother, Mark (Leigh McCloskey, in a role originally slated for James Woods), an American music student in Rome, but when he arrives in New York, Rose has gone missing.

With a budget of $3 million, Argento filmed *Inferno* over 14 weeks from April 1979, beginning in New York and Central Park (for one week), then in Rome, and in Elios and De Paolis Studios. The score by Keith Emerson, formerly of The Nice and the showman keyboardist in Emerson, Lake and Palmer, is a mix of conventional orchestrations (by Godfrey Salmon) and operatic, Goblinesque compositions. Verdi's 'Va Pensiero' from *Nabucco* plays fitfully on a turntable during a power cut. Fulvio Mingozzi again appeared as a taxi driver and Feodor Chaliapin played the wheelchair-bound architect Varelli, who lives in the bowels of the Manhattan apartment building. Asia Pieroni appeared briefly as the beautiful, cat-stroking Mother of Tears, who materialises in Mark's lecture theatre.

Considering the large budget and its predecessor's success, *Inferno* was a disappointment. Argento's series of florid murders only occasionally equal his own high standard and the plot is a maze, like Rose's labyrinthine apartment building. The photography by Romano Albini is Bavaesque in style, with glowing blues and reds. An underwater scene, when Rose dives into an ornate sunken ballroom and is surprised by a floating corpse, is effective. Mark's friend Sara

(Eleonora Giorgi) and her companion Carlo (Gabriele Lavia from *Deep Red*) are stabbed during a power failure in her apartment; Rose is guillotined by a sheet of glass which repeatedly descends on the back of her neck; Rose's neighbour, Contessa Elise Delon Van Adler (Daria Nicolodi), dies in a frenzied attack by a dozen cats and the apartment's caretaker, Carol (Alida Valli), is incinerated. Kazanian tries to rid himself of the bothersome cats and drowns them in a sack in Central Park, but sewer rats devour him alive and a manic hotdog vendor stabs him. The final confrontation between Mark and the Mother of Darkness (Veronica Lazar), as fire licks through the apartment building, falls flat thanks to the ghoul resembling a fancy dress shop Grim Reaper, in cape and skeleton mask. Special effects man Germano Natali was aided by Mario Bava, and Bava's son Lamberto worked as Argento's assistant director. Lamberto went on to direct his own horror movies, *Macabre* (1980) and *A Blade in the Dark* (1983). Lamberto's grisly *Demons* (1985) and *Demons 2* (1987) were produced by Argento.

Inferno was distributed internationally with the tagline 'Terror that's Hotter than Hell!' It was released in truncated form at 83 minutes in the US in 1986, and was cut in the UK to 106 minutes in 1980 to gain an X. The uncut 107-minute version is now available on US DVD and includes a cat eating a live mouse. Surprisingly in the early 1980s it was *Tenebrae* and *Inferno* that made it onto the UK's 'Video Nasty' list and not the more violent *Suspiria* and *Deep Red*. Fans had to wait for the final instalment of the 'Three Mothers' until 2007, when Argento finally released *Mother of Tears*. It starred Asia Argento (Dario and Daria Nicolodi's daughter), Udo Kier, Philippe Leroy and Moran Atias (as Mater Lachrymarum) and fiercely divided Argento's fans and critics. Argento's style has permeated mainstream Hollywood – the blockbusting *The Da Vinci Code* (2003) is simply a Dario Argento movie staged by the Muppets. Apart from partial returns to form, with *Phenomena* (1985 – *Creepers*) and *Opera* (1987), none of Argento's post-*Suspiria* films has equalled its international impact. His fans won't let him get away with murder forever.

Chapter Twelve

A Funny Thing Happened
Italian Comedy

Commedia all'Italiana – 'Comedy Italian-Style' – has enjoyed huge domestic success, but the popularity of screen comedians such as Totò and Franchi and Ingrassia barely radiated beyond Italy's borders, and certainly not beyond mainland Europe. Their style of slapstick humour was often further hampered by ineptly voiced English language dubbing. It wasn't until the breakthrough by Terence Hill and Bud Spencer in the 1970s – working in popular forms such as westerns and cop movies – that Italian comedy cinema enjoyed its greatest global success. Italian cinema has always loved great comics – the last film starring Laurel and Hardy ('Stanlio e Olio' in Italy) was Italian-French co-production *Atol K* (1950 – *Robinson Crusoeland* and *Utopia*) and one of Buster Keaton's final screen appearances was in *War, Italian Style* (1965 – *Two Marines and a General*) opposite Franchi and Ingrassia.

Totò the Clown

The most popular Italian cinema comedian is Totò (real name Antonio De Curtis), who was born in Naples in 1898. Even today you can't move in the city without seeing images of their most famous son. He began in variety and his physical style of comedy was a carryover from the Italian theatrical comedy tradition. Totò's role in 'The Racketeer' episode of Vittorio De Sica's *The Gold of Naples* (1954) is one of his best remembered performances for international audiences, where he co-starred with Sophia Loren and Silvana Mangano. His career spanned the 1930s to the 1960s and in later vehicles he was often teamed with Peppino (actor Peppino De Filippo). Many of Totò's films were parodies of popular movies – *Totò of Arabia* (1965), *Totò against the Black Pirate* (1964) and *Totò against Maciste* (1961). A good example of his style is Sergio Corbucci's *Totò, Peppino and la dolce vita* (1960) which captures the authentic Rome of Fellini, the snap of the paparazzi and the hum of vespas. In one scene Totò and Peppino pick up two young English starlets, Patricia and Alice, on the Via Veneto, and take them to an exotic nightclub. The party descends into a drug-fuelled bacchanalia, with Patricia (who resembles a young Sophia Loren) performing a striptease and Totò pulling funny faces and dancing like a robot.

Totò appeared in Mario Monicelli's spoof heist movie **Big Deal on Madonna Street** (1958 – *Persons Unknown*) as master safebreaker Dante Cruciani, who is hired by a quintet of cretinous crooks for a 'big job': the emptying of a jewel safe in a pawnbrokers on Madonna Street. The gang consists of beefcake boxer Peppe (Vittorio Gassman), photographer Tiberio (Marcello Mastroianni), small-time crook Mario Angelitti (Renato Salvatori), Sicilian Michele Ferribotte (Tiberio Murgia) and aged car thief Capannelle (Carlo Pisacane). They discover from convict Cosimo (Memmo Carotenuto) that the partition wall between the pawnbrokers and a neighbouring apartment is poorly constructed. *Film noir* send-up *Big Deal* is one of the most consistently amusing Italian comedies and Piero Umiliani's strutting jazz score could easily have scored a true *noir*. Tiberio steals a camera from a market by distracting the stallholder with his fake splinted broken arm. Later the stallholder breaks his arm for real, so Tiberio shows up for the robbery with his arm in a cast. On viewing Tiberio's jumpy footage of the safe being opened, Totò comments, 'As a movie, it's lousy'.

Photographed by Gianni Di Venanzo on location in Rome (with interiors at Cinecittà), *Big Deal*'s monochrome cinematography and vignettes of street life recall neorealism, but the humour is international. It enjoyed great notices in the New York press and was nominated for a Best Foreign Film Oscar. Rosanna Rory played Norma (Cosimo's moll), Gina Rovere was Teresa, Tiberio's cigarette-smuggling wife, and Carla Gravina was Nicoletta, maid to the owners of the neighbouring apartment. Claudia Cardinale played Michele's cosseted sister, Carmela, who falls for Mario, creating tension within the gang. During the hilarious heist, the bumbling crooks drill through a water pipe, flood the apartment and demolish the wrong wall. Foiled, they sit down and eat a meal of pasta and beans which they find on the stove. Newspapers the following morning report that the police are looking for 'persons unknown' who perpetrated a strange burglary – they bored a hole through a wall to steal pasta and beans. As the master thief, Totò steals the show and the film is his best-known outside Italy.

In Pier Paolo Pasolini's **Hawks and Sparrows** (1965), Totò and Ninetto Davoli played father and son, two wanderers who encounter a chatty, Marxist crow, which joins them on their meandering odyssey. The crow recounts the story of St Francis of Assisi, who dispatched two monks, Brothers Ciccillo and Ninetto (Totò and Davoli again), to convert the birds to Christianity – they preach the Word of the Lord to the hawks (via whistles) and the sparrows (by hopping around). Pasolini's irreverent parable is one of his lesser works. He includes parody miracles ('You saved me from the wasps', says a local to the monks) and Ninetto recounts Ciccillo's exploits: 'At Zagarolo, [he changed] water to wine, because they liked it...at Sgurgola he changed nothing, everything was fine'. For

Italian Comedy 247

Italian poster for Pier Paolo Pasolini's *Hawks and Sparrows* (1965), starring Totò, Ninetto Davoli and Femi Benussi. Poster courtesy Ian Caunce Collection.

Ennio Morricone's imaginative title track, which blends medieval music, opera, classical strings and rock 'n' roll, Domenico Modugno sings the cast and crew credits and notes: 'In producing it, Alfredo Bini risked his position...in directing it, Pier Paolo Pasolini risked his reputation'.

Totò also starred in Pasolini's contribution to **The Witches** (1966), a five-episode showcase for Silvana Mangano produced by her husband, Dino De Laurentiis. 'The Earth Seen from the Moon' was typical Pasolini surrealism, with Totò (sporting two tufts of fluffy clown's hair) and Ninetto Davoli (with a giant orange quiff) again cast as father and son, in search of an ideal woman for Totò following the death of his wife, Grisantema. In Pasolini's beloved Roman suburbs they encounter Absurdity (Mangano), a green-haired mute woman in a green dress, who marries Totò. Totò's third appearance for Pasolini, in the 'Che cosa sono le nuvole' episode of *Capriccio all'Italiana* (1967), failed to gain widespread international distribution and later that year Totò died, aged 68.

Franco and Ciccio: Two Cine-Idiots

Franco Franchi and Ciccio Ingrassia were a Sicilian variety double act who shot to fame in the early 1960s in a seemingly endless series of slapstick parodies, laughing at the popular film stars and genres of the day. They were heirs apparent to Totò, fusing silent film humour to Italian popular cinema. Franchi was the short, uncouth one, given to pulling faces, gesticulating and falling over, while moustachioed Ingrassia was tall and rather refined. Between 1960 and 1983 they made over 100 films together – as they said, they were united 'first by hunger, then by success'.

Most of Franchi and Ingrassia's films weren't distributed internationally, nor even dubbed into English, though their brand of parody had good production values. They lampooned Visconti with Sergio Corbucci's *Son of the Leopard* (1965) and Fellini with *Satiricosissimo* (1969). They spoofed war movies with *The Shortest Day* (1963), Zorro movies in *The Nephews of Zorro* (1968), sci-fi in *002 Operation Moon* (1965), prison dramas with *Two Escapees from Sing-Sing* (1964) and heist movies in *How We Robbed the Bank of Italy* (1966). They co-starred in *Primitive Love* (1964) with Jayne Mansfield – her striptease from this film can be seen in *The Wild, Wild World of Jayne Mansfield* (1968). They made 'In the Army' parodies such as *The Two Parachutists* (1965) and *How We Got into Trouble with the Army* (1965), gangster spoofs with *Two Public Enemies* (1964) and *The Clan of Two Borsalini* (1971) and spy parodies with *00–2 Most Secret Agents* (1964). *How to Steal an Atomic Bomb* (1967) had the duo up against 'Doctor Yes' and agents Modesty Bluff, Derek Flit and James Bomb.

They also made westerns, 11 in all, including *Two Sergeants of General Custer* (1965), *Two Sons of Ringo* (1966) *Two R-R-Ringos from Texas* (1967), *Ciccio Forgives...I Don't* (1968) and *Two Sons of Trinity* (1972). *Two Mafiosi in the Far West* (1965) is a fine example of their work, a comedy western co-starring Fernando Sancho. The costumes were designed by Carlo Simi (who worked on

Leone's 'Dollars' trilogy) and the Elios Studios western set was deployed, which gives the film an authentically 'spaghetti western' visual style. The title song, 'Fuoco nel cielo' [Fire in the Sky], sung by Giancarlo Guardabassi, could have been written for a real western. *For a Fist in the Eye* (1966) was a *Fistful of Dollars* parody, while their finest western pastiche was *Il bello, il brutto, il cretino* (1967 – 'The Handsome, the Ugly, the Cretinous'), the duo's homage to *The Good, the Bad and the Ugly*.

With the success of Franchi and Ingrassia's Bond parody *The Amazing Dr G* (1965 – featuring Fernando Rey as villain Goldginger) and Vincent Price's US comedy *Dr Goldfoot and the Bikini Machine* (1965), the stars combined for Mario Bava's **Dr Goldfoot and the Girl Bombs** (1966). Price played Dr Goldfoot ('That tongue-in-cheek terrorist' as the trailers put it), so-called because of his gold, curly-toed slippers. Goldfoot, with his Chinese assistants Hardjob (Moa Tahi) and Fong (George Wang), assassinates seven prominent NATO generals using seductive robot women who explode when they kiss their target. Franchi and Ingrassia, plus Bill Dexter (pop singer Fabian), are the SIC (Security Intelligence Command) agents on Goldfoot's trail investigating 'The Case of the Exploding Generals'.

Set somewhere between cold war sci-fi, Bondian espionage and slapstick comedy, *Girl Bombs* is a shambles. Price hams it up and Dexter's love interest, Rosanna, was played by Laura Antonelli. Franchi and Ingrassia were let loose in one of their few English language outings. The production's shoddiness is epitomised by a chase sequence filmed in Luna Park, Rome. As the agents pursue Goldfoot and his henchmen through a fairground, the action is speeded up and narrated by silent movie intertitles – this was necessitated because the sound recordist lost the dubbing track. The film ends with a *Dr Strangelove* parody, as Franchi and Ingrassia attempt to diffuse Goldfoot's Super Hydrogen Bomb aboard a B-52 but are launched from the bomb bay, straddling the device. The original Italian version – titled *Le spie vengono dal semi fredo* [The Spies who Came in from the Semi-cold] or *I due mafiosi dell-FBI* – had a James Bond-style title sequence with Franchi performing the wailing title song, 'Bang Bang Kissene' (by Lallo Gori). The English language release had a groovy new theme song performed by The Sloopys. The film's enduring image is of Goldfoot's arsenal of beautiful pin-ups, clad in gold bikinis and swimsuits, in Goldfoot's underground lair. They were called 'Love Bombs' in the original script but were redubbed 'Girl Bombs'. Bava had a cameo as an angel on a cloud. *Girl Bombs* is infantile sexploitation, but what were audiences expecting from the tagline 'Meet the Girls with the Thermo-Nuclear Navels!'

Franchi and Ingrassia's domestic popularity waned in the early 1970s, as sex comedies took over at the box office. One of their late triumphs was playing the Cat and the Fox in Luigi Comencini's *Pinocchio* (1972). Ingrassia appeared in Fellini's *Amarcord* (1973) as tree-climbing Uncle Teo and they made their final appearance in 'The Jar' episode of the Taviani brothers *Kaos* (1983) – like Totò these two 'cine-idiots' finally made the transformation from 'fleapit' attractions to 'arthouse' respectability.

Two Rode Together: Trinity and Bambino

By far the most internationally successful of Italy's cinema comedians is the 17-film double act of Terence Hill and Bud Spencer. Their success took them from Italy to the US to make comedies in the tradition of a latter-day Laurel and Hardy. The duo made three popular westerns with Giuseppe Colizzi – *God Forgives... I Don't* (1967), *Ace High* (1968) and *Boot Hill* (1969) – before their first comedy, **They Call Me Trinity** (1970). It was concocted by writer-director Enzo Barboni/'E.B. Clucher'. Hill played bean-eating drifter Trinity, a fast-drawing layabout who travels on a travois and Spencer was his half-wit half-brother, Bambino, an ursine outlaw who impersonates a sheriff.

The plot, a parody of *Rio Bravo* and *The Magnificent Seven*, had the duo helping a community of pacifist Mormons led by Brother Tobias (Dan Sturkie) against a land-grabbing horse rancher, Major Harrison (Farley Granger). *Trinity* was shot on location in the Parco Naturale Dei Monti Simbruini, at the waterfalls at Monte Gelato and on the western town at Incir-De Paolis. Barboni fills his film with a rogue's gallery of western clichés – bandido Mescal (Remo Capitani), a madly laughing parody villain; Jonathan Swift (Steffen Zacharias), the sheriff's fastidious housekeeper; Sarah (Gisela Hahn) and Judith (Elena Pedemonte), two pretty Mormon women; Bambino's sneaky henchmen, Weasel (Ezio Marano) and Timid (Luciano Rossi); and a drunken Mexican jailbird (Michele Cimarosa). The major's gang includes stuntman Riccardo Pizzuti, who went on to appear in almost all Hill and Spencer's subsequent teamings. Barboni speeds up Trinity's quick-draw prowess and the fistfights are well integrated into the story, evolving from the narrative like a song in a good musical. In later Hill and Spencer entries, such pugilism was crowbarred into the story. Even Franco Micalizzi's laid-back whistled score and the title song (crooned by David King) are in tune with the send-up's atmosphere. *They Call Me Trinity* was a hit in Italy over Christmas 1970 and was popular in the US when released by Joseph E. Levine in 1971.

Barboni and producer Italo Zingarelli struck again with **Trinity Is Still My Name** (1971). Horse rustler Bambino and turkey rustler Trinity are mistaken for outlaws, then federal agents, by gunrunners Parker (Emilio Delle Piane) and Lopert (Gerard Landry). Parker's gang are in league with a gang of Mexican bandits who are trafficking arms from the San Jose monastery. Barboni filmed entirely in Italy, including the western towns at De Paolis and De Laurentiis Studios. The slim plot is little more than a series of vignettes: a poker game where Trinity demonstrates some nifty shuffling; his slapping game with gunslinger Wildcard Hendricks; Trinity and Bambino's gluttonous meal in a posh French restaurant; and the finale with the heroes dressed as monks in a game of American football against Parker's gang at the monastery. Stunt arranger Giorgio Ubaldi was billed as assistant director, as he was on the first 'Trinity'.

Go West: Bambino and Trinity trample hallowed western myths in Enzo Barboni's *They Call Me Trinity* (1970). Spanish poster artwork depicting Bud Spencer and Terence Hill. Poster courtesy Ian Caunce Collection.

Guido and Maurizio De Angelis provided the folksy score, with the memorable theme song, 'Trinity Stand Tall', sung by Gene Roman (backed by Nora Orlandi's 'Coro 4+4' vocal group). For most of the film Hill and Spencer are dressed in pinstriped suits and bowler hats, which makes them resemble Laurel and Hardy. Yanti Somer, as settler Wendy, was the most memorable of Hill's many onscreen romantic partners. Wendy's baby brother, Ebenezer, farts his way through the film with a bad case of 'aerodogy' (he's christened 'Little Windy' by Bambino). These windy comedies and their progeny were termed *fagioli* (beans) westerns in Italy. When Trinity visits his parents, Harry Carey Jnr and Jessica Dublin, they berate him for not keeping in touch, but he reasons: 'I don't know how to write…and you don't know how to read'. It was particularly satirical of Barboni to cast Carey Jnr, the veteran of so many Hollywood John Ford movies, as Trinity's dad. Less structured and more irreverent than the first film, it became the most successful Italian western ever made when it was released in Italy in 1971.

Big Hitters: Solo Comedy Success

Capitalising on the success of the 'Trinities', Hill starred in two westerns produced by Sergio Leone: Tonino Valerii's *My Name Is Nobody* (1973) and Damiano Damiani's *Nobody's the Greatest* (1975). Hill's 'Nobody' persona was contrasted with Hollywood western archetypes such as living legend gunfighter Jack Beauregard (Henry Fonda), crooked mine owner Sullivan (Jean Martin) and embezzling 'Injun-hating' major Cabot (Patrick McGoohan). *My Name Is Nobody* is the last truly great Italian western. It is filled with in-jokes (at one point Hill name-checks Sam Peckinpah) and cast many US western actors – Neil Summers, Leo Gordon, R.G. Armstrong, Steve Kanaly and Geoffrey Lewis – alongside their spaghetti western counterparts: Benito Stefanelli, Antonio Molino Rojo, Piero Lulli, Mario Brega and Marc Mazza. Both 'Nobody' films were partly shot in the US – in the latter's case Monument Valley – and on Leone's Flagstone City set in Almeria. And both featured bubblegum theme tunes from Morricone. In *My Name* Beauregard shoots it out with the 150-strong 'Wild Bunch' to Wagner's 'Ride of the Valkyries' and in *Greatest*, Nobody leads the Fifth Cavalry a merry dance at Fort Cristobel, to Rossini's 'William Tell Overture'.

Spencer's performance as horse thief Hiram Coburn in Maurizio Lucidi's ***It Can Be Done, Amigo*** (1972 – *The Big and the Bad*) owed much to his moseying Bambino persona. Coburn becomes the guardian of little Chip Anderson (Renato Cestiè), who has inherited ramshackle Welldigger's Roost, a seemingly worthless ranch near Westland. Franciscus (Francisco Rabal), the town's judge, preacher and sheriff, covets the ranch for himself. The ranch is perched on oil-rich land and the film ends with a fistfight between Coburn and Franciscus' men, as oil geysers from the well. Coburn is being pursued by gunslinging pimp Sonny Bronston (Jack Palance), who drives a rickety mobile brothel. He wants Coburn to marry his sister, Mary (Dany Saval), who is expecting Coburn's child. Spencer is in fine form in this gentle western send-up. Luis Enriquez Bacalov provided the parodic score and the bouncy sing-along 'Can Be Done' was performed by Rocky Roberts (from *Django*). Most of the action was shot on location in the Almerian desert. Mini Hollywood was Silvertown and De Laurentiis Studios' western set was Westland. As the film is a spoof of *Once Upon a Time in the West*, it is fitting that Leone's Sweetwater homestead is reused here as Welldigger's Roost. In the German print, entitled *Der Dicke in Mexiko*, Coburn's horse, Rufus, is dubbed with a voice so that it can talk.

Spencer returned to Almeria for Michele Lupo's rumbustious comedy western **Buddy Goes West** (1980), a virtual remake of *Can Be Done*. Buddy (Spencer) and his Native American sidekick, Cocoa (Amidou), find themselves in Yucca City (Mini Hollywood), where Buddy hides from the law, posing as a doctor. They also help the local settlers at Leone's Sweetwater ranch against crooked sheriff Braintree (Joe Bugner), who's in cahoots with outlaw Colorado Slim (Riccardo Pizzuti) and his gang (Romano Puppo, Lorenzo Fineschi, Giovanni Cianfriglia, Fortunato Arena and Benito Stefanelli). Morricone provided the score, which references and parodies his own compositions for *Once Upon a Time in the West*, *Death Rides a Horse* and the 'Nobody' films.

Barboni directed Hill in *Man of the East* (1972) and Spencer in *Even Angels Eat Beans* (1973). Both films were massively popular in Italy. The Yugoslav-shot **Man of the East** reteamed Hill with Yanti Somer, as his lover Candida. Hill played Sir Thomas Moore, a naive Englishman-out-west, who is schooled in frontier ways by three itinerant outlaws, Bull, Holy Joe and Monkey (Gregory Walcott, Harry Carey Jnr and Dominic Barto). He then confronts Morton Clayton (Riccardo Pizzuti), his rival for Candida's affections. G & M De Angelis supplied the sentimental score.

Even Angels Eat Beans was a Depression-era gangster comedy, set (and partly shot) in New York. Spencer played Charlie Smith, who wrestles in a black leotard and Santo mask under the pseudonym The Mystery Man. Giuliano Gemma played budding gangster Sonny. Gemma had proved popular in the caveman comedy *When Women Had Tails* (1970, opposite Senta Berger as a cavegirl with a tail), which spawned *When Women Lost Their Tails* and *When Women Played Ding Dong* (both 1971). Charlie and Sonny fall afoul of Godfather Angelo (Robert Middleton) – having joined Angelo's 'Family' and been dispatched to collect protection money, the duo end up helping their poverty-stricken victims, including grocer Gerace (Steffen Zacharias). Among the gangsters were Riccardo Pizzuti (henchman Cobra), Pietro Ceccarelli (Stonehead), Giovanni Cianfriglia (Mack the Knife) and Mario Brega (Angelo's armourer). Fortunato Arena played a cop, Victor Israel was informer Judah, George Wang was Japanese martial artist Naka Taka and Claudio Ruffini played Jim Baxter, a frantic wrestling referee. The jazzy ragtime score was by G & M De Angelis, with the title song, 'Angels and Beans' (co-written by Spencer) sung by 'Kathy and Gulliver'.

The success of *Even Angels Eat Beans* and the popularity of Paul Newman and Robert Redford's *The Sting* (1973) resulted in Sergio Corbucci's **The Con Artists** (1976 – *High Rollers* and *The Switch*), one of the highest grossing comedies of the 1970s in Italy and Corbucci's greatest commercial success. Anthony Quinn starred as con maestro Philip Bang. His protégé Felix was played by dopey, rubber-faced Italian singer-turned-comedian Adriano Celentano. Bang buys a swamp and creates a bogus archaeological dig for the mythical Nibelungen Treasure (the 'find of the century'), including Siegfried's tomb, to con casino owner Belle Duke (Capucine). Corrine Clery appeared as Bang's wily daughter, Charlotte. Corbucci shot some of the film in Monte Carlo and the original Italian title was *Bluff – storie di truffe a di imbroglioni* [Bluff – Story of Swindles and Cheats].

Bud Spencer capitalised on his newfound fame with *Flatfoot* (1973), a violent cop movie, and played the conman title role in Marcello Fondato's gangster movie *Charleston* (1978). He appeared as Ettore Fieramosca, a mercenary, in *Soldier of Fortune* (1976), a knockabout costume adventure set during the siege of Barletta in 1503, which was influenced by the medieval comedy *L'armata Brancaleone* (1966 – *For Love and Gold*) starring Vittorio Gassman, Gian Maria Volonté, Enrico Maria Salerno and Barbara Steele. Spencer also had hits with films aimed at a juvenile audience, including Michele Lupo's sci-fi comedy *The Sheriff and the Satellite Kid* (1979), and he later portrayed the genie in Bruno Corbucci's modern-day reworking of *Aladdin* (1986).

Spencer played the title role in Lupo's **They Called Him Bulldozer** (1978), which was filmed at Marina Di Pisa, a seaside resort to the west of Pisa. Retired American football star Bulldozer coaches a bunch of skinny, pasty teenage thieves and ne'er-do-wells who hang around 'Papa Galeone's Tavern' in the harbour, to take on the hulking US Rangers' football team at nearby Camp Durban. Raimund Harmstorf played Sergeant Kempfer, a bullying Ranger – as Sergeant Milton he'd tormented Terence Hill in *Nobody's the Greatest*. Gigi Bonos appeared as Bulldozer's boat mechanic, Rene Kolldehoff was the camp's colonel, Nello Pazzafini was a casino bouncer and stuntmen Romano Puppo, Riccardo Pizzuti, Giovanni Cianfriglia and Claudio Ruffini played GIs. *Bulldozer* is essentially *The Mean Machine*-Italian style. Bulldozer retired unexpectedly in 1973 when he discovered match-fixing but joins the fray in the finale, to galvanise his battered team. The irritating theme song, 'Bulldozer', was performed by 'Oliver Onions' (G & M De Angelis) and Spencer plays acoustic guitar and sings 'Como Se Llama'. UK boxer Joe Bugner made his film debut as the Bear, a street thug and lifeguard who is recruited into Bulldozer's team as a blocker. Although no actor, Bugner is great at this type of action film and enjoyed a mini career collaborating with Spencer on several movies.

Meanwhile Terence Hill made a brief break into the international mainstream in Dick Richards's French Foreign Legion epic *March or Die* (1977), opposite Gene Hackman, Max Von Sydow, Catherine Deneuve, Ian Holm and Richard

Kiel. This led to his first American starring role, *Mr. Billion* (1977), co-starring Jackie Gleason, Valerie Perrine, Slim Pickens and Chill Wills, where he played Guido Falcone, an Italian mechanic who attempts to claim an inheritance.

In Sergio Corbucci's US-shot **Supersnooper** (1981 – *Super Fuzz*), rookie Miami motorcycle cop Dave Speed (Hill) is exposed to red plutonium during a NASA test blast near Creektown. The explosion endows him with various superpowers – he can move objects telepathically, run faster than a car, anticipate future events, fly, catch bullets with his teeth and is indestructible. He makes Puma Man look pretty paltry. Dave also discovers that his powers are neutralised by the colour red. Dave and his partner, Officer Willy Dunlop (Ernest Borgnine), investigate a counterfeiting ring run by gangster Tony Torpedo (Marc Lawrence) from a fishing vessel, the *Barracuda*. In the finale, Dave and Willy float to safety on a giant yellow bubblegum bubble. Corbucci shot on location in Miami, including the Orange Bowl football ground. The Oceans performed the irksome disco theme song, 'Supersnooper', composed by Carmelo and Michelangelo La Bionda. When he isn't in uniform, Hill wears a cowboy hat and chequered shirt for much of the action, like a western hero. Sal Borgese appeared as Torpedo's henchman Paradise, Joanne Dru played ageing film star Rosy La Bouche, who is in cahoots with Torpedo, and Julie Gordon played Willy's niece Evelyn, Dave's love interest.

Double Trouble

It was as a team that Hill and Spencer had most success. They followed the 'Trinity' films with the disappointing swashbuckler *The Black Pirate* (1971) and then reunited with Giuseppe Colizzi for **All the Way, Boys!** (1972 – *Plane Crazy*). Plata (Hill) and Salud (Spencer), two freewheeling pilots, fly freight over the Amazon jungle. Their scamming boss tells them to crash the plane deliberately, so that he can collect the insurance money, but they really crash and are marooned in the piranha-infested jungle. They meet miners who scrape a living digging emeralds for exploitative Mr Ears (Rene Kolldehoff) and decide to start up their own business. They fix up an old biplane and begin shipping supplies to the miners, which leads to a clash of interests with Mr Ears.

Since *All the Way* involves Hill, Spencer, producer Zingarelli and director Colizzi, the mediocrity is staggering. Shot on location in Colombia, *All the Way, Boys!* was butchered for its English language release, from 120 minutes to barely 90, but the resultant incoherence doesn't help the sluggish narrative. Hill and Spencer are both good – basically as Trinity and Bambino in a plane – but the material simply puts them through their paces. The irritatingly catchy oom-pah, oom-pah title song, 'Flying Through the Air', was composed by S. Duncan Smith, Spencer and the De Angelis brothers. Respected actor Cyril Cusack played Loco, a lonely old Irish prospector who teams up with the duo and provides the film's most thoughtful moments. Riccardo Pizzuti played a bar owner and Antoine Saint-John a German-accented baddie – both are beaten up by the heroes in

Trinityesque fistfights. The exciting opening sequence introduces the heroes flying their stricken plane – on fire and without brakes – towards a busy airport. Spencer reads a *Popeye* comic while Hill dozes, unperturbed. As they career towards the runway, they leap an oncoming plane and then crash into a hangar, before emerging unscathed. Unfortunately, this provides the film's last moment of genuine excitement.

Marcello Fondato's **Watch Out, We're Mad!** (1973) cast Hill and Spencer as rival rally drivers Kid and Ben. In a rallycross race, they share first prize: a bright red Puma dune buggy. Gangster 'The Boss' (John Sharp) and his advisor the Doctor (Donald Pleasence) plan to take over an amusement park adjacent to Ben's garage and build a skyscraper. The hoods' gang destroy the duo's dune buggy. To help the people who work in the park and to get their buggy replaced, Kid and Ben take on the gangsters. Billed as 'A film ideated by Marcello Fondato' and filmed on location in Madrid and at De Paolis Studios, *Watch Out, We're Mad!* is one of the duo's finest post-Trinity comedies. The plot is an update of their western plots, with the threatened amusement park staff – including love-interest tightrope walker Liza (Patty Shepard) – subbing for distressed farmers. The crime boss sends for Paganini (Manuel De Blas), a virtuoso hitman from Chicago. He wears a long black coat, carries a violin case concealing a rifle and resembles a spaghetti western gunman. The duo also joust with a 10-man black-clad motorcycle hit-squad, which is scored with a Mexican trumpet Deguello.

The film's theme song is the popular pop hit 'Dune Buggy' performed by 'Oliver Onions' (G & M De Angelis), a flatulent, lively footstomper. The heroes' penchant for beans in the Trinity films becomes a beer and hotdogs–eating contest and the finale is a punch up in the gangster's club amid a sea of balloons. Though the fistfights and bizarre sight gags are equal to their western equivalents – including a scene where the duo takes on a gym full of boxers – the film really scores in the car and motorbike chases, which were staged by stunt ace Remy Julienne. Speedy highlights include the opening cross-country stockcar rally and a scene when Hill and Spencer drive their red Ford rally car, on fire, through the city streets into a carwash to extinguish the flames. The heroes plough their car through the gangster's club, destroying the venue, in the film's most impressively destructive scene. This was another hit for the duo and continued their winning streak at the Italian box office.

Franco Rossi's **Two Missionaries** (1974 – the original Italian title translated as 'Turn the Other Cheek') didn't receive widespread international release, despite being produced by Dino De Laurentiis. Filmed in Colombia, it told the story of two missionaries in the Antilles jungle in 1890 – Father Pedro De Léon (Spencer) and Father J (Hill) – who come into conflict with an exploitative coffee plantation magnet's henchmen, led by Menendez (Mario Pilar), and the bourgeois marquis and marquise Gonzaga (Robert Loggia and Maria Cumani Quasimodo). Eventually the missionaries incite the populace to rebel during a festival celebrating the oppressive colonial regime, the Fiesta of Conquistadores.

Terence Hill and Bud Spencer play rival rally racers Kid and Ben in Marcello Fondato's hit comedy *Watch Out, We're Mad!* (1973).

The standard Latin American 'rich-versus-poor' revolution scenario is lifted by the beautiful location work (some of the action looks like outtakes from *Burn!*), by Hill and Spencer's fine performances in atypical roles and by the period costumes and production design: notably the missionaries' battered river steamer and the gangways between the jungle villagers' treetop community. It is one of the duo's best-looking films, thanks to the widescreen cinematography by Gabor Pogany. Jean-Pierre Aumont was baddie Delgado and Riccardo Pizzuti was again beaten up as one of Menendez's henchmen. There is no love interest for Hill or Spencer, which helps the pace, and even the fight scenes are used sparingly, rather than as the film's raison d'être: in one scene, a hammock is used as a catapult. G & M De Angelis provided the upbeat, samba-flavoured score, with the songs 'Mañana' and 'El Barca de San José' performed by Barqueros.

Globetrotting Adventures

Crime Busters (1977 – *Two Supercops*) was the team's first attempt to crack the US market, by setting the action in Miami and filming on location in Florida (with interiors at Incir-De Paolis, Rome). It reunited Hill and Spencer with director Barboni. In Port Everglades, two unemployed drifters – acrobatic Matt Kirby (Hill) and '18-wheeler' Wilbur Walsh (Spencer) – decide to rob the Grand Union supermarket but inadvertently enlist in the Miami police force. Zipping through police training, they are soon star cops and favourites of their superior, Captain McBride (David Huddleston), when they break up a drug-trafficking ring operating from the docks and a bowling alley. Luciano Catenacci was the gang's leader, Fred 'Curly' Cline, and the presence of henchmen Scarface (Riccardo Pizzuti) and stuntmen Giovanni Cianfriglia, Rocco Lerro, Claudio Ruffini and Fortunato Arena gives the film a familiar ring. The film's plot strongly resembles *Trinity Is Still My Name* and once the duo are in uniform, as traffic cops on Harley Davidsons, the gags flow. The De Angelis brothers provided the score and the main theme is a countryish honkytonk.

The film's depiction of America offers interesting clues to Italian filmmakers' views on the US, where seemingly everyone's out to make a buck. It's a country of big shiny cars (most of which get trashed), hotdogs, fries in polystyrene cups, American football and bowling alleys. The heroes live on hamburgers, but with all the fight scenes they also take plenty of exercise. The mayhem escalated in the duo's films throughout the 1970s and the destruction became more grandiose, but they never lost sight of their Laurel and Hardy inspiration: 'A fine mess you made!' Hill tells Spencer when they accidentally smash the doors off their squad car. In a café scrape they take on toughs led by whip-wielding Ezio Marano (from *They Call Me Trinity*) and in the Miami Orange Bowl stadium they beat up a gang of cowboys led by hippy Geronimo (Luciano Rossi, also from *Trinity*) in a Grid Iron football parody. The big finale is a free-for-all in the Bird Bowl bowling alley, with Spencer sending the baddies skidding down the bowling lanes. Hill and Spencer are on top form here, and there are several in-jokes – Matt explains that he was born in Venice (as Hill was in real life) and six-feet-five-inch Spencer asks for an XXXXL uniform – Spencer starred as 'Detective Extralarge' on TV. Hill's love interest is Chinese Susy Lee (Laura Gemser, the star of countless *Emmanuelle* rip-offs) and her Chinese family christen the heroes 'The Great Dragon and the Tiger Cub'. The partnership 'cast one big shadow' and the film proved popular, even in the US on its release in 1980.

In Sergio Corbucci's ***Odds and Evens*** (1978), Lieutenant Johnny Firpo (Hill), a naval intelligence officer, investigates organised crime's control of gambling in Miami. He enlists the help of his half-brother, Charlie Firpo (Spencer), a card sharp and gambler. They take on the mob in a series of gambling challenges until Johnny faces chief villain The Greek (Luciano Catenacci) in a game of high-stakes poker aboard the villain's yacht.

Odds and Evens is where the rot began to set in. Hill is allowed to overact as hyperactive buffoon Johnny, with mugging and face-pulling, especially in an embarrassing scene where he talks 'Dolphinese'. The duo's meal of choice is beans and onions and the protracted fight scenes have become a hindrance to the overlong plot, which takes over half of its 112-minute running time to get going. When Hill sits down to play poker with four Italian stuntmen, you just know someone's going to end up bruised. The funky, synthesiser disco score by G & M De Angelis doesn't help. Spencer at one point appears dressed as a baby, complete with bonnet and dummy. Not to be outdone, Hill hitchhikes disguised as a nun.

Odds was filmed on sunny locales in Miami, Florida (including the Orange Bowl and the Seaquarium) and at De Paolis, Rome. The duo take on the Greek's gang and wreck a floating casino. There's a demolition derby, powerboat racing and even some speeded-up slapping. Woody Woodbury played Admiral O'Connor, Johnny's father, and TV comic Jerry Lester played Mike Firpo, Charlie's dad, who in a running 'gag' pretends to be blind. In a schmaltzy ending, the heroes' winnings save Sister Susanna's (Marisa Laurito) orphanage from closure. A success in Italy, the film was also a massive hit in Germany where the duo had a sizeable following, but there's no concealing the fact that, eight years after the Trinity films, they were still reusing the same plot.

I'm for the Hippopotamus (1979) was directed by 'Trinity' producer Italo Zingarelli and was filmed in Africa, which provided a welcome change of locale for the duo. This may have been inspired by Michele Lupo's popular *Africa Express* (1975) which saw John Baxter (Giuliano Gemma), nun Madeline (Ursula Andress) and Biba the Chimp up against ivory trader Robert Preston (Jack Palance), a Nazi war criminal. In *Hippopotamus*, Slim (Hill) and his cousin Tom (Spencer) tackle game hunters and ivory traffickers, led by ex-boxer Jack 'Hammer' Ormond (ex-boxer Joe Bugner), who is shipping animals to collectors in Ontario. The duo take on Ormond's pugnacious, idiot henchmen in set-piece after thumping set-piece. Remy Julienne performed the vehicle stunts, which include a jeep leaping into a river and a chase between a lorry and Tom's multicoloured, antique tourist bus. Tom runs safaris for big game hunters (but he substitutes their bullets for blanks) and is in league with local native Senghor (Sandy Nkomo), who sells fake 'tribal artefacts' to unsuspecting tourists. Dawn Jürgens played Senghor's daughter, Stella (Slim's love interest), and Ben Masinga was Dr Jason, a butterfly collector. Walter Rizzati composed the buoyant score – especially memorable is the ecological theme song, 'Grau Grau Grau', which is also performed by Spencer during the film.

Hippopotamus has some trademark Hill and Spencer moments: Slim and Tom enjoy a posh meal at Ormond's estate (Slim devours a lobster, shell, claws and all); in a casino Slim demonstrates some dextrous card shuffling; and a jailbreak has Slim spring Tom with a bulldozer. The finale features Ormond herding dozens of animals aboard a river steamer and Slim and Tom releasing them back into the wild, which results in a memorable stampede of ostrich, zebra and impala. Ormond's men jump into the crocodile-infested river rather than face the heroes. Cut by 10 minutes on some DVD releases, the UK video is uncut at 104 minutes.

The title of Sergio Corbucci's **Who Finds a Friend Finds a Treasure** (1981) was inspired by a line uttered by Hill to Spencer in *Crime Busters*. The excruciating reggae theme song, 'Movin' Cruisin', composed by Carmelo and Michelangelo La Bionda and sung by The Oceans prepares the audience for what follows. This is possibly the duo's career nadir and a sorry entry in Corbucci's filmography. Alan (Hill) is on the run from mobster Frisco Joe (Salvatore Basile) and his gang (including Riccardo Pizzuti and Giovanni Cianfriglia). Alan stows away on Charlie O'Brien's sailboat, the *Puffin* – Charlie (Spencer) is single-handedly attempting to circumnavigate the globe, but Alan has a map from his uncle Brady (Herbie Goldstein), which indicates a treasure buried on a South Pacific island.

Alan and Charlie end up marooned on the island, named Bongo Bongo. Before you can say 'embarrassingly offensive racial stereotypes', Alan and Charlie encounter a tribe of natives, including Queen Mama (Luise Bennett) and Chief Anulu (stuntman Sal Borgese, in an afro wig, grass necklace and loincloth). The duo find that the treasure is buried in a stockade defended by Kamasuka (John Fujoka), a Japanese hold-out who thinks World War II is still raging. Alan and Charlie, dressed in US army surplus kit, drive a vintage Type 95 KE-GO Japanese tank at the stockade. The film's lowlights include a band of slaver pirates from Barracuda dressed in leather bondage gear, caps and chaps. Alan and Charlie find over $300 million but hand it over to the US army when they are told it's counterfeit: it isn't. The film was retitled *Keep Your Hands off the Island* in the US and the best gag is the spoof ending which thanks the people and authorities of 'The Island' for their 'courteous and generous collaboration' and states that the filmmakers have promised never to reveal the location of this unspoiled paradise. The film was made at Key Biscayne, Florida, south of Miami.

Back with Barboni for **Go for It** (1983), Hill and Spencer were also reunited with David Huddleston from *Crime Busters*. In a replay of *Trinity Is Still My Name*, 'roller-bum' Roscoe Fraser (Hill), a roller-skating hitchhiker, and recently released convict Doug O'Riordan (Spencer) are mistaken for truck hijackers, then for CIA operatives 'Steinberg' and 'Mason'. Huddleston plays their CIA chief, the Tiger. The twosome are assigned to break up a ring of crooks who are fleecing rich tourists on Miami Beach. Posing as Texan millionaires, Roscoe and Doug arrive in town driving a gold Lincoln Continental, with longhorns on the hood and towing a cow ('Calamity Jane') in a trailer. The crooks, led by Dr Spider (Riccardo Pizzuti) and his vampish moll (stuntwoman Faith Minton), are working with crime overlord K1 (Buffy Dee), who plans to blow up the Space Shuttle with the K-bomb and release a cloud of radiation.

Go for It is proof that the Hill-Spencer comedy team worked best with Barboni. With an above-average script and a coherent plot, the duo are visibly reinvigorated by this spy spoof. There are several good gags involving Roscoe's skills as a ventriloquist. The score was provided by Franco Micalizzi and the title song, 'In the Middle of That Trouble Again', is an up-tempo country twang sung by A. Douglas Meakin. Barboni shot on location in Miami – the heroes check into the luxury Fontainbleau Hilton Resort at Miami Beach. During a scene at Miami's Seaquarium, Hill and Spencer take on a gang of Chinese assassins led by Charlie Chan (Jeff Moldovan) and black-suited Mafia hitmen. The pratfalls and face-pulling are kept to the minimum and superior sight gags prevail. The agents are kitted out with a gadget-laden bullet-proof car, a spray that makes even Spencer irresistible to women and super-strength toilet paper. The villains' henchmen wear t-shirts emblazoned 'I L♥VE K1' and in the film's most Bondian moment, a beautiful barmaid (Susan Teesdale) attempts to kill Roscoe with an exploding cocktail and escapes by paragliding behind a speedboat, with Roscoe in hot pursuit on a jet ski.

Each Hill and Spencer teaming had an angle – there's the one where they play stockcar drivers, the one where they play priests, or crooks-turned-cops, or pilots, or pirates. In Barboni's **Double Trouble** (1984) they play themselves. In Rio De Janeiro, two of the richest men in the world, the Coimbra cousins Bastiano and Antonio (Hill and Spencer), are being targeted by mobsters led by hitman Tango (Nello Pazzafini), who don't want them to sign an important business contract. Two look-alikes – stuntman Elliot Vance (Hill) and sax-playing New Orleans ex-con Greg Wonder (Spencer) – are hired as diversionary bait. They must impersonate the millionaires for seven days, for $1.5 million each. Elliot and Greg's public brawling makes the papers and the millionaires decide that their reputations are being sullied ('I'll never be able to show my face at the yacht club again', moans Antonio), so they fly from hiding in New York to Rio, as a gang of heavily armed mercenaries are employed to kill the cousins. The climax is a massed fight, with the two cousins and their doubles against Commander Van Der Bosch (Dary Reis) and his camouflaged dogs of war mercenaries, who have parodic names like Apocalypse, Sulphurhead, Cobra, Mamba and Rattler. The setting for this fight is the stables of the millionaires' country villa in San Jose. The villain behind the assassination attempts is revealed to be Bastiano's lover, Doña Olympia Chavez (April Clough from *Crime Busters*), because Antonio has financially ruined her father.

Double Trouble was shot on location in Rio, including Christ the Redeemer's statue and Sugar Loaf Mountain in Guanabara Bay. Carnivalesque local colour is established via smoky clubs, booty-shaking extras and a Samba-flavoured score courtesy of Franco Micalizzi, including the song 'Samba é Alegria'. Hill and Spencer enjoy themselves as the two slovenly impersonators, dressed in top hats and evening suits, driving luxury limousines and living in the lap of luxury. Split-screen effects enable all four protagonists to appear together. In one of Hill and Spencer's most famous moments, they emerge from their white limo in wet suits (as Elliot and Greg) and waddle across the beach to a dinghy, to travel to a mobster's island hideout. *Double Trouble* is the only Hill and Spencer vehicle to reference British PM Margaret Thatcher – their look-alike agency have provided doubles for many politicians, including Roosevelt, Churchill, Reagan, Thatcher and Stalin. UK home video prints slightly tone down the violence (according to the BBFC, 'ear claps' were removed from the fight scenes) to gain a PG rating.

The End of the Partnership

The title sequence of **Miami Supercops** (1985) suggests a knockabout comedy. Accompanied by frenetic, punchy synthesiser disco (courtesy of Carmelo and Michelangelo La Bionda), it depicts the sights of Miami: dolphins, speedboats, horse and greyhound races, baseball, beach babes, jet skis and performing parrots riding miniature bicycles and roller-skating. But this is no juvenile comedy – the duo are older, wiser and tougher and are much more likely to settle disputes with guns rather than fists. New York cop Doug Bennett (Hill) is contacted by

In Bruno Corbucci's *Miami Supercops* (1985), Doug Bennett (Terence Hill) and Steve Forest (Bud Spencer) cause havoc when they go undercover as 'Jess Donnell' and 'L.A. Ray' in the Hialeah Police Force.

his old boss Chief Tanney (C.B. Seay) in the Hialeah Police Department, near Miami. Felon Joe Garret (Richard Liberty) has been released from prison. He perpetrated the only case Bennett didn't crack during his time with Tanney: the $20 million robbery of the Detroit First National Bank. Bennett travels to Miami to recruit his old partner Steve Forest (Spencer), now a helicopter instructor in Tampa. Bennett and Forest go undercover on the Hialeah Police Force as uniformed cops – Officers Jess Donnell (Hill) and L.A. Ray (Spencer) – and investigate a trail of dead bodies. Garrett is killed and Garret's partner-in-crime, Ralph Duran, thought to have died in a fire in 1978, is still very much alive. He's had cosmetic surgery and is now Cuban ex-pat businessman Robert Delmann (Ken Ceresne), a wealthy Miami construction magnate.

Miami Supercops is more violent than any other Hill and Spencer comedy, courtesy of director Bruno Corbucci, who made his name with Tomas Milian's poliziotteschi. Spencer and Milian had co-starred in Corbucci's Florida-set comedy *Cats and Dogs* (1983), which is notable for Milian's hilarious turn as rock 'n' roll lothario and jewellery thief Tony Roma. *Supercops* was a 15 certificate in the UK, rather than Hill and Spencer's usual PG or U rating. The duo's mismatched buddy cop routine works well, though admittedly by now they've had enough practice. Spencer calls Hill 'Blue Eyes' (a signature of their films together) with reference to Hill's baby blues. Bennett foils a gunsmith hold-up by posing as a mannequin and the duo effortlessly apprehend bus hijackers. The film was shot on location in Florida, with a trip to the Orange Bowl (for a subplot detailing the kidnapping of a star quarterback) and the football squad stay at the Seville Beach Hotel, Miami. *Miami Supercops* makes you wonder why Hill and Spencer didn't make more crime films like this, with the comedy taking a back seat to the action. The car stunt pyrotechnics were co-ordinated by Mike Warren. Hill's love interest was informant Irene (Jackie Castellano), who turns out to be FBI special agent Irene Allen, while Spencer courts muscly trucker Annabel (Rhonda S. Lundstead); they bond over arm wrestling. William 'Bo' Jim played Native America muscleman Charro, a former cellmate of Garret's in San Quentin, whose Indian saying may be the credo for Hill and Spencer's screen partnership: 'All the money in the world ain't worth a friend'.

By the early 1980s, Hill was also running his production company, Paloma Films. He starred for Barboni in the contemporary western road movie *Renegade* (1987 – *They Call Me Renegade*) as drifter Luke and produced and directed **Lucky Luke** (1991), a live-action version of Goscinny and Morris's cartoon strip, which was scripted by his wife, Lori Hill. Sheriff Lucky Luke (Hill, wearing a long duster, like 'Nobody') and his smart-aleck white horse Jolly Jumper (voiced by Roger Miller, from Disney's *Robin Hood*) save Daisy Town from the four villainous Dalton brothers. Nancy Morgan played saloon gal Lotta Legs and Neil Summers (from *My Name Is Nobody*) was Luke's deputy, Virgil. It was filmed on location in New Mexico and Arizona (including Santa Fe, White Sands and Monument Valley). Luke is quicker on the draw than his own shadow and much of the action resembles the Trinity films. David Grover and Aaron Schröder's countryish score reinforces this, though the soundtrack also uses uncredited cues from Morricone's *The Big Gundown* and *My Name Is Nobody*. The film's best gag involves a spaghetti western gunfight between Luke and the Daltons, which features a parody of the persistent fly in *Once Upon a Time in the West*. An ambling, silly film, *Lucky Luke* spawned an eight-episode TV series in 1992, also called *Lucky Luke* and starring Hill.

Hill and Spencer reunited for **The Troublemakers** (1994), the last roundup for the duo, scripted by Hill's son, Jess, and produced by Spencer's son, Giuseppe Pedersoli. It was filmed under the working title *The Fight before Christmas*. Hill (who also directed) played conman Travis. Spencer was his bounty-hunting brother, Moses, who has a wife and ten children to provide for. The two warring brothers unite for Christmas at the ranch of their 'Maw' (Ruth Buzzi). Neil Summers played bad guy Dodge and Anne Kasprik was Travis' love interest, German veterinarian Bridget. The film was shot on location in New Mexico, including White Sands, the Bonanza Creek Ranch and the Eaves Movie Ranch (as the town of Cross Roads). Pino Donaggio provided the heroic score and Terry Nunn from band Berlin belted out the end title's rock song, 'I'm Coming Home'. The film depicts the duo's manhunt for outlaw Sam Stone (Boots Southerland) but Travis and Moses are Trinity and Bambino in all but name – they even devour pans of beans.

The Christmas Eve climax at Maw's ranch features one final punch-up for the duo, stunt co-ordinated by Giorgio Ubaldi. The unconscious, beaten villains' bodies decorate a giant prairie Christmas tree topped with a Catherine Wheel star. This belated spaghetti western has its moments, especially during a parody of the hangings from *The Good, the Bad and the Ugly*. Moses is about to be executed. As Travis levels his Winchester to shoot the rope, a dog ravages his leg and distracts him. When Moses plunges through the trap door, his weight demolishes the scaffold. Spencer wore a huge shaggy sheepskin jerkin and bowler hat (as in the Colizzi westerns) and Hill donned a long duster coat (from the Nobody films), in homage to their western teamings all those years ago. *Troublemakers* isn't vintage Hill and Spencer, but it's not bad either, though it has proved to be their last foray as a duo.

Hill and Spencer's comedic style is not to everyone's taste but there is no denying their onscreen chemistry. The partnership has entertained audiences for over 40 years and continues to do so even today. In the early 1980s, home video brought Hill and Spencer's humour to a new audience. In the UK, Warner Home Video released *Go for It* and *Crime Busters* in big-box editions and Embassy Home Entertainment put the Trinities on rental shelves. Medusa Home Video released *I'm for the Hippopotamus* (plus Hill's 'Nobody' films) and RCA/Columbia compiled 'The Hollywood Spencer-Hill Collection', which featured *Watch Out, We're Mad!*, *Odds and Evens*, *Who Finds a Friend Finds a Treasure*, *Double Trouble* and *Miami Supercops*. These knockout comedies were staples of any self-respecting video rental store. Even today Hill and Spencer's entire oeuvre is available on DVD and videocassette – it'll take more than fashion and good taste to keep this duo down. In May 2010 they received lifetime achievement David Di Donatello Awards, to celebrate their long and successful careers. Like Totò and Franchi and Ingrassia before them, Hill and Spencer have finally seen their accomplishments acknowledged by Italian cinema's 'establishment'.

Chapter Thirteen

Splats Entertainment
Italian Cinema Eats Itself

The 1970s saw a gradual decline in Italian film production. Adriano Celentano had several huge-grossing comedy hits, but they weren't distributed internationally – most weren't even dubbed into English, as the big hitters in Hollywood began to dictate what was seen in the global entertainment market. Sex comedies became popular in Italy, with Edwige Fenech the most admired star, but they too failed to garner international success. After an initial surge of interest, demand for gialli and poliziotteschi wilted off domestically, and spaghetti westerns also fell out of favour. But the 1970s and the early 1980s produced its fair share of interesting genres. There was a sword and sandal revival in the wake of Arnold Schwarzenegger's 'Conan' films, post-apocalyptic films aping the Mel Gibson vehicle *Mad Max 2*, street gang warfare inspired by Walter Hill's *The Warriors* and mercenary jungle warfare movies derived from *The Wild Geese* and *Apocalypse Now*. The 'zombie' sub-genre traded on the success of George A. Romero's *Night of the Living Dead* (1968) and *Dawn of the Dead* (1979) and 'mondo' movies graphically depicted cultures around the world. And Italian cinema created its own infamous addition to horror, with sickening cannibal movies – a moment when Italian cinema quite literally ate itself.

Western Adios

In an effort to revamp Italian westerns in the early 1970s, martial arts action was added, creating 'east-meets-westerns' such as Terence Young's *Red Sun* (1971 – with Charles Bronson and Toshirô Mifune) and Antonio Margheriti's *The Stranger and the Gunfighter* (1974 – *Blood Money*, starring Lee Van Cleef and Lo Lieh). Mario Caiano's **The Fighting Fist of Shangai Joe** (1973 –*To Kill or to Die*), a kung fu movie set in the American south-west, is essentially 'Enter the Lizard'. In 1882, Chinese martial arts expert Chin Ho (Chen Lee) dreams of becoming a cowboy and heads east from San Francisco. 'Shangai Joe' is a pejorative term

The Season's Most Argued About Film: US poster for Gualtiero Jacopetti's controversial *Mondo cane* (1962). Poster courtesy Ian Caunce Collection.

used for Chin by the racist cowpokes he encounters. Chin works for powerful Texan rancher Stanley Spencer (Piero Lulli) but discovers Spencer's smuggling Mexican peons across the border as slave labour. Spencer puts a $5,000 bounty on Chin's head and hires four notorious killers: Pedro the Cannibal (Robert Hundar), undertaker Burying Sam (Gordon Mitchell), Tricky the Gambler (Giacomo Rossi-Stuart) and Scalping Jack (Klaus Kinski, wearing a knife-lined jacket). Chin dispatches them in turn with boiling rice, a spiked mantrap, eye-socket tearing martial arts and disembowelling knives. Spencer contacts Chin's old nemesis Mijuka (Katsutoshi Mikuriya), who faces Chin in a *Yojimbo/Fistful of Dollars*-style showdown on De Paolis Studio's western town set. *Shangai Joe* has a great score by Bruno Nicolai, which recycles cues from *Have a Good Funeral, Amigo…Sartana Will Pay* (1970). With plenty of gory kung fu action, the film stays close to its Chinese martial arts movie roots and is Caiano's best western.

A gloomier strain of Italian westerns also emerged, dubbed 'crepuscolo' (twilight) westerns, which took the mud, rain and fog of Sergio Corbucci's anti-westerns and added a feudal atmosphere of medieval primitivism and ever more excessive violence. Lucio Fulci's *Four Gunmen of the Apocalypse* (1975) was the most extreme example, with Tomas Milian's outlaw Chaco torturing and raping his way through a party of travellers, including Fabio Testi, Lynne Frederick and Michael J. Pollard. Michele Lupo's pensive *California* (1977) was a death rattle from the genre set in a ruined, post–Civil War west (filmed in Manziana and Almeria). California (Giuliano Gemma) finds himself up against bounty hunter Whittaker (Raimund Harmstorf) and his cohorts (Romano Puppo and Robert Hundar)

Enzo G. Castellari's **Keoma** (1976 – *The Violent Breed, Django Rides Again* and *Django's Great Return*) starred Franco Nero as Keoma, a 'half-breed' Native American who is raised by rancher Shannon (William Berger). Following the Civil War, Keoma returns to his plague-wracked hometown of Skidoo City (the Elios Studios set), which is now ruled by Caldwell (Donal O'Brien). Keoma confronts his three stepbrothers – Butch (Orso Maria Guerrini), Lenny (Antonio Marsina) and Sam ('Joshua Sinclair'/Gianni Loffredo) – and when Caldwell murders Shannon, the trio blame Keoma. They kill Caldwell and take over the town, triggering a confrontation with Keoma.

Keoma was originally envisioned as a sequel to Corbucci's *Django* and was based on a story by actor Luigi Montefiori. There was no need to redress the Elios Studios western town set, as Corbucci had in 1966. As the western fad died, so did Elios and the set was in ruinous disrepair. Castellari filmed his location scenes at Camposecco, near Camerata Nuovo, Lazio and in the misty high country of Campo Imperatore, near L'Aquila in the Abruzzo National Park. Woody Strode played bowman George (Keoma's mentor) who is driven to alcoholism in Skidoo City's troubled times. Olga Karlatos played expectant mother Lisa, whom Keoma protects from Caldwell and who dies in childbirth. Throughout the film a witch (Gabrielle Giacobbe) makes a series of unnerving appearances, as though controlling Keoma's fate.

Nero gives a very different performance to his other western portrayals and Keoma's primary motivation is to help others. Castellari said, 'I think that to have an actor like Franco Nero is one of the best things that can happen to a director... if it had been possible, I would have made all my films with him'. If *Keoma* has a failing it is its weird score by G & M De Angelis, which deploys haunting songs to narrate the action. 'Keoma' and 'In Front of My Desperation' are performed by Sybil and Guy – her voice quiveringly shrill, his a froggy croak. For the stylised action scenes, Castellari imitated Sam Peckinpah's style, distending death throws into a blood-spurting ballet. The bad guys spin and twist from bullet impacts in slow motion – there are more pirouettes in *Keoma* than in *Swan Lake*. A moderate success in Italy at the time, *Keoma* has since seen its reputation grow considerably, though its gloomy style fiercely divides aficionados.

In Sergio Martino's superior **A Man Called Blade** (1977 – *Mannaja*), Maurizio Merli played the tomahawk-throwing Blade (Mannaja in the Italian print), who arrives in the decrepit town of Suttonville (the Elios set) to take revenge on the man who caused the death of his father, Gerald Merton (Rik Battaglia). The culprit is wheelchair-bound mine owner McGowan (Philippe Leroy). McGowan's henchman Voller (John Steiner) covets McGowan's empire and arranges for McGowan's daughter, Deborah (Sonia Jeanine), to be kidnapped by outlaw Allman (Antonio Casale). Blade is recruited by McGowan to get her back.

G & M De Angelis provided another doom-laden wailing harmonica and twanging guitar score, including the song 'Snake' by Dandylion. Merli's Blade, a solitary man, looks the part and Martino's deliberate pacing is right for this fatalistic morality tale. The murky, muddy cinematography also helps. *Blade* was shot on location in wintry Lazio, at Camposecco, in a valley at Tolfa, at Caldara Di Manziana and the quarries of Magliana. A subplot has Blade buried in a rock fall and being nursed back to health by a party of travelling prostitutes and their pimp, Johnny Johnny (Salvatore Puntillo). Steiner, dressed in a black cape and leading two snarling Dobermans, is a fine villain. As with *Keoma*, the violence is strong: the prostitutes are flogged in the main street of Suttonville by Voller's men and outlaw Burt Craven (Donal O'Brien) is apprehended in a swamp when Blade severs his gun hand with a throwing axe. Blade is buried up to his neck and has his eyelids pinned open in the hot sun. This leaves him temporarily blind, but he recovers for the final showdown, where he dispatches Voller with a hatchet to the chest.

The title of Monte Hellman's **China 9, Liberty 37** (1978) refers to a signpost between two towns. In China, condemned gunfighter Clayton Drumm (Fabio Testi) is released from jail. He's offered an amnesty and bounty reward by railroad boss Williams (Luis Prendes) if he kills farmer Matthew Sebanek (Warren Oates), whose land stalls the progress of the Great Texas Railroad. When Clayton arrives to kill the farmer, he falls in love with Matthew's wife, Catherine (Jenny Agutter). She stabs her husband and the two lovers head toward the town of Liberty. But Matthew survives and with his brothers, he sets out after Clayton, who is also now the target of Williams' railroad hired guns – their boss doesn't want to pay up for Matthew's murder.

Photographed by Giuseppe Rotunno in a twilit Almeria, *China 9* is a melancholic, low-key anti-western. Hellman movingly dedicated the film to his father and it shares themes and settings with Leone's *Once Upon a Time in the West* (the railroad regulators, the picnic tables at Sebanek's farm, the Almerian desert) and the westerns of Sam Peckinpah. Peckinpah himself appears, dressed in a long duster coat, as ageing dime novelist Wilbur Olsen, who offers to buy Clayton's story. China and Liberty are played by the Texas-Hollywood town, while a Mexican settlement is the pueblo district of the same set (with interiors at DEAR Studios, Rome). In the final ambush of Matthew and Catherine at their farm by Williams' regulators, Clayton intervenes with some accurate Sharps rifle marksmanship and then departs. Matthew and Catherine torch their ranch and move on, a symbolic new beginning – the opposite of most westerns, which see the creation of a home. The film was also released as *Clayton Drumm* and *Clayton and Catherine*. Most prints cut Agutter's nude scenes, some violence and a sex scene. The score was by Pino Donaggio, who incorporated a lazy harmonica cue, romantic orchestrations and the aching 'China 9 Love Ballad' performed by singer Ronee Blakley (from Robert Altman's *Nashville*).

Klondike Gold Fever: Towers and London

Italy also produced a popular series of snowbound Klondike pseudo-westerns based on Jack London's novels *Call of the Wild* (1903) and *White Fang* (1906). **The Call of the Wild** (1973) was the cinematographic equivalent of spread betting. It was a UK-Italian-West German-Spanish-French co-production – produced by Harry Alan Towers and directed by Ken Annakin – shot on location in Norway and Spain. The film told the story of Alsatian Buck, a Californian house dog who finds himself in the Yukon Gold Rush pulling Charlton Heston's sled. Heston starred as John Thornton, who with his partner Pete (Raimund Harmstorf) transports the mail on an arduous 600-mile trek from Skagway port to boomtown Dawson City. Thornton falls for saloon proprietor Calliope Laurent (Michele Mercier) and falls foul of liquor importer Black Burton ('George Eastman'/Luigi Montefiori). Buck survives various adventures and owners and eventually settles down with a she-wolf for the fadeout, after Thornton and Pete are killed by Indians. Maria Rohm played a spoilt heiress, Rik Battaglia played dog trader Dutch Harry and Sancho Gracia was Pete's gold-prospecting partner, Taglish Charlie, who tells tales of Yellow Moon (a mythical gold deposit). The dog fights and general barbarity towards Buck make the film a little strong for its UK 'PG' rating. The spectacular scenery, good pace and intelligent script lift it above other Yukon entries. Carlo Rustichelli's romantic score adds to the film's epic feel and *Call of the Wild* was a great success in Italy. During this period, successful producer Towers also bankrolled a boisterous adaptation of the buccaneering tale *Treasure Island* (1972) starring Orson Welles as peg-legged Long

John Silver, alongside Lionel Stander, Rik Battaglia, Aldo Sambrell and Angel Del Pozo. Welles also co-scripted as 'O.W. Jeeves'.

Towers returned to the Yukon for Lucio Fulci's **White Fang** (1973). The story begins where *Call of the Wild* left off, with old Buck dying and his son – half-dog, half-wolf – being adopted by Indian Charlie (Daniel Martin) and his son, Mitsah (Missaela Chiappetta). They christen him White Fang. When Mitsah falls into a lake, Charlie takes him to Dawson City for treatment at a hospital run by Sister Evangelina (Virna Lisi). Charlie is stabbed to death by Chester (Daniele Dublino), a henchman of town tyrant Beauty Smith (John Steiner), and Mitsah and White Fang are adopted by journalist Jason Scott (Franco Nero) and Evangelina. Smith has been buying the miners' gold with worthless promissory notes. When gold is discovered in Nome, Smith's deception is discovered and he's killed in an explosion as he blows up a dam.

Nero is teamed with mining representative Kurt Jansen (Raimund Harmstorf). Fernando Rey played Dawson's alcoholic parson, Oatley, Carole Andre was his daughter, saloon singer Krista, Rik Battaglia was Hall (Smith's henchman) and Maurice Poli and John Bartho were Mounties. With spectacular snowbound locations in Norway, Spain and Italy, and interiors at Cinecittà, *White Fang* is the best of the Klondike crop. Rustichelli again provided a rousing, traditional score. Fulci, a director better known for his bloody horror movies, crafted an 'adult' family adventure film. The bloody dog fights, particularly in scenes where Fang is pitted against Satan (Smith's vicious black hound) and a bear, are realistically staged and are not suitable for children. *White Fang* was a smash in Italy (it took almost 2.5 billion lira) and spawned *The Challenge to White Fang* (1974), again directed by Fulci, which reused many of the same cast and resurrected villain Beauty Smith (Steiner again).

Tonino Ricci, Fulci's second unit director on the 'White Fang' movies, took the helm for **White Fang to the Rescue** (1974). Exteriors were filmed in the snowscape of Cortina D'Ampezzo (from *The Big Silence*). Interiors were filmed at De Paolis and the mining town of Shelby was the ATC Studios western set, dressed with fake snow. Burt Holloway (Maurizio Merli), a miner, lives in the wilderness with his partner, Ben Dover, and their dog, White Fang. When Ben is murdered by ruffians (Donal O'Brien and Luciano Rossi), Burt assumes Ben's identity as he searches for his friend's killers. Ben's son, Kim, arrives to live with his father and Burt adopts the boy. Burt also becomes involved with saloon proprietor Katie (Gisela Hahn) and is falsely accused of Ben's murder. The villains steal a treasure map, kidnap Kim and set off to locate Ben's gold strike. The film's heavies were Nelson (Henry Silva) and his sidekick Jackson (Benito Stefanelli). Riccardo Pizzuti and Pietro Torrisi featured in Nelson's gang and Renzo Palmer played an Irish Mountie sergeant. The music was composed by Rustichelli and stunt dog Saccha played Fang, who in one brutal scene convincingly fights a bear (Canadian performing bear Bobo). Fang also crashes through a glass window, a stunt trademark of the Italian Klondike films. The film's opening scene, when

Ben is ambushed, resembles *The Big Silence* re-imagined as a Lassie film. Fang saves Kim in the cliffhanging finale but falls into a raging torrent. Kim is now the rich owner of a gold mine, but like all boys all he really cares about is his missing dog, which makes Fang's reappearance (limping into town in the dénouement) more effective.

Gianfranco Baldanello's ***The Great Adventure*** (1975 – *Cry of the Wolf*) starred Joan Collins as Last Chance saloon singer Sonia Kendall and Jack Palance as Dawson City town tyrant William Bates. Palance is the best Klondike villain in these Italian adventures. The climax has Bates employ three specialists from Circle City (a gunman, a dynamiter and a safecracker) to clean out the Dawson bank on Christmas Day. The film was shot in Spain, with the Madrid 70 western set at Alcobendas deployed as Dawson. Manuel De Blas and Remo De Angelis were the heroic brothers John and Hank McKenzie, who help young orphans Jim and Mary Chambers (freckle-faced Fred Romer and forthright Elisabeth Virgil) set up a newspaper, *The Nugget*. Jose Canalejas was Bates' henchman and Riccardo Palacios played Irish bartender Charlie. Wolf-dog Buck contributed his usual doggy heroics – some of the shots of him running with a wolf pack harassing caribou are stock footage from *Call of the Wild*. The beautiful snowscapes, howling wolves and Stelvio Cipriani's score (which recycles cues from *The Stranger Returns*) create a fine atmosphere for this undemanding, eventful 'north-western'. Only the saccharin ballad 'The Sound of the Wild' sung by Joseph Allegro marks the film out as juvenile fare.

Apocalypse Now: Before and After the Bomb

Following in the tyre tracks of the futuristic *Mad Max 2* (1981 – *The Road Warrior*) and also influenced by *The Warriors* (1979) and *Escape from New York* (1981), came the last gasp of Italian sci-fi. Enzo G. Castellari made three anarchic movies with producer Fabrizio De Angelis: *1990: The Bronx Warriors* (1982 – *Bronx Warriors*), its sequel *Escape from the Bronx* (1983 – *Bronx Warriors 2* and *Escape 2000*) and *The New Barbarians* (1983 – *Warriors of the Wasteland*).

1990: The Bronx Warriors begins with Ann Fisher (Stefania Girolami, Castellari's daughter), a wealthy heiress, fleeing Manhattan to the Bronx. By 1990, the borough has been declared a 'no man's land' and is ruled by biker gang the Riders, led by Trash (Mark Gregory). Ann falls in love with Trash, which angers his lieutenant Ice (Gianni Loffredo). Ann is approaching her eighteenth birthday and is about to inherit the Manhattan Corporation, a global arms manufacturer. Her father, Samuel Fisher (Castellari's brother, Enio Girolami), and Farley, the company's vice-president (Castellari himself), send in rogue cop Hammer (Vic Morrow) to get her back. Things are complicated when Ann is kidnapped by the Zombies, led by Golan (George Eastman), so Trash and Ogre (black action icon Fred Williamson) join forces to save her.

Bronx Warriors, Castellari's most sustained piece of insanity, is backed by an atmospheric urban synth score by Walter Rizzati. Though its graffiti-sprayed

US poster for Enzo G. Castellari's *1990: The Bronx Warriors* (1982), depicting (right) Ogre (Fred Williamson) and Witch (Betty Dessy). Mark Gregory takes centre stage as biker leader Trash.

interiors were shot at De Paolis, much of the films' location footage was shot in New York, in Brooklyn and the Bronx – the Brooklyn Bridge and other New York landmarks appear on the skyline. The crumbling tenement blocks and general decay look convincingly apocalyptic, though in the background – as police vans and bikers cruise the streets – locals can be seen going about their daily business and driving cars in the supposedly 'no go' zone.

Gregory's Trash invokes the beefy street hustler chic of Joe Dallesandro in Andy Warhol's *Flesh*, *Trash* and *Heat*. Producer De Angelis discovered Gregory (real name Marco De Gregorio) exercising in a gym. Barely constrained by his waistcoat and tight jeans, long-haired, pouting Gregory resembles the front man of a 1970s rock band. His men are a rugged bunch of hairy, tattooed bikers, who ride machines decorated with glowing skulls. Scenes of gladiatorial combat deploy knives, swords, spears and spiked elbow pads, and a motorcycle beheads victims with its scythed wheels. The stunts were performed by 'Rocky's Stuntmen Team' and 'The Hell's Angels'. Williamson's gang, the Tigers, drive customised vintage jalopies (inspired by *Escape from New York*). Christopher Connelly played trucker Hot Dog, who sides with Hammer and power-hungry Ice. Morrow, as tough cop Hammer (who is described as 'just an asshole who thinks he's God'), has quality dialogue such as, 'I believe in nothing – I'm Hammer, the exterminator'. Rocco Lerro and Massimo Vanni played Rider bikers Hawk and Blade, Angelo Ragusa was Ogre's Dracula-like chauffeur, Leech, and Betty Dessy was Ogre's blonde whip-wielding sidekick Witch, wearing fishnets and a cape. The Zombies are roller-skating hockey players in white World War II German helmets and the Scavengers are rag-clothed, grunting subhumans. Carla Brait led the Iron Men, tap dancers with canes and metal bowler hats, who seem to have pranced off the set of *All That Jazz*. In *Bronx Warriors*' extraordinary finale, Hammer leads New York's Special Vigilante Force in Operation Burnt Earth: an attack on Ogre's lair. The cops arrive in helicopters and vans, and mounted police in crash helmets use flamethrowers to flush out the thugs. Ogre, Ann and Witch are shot and Trash skewers Hammer with a grappling hook, before dragging the cop's corpse in triumph behind his bike – as Achilles dragged Hector at Troy.

Bronx Warriors runs uncut at 92 minutes. Beware the tamer 79-minute version, which also misses a conversation between Trash and Ann on a beach, the Viking-like cremation of Riders Sandy and Speedy and the scattering of their ashes on the Hudson River. *Bronx Warriors* was advertised with the tagline 'The first to die were the lucky ones!' Many film critics wholeheartedly agreed.

The film's huge success – even in the US – spawned an immediate sequel: **Escape from the Bronx** which followed the further adventures of Trash. The General Construction Corporation (GCC) is redeveloping the Bronx. The media are informed that the Bronx gangs are being relocated to New Mexico, but in reality the silver-suited, flamethrower-brandishing Disinfestation Annihilation Force (DAS) are killing as many of the population as possible. Eventually Trash and renegade Strike (Timothy Brent) kidnap the GCC president, Henry G. Clark (Enio Girolami), for ransom, so the DAS launch an attack to wipe out the gangs. Henry Silva played ruthless DAS leader Floyd Wangler, Antonio Sabato was piratical Bronx gang leader Doubloon, Carla Brait reappeared as the leader of the Iron Men and Castellari himself can be seen as a moustachioed radio operator in the DAS command centre. Francesco De Masi provided the synth score and the film was again shot on location in New York and at De Paolis Studios, Rome. Romano Puppo has a brief cameo as Trash's father, who with his wife is torched by DAS flamethrowers, giving Trash more than enough excuse to blow Wangler to smithereens.

The New Barbarians (1983) is Castellari's carmageddon *Mad Max* rip-off, with lone warrior Scorpion (Timothy Brent) closely resembling Mel Gibson's Max. In 2019, a nuclear war has destroyed the Earth. Roving bands of Templars headed by One (George Eastman) ravage the land, seeking out pockets of survivors. Scorpion saves Alma (Anna Kanakis) from the Templars and teams up with Nadir (Fred Williamson) to vanquish the raiders when they threaten a caravan of Christians led by Father Moses (Venantino Venantini).

Castellari created his futuristic world in the quarry pits and building sites of Lazio. Especially effective are the night time scenes (a blur of neon and throbbing colour) and interiors were lensed at De Paolis Studios. Williamson's Nadir – packed into black leather and toting a lethal bow with exploding arrow points – completely overshadows Scorpion. Castellari's brother Enio played One's sidekick Shadow, Massimo Vanni was Mako (a Templar with a Mohawk hairstyle) and Iris Peynado was Nadir's love interest, Vinya. Castellari had a cameo as a mortally wounded scavenger. The pumping synthesizer score was composed by Giorgio Simonetti of Goblin fame and that's Simonetti's wife, Kanakis, a 'Miss Italy', playing Alma. The film's futuristic costumes are suitably preposterous. Leather, rubber and PVC predominate, with codpieces seemingly the essential post-apocalyptic fashion accessory. The film's finest achievement is the futuristic, customised jalopies and motorcycles. In imitation of Max's Interceptor, Scorpion drives a souped-up Mustang with a domed roof and a skull on the bonnet (recycled from *Bronx Warriors*). Castellari had only six cars (built on VW chassis) which are cleverly deployed to appear more numerous. The stunts are impressive and extremely dangerous, resembling the cartoon show *Wacky Races*. The survivors of the apocalypse don't last long, with death by grenades, rockets, limpet mines, machine guns, flamethrowers and laser guns (actually children's guns bought by Castellari from a toy shop). When Scorpion's car isn't running properly, his young mechanic (Giovanni Frezza) discovers a human ear jammed in the engine. Rotating knives decapitate victims, corkscrews and lances skewer bodies and exploding arrow points erupt in slow-motion explosions of freefalling stuntmen, rolling heads and flying liver.

Other Italian sci-fi rip-offs include *Exterminators of the Year 3000* (1983), *The Final Executioner* (1983 – a cross between *The 10th Victim* and *Mad Max*), *Raiders of Atlantis* (1983 – *Atlantis Interceptors*) and *Rome 2033 – The Fighter Centurions* (1984 –*The New Gladiators*). Set in the 'Year 23 – After the Cancellation', *She* (1983) welded 'Conan'-style swordsmanship to *Bronx Warriors* nihilism, via Amazons-versus-chainsaws combat, medieval knights, gladiators, fanatical monks, werewolves and pounding rock music from Rick Wakeman, Justin Hayward and Motorhead. Amazon warrior She (Sandahl Bergman) faced The Norks, a renegade street gang led by Hector (Gordon Mitchell), a face-off which made this a 'sword and Sandahl' epic.

In Sergio Martino's *2019: After the Fall of New York* (1983), 20 years after the European Afro-Asian Confederation (EURAC) has destroyed the world, the president of the Pan-American Confederacy (Edmund Purdom) sends chisel-jawed Mad Max impersonator Parsifal (Michael Sopkiw) on a mission of mercy to New York to save Melissa, civilisation's only fertile woman. Since World War III there has been zero population growth. Parsifal is accompanied by Bronx (Vincent Scalondro) – who has a claw for a hand – and Ratchet (Romano Puppo), a cyborg wearing an eye patch. Most of the film is set amid desolate smouldering streets and rat-infested subterranea (interiors were lensed as RPA Elios and

De Paolis studios). The trio encounter the EURAC forces: mounted police in Roman-style helmets and cloaks, armed with crossbow laser guns. They must also do battle with roving gangs: the Harlem Hunters, the Needle People (who feast on rats) and Big Ape (George Eastman, in a buccaneer costume and hairy face make-up) and his simian gang (which recall *Planet of the Apes*). Aided by Big Ape and one of the Tiny People, a dwarf named Shorty (Louis Ecclesia), Parsifal finds Melissa in hibernation and they escape through the Lincoln Tunnel.

2019 seems assembled from leftovers of all the Italian genres that preceded it. The mounted police and flamethrowers are from *Bronx Warriors*. There are guns from *Barbarella*, the Lazio quarry from sword and sandal epics, spaceship interiors from sci-fi movies, and costumes from genres including westerns and swashbucklers. Parsifal wears boots, a headband and a chain mail vest, and some of the action footage looks like the front-row scramble at a Duran Duran gig. Valentine Monnier was Parsifal's love interest Giara, Anna Kanakis was Anya (a vicious EURAC operative) and Ray Saunders was a lonely trumpeter, busking a requiem for New York. G & M De Angelis provided the effective, doom-laden synthesiser score and mournful harmonica theme. A Lazio gravel pit was the setting for a scene at the Nevada Race Track (when Parsifal takes on Giovanni Cianfriglia in a no-holds-barred stock car race) and Parsifal rides his chopper through Monument Valley. John Ford would have been proud. By combining blood, guts, plucked out eyes, bleeding ears, decapitations and a plot that delivers some surprises, Martino made a decent film. The scene when the heroes run the gauntlet of the mined Lincoln Tunnel in an estate car with sheet steel chained to the roof is impressive. The survivors – Parsifal and Melissa – are fired into space to colonise a planet in Alpha Centauri, unaware that Big Ape has impregnated her.

Plagiarism Inc.: Hollywood Blockbusters, Italian-style

Whenever there was a big international success from Hollywood, there would be at least one – but usually a dozen – Italian copies. When *Raiders of the Lost Ark* (1981) was a hit, the Italian derivatives included Antonio Margheriti's *Jungle Raiders* (1984 – *Captain Yankee*) starring Christopher Connelly and Lee Van Cleef, *Ark of the Sun God* (1983) with David Warbeck and John Steiner, *Massacre in Dinosaur Valley* (1985) with Michael Sopkiw and the Tony Anthony vehicle *The Treasure of the Four Crowns* (1982). David Cronenberg's *The Fly* (1986) metamorphosed into George Eastman's *Metamorphosis* (1989). *Alien* (1979) was reworked as Luigi Cozzi's *Alien Contamination* (1981), starring Ian McCulloch, Louise Monroe and Martin Mase, with music by Goblin. Perhaps the most imaginatively titled Italian sci-fi cash-in was Mario Garriazzo's sexploitative *Very Close Encounters of the Fourth Kind* (1979). *The Terminator* (1984) was recreated in Giannetto De Rossi's *Cyborg* (1989). Fabrizio De Angelis' *Thunder Warrior* (1983) pitted Native American Thunder (Mark Gregory) against a racist sheriff (Bo Svenson) in an explosive, Arizona-set remake of *First Blood* (1982).

The Omen (1976) spawned Alberto De Martino's big-budget **Holocaust 2000** (1977 – *The Chosen* or *Rain of Fire*), an Italian-UK co-production. Kirk Douglas starred as an industrialist, Robert Caine, who plans to build a thermonuclear plant in the Middle East (actually filmed in Tunisia). He discovers that his son, Angel (Simon Ward), is the Antichrist – 'From your seed comes evil' – and the plant's seven turbine towers represent a seven-headed dragon, the harbinger of the coming apocalypse. Morricone provided a suitably nerve-jangling score for this entertaining 1970s potboiler which featured Anthony Quayle, Romolo Valli, Adolfo Celi, Ivo Garrani, Virginia McKenna (as Angel's mother, Eva) and Agostina Belli (Richard's lover, Sara Golan). As Nobel Prize-winning professor Ernst Meyer (Alexander Knox) warns, moments before he drowns in the incoming tide off Burgh Island, Devon, 'The cup of catastrophe is filled to the brim!'

When *The Exorcist* (1973) made a fortune, Mario Gariazzo made *The Devil's Obsession* (1974 – *The Sexorcist* and *Obsessed*). 'Oliver Hellman'/Ovidio Assonitis' *Chi sei?* (1974 – *The Devil Within Her* and *Who?*) – starring Juliet Mills as possessed Jessica – ripped-off *The Exorcist* and *Rosemary's Baby* (1968). It was a huge success in the US retitled *Beyond the Door*. **Shock** (1977), Mario Bava's last film, was released in the US as *Beyond the Door II*, though it more closely resembles *The Omen*, *Repulsion* (1965) and Poe's 'The Black Cat'. Dora (Daria Nicolodi) and her son, Marco (David Colin Jnr, from *Chi sei?*), return to their coastal villa after an absence of seven years. Dora's first husband, Carlo (Nicola Salerno), who is Marco's drug-addicted father, vanished during a boat trip; his disappearance was presumed suicide. Dora has suffered a mental breakdown and spent six months in a sanatorium but has now recovered. She's married to airline pilot Bruno Baldini (John Steiner). When he's away she experiences strange apparitions and occurrences, seemingly orchestrated by seven-year-old Marco. It is revealed that Dora murdered Carlo. To save his wife from prosecution, Bruno bricked up Carlo's corpse in the basement, but Carlo has possessed Marco, who now wants to kill his mother.

Though *Shock* appears to be yet another grainy, low-budget 1970s horror rip-off, it is made with some style. It was directed by Bava, who emerged from retirement to work with his son, Lamberto. The house exteriors were filmed at actor Enrico Maria Salerno's villa in Rome, with interiors at Vides S.p.A (Rome). The beach and headland exteriors were filmed, as always, at Tor Caldara. The point-of-view camera prowls the villa and its sunny grounds malevolently. Marco's garden swing recalls Melissa's in *Kill, Baby… Kill!* (which depicts another vengeful child-aggressor). Though Alberto Spagnoli's cinematography lacks the vivid colour schemes of Bava's earlier films, the nightmarish imagery provokes some jump-out-of-your-seat shocks. Dora discovers her bedroom window walled up, is sent flowers from beyond the grave and trips on a garden rake as a hand clutches her ankle from beneath the lawn. Blood seeps through a wall and across a piano keyboard, a Stanley knife strikes through the darkness, a 'Slinky spring' toy descends a staircase, a razorblade is discovered between piano keys and a porcelain sculptured hand reaches from the sofa. In the finest special effect, Nicolodi's hair swirls, medusa-like, as she lies on a bed during a visitation from Carlo.

I Libra's score veers from Goblinesque pounding to poetic piano cues, uniting Argento's 1970s horrors with Bava's 1960s work. Nicolodi gives her best performance as demented Dora, while Steiner, Colin Jnr and Ivan Rassimov (as Dr Aldo Spidini, a psychologist) do well. When Bruno smashes down the wall in the basement to dispose of Carlo's body, Dora kills Bruno with a pickaxe and then slashes her own throat. Marco sits at a table in the garden making a cup of tea for his father, whom we presume occupies the empty chair opposite him.

Watery Graves: Terrors from the Deep

The success of Steven Spielberg's *Jaws* (1975) and Joe Dante's *Piranha* (1978) spawned several fishy imitators. Antonio Margheriti's *Killer Fish* (1978 – *Deadly Treasure of the Piranha*) starred Lee Majors, Karen Black, Margaux Hemmingway and James Franciscus, in a shot-in-Brazil production which featured stolen jewels hidden in a piranha-infested lake. *Monster Shark* (1984 – *Devil Fish*) starred Michael Sopkiw, William Berger, Gianni Garko and Dagmar Lassander. Lamberto Bava directed it as 'John Old Jnr' in homage to his father. Sergio Martino's *Island of the Fish Men* (1978) deployed webbed, scaly monsters that were reminiscent of *The Creature from the Black Lagoon* (1954). *Island* starred Joseph Cotten as the biologist who creates the 'fish men' and Barbara Bach played his daughter. Bach was back in Martino's lively *Big Alligator River* (1979 – *The Great Alligator*), a displaced *Jaws* rip-off shot in Sri Lanka, where Mel Ferrer's jungle tourist resort is threatened by a giant crocodile.

Unofficial *Piranha* sequel **Piranha II Flying Killers** (1981 – *Piranha Part Two: The Spawning*), an Italian-US co-production produced by Ovidio G. Assonitis, was directed by James Cameron (*The Terminator*, *Titanic* and *Avatar*) on location in Jamaica. At the hotel resort Club Elysium (shot at the Mallard Beach Hyatt Hotel), flying piranhas cause havoc at the 'Annual Fish Fry Beach Festival'. They are escaped genetic experiments which were to have been deployed in the rivers of Vietnam by the US army. The film's love triangle is between diving instructor Anne Kimbrow (Tricia O'Neil), her estranged husband, police officer Steve (Lance Henriksen), and Tyler Sherman (Steve Marachuck), who was involved in the army's project. Ted Richert was Raoul, the resort's camp manager who refuses to suspend the events calendar. Carole Davis and Connie Lynn Hadden were two of the piranhas' shapely snacks, Jai and Loretta. The piranhas can fly and breathe out of water and their attack on the Caribbean beach festival is not to be missed: a percussive reggae band 'call to the fish' and the crowd chant 'We want fish!' as the predators fly in. Stelvio Cipriani composed the music behind a pseudonym ('Steve Powder') but it's not that bad. Often slated by critics as a bomb, *Piranha II* has some good scares and Giannetto De Rossi's gory special effects, including prosthetics of nibbled victims, stifle any laughs. The ridiculous flapping piranha swing into shot on strings and still fly more convincingly than Puma Man.

One Italian *Jaws* imitation stands out for its audacity. Enzo G. Castellari's ***The Last Shark*** (1981) sailed so close to the wind in its plagiarism of Spielberg's movie and its sequel *Jaws 2* (1979) that it was withdrawn shortly after its US release (as *Great White*) at the behest of Universal Pictures. Like many Italian imitations of Hollywood movies, *Last Shark* is like watching the original film in a parallel dimension. In the run-up to their Centennial Week celebrations, which will include a windsurfing competition, the US resort of South Bay is menaced by a great white shark. Mayor Bill Wells (Joshua Sinclair), who harbours ambitions to become governor, is determined that the event will go ahead. This is against the advice of bookish marine writer Peter Benton (James Franciscus) and grizzled Scottish shark hunter Ron Hamer (Vic Morrow), a characterisation so close to Irishman Robert Shaw's Quint in *Jaws* as to defy belief.

Castellari builds the tension well. The monster takes a bite out of a windsurfer's board and a listing fishing boat is found with a severed arm on deck. Despite the installation in the harbour of submerged shark-proof nets, the beast has a field day at the all-you-can-eat teen buffet regatta. The mayor attempts to reel the monster in with a joint of meat and a helicopter winch, but the shark downs the helicopter and chews off Wells' legs. A local surveys an abandoned boat towed into the harbour and notes, 'There's something fishy here', while slow-motion throngs of beach party extras provide bikinied meals. The film was partially shot on Malta (with interiors at Elios Studios), but you'd never know, as Castellari's depiction of his US setting is convincing. G & M De Angelis composed the ominous John Williams-style soundtrack, plus three pop songs – 'Hollywood Big Time', 'The Melody Plays' and 'You've Changed the World for Me' (sung by Yvonne Wilkins). Micky Pignatelli, sporting a Farrah Fawcett hairdo, played Gloria Benton, Peter's wife. Castellari's daughter Stefania was Benton's daughter Jenny, who loses her leg to the predator. Castellari's brother Enio was regatta organiser Matt Rosen, who suffers a spectacular demise when he and his boat are devoured. Timothy Brent was opportunistic news reporter Bob Martin and Massimo Vanni played Jimmy, his cameraman. Romano Puppo, sporting a cowboy hat, showed up for the finale as ace marksman Brierly. A harbour jetty packed with locals is towed out to sea by the shark, in an imaginatively scary sequence. Both Jimmy and Brierly are gorily chomped. The giant-sized model shark was constructed and operated by Giorgio Ferrari and Giorgio Pozzi and was intercut with stock marine footage of a real shark. Only in the finale, when Benton blows up the beast with Hamer's dynamite-loaded corpse as bait, does the film flounder, as the expected spectacular explosion is little more than a fart in a fishtank.

The most entertaining Italian 'Jaws' imitator was ***Tentacles*** (1976), directed by 'Hellman'/Assonitis. On the Californian coastline, a baby is snatched from the seafront and a fisherman is stripped to the bone. Further disappearances cause Sheriff Robards (Claude Akins) to investigate with help from journalist Ned Turner. Marine expert Will Gleason (Bo Hopkins) and his wife, Vicky (Delia Boccardo), from the oceanographic institute are called in. With considerable understatement Will surmises, 'Something set this one off'. They eventually deduce that the culprit is a giant octopus, which is provoked by radio waves. The Trojan Tunnel Company are working in the bay, using sound levels beyond the legal limit which kill marine life – divers find the ocean floor littered with dead fish.

Tentacles was filmed in widescreen on location in California, at Oceanside, Pismo Beach and the oceanarium Marineland of the Pacific (which has since closed down). The spectacular underwater sequences staged by Nestore Ungaro depict a picturesque azure netherworld. Stelvio Cipriani's score introduces a harpsichord trill leitmotif for the octopus and the pounding, rolling theme heard in the action scenes is from *What Have they Done to Your Daughters?* For a film about a giant octopus, *Tentacles* assembled an impressive cast. Ned Turner is played by film director John Huston and his sister Tillie is Shelley Winters, modelling a bizarre array of headgear, including a sailor's hat and a giant straw sombrero. Trojan foreman Corey (Cesare Danova) is brought to task by his boss, Mr Whitehead, played by Henry Fonda. Fonda once recounted why Sergio Leone cast him as hired killer Frank in *Once Upon a Time in the West*. When Fonda first appeared, having massacred a family of settlers, Leone intended his audience to gasp, 'Jesus Christ, it's Henry Fonda!' Fonda's first appearance in *Tentacles* elicits the same reaction.

The action – as the octopus squirts clouds of black ink, smashes boats and devours the cast – was staged with model craft, a real octopus and fake rubber tentacles. When the octopus eats Vicky, Will takes it personally. Will and two killer whale companions (with which he can communicate) take on the octopus in its cave lair in a bout that ends Whales 1, Octopus 0. The film's highlight is Solana Beach's Annual August Junior Yacht Race, which Tillie's little son, Jaime, and his friend Tommy have entered. Their big mistake is to use their walkie-talkies. Coastguards belatedly try to warn the contestants that attack is imminent. Assonitis intercuts the parents – watching a children's entertainer and enjoying a picnic, blissfully unaware of the impending disaster – with the massacre that unfolds out in the open sea, as the octopus (its two eyes speeding through the water like a motorboat) wreaks havoc, scattering and toppling the sailboats. This visceral scene and its aftermath is undeniably powerful. *Tentacles* was presented by Samuel Z. Arkoff in the US with the tagline 'It's turning the beach into a buffet'. It was distributed via AIP, which had made its name in the 1950s with Roger Corman's creature features, to which *Tentacles* is a true heir.

The bizarre seafaring/sci-fi hybrid **Encounters in the Deep** (1979) highlighted another popular 1970s plotline – disappearances of ships in the Bermuda Triangle. When Mary (Carole Andre) vanishes during a cruise, her father, Mr Miles (Gabriele Ferzetti), employs oceanographers Peters (Manuel Zarzo), Mike

(Gianni Garko) and Scott (Andrés Garcia), plus oldster Pops (Alfredo Mayo), to investigate. Peters theorises that extraterrestrials are living beneath the ocean and eventually his drivel is proved right, as the divers discover a mysterious race of bulbous-headed aliens in an underwater cavern. In the finale a spaceship takes off with the entire cast on board, except Pops who is left wondering what he has witnessed, as are we. *Encounters* boasts a Cipriani score far superior to the film it accompanies. Hunky James Caan look-alike Andrés Garcia – the nominal hero who is apparently sponsored by Adidas – became a pin-up of these adventures, appearing in the sharksploitation movie *Tintorera!* (1977), Tonino Ricci's *Cave of the Sharks* (1978) and in *The Bermuda Triangle* (1978), with John Huston and Claudine Auger.

Green Hell: Jungle Mercenaries and Revolutionaries

Deriving from *The Deer Hunter*, *The Wild Geese* and *Apocalypse Now*, Italian exploitation filmmakers mounted a series of action movies which sent their 'dogs of war' mercenaries on missions of mercy to exotic, revolution-wracked locales. Master of this sub-genre was journeyman director Antonio Margheriti/'Anthony M. Dawson', who made *The Last Hunter*, *Codename Wildgeese*, *Commando Leopard* and *The Commander*.

Set in Vietnam in 1973, ***The Last Hunter*** (1980 – *Hunter of the Apocalypse*) starred David Warbeck as Captain Harry Morris, who is assigned a top-priority secret mission to blow up a radio installation which is transmitting Vietcong propaganda. Morris's journey resembles *Apocalypse Now*'s odyssey, without the protracted Marlon Brando epilogue. Margheriti also aped *The Deer Hunter*: at one point, Morris is imprisoned in a fetid bamboo cage partially submerged in a river, where he endures rat attacks. Morris suffers nightmarish flashbacks depicting his best friend Steve's suicide. They shared a lover, Carol (Margi Eveline Newton), who in a ridiculous twist is revealed to be the voice of the propaganda broadcasts.

The Last Hunter was filmed in the Philippines, where long-serving Italian cinematographer Riccardo Pallottini was killed in a plane crash on location. *Last Hunter* is one of Margheriti's most relentlessly violent films, with the Vietcong waiting in ambush at every turn. War correspondent Jane Foster (Tisa Farrow) is almost assaulted by doped-out GIs, the rotting corpse of a parachutist dangles from a tree and bamboo booby traps and spiked pits pick off US soldiers in 'Nam's green hell. These grisly effects feature blood-spurting eyes, severed limbs and flamethrower-scorched bodies. Margheriti's son Edoardo played soldier Stinker Smith, who is disembowelled on a bamboo rig, Luciano Pigozzi was an army doctor and Tony King and Bobby Rhodes were Morris's black squad members, George Washington and Carlos. John Steiner cameoed as Colonel William Cash, the insane commanding officer of a US emplacement in a cave, who is clearly modelled on Lieutenant-Colonel Killgore (Robert Duvall) in *Apocalypse Now*. The score is inappropriate funkadelic cues from Franco Micalizzi.

British actor Lewis Collins was well-suited to these tough jungle adventures. He'd previously appeared in the UK TV cop show *The Professionals* and the SAS movie *Who Dares Wins* (1982 – *The Final Option*). The success of all-star Hollywood mercenary movie *The Wild Geese* (1979) inspired Margheriti's **Codename Wildgeese** (1984). Along the way it was forgotten that 'Wild Geese' were Irish historical mercenaries. Captain Robin Wesley (Collins) is recruited by rich Hong Kong businessman Charlton (Klaus Kinski) to lead a raid into the Golden Triangle to 'burn a little opium'. Their opponents are General Khan, a warlord, and his fanatical army. Wesley's party includes mercenaries Klein (Manfred Lehmann) and Stone (Frank Glaubrecht), and ace helicopter pilot 'China' Travers (Lee Van Cleef). They destroy the general's opium refinery, but their helicopter is destroyed and they head cross-country on foot. They travel with Kathy Robson (Mimsy Farmer), who has been held captive in the refinery and is now a junkie. They discover that there is another depot and computer disk data reveals that Charlton is its owner – he plans to inflate the price of heroin. The ever-dwindling group of mercenaries find themselves caught between the general's army and Charlton – a crossfire from which only Wesley, China and Kathy survive.

Codename Wildgeese was shot on location in Hong Kong and the Philippines. Margheriti's convincing special effects include a train blown off a bridge and a helicopter fitted with a flamethrower. Ernest Borgnine played drugs enforcement agent Fletcher and Harmut Neugebauer was Wesley's boss, William Brenner, who is also involved in the trafficking. Wesley's son died as a result of heroin abuse and Wesley aims to root out the culprits. Jan Nemec's synthesizer score was played by German prog-rock band Eloy (H. Arcona, H.L. Folbert and K.P. Matatzoil) on Yamaha equipment. The Far-Eastern-flavoured cues (resembling 1980s pop band Japan) deployed hollow, fretless bass, pan flutes and synth strings. *Codename* also displays influences from *Apocalypse Now* (Wesley's men travel the river on an armoured gunboat) and anticipates *Rambo: First Blood Part II* (1985), with the sweaty, heavily armed mercenaries swathed in coils of ammo bandoliers. Van Cleef, who wears a cowboy hat and is referred to as 'Wyatt Earp', is obviously pleased to be back in action, in a familiar paternal role. Kinski is typically unhinged as Charlton, who dies engulfed in flames as his opium empire goes up in smoke, though he is dubbed with an inappropriate English accent in the international print. 'Alan Collins'/Luciano Pigozzi had a memorable cameo as a Swiss missionary who helps the mercenaries and is crucified alive by the general. A worldwide success, *Codename Wildgeese* was a mainstay of video stores in the 1980s – it seemed that every rental shop in the UK had a copy – and has worn surprisingly well.

Kinski and Collins were reunited on Margheriti's **Commando Leopard** (1985). This has superior special effects to its predecessor, staged in miniature by Margheriti and his son, Edoardo (now working as his father's assistant director). The opening sequence depicts a guerrilla raid on a dam, accompanied by Goran Kuzminac's atmospheric score: pan pipes, strings and jungle echoes.

The raiders blow up the dam as they shoot it out with a helicopter gunship and the torrent of water washes away a government refuelling convoy crossing a bridge. The locale is an unspecified, revolution-torn Latin American country – Margheriti shot on location in the Philippines and Venezuela. Collins is excellent as the idealistic freedom fighter Carrasco. His dogged band of rebels, including Maria (Cristina Donadio) and Scottish mercenary Smithy (John Steiner), battle the government troops who comb the jungle for opposition to dictator, President Ramon Homoza (Subas Herrera). The president's anti-guerrilla militia is headed by a fanatical colonel, Silveira (Kinski). Luciano Pigozzi played an old comrade of Carrasco's father, Hans Leutenegger was Silveira's moustachioed right-hand-man and Manfred Lehmann played Father Julio, who runs a hospital in San Juan.

According to producer Erwin C. Dietrich, *Codename Wildgeese* and *Commando Leopard* had considerable budgets: 15 million Swiss francs each. In *Leopard*'s case, half of this was spent on special effects. In addition to the dam-busting opening, there's the militia's helicopter flamethrower attack on a defenceless village; a raid on the Marbella oil depot (which Carrasco blows up with a train); and a shootout in an abandoned monastery, with berserk Kinski running amok. The film's radical politics are startling within this action scenario. The government villains burn down a hospital and gun down defenceless refugees when their bus is trapped in a minefield. At an airport Carrasco plans to down a passenger jet carrying President Homoza. He is foiled, but one of Silveira's militia blasts it out of the sky with a missile launcher. It is later revealed that the plane was carrying 185 children, not the president, and Carrasco is branded a terrorist by Silveira for this atrocity. The score adds depth to the drama: in addition to Kuzminac's original music, the film uses uncredited cues from Morricone's *Battle of Algiers*, and the end titles play out over a duet between Bob Dylan and Joan Baez.

Margheriti's **The Commander** (1988) co-starred Collins and Van Cleef as adversaries. Like *Codename Wildgeese*, it was an Italian-German co-production shot in the Philippines. Colonel Mazzarini (Van Cleef), a gunrunner, dispatches mercenaries led by Major Jack Colby (Collins) into Cambodia to attack the opium depots of General Dong, though the plan is a ruse by Mazzarini, who is in league with Dong. Colby and his men, including Wild Bill Hickok (Manfred Lehmann), succeed in their mission, before killing Mazzarini. The supporting cast features Donald Pleasance, Brett Halsey, John Steiner, Paul Muller and Romano Puppo (Van Cleef's stunt double from spaghetti western days) and some of the explosions are stock footage from *Codename Wildgeese*.

Margheriti also made *Indio* (1988) and *Indio II: The Revolt* (1990) – Ramboesque adventures set in South America. Francesco Quinn (Anthony's son) played the title role, an ex-marine. Boxer 'Marvellous' Marvin Hagler appeared as Sergeant Iron. Brian Dennehy was the villainous developer in *Indio* and Charles Napier was a road builder in the sequel. The films were noted for their 'ecological' themes: Indio is seen to be protecting the rainforests from destruction by rapacious corporate exploiters, who tear through the forests with bulldozers and chainsaws. A signature of this 'Rambo' sub-genre was heroes dressed in camouflaged gear, their sweaty torsos draped in ammunition belts. These 'Camo and Ammo' adventures were popular worldwide and inevitably came in for the Italian treatment, with such fare as Ferdinando Baldi's *Warbus* (1985) where mercenaries and refugees embark on a cross-country escape through rebel territory in a yellow school bus.

Hercules Unchanged: The Muscleman Revival

Throughout the 1970s and early 1980s, Italian filmmakers attempted to revive pepla. A good example of a sub-genre bereft of ideas was 'Al Bradley'/Alfonso Brescia's ***The Beauty of the Barbarian*** (1973 – *Battle of the Amazons*), yet another remake of *The Magnificent Seven* in period costume. Here the period is an undefined blend of Ancient Greece and the Dark Ages. Zeno (Lincoln Tate), with a trio of brigands led by Medontis (Riccardo Pizzuti), is enlisted to protect a village from rampaging Amazons. The supporting cast included Frank Braña, Alberto Dell'Aqua, Benito Stefanelli and his son Marco. This is the kind of film that gives exploitation a bad name. Not only is it badly made and acted, it commits the cardinal sin of being dull. Only in the finale when the Amazons attack the village does the film liven up. The Amazons wear facemasks, enabling an army of stuntmen to perform their fight scenes in the actresses' place, which would have worked if it weren't for the stuntmen's hairy muscled legs, lack of breasts and bulging scrota.

The success of Arnold Schwarzenegger's *Conan the Barbarian* (1982) and *Conan the Destroyer* (1984) gave Italian producers the opportunity to revisit pepla from a new angle. Schwarzenegger's bodybuilding heroes had been Steve Reeves and Mickey Hargitay, and *Barbarian* had been filmed on location in Spain (including the Cuidad Encantada near Cuenca). Schwarzenegger's film debut in *Hercules in New York* (1970) billed him as 'Arnold Strong'. Dino De Laurentiis' production *Red Sonja* (1985) starred Brigitte Nielsen as the title heroine and Schwarzenegger as swordsman Kalidor. It was filmed in the hills of L'Aquila and Lazio, had costumes by Danilo Donati and a trumpet and choral score by Morricone.

The closest in tone to the 'Conan' films were the Italian 'Ator' series, starring Miles O'Keefe, who had swung to fame as Bo Derek's Tarzan in *Tarzan the Ape Man* (1981). 'David Mills'/Aristide Massaccesi's ***Ator the Fighting Eagle*** (1982) was the first and best of the four-film series. It was shot in Italy, including at the Monte Gelato falls and the Grotte Di Salone. In the Age of Darkness, Ator (O'Keefe) embarks on a trail of revenge when his village is destroyed and his newlywed bride, Sanya (Ritza Brown), is abducted by Dakar, the high priest of the Spider (played by peplum actor Dakar). Impressively photographed by former cinematographer Massaccesi, *Ator the Fighting Eagle* benefits from imaginative costuming and special effects, and a good-looking cast. Hunky, rock-jawed O'Keefe may have the charisma and easy grace of a zombified catwalk model, but with his lion's mane of hair, armour and broadsword, he looks the part. Ritza Brown is his shapely, mini-skirted love interest and Edmund Purdom played Ator's mentor, Griba. Ator's travelling companion, blonde Amazon Roon, was played by statuesque Sabrina Siani, while Laura Gemser appeared as seductive, bejewelled sorceress Indun, who waylays Ator. The best aspect of the film is Ator's sidekick, a baby bear called Kiop, who trundles along in the background and steals every scene simply by being cute.

Ator fights Amazons, brigands, the Spider King's Black Knights and a Shadow Warrior (who is literally just a shadow on the wall). Ator ventures into the Land of the Walking Dead (where he faces zombies), to the Volcano of Shadows, to take possession of the Shield of Mordor (which bestows invincibility), and to the Caverns of the Blind Warriors, who toil in their forge. In the finale the giant Tarantula King puppet wiggles its legs menacingly when Sanya is caught in its web and then Ator takes on the beast in the ruined amphitheatre of the Temple of the Ancient Ones. The epic score was composed by Carlo Maria Cordio and the slushy ballad 'Now that I've Found You' plays over the end titles. Three sequels followed: *The Blade Master* (1982 – Ator the Invincible), *Iron Warrior* (1985 – Echoes of Wizardry) and *Quest for the Mighty Sword* (1989 – Ator III: The Hobgoblin).

On initial inspection, Antonio Margheriti's ***Yor – The Hunter from the Future*** (1983) appears to be a caveman drama. It opens with loinclothed, medallion-wearing Yor (blond ex-football player and boxer Reb Brown) trapped in a *One Million Years BC* scenario and saving cavegirl heroine Kala (Corrine Clery) from becoming a triceratops' lunch. Yor, plus Kala and her guardian, Pag (Alan Collins), trek across the wasteland – by foot, raft and boat – on a quest to discover Yor's ancestry, which leads them into the desert of the Land of the Diseased and to an island ruled by the Overlord (John Steiner) and his army of androids (who resemble Darth Vader). It is eventually revealed that this isn't a prehistoric world, but a post-nuclear one following the Great Destruction. The cave and desert people are the survivors, existing in the fall-out. The Overlord plans to invade the mainland with his androids and repopulate the world with progeny sired by Yor and Kala. 'When you have inseminated this woman, you will die!' Overlord cheerfully informs Yor.

In a surprisingly well-constructed narrative, *Yor* unites Italian filmmakers' twin preoccupations with peplum heroes and post-nuclear sci-fi. Margheriti filmed on location in Turkey, at Cappadocia and Goreme (from Pasolini's *Medea*). From the Duran Duran-meets-David Bowie title song, you know Yor in trouble. The song – 'Yor's World' – is by G & M De Angelis. *Il mondo di Yor* was originally a four-part TV series for Italian TV, which was whittled down to an hour-and-a-half English language feature. This abridged version partially replaces the original score with new cues by John Scott. He-man Yor deploys a stunned giant bat as a hang-glider and performs a trapeze act with Pag to cross a chasm. The climax has the survivors of another explosion flying back to the mainland in a jet fighter. Carole Andre played Ena, a rebel planning to overthrow Overlord, and Ayshe Gul was desert princess Rea, Yor's love interest when he's not dating Kala. Like many of these 1980s Italian films, it now has a sizeable cult following as a guilty pleasure.

Bodybuilder Lou Ferrigno was Mr Universe 1973 and 1974 and gained fame playing *The Incredible Hulk* on US TV. In Italy he appeared in a *Magnificent Seven* remake, *The Seven Magnificent Gladiators* (1983), which deployed several peplum stalwarts (Brad Harris, Giovanni Cianfriglia, Sal Borgese and Dan Vadis) and Mandy Rice-Davis (of Profumo Scandal fame). Ferrigno was also cast as Hercules in two Golan-Globus reworkings of Steve Reeves' classics. Luigi Cozzi's **Hercules** (1983) is a garish comic book sci-fi/peplum which owes little to mythology and plenty to Cozzi's penchant for disco-light special effects. In 'Thebes in the Bronze Age, 4000 years ago', Hercules is called to rescue Cassiopea (Ingrid Anderson) and the Sacred Sword of Thebes from the Island of Thera, where King Minos (William Berger) rules the city of Atlantis with his evil sidekick Adriana (ubiquitous, amazonian Sybil Danning, familiar from many such outings).

Hercules is a surreal cinema experience, with all logic suspended, as though the scriptwriters placed elements from twenty unrelated films in a hat and drew them out at random. There are references to Conan, the legend of Excalibur, Genesis and Moses in *The Bible*, *Star Wars*, pepla, westerns and reams of garbled mythology (including Pandora's Jar). In *Hercules*, gods Zeus (Claudio Cassinelli), Hera (Rosanna Podesta) and Athena (Delia Boccardo) live on the moon, not Olympus.

Hercules was filmed at De Paolis Studios, RPA Elios and Laboratory Valcauda, and in Lazio peplum locations: the gorge at Tolfa and the Grotte Di Salone. The colourful production design and garish cinematography resemble Dino De Laurentiis' *Flash Gordon* (1980). Pino Donaggio's blaring score closely resembles *Star Wars*'s music and the star fields, planets and meteorites are leftovers from *Starcrash*, Cozzi's *Barbarella* rip-off. The Technicolor visuals are awash with candy colours, depicting rainbow bridges, misty caverns and the green-hued harbour of Atlantis with its Colossus of Rhodes-style statue. A solemn narration repeats every plot point with grim regularity. On his intergalactic travels Hercules battles a giant robotic fly, a three-headed robot hydra, a volcanic phoenix and a mechanical centaur. He visits Hell's Skull Mountain, throws bears into outer space, flies through the cosmos in Prometheus' Winged Chariot and instigates continental drift when he parts Europe and Africa.

Ferrigno's cult popularity, the dinky special effects and several revealing costumes (Cassiopea's miniscule sacrificial outfit and Danning's low-cut numbers) have assured continued interest in *Hercules*. Ferrigno certainly possesses screen presence and *Hercules* remains the best of these latter-day pepla. Whenever Hercules performs feats of strength, Cozzi switches to slow-motion for added emphasis. The strong supporting cast included Brad Harris (King Augeias),

Mirella D'Angelo (sorceress Circe), Gianni Garko (evil Valcheus), Raf Baldassarre (henchman Sostratos) and Eva Robbins (Minos' minion, Dedalos). The presence of peplum actors Garko, Baldassarre, Harris and Podesta (Helen in the 1955 version of *Helen of Troy*) adds to the fun.

Having perished in a fiery, multicoloured swordfight, King Minos was resurrected for Cozzi's **The Adventures of Hercules** (1984 – Hercules II). Hercules (Ferrigno) must recover Zeus' seven thunderbolts, which have been stolen by renegade gods Flora (Laura Lenzi), Hera (Maria Rosaria Omaggio), Aphrodite (Margi Newton) and Poseidon (Nando Poggi). The quartet revive Minos, a progenitor of Evil Science, who teams up with Dedalos (Eva Robbins) and sets the Moon on a collision course with Earth. Though it shares much stock footage with its predecessor, this sequel isn't as entertaining. The spangly disco visuals induce migraines, as does Donaggio's fanfare score (reused in its entirety from the first film). Hercules battles an array of monsters including the electrified fire god Antius, the slime people, an ape, gorgon Euryale (Serena Grandi), knight Tartarus in the Forest of Dangling Souls (a scene which resembles *Monty Python*), phosphorescent cave dwellers and Amazons led by spider queen Aracne (Pamela Prati). Hercules is accompanied by Urania (Milly Carlucci) and Glaucia (Sonia Viviani), the last of the Maidens of Phagesta, neither of whom compensates for the absence of Danning. Cassinelli returned as Zeus, Raf Baldassarre played warrior Gorus, Venantino Venantini was the high priest of Antius and Carla Ferrigno (billed as 'Carlotta Green'), Ferrigno's wife and manager, played goddess Athena. End credits inform us that 'Lou's training was done at the American Health Club, Rome', which is presumably where they mislaid the script.

Another strand of these reinvented pepla aped Tinto Brass's *Penthouse*-financed epic *Caligula* (1979), a 'sex and sandals' rip-off of *Fellini Satyricon*, which starred Malcolm McDowell, Peter O'Toole, John Gielgud, Helen Mirren and Teresa Ann Savoy. This sired the expected sequels – Bruno Corbucci reused Ken Adam's sets at DEAR Studios and Danilo Donati's costumes from Brass's film for his sex comedy hit *Messalina, Messalina!* (1977 – *Caligula: Sins of Rome* and *Caligula II*). Typical of these films was **Warrior Queen** (1986) starring Sybil Danning as Berenice, an ambassador visiting Pompeii on 22 August 79 AD. Donald Pleasence played ruler Clodius, Richard Hill was muscular hero Marcus, Marco Tulio Cau was his adversary Goliath, and the scantily clad cast were *Playboy* centrefolds and oiled male models. The plot is essentially the same as that of 1960s pepla – involving slaves, orgies and gladiatorial combat – but these sex and sandals movies were more explicit in their nudity and gore. The volcanic eruption climax in *Warrior Queen* is lifted in its entirety from *The Last Days of Pompeii* (1959), complete with shots of Steve Reeves.

Pleased to Eat You: Mondo and Cannibal Movies

Cannibal movies are the most controversial cycle of films to emerge from Italian exploitation cinema. Several were rightly labelled Video Nasties in the UK and continue to provoke, enrage and divide audiences. Set in uncharted jungles, these films pitted their interloping white 'heroes' against indigenous 'lost tribes'. The intrusive foreigners exploit and brutalise the local natives, who take horrific revenge on their oppressors, often by cooking and eating them.

Italian cannibal movies grew out of the 1960s taste for 'shockumentaries' depicting human and animal behaviour throughout the world – so-called mondo cinema. These docu-features with voice-over narrations depicted everything from wildlife footage, tribal rituals and culinary grotesquery, to headhunters, slave markets, strippers and transvestism. Gualtiero Jacopetti's **Mondo cane** (1962) was the trigger film. Its hit theme song 'More' by Riz Ortolani – which has been covered by Frank Sinatra, Alma Cogan, Roy Orbison and Doris Day, among many others – was nominated for a Best Song Oscar. Jacopetti followed this with *Mondo cane No.2* (1963 – *Mondo pazzo*). The two movies were shown as a double bill in the US presented by Jerry Gross as 'The Most Sensational Exposé of the Freak Side of Life'. *Mondo cane* boasts 'Naked Witchcraft Murders' and 'See The Chicken That Smokes', while *No. 2* promised 'See Priests on Fire!' and 'Today's Cannibalism!'

Mondo filmmakers trawled their cameras around the world, searching for ever more extreme footage. Jacopetti's *Africa addio* (1966) was retitled *Africa Blood and Guts* for the US exploitation market. Other mondos include *Taboos of the World* (1963 – narrated by Vincent Price) and *Mondo balardo* (1963 – narrated by Boris Karloff). Extravagant ads for *Kwaheri* (1965) claimed the film was 'Better than a $10,000 Vacation!' and promised audiences that they would 'See the unseen' in 'The land of thatched huts and hatched nuts'. *Slave Trade in the World Today* (1964) depicted skeletons of escaped slaves washed up onshore being dragged off by giant crabs. Paolo Cavara, co-director of *Mondo Cane*, blurred the lines between real and faked footage, controversy that would dog later cannibal movies. His *Wild Eye* (1967) starred Philippe Leroy as a filmmaker faking mondo scenes in Africa, Asia and Vietnam.

Emerging alongside these shockumentaries was a series of 'exposes' of the World by Night, again purporting to comprise real footage. Jacopetti contributed to *Europe by Night* (1959) and then wrote *The World by Night* (1960), which featured the Crazy Horse Saloon in Paris and the Queen Bee Cabaret in Tokyo. *The World by Night No.2* and *No.3* were edited together in the US as *Ecco* (1965). *Women of the World* (1963), *Mondo nudo* (1963), *Sexy probitissimo* (1963), *Go! Go! Go! World* (1964), *Malamondo* (1964), *Mondo erotico* (1977) and the celebrated 'biopic' *The Wild, Wild World of Jane Mansfield* (1968) were more of the same. The cannibal sub-genre stirred together disparate mondo ingredients – nudity, jungles, animal footage, gore and rituals – into one abhorrent jungle brew.

The first significant cannibal movie was Umberto Lenzi's **Deep River Savages** (1972 – *The Man from Deep River* and *Sacrifice*). British wildlife photographer John Bradley (Ivan Rassimov) flees Bangkok when he stabs a man in a barroom fight and heads into the jungle where he's captured by a primitive river tribe. Due to his wetsuit and flippers, they think he's an aquatic monster and truss him up in a net. Through his relationship with native girl Maraya (Mi Mi Lai), he gains respect, eventually marrying her and becoming tribal chief.

Deep River is essentially a remake of the endurance western *A Man Called Horse* (it could have been called 'A Man Called Croc') with Bradley suffering various trials. He is crucified in a revolving bamboo structure with a head restraint which resembles death-by-birdbox, while warriors shoot at him with blowpipes. There are several scenes of animal mistreatment and death (which are removed from UK prints of the film) and much nudity, particularly from former TV presenter Lai, whose Eurasian prettiness stands out amongst the river people. The cannibalistic aspect of the film is small but crucial, as a neighbouring tribe of flesh-eating 'savages' burn the village, leaving Bradley to rebuild the community after the death of Maraya. The lush Europop score by Daniele Patucchi is more appropriate for a groovy lounge cabaret spot and Riccardo Pallottini's widescreen cinematography captures Thailand in sun-drenched travelogues.

Cannibalistic journeys into 'lost worlds' soon found their feet – and other bits of anatomy – with the appearance of Ruggero Deodato's **Last Cannibal World** (1977 – *The Last Survivor*, *Cannibal!* and *Jungle Holocaust*). An oil company searching for missing prospectors on a Filipino island find more than they bargained for, encountering and then being tortured and eaten by primitive tribesmen. Lai again played a native girl and Massimo Foschi and Ivan Rassimov were the heroes – not so much star and second lead, but rather starter and main course.

Deodato followed this with **Cannibal Holocaust** (1979), the sub-genre's most infamous entry. A documentary film crew – Alan Yates (Gabriel Yorke), Faye Daniels (Francesca Ciardi), Mark Tamaso (Luca Barbarschi) and Jack Anders (Perry Pirkanen) – have vanished in the Amazon jungle. When the search party find the remains of the journalists, they also find the footage they have shot; it chronicles in graphic detail the party's horrific demise at the hands of cannibals – the journalists provoked the natives into violence and the natives turned on their exploiters. This is true exploitation filmmaking and the extreme violence and cruelty were shocking in 1979 and remain so today. The 'film-within-a-film' shaky-cam vérité style was reused to lesser effect by *The Blair Witch Project* (1999), though the discovery of a filmed document of an expedition dates back to Mario Bava's *Caltiki* (1959). Deodato's film caused outrage on its release and it was one of the key Video Nasties, a distinction which cemented its reputation as the strongest and most controversial of gore films. It is often cited as a scathing indictment of the media, but Deodato claimed that he just wanted to make a film about cannibals.

Cannibal films' recurrent motifs include jungle hazards and wildlife, shock editing, strong violence, zooming camerawork and blood and guts. The violence, assault and torture of the white protagonists by the cannibals are the 'entertainment highlights' of each entry – a messy combination of amputation, mutilation,

Sergio Martino's *The Mountain of the Cannibal God* (1978), under one of its alternative titles, stars Ursula Andress on a search in the snake-infested jungles of New Guinea. US poster courtesy Ian Caunce Collection.

copulation, evisceration and several other '-ations'. Lenzi returned to the genre with *Eaten Alive!* (1980 – also with Rassimov and Lai), which featured a search by Sheila Morris (Janet Agren) and mercenary Mark Butler (Robert Kerman) for Sheila's sister, who has gone missing in New Guinea. Lenzi also made *Cannibal Ferox* (1981) which is more like 'Cannibal Xerox' – a carbon copy of earlier films strung around the flimsiest of narratives. It was also known as *Make Them Die Slowly*. Antonio Margheriti jumped on the bandwagon with *Cannibal Apocalypse* (1980), which fused cannibal horror to Vietnam War action. Jesus Franco couldn't let this genre pass him by – no other had – and contributed *Mondo Cannibale* (1979) and *The Man Hunter* (1980). Laura Gemser played journalist Emanuelle in *Emanuelle and the Last Cannibals* (1977 – *Emanuelle's Amazon Adventure*), co-starring her husband, Gabriele Tinti, Donal O'Brien and 'Susan Scott'/Nieves Navarro, in a search for a lost tribe of cannibals in the Amazon jungle.

Sergio Martino's **The Mountain of the Cannibal God** (1978 – *Prisoner of the Cannibal God* and *Slave of the Cannibal God*) is a relatively up-market cannibal movie, with Susan Stevenson (Ursula Andress) and her brother, Arthur (Antonio Marsina), searching for her husband on an island in New Guinea. Dr Edward Foster (Stacy Keach) is their guide. The score was by G & M De Angelis and a credit attributes 'Miss Andress's Leatherwear' to Albanese. It is in this film that Andress is proclaimed a cannibal god by the muddy, straggly haired locals and her naked body is smeared in brown paint. In its cut version the film is a mainstream jungle adventure – all that's missing is Tarzan. The cannibal sub-genre was short-lived but shocking and the censors stamped on them quickly. In cannibal movies, violence is frequent and strong, and the animal cruelty is real and upsetting. Other Italian horror fads – such as zombies or gialli – are violently gory, but you can always tell yourself, 'It's only a movie. No zombies were hurt in the making of this picture'.

Industrious Corpses: Morto Viventi

Less prolific than the Italian-style cannibal movies, though no less visually repulsive, were Italian zombie films featuring *morto viventi*: the living dead. The Hammer Horror *Plague of the Zombies* (1966) had voodoo zombies working a Cornish tin mine, but it was George A. Romero's US-made *Night of the Living Dead* (1968) that really proved that there was life after death, as decomposed, flaky cadavers reanimated to feast on the living. The Spanish-Italian **The Living Dead in the Manchester Morgue** (1974) pitted cop Arthur Kennedy against Ray Lovelock in the Lake District. The zombies here are resurrected by an untried insecticide. To Italian producer Edmondo Amati, Manchester was 'a distant, mysterious place', though director Jorge Grau wanted to film in Glasgow. Most of the eerie Lake District scenes were actually shot in the Peak District. Romero's sequel to *Night of the Living Dead*, entitled *Dawn of the Dead* (1978), was an Italian-US co-production, part-financed by Claudio Argento and Alfredo Cuomo. Dario Argento was script consultant and Italian posters proclaimed

Italian Cinema Eats Itself 293

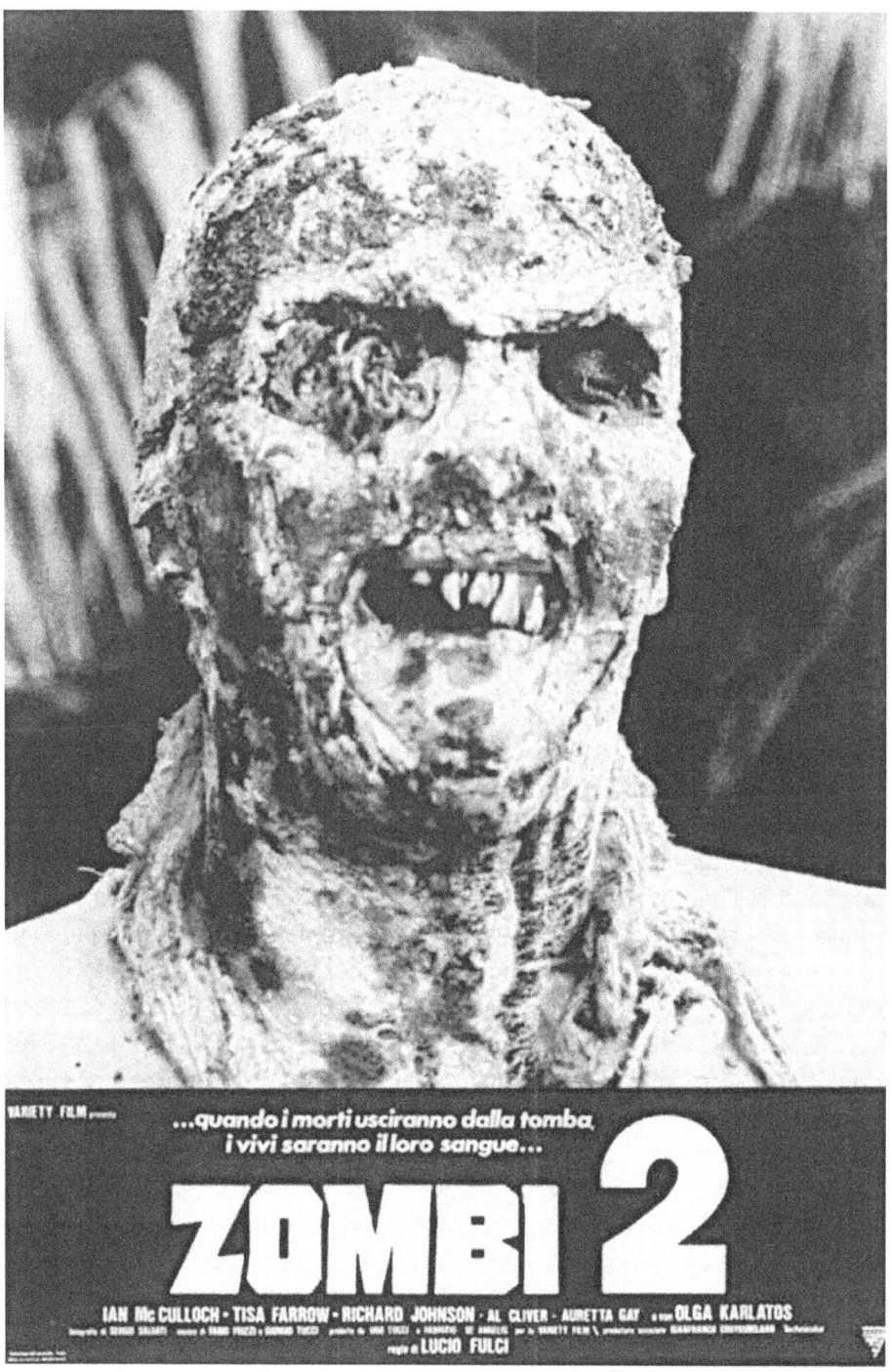

Italian poster for Lucio Fulci's *Zombi 2* (1979) – also known as *Zombie Flesh Eaters* – highlights the wormy-eyed special effects work of maestro Giannetto De Rossi.

'Dario Argento Presenta'. Goblin provided the score and their music featured more prominently in the Italian print, entitled *Zombi*.

Variety Film producers Ugo Tucci and Fabrizio De Angelis approached Enzo Castellari to direct a sequel to Romero's movie, but he refused. Lucio Fulci, a director already known for unsettling horror films such as *Don't Torture a Duckling*, took the helm. The film was originally titled 'Island of the Living Dead', but it premiered in Italy in 1979 as *Zombi 2*, in Germany as *Woodoo*, in the US as *Zombie* and in the UK by its most provocative title, ***Zombie Flesh Eaters***.

A mysterious sailboat drifts into New York harbour. When the coastguard investigates, they are attacked by a fat zombie (Captain Arthur Haggerty), who kills one man and disappears. Journalist Peter West (Ian McCulloch) is dispatched by his editor (Fulci himself) to investigate. West meets Anne Bowles (Tisa Farrow, Mia's sister), whose father owns the boat and has vanished in the Caribbean Antilles Islands. Her father had visited the uncharted island of Mantul, so Peter and Anne hitch a lift with marine photographers Brian Hull ('Al Cliver'/Pier Luigi Conti) and his wife, Susan ('Auretta Gay'/Auretta Giannone). On Mantul, Dr David Menard (Richard Johnson) is struggling to cope with an epidemic which the local population blames on voodoo – the dead are rising and eating the living. Menard's wife, Paola (Olga Karlatos), is killed and devoured in her home (in savage scenes that are truncated in many prints of the film). With the arrival of Peter and company, the dead besiege Menard's hospital.

Zombie Flesh Eaters is Fulci's masterpiece: a sustained, visceral horror movie, with exceptional special effects and convincing mise-en-scène. Fulci 'exoticised' *Dawn of the Dead* – there's no shopping mall here, but a palm tree–littered tropical paradise. The sunny Antilles locations – the wooden hospital and ramshackle village – add much to the film. *Flesh Eaters* was photographed from June to July 1979 in 2.35:1 widescreen by Sergio Salvati on location in New York and Santo Domingo in the Antilles. Interiors were recreated at Elios Studios, Rome. A flashback depicts Menard's hospital before the epidemic – hygienic, bright and white. Now it is fetid squalor filled with shrouded corpses. Fabio Frizzi and Giorgio Tucci's score ranges from haunting, ebbing percussive voodoo, to the creeping title music. Subdued, almost hymnal in tone, it builds to relentless, Goblinesque electronica. The supporting cast included Dakar as Menard's assistant Lucas, Stefania D'Amario as a nurse, and Franco Fantasia as Father Mattias; many of the zombies were played by the Dell'Aqua brothers – Alberto, Arnaldo, Roberto and Ottaviano – who were stuntmen.

The zombies' grotesque flaky makeup was created by Giannetto De Rossi, who worked on *Cleopatra*, *The Leopard*, *Once upon a Time in the West* and *1900*. The *morto viventi* in Fulci's film are more repulsive than any cinema zombie before or since. Their excessive violence is convincing: if you should ever happen to witness someone bitten and eaten by a zombie in real life, this is what it would look like. There are some eye-popping special effects – quite literally in the film's most infamous moment, when Olga Karlatos has her eye poked out in close-up by a long, sharp wooden splinter. Diver Susan witnesses a sub-aqua zombie rip a chunk out of a shark, during an encounter which is photographed in rippling azure hues. When the 'earth spits out the dead', Fulci and crew staged a memorable set piece. From an ancient graveyard, serenely dappled in sunlight and shadow, long-dead Spanish conquistadors, their eyes wormy, their disintegrating bodies putrid, cleave and rise from the mouldering earth. Unleashed, they roam the village's deserted streets and attack the hospital, which catches fire. The hospital's deceased patients rise too and only Peter, Anne and Brian escape. Brian has been bitten. As the survivors head seaward, breaking news reports that zombies have overrun New York and the final image is of the Brooklyn Bridge engulfed by a shambling undead attack.

Not so much released as escaped, *Zombie* stumbled into US cinemas in 1980, presented by Jerry Gross. Taglines included, 'The Dead Are Among Us!' and 'We Are Going to Eat You!' It took $30 million worldwide – outgrossing even *Dawn of the Dead* – but ran into censorship difficulties, especially on the home video market in the UK, which dumped it on the banned Video Nasties list. It has since been released uncut at 91 minutes on DVD and remains the most repulsive – that is to say the best – zombie movie ever made.

The expected imitators ensued, but none equalled Fulci's tour de gore. Andrea Bianchi's *Nights of Terror* (1980) was released as *Zombi 3* in some territories, though it failed to equal either of its predecessors, despite De Rossi providing the graphic makeup effects. Fulci himself made an inferior sequel, also called *Zombi 3* (1988). Umberto Lenzi's *City of the Walking Dead* (1980) saw a planeload of zombies flooding into an American city; Marino Girolami's *Zombi Holocaust* (1980), starring Ian McCulloch and Alexandra Delli Colli, mixed zombies, cannibals and experimental transplants; and Bruno Mattei's *Zombie Creeping Flesh* (1981) located its action in the jungle. Fulci's grisly *City of the Living Dead* (1980) and *The House by the Cemetery* (1981) melded living dead themes to contemporary, supernatural gothic narratives. Here the wormy living dead roam modern America, clawing out brains and disgorging guts.

Italian horror's influence on US cinema can be seen in the films of George A. Romero and John Carpenter. For example, Carpenter's *The Thing* (1982) owes much to Italian cult cinema: the snowy whiteouts of *The Big Silence*, swathes of vivid red and blue colour from Bava and Argento, and the ultra-gore of Fulci's movies. Kurt Russell's monosyllabic hero even drinks J&B Whisky.

Fulci also made **The Beyond** (1981), the Italian splatter film par excellence. In a Louisiana hotel being renovated by Liza Merill (Catriona MacColl), a painter falls from a scaffold and a plumber vanishes in the flooded basement. With help from Dr John McCabe (David Warbeck), Liza unravels the flimsily constructed plot – which involves a book entitled *Eibon* and mysterious 'Room 36' – and discovers that the basement is one of the Seven Gateways into Hell: the Beyond. The hotel and McCabe's hospital become the site of several visceral set pieces, as the forces of evil burst forth – as do blood, heads, eyeballs and a sea of spiders.

A library is the setting for the film's most revolting scene, when architect Martin Avery (Michele Mirabella) is devoured by tarantulas in close-up; Fulci has a cameo here as the librarian. Fulci's orchestration of his shocks (of which there are many) is skilful and he stages some memorably nightmarish imagery, such as the sudden appearance of blind woman Emily ('Sarah Keller'/Cinzia Monreale) and her Alsatian in the middle of a desolate causeway.

Fulci shot on location in Louisiana (interiors at Incir-De Paolis Studios), which provided a convincing milieu for the fantastical action. *The Beyond* is a virtually plotless splatterfest, with the violence depicted in gruesome detail by Giannetto De Rossi's horribly well-done special effects. Fulci goes 'beyond' good taste, lingering on the stomach-churning violence. Set in the 'present day' of 1981, the story begins with a sepia-tinted 1927 prologue, when an accused warlock (Antoine Saint-John) is crucified and sizzled with quicklime by torch-bearing locals in the bedevilled hotel's basement. He is the author of a strange painting which depicts a corpse-strewn landscape – the 'Sea of Darkness' – which is key to unlocking the hotel's secrets. In the nonsensical finale, while battling the risen dead in the hospital, Liza and John suddenly find themselves back in the hotel basement. Through mist, they wander into the landscape which is depicted in the painting – an empty wasteland from which there is no escape. It's a genius ending to a crazy film. Their entry into 'the beyond' of Hell is delicately scored by Fabio Frizzi's flute and piano theme, while the title music features monastic chanting over a funky bassline. The film was released in the US as *Seven Doors of Death* in 1983, abridged and with a different soundtrack by Mitch and Ira Tuspeh. The fully uncut version with Frizzi's original score is now available on DVD.

'Joe D'Amato'/Aristide Massaccesi put an emphatic full-stop to Italian horror exploitation cinema with his *Anthropophagus* (1980 – *Anthropophagous The Beast*, *Man Eater* and *The Grim Reaper*), another Video Nasty. It featured 'George Eastman'/Luigi Montefiori as a marooned cannibal who roams a Greek island seeking out prey. For the climax, having been disembowelled with a pickaxe, the beast eats his own guts, indulging in a blood feast which bizarrely visualises the fashion in which Italian cinema consumed itself.

Italian cinema had enjoyed a 1950s heyday of almost 820 million patrons in 1955 (the peak year). This fell gradually throughout the 1960s and plummeted in the late 1970s to around 200 million patrons per year. TV and video also ate away at Italian cinemagoing figures. Video was initially a boon, with Italian films being specifically tailored to the foreign videotape market, but this was short-lived. As their audiences continued to dwindle – and faced with rising production costs and the global downturn in film production in the 1980s – Italian studios shut down. With every film genre appropriated and every star impersonation exploited, Italian cinema finally ran out of steam. The banquet, which had endured for almost a quarter of the twentieth century, was over, but it had been an amazing feast.

BIBLIOGRAPHY AND SOURCES

Bergen, Ronald, *The United Artists Story* (Octopus, 1986)
Bertolino, Marco & Ridola, Ettore, *Bud Spencer & Terence Hill* (Gremese Editore, 2002)
Betts, Tom, *Westerns All'Italiana!* (Anaheim, California 1983–present)
Black, Andy, *Necromicon – Book One* (Creation, 1996)
Bosworth, Patricia, *Marlon Brando* (Phoenix, 2002)
Bowra, C.M., *Classical Greece* (Time-Life, 1970)
Brode, Douglas, *Money, Women, and Guns* (Citadel, 1995)
Bruckner, Ulrich P., *Für ein paar Leichen mehr* (Schwarzkopf & Schwarzkopf, 2002)
Bruschini, Antonio & Federico De Zigno, *Western All'Italiana – Book Two* (Glittering Images, 2001)
Bruschini, Antonio & Federico De Zigno, *Western All'Italiana – Book Three* (Glittering Images, 2006)
Buford, Kate, *Burt Lancaster – An American Life* (Aurum, 2001)
Cavendish, Richard, *Mythology – An Illustrated Encyclopedia* (Silverdale, 2003)
Chapman, James, *Licence to Thrill – A Cultural History of the James Bond Films* (I.B.Tauris, 2007)
Chatman, Seymore and Paul Duncan, *Michelangelo Antonioni – The Complete Films* (Taschen, 2004)
Connolly, Peter, *The Roman Army* (Macdonald, 1978)
Connolly, William, *Spaghetti Cinema* (Hollywood, California 1984–present)
Costantini, Costanzo, *Conversations with Fellini* (Harcourt Brace, 1995)
Cotterell, Arthur, *World Mythology* (Parragon, 1999)
Crawley, Tony, *Bébé – The Films of Brigitte Bardot* (BCA, 1979)
De Fornari, Oreste, *Sergio Leone* (Gremese, 1997)
Dunford, Martin *The Rough Guide to Rome* (Rough Guides, 2005)
Eames, John Douglas, *The MGM Story* (Octopus, 1977)
Eames, John Douglas, *The Paramount Story* (Octopus, 1985)
Eleftheriotis, Dimitris, *Popular Cinemas of Europe* (Continuum, 2001)
Elley, Derek, *The Epic Film – Myth & History* (Routledge & Kegan, 1984)
Everman, Welch, *Cult Science Fiction Films* (Citadel Press, 1995)
Forshaw, Barry, *The Pocket Essential Italian Cinema* (Pocket Essentials, 2006)
Fox, Keith & Maitland McDonagh, *The Tenth Virgin Film Guide* (Virgin, 2001)
Frayling, Christopher, *Sergio Leone – Something to Do with Death* (Faber & Faber, 2000)

Frayling, Christopher, *Spaghetti Westerns – Cowboys and Europeans from Karl May to Sergio Leone* (I.B.Tauris, 2006)
Gallant, Chris, *Art of Darkness – The Cinema of Dario Argento* (FAB Press, 2000)
Giré, Jean-François, *Il Était une Fois... Le Western Européen* (Dreamland, 2002)
Goldstein, Norm, *Henry Fonda* (Michael Joseph, 1982)
Hadas, Moses, *Imperial Rome* (Time-Life, 1971)
Hardy, Phil, *The Aurum Encyclopedia of Science Fiction Movies* (Aurum Press, 1984)
Hardy, Phil, *The Aurum Encyclopedia of Horror* (Aurum Press, 1985)
Hardy, Phil, *The Aurum Film Encyclopedia – Gangsters* (Aurum Press, 1998)
Henry, Marilyn and Ron DeSourdis, *The Films of Alan Ladd* (Citadel, 1981)
Hirschhorn, Clive, *The Warner Bros. Story* (Octopus, 1983)
Hochkofler, Matilde, *Marcello Mastroianni – The Fun of Cinema* (Gremese, 2001)
Hotchner, A.E., *Sophia – Living and Loving* (Corgi, 1980)
Howarth, Troy, *The Haunted World of Mario Bava* (FAB Press, 2002)
Hyams, Jay, *War Movies* (Gallery Books, 1984)
Katz, Ephraim, *The Macmillan International Film Encyclopedia* (HarperCollins, 1998)
Kezich, Tullio, *Federico Fellini – His Life and Work* (I.B.Tauris, 2007)
Kinski, Klaus, *Kinski Uncut* (Bloomsbury, 1996)
Lampedusa, Giuseppe Di *The Leopard* (Wm. Collins Sons and Co., 1960)
Levy, Alan, *Forever Sophia – An Imitate Portrait* (Magnum, 1979)
Lloyd, Ann, *Good Guys & Bad Guys* (Orbis, 1982)
Lloyd, Ann, *Movies of the Fifties* (Orbis, 1982)
Lloyd, Ann, *Movies of the Sixties* (Orbis, 1983)
Lloyd, Ann, *Movies of the Seventies* (Orbis, 1984)
Lloyd, Ann and Graham Fuller, *The Illustrated Who's Who of the Cinema* (Orbis, 1983)
Luck, Steve, *Philip's Compact Encyclopedia* (Chancellor Press, 1999)
Madsen, Axel, *John Huston – A Biography* (Robson Books, 1979)
Malloy, Mike, *Lee Van Cleef – A Biographical, Film and Television Reference* (McFarland, 1998)
Maltin, Leonard, *2001 Movie and Video Guide* (Penguin, 2001)
Mann, May, *Jayne Mansfield* (Mayflower, 1975)
Masi, Stefano & Lancia, Enrico, *Italian Movie Goddesses* (Gremese, 1997)
Mathews, Tom Dewe, *Censored – The Story of Film Censorship in Britain* (Chatto and Windus, 1994)
McCarty, Nick, *Troy – The Myth and Reality behind the Epic Legend* (Carlton, 2004)
McGilligan, Patrick, *Clint – The Life and Legend* (HarperCollins, 1999)
Müller, Jürgen, *Movies of the 60s* (Taschen, 2004)
Newman, Kim, *Nightmare Movies – A Critical History of the Horror Film, 1968–88* (Bloomsbury, 1988)
Newman, Kim, *Apocalypse Movies: End of the World Cinema* (St Martin's Griffin, 2000)
Nourmand, Tony & Graham Marsh, *Film Posters of the 60s: The Essential Movies of the Decade* (Aurum, 1997)
Nourmand, Tony & Graham Marsh, *Film Posters – Horror* (Evergreen, 2006)
Nourmand, Tony & Graham Marsh, *Film Posters – Science Fiction* (Evergreen, 2006)
Nowell-Smith, Geoffrey, *The Companion to Italian Cinema* (Cassell, 1996)
Palmerini, Luca M. and Gaetano Mistretta, *Spaghetti Nightmares* (Fantasma, 1996)
Pasolini, Pier Paolo, *Oedipus Rex* (Lorrimer, 1971)
Pfeiffer, Lee & Dave Worrall, *The Essential Bond: The Authorised Guide to the World of 007* (Boxtree, 1998)
Robinson, Jeffrey, *Bardot – An Imitate Portrait* (Primus, 1996)
Ross, Jonathan, *The Incredibly Strange Film Book* (Simon & Schuster, 1993)
Scheuer, Steven H., *Movies on TV* (Bantam Books, 1977)
Schwartz, Barth David, *Pasolini Requiem* (Pantheon Books, 1992)
Sciascia, Leonardo, *The Day of the Owl/ Equal Danger* (Paladin, 1987)

Secchiaroli, Tazio, *Fellini 8½* (Te Neues, 1999)
Shipman, David, *The Movie Makers: Brando* (Macmillan, 1974)
Siciliano, Enzo, *Pasolini* (Bloomsbury, 1987)
Sifakis, Carl, *The Mafia Encyclopedia* (Checkmark, 1999)
Slater, Jay, *Eaten Alive – Italian Cannibal and Zombie Movies* (Plexus, 2002)
Slide, Anthony, *De Toth on De Toth* (Faber and Faber, 1996)
Sophocles, *The Theban Plays* (Penguin, 1984)
Stewart, John, *Italian Film: A Who's Who* (McFarland, 1994)
Tchernia, Pierre *80 Grands Succés Du Cinema Policier Français* (Casterman, 1989)
Thrower, Stephen, *Beyond Terror – The Films of Lucio Fulci* (FAB Press, 1999)
Time-Life History of the World: *Barbarian Tides* (1987), *The Age of God-Kings* (1987), *Empires Besieged* (1988) *Light of the East* (1989) *A Soaring Spirit* (1988)
Tornabene, Francesco, *Federico Fellini – Fantastic Visions of a Realist* (Taschen, 1990)
Tyler, Parker, *Early Classics of the Foreign Film* (Citadel Press, 1962)
Vincendeau, Ginette, *Encyclopedia of European Cinema* (Cassell, 1995)
Weisser, Thomas, *Spaghetti Westerns – the Good, the Bad and the Violent* (McFarland, 1992)
Weldon, Michael J., *The Psychotronic Video Guide* (St Martin's Griffin, 1996)
Whitney, Steven, *Charles Bronson, Superstar* (Dell, 1975)
Wiegand, Chris, *Federico Fellini – The Complete Films* (Taschen, 2003)

Internet Sources

The Internet Movie Database (www.imdb.com), the official British Board of Film Classification site (www.bbfc.co.uk), Amazon UK (www.amazon.co.uk), You Tube (www.youtube.com) and the Motion Picture Association of America (www.mpaa.org)

INDEX OF KEY DIRECTORS

Antonioni, Michelangelo ix, xiv, 67, 110, 119–122
Argento, Dario ix, xiv, 81, 122, 228–233, 238–244, 279, 292, 294, 295
Assonitis, Ovidio G./Oliver Hellman xiv, 278–281

Baldi, Ferdinando xiv, 33, 55, 68, 70, 150, 157, 162, 285
Barboni, Enzo (E.B. Clucher) xiv, 24, 32, 54, 65, 89, 154, 162, 250–253, 258, 260–261, 263
Bava, Mario xiii, xiv, 2, 4, 8–9, 14, 30–33, 36, 49–50, 69–70, 77–84, 89, 91, 95, 97–99, 101, 103, 106, 110–115, 134, 174, 182, 223–228, 230, 233, 240, 242–244, 249, 278, 279, 290, 295
Bertolucci, Bernardo xiv, 139, 191, 196–199, 237

Caiano, Mario 18, 32, 58, 62, 88, 145, 267, 269
Castellari, Enzo G./Enzo Girolami xiv, 117, 155, 167–168, 183–185, 187–189, 215, 220–221, 236, 269–270, 273–276, 280, 294
Colizzi, Giuseppe 165–166, 250, 255, 264
Corbucci, Sergio xi, xiv, 9–10, 41, 54, 64–65, 86, 152–155, 157, 162, 164, 171, 195, 245, 248, 254–255, 258, 260, 269
Cottafavi, Vittorio xiii, 6–7, 68
Cozzi, Luigi 115, 277, 287–288

Dallamano, Massimo 147, 236–238
Damiani, Damiano 191, 194–197, 252

De Martino, Alberto xiv, 20, 23, 60–61, 150, 155, 167, 172, 175–176, 181, 213–214, 278
De Sica, Vittorio 36, 43, 96, 119, 123, 126–127, 130, 164, 245

Fellini, Federico ix, x, xiii, xiv, 59–60, 71, 93–94, 112, 119, 122, 127–136, 245, 248–249, 288
Ferroni, Giorgio xiv, 14, 51, 54–55, 69, 89, 152, 214
Francisci, Pietro 2–6, 56
Freda, Riccardo xiii, xiv, 6, 11, 33–34, 60, 67, 84–85, 89, 103, 242
Fulci, Lucio xiv, 234–235, 269, 272, 293–296

Leone, Sergio ix, xi, xiv, 50–51, 54, 65, 70–71, 144–149, 152–153, 156, 158, 165, 177, 195, 228, 240, 249, 252, 253, 271, 281
Lizzani, Carlo 157, 219
Lupo, Michele 21–23, 118, 180, 253–254, 259, 269

Margheriti, Antonio/Anthony Dawson xiii, xiv, 13, 37, 57, 85–86, 89, 91, 95, 102–105, 110, 117, 169, 221, 267, 277, 279, 282–284, 286, 292
Martino, Sergio 229, 233, 270, 276–277, 279, 291–292
Monicelli, Mario 133, 246

Paolella, Domenico 35–36, 62
Parolini, Gianfranco ix, 16–17, 62, 66, 159–160, 174, 210, 216

Pasolini, Pier Paolo ix, xiii, 25–27, 72–75, 93, 136, 139–140, 147–148, 197, 246–248, 286
Petri, Elio 109, 191, 202–203, 230
Pontecorvo, Gillo xiv, 191–194

Questi, Giulio xiv, 129, 156

Rosi, Francesco xiv, 191, 200–202, 204–207

Sollima, Sergio xiv, 39, 170, 178–180, 183, 195, 221

Tessari, Duccio xiv, 9, 18, 54, 65, 150–152, 171–172, 181

Visconti, Luchino ix, xiii, 44–47, 130, 136, 138, 141, 148, 158, 204, 239, 248

INDEX OF FILM TITLES

Films are listed by their best-known English language title, unless they were not released internationally, or there is no English title available. Alternative titles are listed in parenthesis. Page numbers in bold denote an illustration. TV = television series, miniseries or episode.

Accattone 139, 197
Ace High (Revenge at El Paso) 165–166, 250
Adios Gringo 152
Adios Sabata (The Bounty Hunters) 160
Adventures of Hercules, The (Hercules II) 288
Africa addio (Africa Blood and Guts) 289
Africa Express 259
Ali Baba and the Seven Saracens 38
Alien Contamination 277
All the Way, Boys! (Plane Crazy) 255–266
Almost Human 182–183
Amarcord 59, 135–136, 249
Amazing Dr G, The 249
And God Said to Cain 157
Angel for Satan, An 89, **90**
Anthar the Invincible (The Devil of the Desert Against the Son of Hercules) 37
Anthropophagus (The Anthropophagous Beast/Man Eater/The Grim Reaper) 296
Anzio 216
Arabian Nights 140
Ark of the Sun God 277
Arm of Fire (The Colossus of Rome) 55
Arriva Dorellik (How to Kill 400 Duponts) 115
Assassination in Rome 169
Assignment: Outer Space (Space Men) 103–104

Asylum Erotica 236
Atlas in the Land of the Cyclops (Monster from the Unknown World) 11, 15
Atlas versus the Czar 34
Atol K (Robinson Crusoeland/Utopia) 245
Atom Age Vampire 103
Ator the Fighting Eagle 285–286
Attack of the Normans 30
Attila the Hun 2
Avenger of the Seven Seas 40

Bacchantes, The 14
Barabbas 72, 164
Barbarella 93, 112, 277, 287
Baron Blood 97–98, 237
Battle Giants, The (The Fall of the Giants/Attack Force Normandy) 217–218
Battle of Algiers xiii, 191–193, **192**, 221, 284
Battle of Austerlitz, The 43
Battle of El Alamein, The 214–215
Battle of Neretva, The (The Battle on the River Neretva) 218–219
Battle of the Commandos, The (The Legion of the Damned) 217–218, 228
Battle of the Last Panzer, The 212
Battle of the Worlds 102, 104–105
Bay of Blood, A (Blood Bath/ Carnage/ Twitch of the Death Nerve/Last House – Part II) 227–228, 237

Beauty of the Barbarian, The (Battle of the Amazons) 174, 285
Before the Revolution 197
Bello, il brutto, il cretino, Il (The Handsome, the Ugly, the Cretinous) 249
Ben-Hur 51, 60, 65
Bermuda Triangle, The 282
Betrayed 203–204
Beyond, The 295–296
Beyond the Door (Chi sei?/The Devil Within Her/ Who?) 278
Bible...in the Beginning, The 71, 149, 287
Bicycle Thieves, The (The Bicycle Thief) 123
Big Alligator River (The Great Alligator) 279
Big Deal on Madonna Street (Persons Unknown) 246
Big Gundown, The 195, 221, 264
Big Racket, The 188–189
Big Silence, The (The Great Silence) xiv, 154–155, 272, 273, 295
Biggest Battle, The (The Greatest Battle/ The Great Battle/Battle Force/Battle of Mereth) 219
Bird with the Crystal Plumage, The (The Phantom of Terror/The Gallery Murders) xi, xiv, 228–230, **229**
Bitter Rice 26
Black Belly of the Tarantula, The 235–236
Black Cat, The 234
Black Duke, The 41
Black Pirate, The (Blackie the Pirate) 42, 255
Black Sabbath 79–81, **80**, 226
Blade in the Dark, A 244
Blade Master, The (Ator the Invincible) 286
Blood and Black Lace xiv, 87, 224–226, **225**
Blood for Dracula 95–96
Bloody Judge, The (Night of the Bloody Monster) 94–95
Bloody Pit of Horror (A Tale of Torture/The Crimson Executioner) 92
Blowup (Blow-up) xiv, 120–122, **121**
Boccaccio 70 **130**, 131
Boot Hill (Boots Hill) 165, 166, 250
Boss, The 182
Bram Stoker's Count Dracula 95
Brennus Enemy of Rome (Battle of the Spartans) 58
Buddy Goes West 253
Buffalo Bill, Hero of the Far West 143–144
Bullet for the General, A (El Chuncho: Quien sabe?) 194–195
Burn! (Battle of the Antilles) 44, 118, 193–194, 196, 257

Cabiria 13
Caesar the Conqueror 57
California 269
Caligula 288
Call of the Wild, The 271–272, 273
Caltiki – The Immortal Monster 103, 290
Cannibal Apocalypse 292
Cannibal Ferox (Make Them Die Slowly) 292
Cannibal Holocaust 290
Canterbury Tales, The 140
Capriccio all'Italiana 248
Captain Falcon 40
Carthage in Flames 23, 56–57
Casanova '70 133
Case of the Bloody Iris, The (What are Those Strange Drops of Blood on the Body of Jennifer?) 232–233
Case of the Scorpion's Tail, The 233
Castle of Blood (La Danza Macabra/The Castle of Terror) xiii, 85, 86, 95
Castle of the Living Dead, The xiv, 91–92
Cat O'Nine Tails, The 230–231
Cavaliers of Devil's Castle, The 42
Cave of the Sharks 282
Challenge to White Fang, The 272
Charleston 254
China 9, Liberty 37 (Clayton Drumm/ Clayton and Catherine) 270–271
Christ Stopped at Eboli 202
Ciccio Forgives...I Don't 248
Cinema Paradiso 136
City of the Living Dead 295
City of the Walking Dead 295
Clan of Two Borsalini, The 248
Cleopatra 49, 67–68, 294
Cleopatra's Daughter 68
Codename Wildgeese 282–284
Cold Eyes of Fear (Desperate Moments) 236
Cold Steel for Tortuga 38
Colossus and the Amazon Queen (Love Slaves of the Amazons/Queen of the Amazons) 17–18
Colossus and the Headhunters 20
Colossus of Rhodes, The 50–51, 62, 63
Commander, The 282, 284
Commando Leopard 282, 283–284
Commandos 211, 228
Compañeros 195
Con Artists, The (High Rollers/The Switch) 254
Confessions of a Police Captain 196–197
Conformist, The xiv, 197–200, **198**, 237

Index of Film Titles

Conqueror of Atlantis, The (Kingdom in the Sand) 106–107, 116
Conqueror of the Orient, The 36
Constantine and the Cross (Constantine the Great) 12, 67
Contempt (Le Mépris) xiii, 124–126, **125**, 199
Convoy Busters 188
Cop in Blue Jeans, The 186–187
Cosmos: War of the Planets 116
Crime Boss 181
Crime Busters (Two Supercops) 258, 260, 261, 264
Crimson Pirate, The 38
Crypt of Horror 91
Cyborg 277
Cynic, the Rat and the Fist, The 188

Damon and Pythias 53
David and Goliath xiii, 70
Dawn of the Dead (Zombi) 267, 292, 294, 295
Day of Anger 147, 152
Day of the Owl, The 196
Day the Sky Exploded, The 101–103
Deadlier than the Male 170–171
Death at Owell Rock 157
Death in Venice 141–142
Death Rides a Horse 147, 221, 253
Decameron, The 139
Decameroticus 140
Deep Red (Profondo Rosso/The Hatchet Murders) xiv, 122, 237, 238–240, 244
Deep River Savages (The Man from Deep River/Sacrifice) 289–290
Demons 244
Demons 2 244
Desert Battle (Desert Assault/Battle in the Desert) 211
Desert Commandos 209–211
Desert Tigers 211–212
Designated Victim, The 233–234
Devil's Cavaliers, The 42
Devil's Nightmare, The (The Devil's Longest Night) 96–97
Devil's Obsession, The (The Sexorcist/Obsessed) 278
Devils of Spartivento, The 42
Diabolik (Danger: Diabolik) xiv, 112–115, **113**, 169, 174, 227
Dirty Heroes, The 213–214, 220
Divorce – Italian Style 127
Django xiv, 153–154, **154**, 157, 162, 164, 253, 269
Django against Sartana 163

Django, Kill! If You Live Shoot! xiv, 129, 156–157, 162
Django Shoots First (He Who Shoots First) 155–156
Django Story, The (Reach You Bastard!) 164
Django Strikes Again (Django 2: Il Grande Ritorno) 164–165
Django the Bastard (The Stranger's Gundown) 162–163
Dr Goldfoot and the Girl Bombs 249
Dolce vita, La **x**, xi, xiii, 127–131, **128**, 224
Dollar of Fire, A 152
Don't Torture a Duckling 234–235, 294
00-2 Most Secret Agents 248
002 Operation Moon 248
Double Trouble 261–262, 264
Duck You Sucker (A Fistful of Dynamite) 195
Duel of Champions 55
Duel of the Titans (Romulus and Remus) 54

Eagles Over London 215, 220
Eaten Alive! 292
Ecco 289
Eclipse, The 120, 137
8½ 131–133, **132**
Emanuelle and the Last Cannibals (Emanuelle's Amazon Adventure) 292
Embalmer, The (The Monster of Venice) **xii**, 92–93
Emergency Squad 187
Encounters in the Deep 281–282
Erik the Conqueror (Fury of the Vikings/The Invaders/Viking Invaders/Conquest of the Normans) 23, 30–32, **31**
Erik the Viking (Vengeance of the Vikings) 32
Escape from the Bronx (Bronx Warriors 2/Escape 2000) 273, 275
Espionage in Tangiers 168–169
Esther and the King 69
Europe by Night 289
Even Angels Eat Beans 253–254
Executioner of Venice, The (Blood of the Executioner) 42
Exterminators of the Year 3000 276

Fabiola 65
Face to Face 195
Fantastic Argoman, The 175
Fantastic Three, The (Three Fantastic Supermen) 174
Fear in the City 188
Fellini Satyricon xiv, 59–60, 134, 288

Few Dollars for Django, A 155
Fifth Cord, The 232
Fifth Day of Peace, The (Crime of Defeat/ Gott Mit Uns) 218
Fighting Fist of Shangai Joe, The (To Kill or To Die) 267–269
Final Executioner, The 276
Fire Monsters against the Son of Hercules (Colossus of the Stone Age) 19–20
Fistful of Dollars, A xi, 144–147, **146**, 149, 150, 153, 156, 249, 269
Fists in the Pocket (Fist in His Pocket) xiii, 137–138
Five Dollars for Ringo 152
Five Dolls for an August Moon 226–227
Five for Hell **210**, 216
Five Graves for a Medium (Terror-Creatures from the Grave) 87–88
Five Man Army, The 228
Flatfoot 185–186, 254
Flatfoot in Africa 186
Flatfoot in Egypt 186
Flatfoot in Hong Kong 186
Flesh for Frankenstein 95–96
Footprints 232, 237
For a Few Dollars More 147–148, 162
For a Fist in the Eye 249
Fort Yuma Gold 152
Four Flies on Grey Velvet 231–232, 239
Four Gunmen of the Apocalypse 269
Four Musketeers, The 42
Frankenstein '80 96
Frankenstein's Castle of Freaks 96
From Hell to Victory 219–220
From the Orient With Fury 167
Fury of Achilles (Achilles) 52–53
Fury of Hercules, The 17

Garden of the Finzi-Continis, The 164
Gatling Gun 157
Genghis Khan 36
Gestapo's Last Orgy 220
Get Mean xiv, 150
Ghost, The (The Spectre) 84, 85
Giant of Marathon, The 49–50
Giant of Metropolis, The 14, 106
Giants of Rome, The 57–58
Giants of Thessaly, The 6, 26
Girl Who Knew Too Much, The (Evil Eye) 223–224
Gladiator of Rome (Battles of the Gladiators) 62
Gladiators Seven (Gladiators 7) 60–61
Go For It 260–261, 264

Go! Go! Go! World 289
God Forgives... I Don't (Blood River) 165–166, 250
Gold of Naples, The 245
Golden Arrow, The 37
Goliath and the Barbarians (Colossus and the Golden Horde) 33
Goliath and the Dragon 6–7
Goliath and the Sins of Babylon 21–23, **22**
Good, the Bad and the Ugly, The xiv, 74, 114, 148–149, 166, 196, 249, 264
Gordon the Black Pirate 38–39
Gospel According to St Matthew, The xiii, 73–75, **73**
Grand Slam 176–177
Great Adventure, The (Cry of the Wolf) 273
Gunfight in the Red Sands (Gringo/Gunfight at Red Sands/Duello nel Texas) 143
Guns of the Black Witch 38

Hands over the City 201
Hannibal 12, 13, 55–56, 63
Hatchet for the Honeymoon (Blood Brides) 226–227
Have a Good Funeral, Amigo... Sartana Will Pay 160, **161**, 269
Hawk of the Caribbean 40
Hawks and Sparrows 246–248, **247**
Helen of Troy 1, 49, 288
Hell Below Deck (Queen of the Seas) 40
Hell Commandos 212–213, 220
Hell in Normandy 212
Hellbenders, The 157
Hercules (1958) xi, 2–3, 5, 6, 26, 27, 74, 124, 287
Hercules (1983) 287–288
Hercules against Moloch (The Conquest of Mycenae/Hercules' Challenge) 14
Hercules against the Barbarians 35–36
Hercules against the Mongols 35, 36
Hercules against the Moon Men 107
Hercules against the Sons of the Sun 2, 21
Hercules and the Black Pirate 40
Hercules and the Masked Rider 43
Hercules and the Princess of Troy (TV episode) 24
Hercules Conquers Atlantis (Hercules and the Captive Women) xiii, 7–8, 24, 106
Hercules in New York 285
Hercules in the Centre of the Earth (Hercules in the Haunted World) 8–9, 24, 30, 36
Hercules Prisoner of Evil 13
Hercules Returns 25

Hercules, Samson and Ulysses 5
Hercules, Samson, Maciste and Ursus the Invincibles (*Samson and the Mighty Challenge*) 24–25
Hercules the Avenger 24
Hercules Unchained 3–5, **3**, 23, 25, 107
Hero of Babylon, The (*The Beast of Babylon Against the Son of Hercules*) 23
Herod the Great 71–72
Heroes Without Glory 211
Heroin Busters, The 189
Hills Run Red, The 157–158
Histoires Extraordinaires (*Force of Evil/Tales of Mystery and Imagination/Spirits of the Dead*) 93–94, 135
Hitch-hike 182
Holocaust 2000 (*The Chosen/Rain of Fire*) 278
Hornets' Nest 218
Horrible Secret of Dr Hichcock, The (*The Horrible Dr Hichcock/ The Terror of Dr Hichcock/Raptus – The Secret of Dr Hichcock*) xiii, 84–85
House by the Cemetery, The 295
House of Exorcism, The 99
How to Steal an Atomic Bomb 248
How We got into Trouble with the Army 248
How We Robbed the Bank of Italy 248
Human Duplicators, The 117
Humanoid, The 117–118
Hunter of the Unknown (*Agent 3S3: Massacre in the Sun*) 170

I Am Sartana… Trade Your Pistol for a Coffin (*Fistful of Lead*) 160
I'm for the Hippopotamus 259–260, 264
If You Meet Sartana… Pray for Your Death 159–160
Illustrious Corpses xiv, 205–207, **206**
Indio 284–285
Indio II: The Revolt 284–285
Inferno 243–244
Inglorious Bastards, The (*The Counterfeit Commandos*) xiv, 220–221
Investigation of a Citizen above Suspicion 202–203, **202**
Invincible Gladiator, The 61
Iron Warrior (*Echoes of Wizardry*) 286
Island of the Fish Men 279
It Can Be Done, Amigo (*The Big and the Bad*) 252–253

Jason and the Argonauts 6
Juliet of the Spirits 133–134
Jungle Raiders (*Captain Yankee*) 277

Kaos 249
Keoma (*The Violent Breed/Django Rides Again/Django's Great Return*) 269–270
Kill, Baby… Kill! (*Curse of the Dead*) 82–84, **83**, 98, 235, 278
Killer Fish (*Deadly Treasure of the Piranha*) 279
Kindar the Invulnerable 37–38
King of Kings 15, 18
Kiss Kiss Bang Bang 171–172
Knives of the Avenger 32
Kriminal 115

Lady Frankenstein 96
Last Cannibal World (*The Last Survivor/Cannibal!/Jungle Holocaust*) 290
Last Days of Pompeii, The 62, 63, 65–66, 67, 288
Last Days of Pompeii, The (TV miniseries) 66
Last Days of Sodom and Gomorrah, The (*Sodom and Gomorrah/Sodom and Gomorrah: Twin Cities of Sin*) 32, 70–71
Last Glory of Troy, The (*War of the Trojans/The Avenger*) 14, 53–54
Last Hunter, The (*Hunter of the Apocalypse*) 282
Last Man on Earth, The xiv, 107–109, **108**
Last of the Vikings 29–30, 32
Last Shark, The (*Great White*) 280
Last Tango in Paris 199
L'avventura (*The Adventure*) 119–120
Legions of the Nile 68
Leopard, The ix, xiii, **45**, 46–47, 75, 137, 148, 204, 294
Light the Fuse… Sartana's Coming (*Run Man Run… Sartana's in Town!*) 160
Lightning Bolt (*Operation Goldman*) 169–170
Lights of Variety 133
Lion of Saint Mark, The (*The Marauder*) 40
Lion of Thebes, The 69
Lisa and the Devil 98–99
Living Dead in the Manchester Morgue, The 292
Lizard in a Woman's Skin, A 234
Long Arm of the Godfather, The 181
Long Days of Vengeance, The 152
Long Hair of Death, The 85, 87
Lost Command 193
Loves of Hercules, The (*Hercules Versus the Hydra*) 5–6, 17
Lucky Luciano 204, 205
Lucky Luke 263–264
Lusty Wives of Canterbury, The 140

Macabre 244
Machine Gun McCain 177–178
Maciste against the Vampire (Goliath and the Vampires) 9–11, **10**
Maciste, Gladiator of Sparta (The Terror of Rome against the Son of Hercules) 62
Maciste in Hell (The Witch's Curse) xiv, 2, 11–12, 14, 34, 36, 58, 107
Maciste in King Solomon's Mines 24
Magnificent Gladiator, The 62
Magnum Cop 188
Malamondo 289
Man called Apocalypse Joe, A 163
Man Called Blade, A (Mannaja) 270
Man Hunter, The 292
Man of the East 253
Man Who Laughs, The 41
Manhunt 181–182
Marco Polo 34
Marriage, Italian Style 127
Marseilles Connection, The (High Crime) xiv, 183–185, **184**, 187, 188
Mars, God of War (The Son of Hercules versus Venus) 19
Mask of Satan, The (Black Sunday/Revenge of the Vampire) xiii, 77–79, **78**, 81, 91
Mask of the Musketeers (Zorro and the Three Musketeers) 42
Masked Man Against the Pirates, The (The Black Pirate) 40
Massacre in Dinosaur Valley 277
Massacre in Rome (Rappresaglia) 219
Mattei Affair, The 201
Mean Frank and Crazy Tony (Escape from Death Row) 180–181
Medea 26–27, 286
Messalina against the Son of Hercules 62
Messalina, Messalina! (Caligula: Sins of Rome/Caligula II) 288
Metamorphosis 277
Miami Supercops 262–263, **262**, 264
Milan Calibre 9 xiv, 181–182
Mill of the Stone Women 89–91
Minnesota Clay 153
Mission Bloody Mary 167
Mr. Billion 255
Mole Men against the Son of Hercules 12, 14–15, 23
Mondo balardo 289
Mondo cane **268**, 289
Mondo cane No.2 (Mondo pazzo) 289
Mondo Cannibale 292
Mondo erotico 289
Mondo nudo 289

Monster Shark (Devil Fish) 279
More Sexy Tales from Canterbury 140
Morgan the Pirate 39
Moses xiii, 70
Moses the Lawgiver (TV miniseries) 69–70
Mother of Tears 244
Mountain of the Cannibal God, The (Prisoner of the Cannibal God/ Slave of the Cannibal God) **291**, 292
Moving Target (Death on the Run) 171
Musketeers of the Seas 40
Mussolini: The Last Days (The Last Four Days) 219
My Name is Nobody xiii, 252, 263, 264

Navajo Joe 157
Nefertite – Queen of the Nile 68
Nephews of Zorro, The 248
New Barbarians, The (Warriors of the Wasteland) 273, 275–276
New York Ripper, The 234
Night of the Doomed (The Faceless Monster/ Nightmare Castle) 88–89
Night of the Living Dead 109, 267, 292
Nights of Cabiria 123, 129
Nights of Terror 295
1900 xiii, 199, 294
1990: The Bronx Warriors (Bronx Warriors) xiv, 135, 189, 273–274, **274**
No Room to Die (A Noose for Django) 162
Nobody's the Greatest 252, 254
Notte, La 120

Odds and Evens 258–259, 264
Oedipus Rex 25–26, 139
OK Connery (Operation Double 007/ Operation Kid Brother) 172–173
Once Upon a Time in the West xiii, 71, 158, 166, 197, 218, 228, 240, 253, 264, 271, 281, 294
One Damn Day at Dawn...Django Meets Sartana! 163–164
$100,000 for Ringo 150, 152
One on Top of the Other 234
One Silver Dollar 152
Opera 244
Ossessione (Obsession) 239
Other Canterbury Tales, The 140

Partner 197
Passenger, The 122
Passport to Hell 170
Perseus the Invincible (Perseus against the Monsters/The Medusa against the Son of Hercules) 20–21

Phenomena (Creepers) 224
Pinocchio 249
Piovra, La (The Octopus – TV series) 197
Piranha II Flying Killers (Piranha Part Two: The Spawning) 279–280
Pirate and the Slave Girl, The 40
Pirate of the Black Hawk 40
Pirates of Malaysia, The 39
Pirates of the Coast 40
Pistol for Ringo, A 150, **151**, 195
Pistols Don't Argue (Bullets Don't Argue) 144–145, 150
Place in Hell, A (Commando Attack) 213
Planet of the Vampires (The Demon Planet) 110–112, **111**
Pontius Pilate 72
Postino, Il 154
Price of Death 160
Price of Power, The 195
Pride and the Passion, The 43–44
Primitive Love 248
Probability Zero 228
Professional Gun, A (The Mercenary) 44, 195, 221
Puma Man ix, xiv, 175–176, 255, 280
Purple Noon (Plein Soleil/Lust for Evil/Blazing Sun) 137

Queen for Caesar, A 68
Queen of the Pirates 40
Queen of the Tartars (The Huns) 34
Quest for the Mighty Sword (Ator III: The Hobgoblin) 286
Quiet Place in the Country, A 230
Quo Vadis 1, 49

Rabid Dogs (Kidnapped) 182
Raiders of Atlantis (Atlantis Interceptors) 276
Rebel Gladiators, The 62
Red Desert 120
Red Nights of the Gestapo 220
Red Sonja 285
Red Sun 267
Redneck 182
Renegade (They Call Me Renegade) 263
Return of Ringo, The 152, 221
Return of Sabata 160
Revenge of the Musketeers 42
Revolt of the Pretorians 59
Revolver (Blood in the Streets) 179–180, 221
Ringo and his Golden Pistol (Johnny Oro) 152–153
Risking 186

Rita of the West (Little Rita of the West/Rita the Kid) 157
Rocco and his Brothers 136
RoGoPaG 72–73
Roma 134–135
Romanzo Criminale 183
Rome 2033 – The Fighter Centurions (The New Gladiators) 276
Rome, Open City 134
Rome Against Rome (Night Star: Goddess of Electra/War of the Zombies) 12–13
Romulus and the Sabines 54–55
Rose Tattoo, The 123
Rulers of the City (Mister Scarface) 187
Run, Man, Run 195

Sabata 160
Sabata the Killer (Viva Sabata!) 160
Sacco and Vanzetti 202
Salon Kitty 220
Salt in the Wound (The Liberators/War Fever/The Dirty Two) 216–217
Salvatore Giuliano 200–202
Samouraï, Le 137, 181
Samson 17
Samson and the 7 Miracles of the World 11, 34–35
Samson and the Treasure of the Incas 43
Sandokan (TV miniseries) 39
Sandokan Against the Leopard of Sarawak 39
Sandokan Fights Back 39
Sandokan the Great 39
Sartana, If Your Left Arm Offends, Cut it Off (Django and Sartana are Coming… It's the End) 164
Sartana in the Valley of Death 160
Sartana the Gravedigger (I Am Sartana… Your Angel of Death) 160
Satanik 112, 115
Satiricosissimo 248
Scipio Africanus 56
Secret Mark of D'Artagnan, The 42
Secret of the Black Falcon 40
Senso (Wanton Contessa/The Wanton Countess) 44
Seven Guns for the MacGregors 157
Seven Hours of Gunfire 144
Seven Magnificent Gladiators, The 287
Seven Seas to Calais 40
Seven Winchesters for a Massacre 155
Seven Women for the MacGregors 145
79 AD (The Destruction of Herculaneum/The Last Days of Herculaneum) 66

Sexy Probitissimo 289
She 276
She Beast, The (Revenge of the Blood Beast) **xii**, 88, 93
Sheriff and the Satellite Kid, The 118, 254
Shock (Beyond the Door II) 278–279
Shortest Day, The 248
Sicilian Clan, The 206
Siege of Syracuse, The 56
Sign of the Gladiator 63, 66–67
Silent Stranger, The (The Stranger in Japan) 150
Sins of Rome 60
Slave Trade in the World Today 289
Snow Devils, The (Space Devils) 105
Solomon and Sheba 123
Son of Captain Blood, The 41
Son of Cleopatra 68
Son of Django 163
Son of Hercules in the Land of Darkness 12
Son of Samson (Maciste the Mighty/Maciste in the Valley of the Kings) 13–14
Son of Spartacus, The (The Slave) **64**, 65
Son of the Leopard 248
Son of the Red Corsair 40
Sons of Thunder (My Son, the Hero) xiv, 18–19
Spartacus 60, 65
Spartacus and the Ten Gladiators (Day of Vengeance) 62–63
Spartan Gladiators, The (The Secret Seven) 63
Special Cop in Action, A 188
Special Mission Lady Chaplin xiv, 167–168
Spider's Stratagem, The (TV movie) 200
SS Experiment Love Camp 220
SS Extermination Love Camp 220
SS Girls 220
Starcrash 115–116, 287
Strada, La 122, 129
Stranger and the Gunfighter (Blood Money) 267
Stranger in Sacramento, A 149
Stranger in Town, A (For a Dollar in the Teeth) 149
Stranger Returns, The (A Man, A Horse, A Gun/ Shoot First, Laugh Last) 149
Stranger that Kneels Beside the Shadow of a Corpse, The 164
Strangler of Vienna, The 97
Super Stooges versus the Wonder Women 174
Superago against Diabolicus 173–174
Superargo (Superargo and the Faceless Giants/The King of Criminals) 174

Supersnooper (Super Fuzz) 255
Suspiria xiv, 81, 240–243, **241**, 244
Swindle, The 129
Swordsman of Sienna 42–43

Taboos of the World 289
Tartars, The xiii, 33–34
Tartars, The (Plains of Battle/Taras Bulba, the Cossack) 34
Ten Gladiators, The 62
$10,000 Blood Money 267
Tenebrae (Unsane) 240, 244
Tentacles xiii, xiv, 238, 280–281
10th Victim, The 109–110, 276
Tepepa (Blood and Guns) xiii, 196
Terra Trema, La (The Earth Trembles) 136
Terror of the Black Mask 42
Terror of the Red Mask 42
Texican, The 152
Theorem 139
They Call Me Trinity xiv, 250, **251**, 258, 264
They Called Him Bulldozer 254
Thief of Baghdad, The 36
Thing, The 295
Third Man, The 97, 170
Thor and the Amazon Women 23
Three Avengers, The 16–17
3 Bullets for Ringo 38
Three Stooges Meet Hercules, The 16
Three Supermen in the West 174
Three Supermen in Tokyo 174
Thunder Warrior 277
Tiger of the Seven Seas 40
Tintorera! 282
Today It's Me...Tomorrow You! 228
Tony Arzenta (Big Guns) 181
Torso 229
Totò against Hercules 124
Totò against Maciste 245
Totò against the Black Pirate 245
Totò and Cleopatra 69
Totò of Arabia 245
Totò, Peppino and la dolce vita xi, 245
Totò Versus Maciste 68–69
Tough Ones (Rome Armed to the Teeth) 188
Treasure Island 271–272
Treasure of the Four Crowns, The 277
Trinity is Still My Name 250–252, 258, 260, 264
Triumph of Hercules, The 23
Triumph of Maciste, The (Triumph of the Son of Hercules) 14
Triumph of the Ten Gladiators 63

Trojan War, The (The Trojan Horse/The Wooden Horse of Troy) xiv, 14, 51–52, **51**, 53, 54, 69
Troublemakers, The 264
Two Escapees from Sing-Sing 248
Two Gladiators, The (Fight or Die) 58–59
Two Mafiosi in the Far West 248–249
Two Missionaries 256–257
Two Parachutists, The 248
Two Public Enemies 248
Two R-R-Ringos from Texas 248
Two Sergeants of General Custer 248
Two Sons of Ringo 248
Two Sons of Trinity 248
2019: After the Fall of New York 276–277
Two Women 122–124

Ulysses against the Son of Hercules (Ulysses against Hercules) 18
Ursus (The Mighty Ursus/Ursus Son of Hercules) 15
Ursus and the Tartar Princess 34
Ursus in the Land of Fire 12, 16
Ursus in the Valley of the Lions 16–17, 23

Valachi Papers, The 204–205
Vampiri, I (The Devil's Commandment/Lust of the Vampire) 84
Vengeance of Ursus 16
Very Close Encounters of the Fourth Kind 277
Vikings, The 29
Violent City (The Family) xiv, 178–179, **178**
Violent Naples 188
Violent Professionals, The 188
Violent Rome (Forced Impact) 187–188
Virgin of Nuremberg, The (The Castle of Terror/Horror Castle) 85–86
Viva Django! (Django Get a Coffin Ready) 145, 162
Vulcan Son of Jupiter 19

Wanted 152
War and Peace 43
War Between the Planets (Planet on the Prowl) 105
War Devils, The 213
War, Italian Style (Two Marines and a General) 245
War of the Planets (The Deadly Diaphanoids) 105
War of the Robots, The 116–117
Warbus 285
Warrior Queen 288
Watch Out, We're Mad! 256, **257**, 264
Waterloo 44
Web of the Spider 95
What Am I Doing in the Middle of a Revolution? 195–196
What Have They Done to Your Daughters? 237–238, 281
What Have You Done to Solange? (Terror in the Woods) 237–238
When Women Had Tails 253
When Women Lost their Tails 201, 253
When Women Played Ding Dong 253
Whip and the Body, The (Night is the Phantom/What) 81–82
White Comanche 158–159
White Fang 272
White Fang to the Rescue 272–273
White Warrior, The 33
Who Finds a Friend Finds a Treasure 260, 264
Who Saw Her Die? 236–237
Why Did You Pick on Me? 118
Wild Eye 289
Wild, Wild Planet, The xiv, 105–106, 169
Wild, Wild World of Jayne Mansfield, The 6, 248, 289
Witches, The 138, 173, 248
Women of the World 289
Wonders of Aladdin, The 36, 37
Working Class Go to Heaven, The (Lulu the Tool) 202
World by Night, The 289

Yesterday, Today and Tomorrow 126
Yojimbo 145, 150, 153, 269
Yor – The Hunter from the Future 286–287

Zabriskie Point 122
Zombi 3 295
Zombi Holocaust 295
Zombie Creeping Flesh 295
Zombie Flesh Eaters (Zombi 2/Woodoo/Zombie) xiv, **293**, 294–295
Zorro against Maciste (Samson and the Slave Queen) 43

www.ingramcontent.com/pod-product-compliance
Lightning Source LLC
Chambersburg PA
CBHW080542230426
43663CB00015B/2683